ISAAC ASIMOV'S
BOOK OF FACTS

ISAAC ASIMOV'S
BOOK OF FACTS

WINGS BOOKS
New York

This 1997 edition is published by Random House Value Publishing, Inc., 201 East 50th Street, New York, New York 10022, by arrangement with Barricade Books.

Random House
New York • Toronto • London • Sydney • Auckland
http://www.randomhouse.com/

Printed and bound in the United States of America

Library of Congress Cataloging-in-Publication Data
Asimov, Isaac, 1920–1992
Isaac Asimov's Book of facts.
1. Encyclopedias and dictionaries.
I. Title. II. Title: Book of facts.
AG6.A84   1981   031'.02   81-12279
ISBN 0-517-06503-7   AACR2

12 11 10 9 8 7 6 5

A Few Opening Remarks

I've always been slightly drunk with facts, and almost all of my more than two hundred books have dealt, at least incidentally, with facts. Now I've compiled and edited this book that deals only with facts—a special collection for those who love facts as much as I do.

Here are three thousand facts of all kinds—facts that are offbeat but true, facts you never knew, facts you can't believe, "facts" you always believed but that happen to be wrong—facts that will teach you, amaze you, and tickle your funny bone.

Perhaps you, too, are "turned on" by learning that: Karl Marx thought communism would not catch on in Russia . . . the father of gerontology lived to be nearly 103 years old . . . Jimmy Carter is the first U.S. President to be born in a hospital . . . brothers-in-law of Abraham Lincoln fought for the Confederacy . . . the Nile River has been known to freeze over . . . no scientist and no science fiction writer—myself included—predicted that Mars was cratered.

The Nobel Prize winner Ivan Petrovich Pavlov said, "Learn, compare, collect the facts." Well, Ivan, I've been up to my sideburns in them. In all, I examined and sifted just over six thousand (from the tens of thousands evaluated by our researchers) and finally selected three thousand beauties for this first volume of *Isaac Asimov's Book of Facts*.

There's a delectable mix here, a panorama of facts dealing with practically every aspect of the universe, human and nonhuman, animate and inanimate, on Earth and beyond.

Your pleasure can begin absolutely anywhere. You can start on page one and zip right through to the very last page. Or you can start in the categories of particular interest to you, and then roam through the book. Or from the very first you can simply poke around, hither and yon, where and when, picking out new and amazing facts and boggling the mind. I'll be surprised if you don't find surprises on every single page. (I did!)

ISAAC ASIMOV

Isaac Asimov died in New York City on April 6, 1992.

Contents

ABOUT KINGS

Uninterruptedly since the sixth century, the Japanese throne has been occupied by a member of the same family. The present emperor, Hirohito, is the 124th in succession.

———

The palace of Versailles cost 5 million livres out of a total state budget of 120 million livres during the first year of its construction, in the late seventeenth century. The cost then went up to 15 million and then to 25 million livres a year. In 1682, 22,000 workers were laboring on it; the next year, there were 36,000. In 230 acres of gardens, 1,400 fountains were installed, and 25,000 full-grown trees were transplanted in one year so that Louis XIV would not have to wait for saplings to grow. The waters of the Seine were raised to supply the waterworks, consisting of fourteen hydraulic wheels and 223 pumps.

———

From the monarchs' investment of $6,000 in Columbus's first voyage, Spain had a return of $1,750,000 in gold after only one century.

———

Royalty has not been noted for contributions to science. But Ferdinand II, Grand Duke of Tuscany, devised the first sealed thermometer in 1654. This was the forerunner of the common mercury thermometers of today.

———

When Sir Walter Raleigh introduced tobacco into England in the early 1600s, King James I wrote a booklet arguing against its use. This early example of attempted government regulation of smoking failed. The "sotweed" caught on immediately as an overwhelmingly popular habit.

———

The father of Frederick the Great had a famous private guard company—the Potsdam Grenadiers. He would bribe, buy, or even kidnap tall men, close to seven feet in height, to get them for the Grenadiers;

1

he made the giant men marry giant women so he could "raise" his own giants.

———

The longest reign in recorded history was that of Pepi II, who had succeeded to the throne of Egypt in 2272 B.C. It lasted, according to all the evidence, for ninety years, which means that he must have been a mere infant on succeeding to the throne. Within two years of Pepi's death, in 2182 B.C., Egypt fell apart.

———

Edward, Prince of Wales, was not known as "the Black Prince" during his lifetime (the middle of the 14th century). The first recorded use of the nickname came two centuries after his death, and it is as the Black Prince that he is universally now known. No one knows how the nickname developed. There is no evidence that he wore black armor, for instance.

———

Czar Nicholas II considered the construction of an electric fence around Russia and expressed interest in building a bridge across the Bering Straits.

———

Louis XIV, the Sun King, was an active and ardent admirer of the dance from the time he was thirteen years old. Before he became too old and too obese to continue, he performed in thirty ballets for which Jean Baptiste Lully composed the music.

———

From the history of Babylonia comes the story of Enlil-Bani, King Erra-Imitti's gardener, who was chosen by him to be the "king for a day" as part of a New Year's celebration. According to custom, each mock king, after ruling for his day, was sacrificed to the gods. In Enlil-Bani's case, however, Erra-Imitti died during the celebration, and Enlil-Bani remained on the throne. He ruled well, for at least twenty-four years.

———

Holy Roman Emperor Charles V said, "I speak Spanish to God, Italian to women, French to men, and German to my horse."

———

Czar Peter III of Russia ruled six months, then was murdered in June 1762 at the age of thirty-four by conspirators of his wife, Catherine. He was not crowned until thirty-five years after his death, when his coffin was opened expressly for that purpose.

———

William of Orange faced an insoluble legal dilemma when he sought the crown of England in 1689 after the flight of James II. Only Parliament could declare William king, but only the king could summon Parliament. A hurriedly gathered convention got around the dilemma by simultaneously offering William the crown and declaring itself a Parliament.

The Hapsburg Empire of early modern times was founded not so much by war as by an astounding series of dynastic marriages. In 1469, Ferdinand of Aragon married Isabella of Castile, thus unifying Spain; their daughter was Joanna the Mad. In 1477, Maximilian of Hapsburg married Mary of Burgundy, uniting Austria and parts of France and the Low Countries; their son was Philip the Handsome. Philip married Joanna, and their son, Charles V, became Holy Roman Emperor in 1519, inheriting an empire stretching from Vienna to the English Channel and from the Pyrenees to the Andes. To the empire were added vast conquests in the Americas.

Hitler, hoping to isolate and demean the Jews in Denmark, as he had elsewhere, ordered all of them to wear a Star of David armband. His plan was foiled by the courageous and compassionate action of the Danes. Within hours of the order, Danish citizens of all religions were wearing the armband. King Christian X declared, "*I am my country's first Jew.*"

A Pope gave Ireland to the King of England. Alexander III, wanting to eradicate Irish customs that conflicted with the teaching of the Catholic Church, declared Henry II to be the rightful sovereign of Ireland. This papal declaration, in 1172, led to the English conquest of Ireland. It took seven and a half centuries for the Irish to regain their freedom.

King George III harassed the American colonists by calling assemblies at peculiar locations and difficult hours. They construed this as a Machiavellian strategy to disrupt their sleep schedules, thereby rendering them psychologically vulnerable. This form of harassment was listed as one of the colonists' grievances in 1776: "He has called together legislative bodies at places unusual, uncomfortable and distant . . . for the sole purpose of fatiguing [us] . . . "

If the arm of King Henry I (1068–1135) of England had been forty-two inches long, the unit of measure of a "foot" today would be fourteen inches. But his arm happened to be thirty-six inches long, and he decreed that the standard "foot" should be one-third that length—twelve inches.

A plan was afoot in New Orleans to rescue Napoleon from the South Atlantic island of St. Helena and bring him back to the Louisiana city and install him in the residence of the mayor, Nicholas Girod. But before an expedition could be organized under the command of Dominique You, a former pirate and a hero of the Battle of New Orleans, Napoleon died. The mayor's house still stands in New Orleans and is celebrated there as the "Napoleon House."

In one ten-day period late in his reign (1368–98), the first Ming Emperor, Hung Wu, had to approve 1,660 documents dealing with 3,391 separate matters.

Edward III of England, angry at the eleven months of resistance by inhabitants of the French town of Calais, had undiscriminating slaughter in mind when the town surrendered in August 1347. He promised to spare the town if six prominent citizens offered their lives. When his queen, Philippa, interceded, Edward III spared the six men and the town. Calais remained in English hands until 1558.

Each of the two marriages of Eleanor of Aquitaine created a powerful political entity. When in 1137 she married Louis VII, King of France, he gained title to her lands south of the Loire. When the marriage was annulled, Eleanor regained her territory; and it was part of her dowry in 1152 when she married Henry II, King of England. The marriage made Henry ruler of the Angevin Empire, which included England and Aquitaine.

The reign of Czar Nicholas II of Russia started, and ended, with misfortune. At the coronation ceremony in Moscow, presents were given to all the people who attended. While these people were waiting to get their presents, which were laid out on stands at Khodinka field, a rumor started that there were not enough to go around. A stampede to the stands began, and hundreds of women and children were trampled and killed. The czar's reign ended with the Russian Revolution and his execution.

Ludwig II, King of Bavaria, had an overwhelming obsession to build beautiful, fantasylike castles. Because of his compulsion he went deeply into debt. Emperor Wilhelm I, a relative of Ludwig's, offered him a loan of 10 million marks, but Ludwig refused because the loan was to be given on the condition that it be used to repay debts and not for more construction. Ludwig unsuccessfully asked the kings of Sweden and Norway for a loan. He became so desperate that he was prepared to imprison anyone who would not help him raise money to build his dream castles.

One medieval ruler who was an open atheist was the Holy Roman Emperor Frederick II, who died in 1250. He set up a cultured court to which he welcomed learned Jews and Muslims on an equal basis with Christians. He found Muslim mercenaries useful in his battles against the Pope.

By the time of the French Revolution, a single family of kings that descended from Hugh Capet had ruled France for almost four centuries (967–1328). Related branches of the Capet family, the Valois and the Bourbons, succeeded the Capets and ruled France until the nineteenth century.

Charlemagne, the Frankish Emperor (742–814 A.D.), never learned to write; even though he practiced on tablets, he admitted he couldn't master the skill. He learned to read, however. He was ahead of nearly all other rulers of his time, who considered such skills beneath their dignity and left them to underlings and monks.

In 695 A.D., Leontius put himself at the head of rebellious Constantinopolitans and seized the emperor, Justinian II. He had Justinian's nose cut off, believing that with such a grotesque disfigurement Justinian would never again aspire to the imperial throne. After three years, Leontius was himself overthrown, by troops under General Tiberius III, who became emperor in 698 A.D., and who in turn cut off Leontius's nose. Justinian, after an exile of ten years, then retook the throne and publicly humiliated and executed both Leontius and Tiberius.

Two kings have ruled for seven decades—Shapur II of the Persian Sassanids ruled from 309 to 379 A.D. (his entire life, as he was born after his father's death), and, thirteen and a half centuries later, Louis XIV of France ruled from 1643–1715. Holy Roman Emperor Francis Joseph I of Austria ruled for sixty-eight years, from 1848 to 1916. Queen Victoria ruled for sixty-four years, from 1837 to 1901.

Louis IX was the Capetian saint-king. His Christian virtues are exemplified by his faithfulness to his wife (who bore eleven children), which was not the royal custom in those days, the thirteenth century. Louis wore a hair shirt, which helped, he said, to keep his mind on higher things. As a gesture of humility, he would kiss lepers and have poor people dine with him. So badly did some of the invited dregs of society smell that the soldiers of the guard (no flowers themselves) objected. Louis abolished trial by combat and insisted on using actual evidence to judge between the right and wrong of an affair. He promulgated stiff laws against blasphemy, gambling, and prostitution, but he also insisted on the most barbarous treatment of Jews and heretics. In 1297, twenty-seven years after he had died in Tunis of the plague, he was canonized as St. Louis.

For twenty centuries after the assassination of Julius Caesar, his name lived on among the rulers of the world. In modern times the emperors of Germany and Austria-Hungary were called *Kaiser,* the German spelling (and almost the correct pronunciation) of the Latin *Caesar.* The Russian word *Tsar* or *Czar* is also a form of *Caesar.* As late as just over thirty years ago, Bulgaria was ruled by Tsar Semeon II, and until 1947 the British Emperors of India bore the title *Kaiser-i-Hind.*

Peter the Great hated the Kremlin, where, as a child, he had witnessed the brutal torture and murder of his mother's family. When he built his capital at St. Petersburg, he forbade even the slightest repair on stone buildings in Moscow, asserting that every mason was needed in the new city.

Pepin the Short, King of the Franks from 751 to 768 A.D., was short indeed—all of four feet six inches. Yet he carried a six-foot-long sword and was a mighty warrior—and the father of Charlemagne. His wife, by contrast, was known as Bertha of the Big Foot.

The Shah of Persia, in 1889, was known to be a difficult royal guest. On a trip to London, he attempted to buy the Marchioness of Londonderry. During the same trip, when he was in a crowded room with the Prince of Wales, he asked him if the women there were his wives and suggested that the Prince have them beheaded and find himself prettier ones.

King Edward VII established the custom of keeping all clocks at the royal residence, Sandringham, set half an hour fast. He wanted his guests to rise early for the best shooting. In 1936, when his son, George V, lay dying at Sandringham, several mistakes were made because of the discrepancy between real time and Sandringham time. In a rage, the Prince of Wales (soon to be Edward VIII) ordered the clocks set immediately to Greenwich Mean Time. It took a local clockmaker from midnight to dawn to accomplish this.

———

A consul and coregent of Rome was a horse—Emperor Caligula's favorite, Incitatus, who was accorded honor at every turn. Caligula's successor, Claudius, did not invite Incitatus in to dine, as had Caligula, but the horse still was decently treated, in his ivory manger, with a golden drinking goblet for partaking of wine.

———

When George Washington became President, in 1789, a king ruled France, a Holy Roman Emperor ruled much of Europe, a czarina ruled Russia, a shogun ruled Japan, and an emperor ruled China. Of these, only the office of President remains.

———

At the age of seventy-four, Narses, a eunuch, destroyed the Ostrogoths and established Byzantine rule over all of Italy, making Ravenna his capital in the mid-sixth century A.D. When he was ninety years old, he was still governing Italy from Ravenna.

———

The first six Mogul Emperors of India ruled in an unbroken succession from father to son for nearly 200 years, from 1526 to 1707. This was remarkable, for there was no tradition of primogeniture and the contest for the throne was often bloody.

———

When Henry III of France visited Venice in 1574, the Venetians erected over the whole area of St. Mark's Square a vast blue awning painted with stars and covered the entire pavement with oriental rugs. They were anxious to secure France as an ally because Spain had shortly before conquered most of the Italian peninsula.

———

The first Ming emperor, Hung Wu, was so afraid of the malign influence of a former ruler's vital force, a force he believed resided in Peiping, the former Yuan Dynasty capital, that he ordered the city leveled, in 1368. But first he had his officials catalog the beauty and grandeur of the Yuan Great Interior, the imperial palace.

———

Akbar, third Mogul Emperor of India (1556–1605), was a brilliant general and ferocious fighter—but that was not all. He imported rare plants and grasses, grafted trees, crossbred doves, maintained zoological notebooks, sent for a Western pipe organ and taught himself to play it, commissioned translations of Aristotle and other Greek philosophers, wrote letters to the Pope and to two Spanish kings, and initiated the first Anglo-Indian diplomatic relationship when he corresponded with Queen Elizabeth I.

When Ivan the Terrible of Russia decided to marry, he directed all the nobles in his realm—those who refused faced execution—to send their marriageable daughters to Moscow. About 1,500 maidens were gathered in a huge building, where they slept twelve to a room. Ivan made his choice after inspecting the entire seraglio and presenting each with a gift, a kerchief embroidered with gold and gems. After the deaths of his first wife, whom he seems to have truly loved, and his second, he selected a third in a similar manner. She became mortally ill when she learned of the czar's decision to choose her and died in 1569 before the marriage was consummated.

In the winter of 1724, while on an outing at sea, Peter the Great of Russia caught sight of a foundering ship, jumped into the water, and helped in the rescue. He caught cold, suffered from high fever, and died several weeks later.

King Charles VII, who was assassinated in 1167, was the first Swedish king with the name Charles. Charles I, II, III, IV, V, and VI never existed. No one knows why. To add to the mystery, almost 300 years went by before there was a Charles VIII (1448–57).

For three years at the end of the eighteenth century, a future King of France was living in one room over a bar in Philadelphia. Louis Philippe, King of the French (1830–48), had joined the army of the French Revolution, but deserted in 1793. For the next twenty years he lived in exile. When the Bourbons were restored to the throne, he returned to France. In the revolution of 1830, with the support of the Marquis de Lafayette, Louis Philippe was chosen "King of the French."

Marco Polo discovered that Kublai Khan maintained 5,000 resident court astrologers. Their duties included the hazardous task of weather prediction, with unforeseeable consequences for those who guessed wrong.

When Mohammed VI (1861–1926) became Sultan of Turkey in 1918, he had been a prisoner for fifty-three years, having been put under strict house arrest at the age of four. Arrest was not uncommon in some countries for royal family members who might aspire to the throne and thereby present a threat to the current ruler. Mohammed went from prison to throne in less than a day.

The Plantagenet dynasty of English kings got its name from a sprig of broom—*planta genista*—that Geoffrey the Handsome of Anjou is said to have worn on his helmet.

Louis XIV of France, in an effort not to be outdone by the splendor of his visitor, once received the Siamese ambassador in the Hall of Mirrors at Versailles while stumbling under the weight of a fur robe that was encrusted with diamonds valued at one-sixth the cost of Versailles itself.

King Alfonso of Spain, who reigned from 1886 to 1931, was so tone-deaf that he had one man in his employ known as the Anthem Man. This man's sole duty was to tell the king to stand up whenever the Spanish national anthem was played, because the monarch couldn't recognize it.

Czar Nicholas II of Russia faithfully wrote in his diary every day. Though his reign was filled with political change and social upheaval, the entries usually consisted merely of descriptions of walks and teas. On the day in 1906 that he dissolved the Duma (the Russian legislature) when a majority of opposition candidates were elected to the representative body, Nicholas described the weather, his walk, his dinner, and his evening reading. There was only one sentence about the day's highlight news: "Signed a decree dissolving the Duma."

A mad monarch enabled Richard Wagner to compose and stage his *Ring of the Nibelung*. Ludwig II of Bavaria, who granted the composer a pension and a villa, suffered from mental problems that eventually caused him to commit suicide by drowning in 1886. The annual music festival at Bayreuth is his monument, as well as Wagner's.

Nero and Henry VIII were both relatively good rulers when they assumed power, but both became bloodstained tyrants. Each killed a philosopher who had been a good influence at the start of the reign, Nero compelling Seneca to commit suicide and Henry having Thomas More beheaded.

Napoleon, who called Charlemagne his forerunner, avoided Charlemagne's example in one vital respect. The Frankish Emperor had been crowned by Pope Leo III in 800 A.D.—an act that remained significant in the rivalry between emperors and popes throughout the Middle Ages. Napoleon, at his own coronation, in 1804, refused to be crowned by Pope Pius VII. He crowned himself, to show his independence of the Church.

George I, King of England from 1714 to 1727, could neither speak nor write the English language. This German prince from Hanover and heir to the throne succeeded Queen Anne when he was fifty-four years old. He had no desire to learn the language of his new country and made no attempt to do so in the thirteen years he ruled.

When it was first suggested that Constantinople be electrified, it was explained to the Sultan of Turkey that it would be necessary to install dynamos. The Sultan, not a man of advanced education, knew only that *"dynamo"* sounded distressingly like *"dynamite,"* and he knew what dynamite was. The Sultan vetoed the project, and Constantinople had to wait several additional years for its electricity.

Forty-seven czars are buried within the Kremlin.

Despite the fact that the Declaration of Independence stated that "governments derive their just powers from the consent of the governed," Louis XVI supported the colonists in their revolt against the British. In so doing, he contributed to the spread of the revolutionary spirit that toppled his own throne twelve years later.

William the Conqueror always insisted that he had not come to England as a foreign invader. He argued that, as a close relative of the English royal family, cousin to Edward the Confessor (King of England 1042–60), he had been promised the crown. The Norman Conquest thus became, in his eyes, simply a case of the rightful King of England making good his claim to the throne.

Napoleon favored mathematicians and physical scientists, but excluded humanists from his circle, believing them to be troublemakers.

ABOUT QUEENS

Queen Victoria's first act after her coronation was to remove her bed from her mother's room.

One queen of England never lived there or even visited there. She was Berengaria, who married Richard I, the Lion-Hearted, in 1191.

Rules for parties during the reign of Catherine I of Russia (1725–27) declared that no gentleman was to get drunk before nine o'clock and that no lady was to get drunk at any hour. The Princess Elizabeth, Catherine's daughter, and the other young ladies of the court reveled in transvestite balls, thus enabling them to circumvent the rules.

Princess George of Greece and Denmark, née Princess Marie Bonaparte—an aunt of Queen Elizabeth II—paid the Nazis a bribe, or ransom, of roughly £20,000 that allowed the eighty-two-year-old Sigmund Freud to move in 1938 from Austria to England. The occupying authorities had demanded the money, falsely stating he owed income tax, and threatened to confiscate Freud's library and collection. Freud repaid the Princess after arriving in England, having been able (also with her aid) to get gold out of Austria. Freud lived for fifteen months in England before dying of cancer.

Queen Elizabeth II wore three different crowns on the day of her coronation, in 1953. On the way to Westminster Abbey, she wore Queen Victoria's diamond circlet diadem. The official act of crowning was done with the heavy St. Edward's Crown, which is made of solid gold with pearl-studded arches. For the procession from the abbey, her crown was the Imperial Crown of State, which has silver arches and a thick ermine fringe.

Elizabeth I was all for bowling and dice and playing cards and fencing clubs; the mayor and aldermen of London weren't. Bowling and dice and playing cards and fencing clubs were allowed. Elizabeth also vetoed a bill that had been passed in 1585 by both houses of Parliament that would have restricted such Sunday pastimes as shooting matches and playgoing. What was good enough for their Queen, she reasoned, was good enough for her subjects. Besides, the government would make a profit on the money that was being spent in pursuit of pleasure.

———

Queen Austrichildia, the wife of the Frankish King Guntram, was ill with dysentery in the year 580 A.D. She felt that her two physicians were not trying hard enough to cure her, so she extracted a promise from King Guntram to kill them, on her grave, if she died. The Queen did die, and the doctors were executed as she wished, and in the presence of the other court doctors.

———

During her tour of the Russian provinces in 1787, Catherine the Great, seeing joyful people and prosperous villages, believed she had succeeded in making her subjects happy. She did not realize it was all a sham concocted by her prime minister, the one-eyed Gregory Potemkin, who had "Potemkin villages" prepared along the royal route. He had ordered the people to clean the streets, paint the fronts of their houses, wear their best clothes, and smile. The Empress never noticed the misery and squalor behind the facade.

———

Every day for forty years after her Prince Consort had died, Queen Victoria ordered that his evening clothes be laid afresh on his bed in his suite at Windsor Castle.

———

The first permanent settlement in the Old Northwest, founded in 1788 among mound builders' earthworks, was named for the hedonistic Queen of France who was later convicted of treason and guillotined. Marietta is the city, in southeast Ohio, and the Queen was Marie Antoinette.

———

Eleanor of Aquitaine, as Queen of England, presided over one of history's most extraordinary institutions, the medieval Courts of Love. Problems of amorous passion—e.g., "Is connubial love possible?"— were brought before her and a "jury" of great ladies, who rendered solemn judicial decisions. (The aforementioned question was answered negatively.)

———

The leader of England's "Bedchamber Plot" of 1839 was Queen Victoria, who refused to let Robert Peel, named to be Prime Minister, replace her ladies of the bedchamber with his own choices. Peel had to step aside, but in 1841 he became Prime Minister with authority to remove those around the Queen. The Bedchamber Plot was the last successful attempt of a British sovereign to overrule a Prime Minister.

A female pharaoh was unknown in Egypt before Hatshepsut, who began her reign in 1502 B.C. In order not to shock convention, she had herself portrayed in male costume, with a beard, and without breasts.

When Elizabeth I of Russia died in 1762, 15,000 dresses were found in her closets. She used to change what she was wearing two and even three times of an evening.

One of the many details to be taken care of for a British coronation is the preparation of the proper anointing oil. Elizabeth I said of hers that it was "nasty grease and smelt ill." Charles I had a special formula, including orange flowers, roses, cinnamon, jasmine, sesame, musk, civet, and ambergris. Traditionally, the oil is made in a quantity large enough to last for several coronations. By the time Elizabeth II was to be crowned, in 1953, the supply of oil had been destroyed by bombs, and the firm that had prepared it since Victoria's time had gone out of business. A Bond Street chemist volunteered to make a new mixture. To be sure that his sense of smell was perfect, he gave up smoking for a month before starting work.

English was not the mother tongue of Queen Victoria. Her mother, the daughter of a German duke, spoke German in the home, and Victoria—though she ruled England for sixty-four years—was never able to speak English perfectly.

In 1819, the year Queen Victoria was born, not one of the seven sons and five daughters of her reigning grandfather, King George III, had a single legitimate child who could inherit the throne. Victoria, who was born to George's fourth son, Edward, became Queen following the death of her uncle William IV, in 1837.

A couple of royal banquets cost Queen Isabella just as much as it did to sponsor Columbus's first expedition to the New World.

_____

When Catherine the Great traveled from St. Petersburg to Moscow for her coronation ceremony, the court followed in fourteen large sleighs and nearly 200 smaller ones. One of the sleighs was a miniature palace on runners. It contained salon, library, and bedroom. In it, eight people could stand side by side.

_____

When Mary, Queen of Scots married her first husband, Francis Dauphin of France, she wore a white wedding gown, because white was her favorite color. Today, no one would be surprised at such a choice, but at that time Mary was defying tradition: white was the traditional color of mourning for French queens. In wearing white, she foreshadowed her young husband's death two years later, and her own tragic end.

_____

When anesthesia was first used to diminish the pains of childbirth in the late 1840s, churchmen (all males) objected because in the Bible Eve was told, "in sorrow thou shalt bring forth children," as one of the punishments for eating the forbidden fruit. In 1853, however, Queen Victoria allowed herself to be chloroformed while giving birth to her seventh child, and all criticism stopped. None of the churchmen had the nerve to criticize the Queen.

_____

Mary Stuart became Queen of Scotland when she was only six days old. When she was born, on December 8, 1542, her father, James V, was on his deathbed. The baby Queen was formally crowned in the chapel of Stirling Castle when she was only nine months old—too young to wear the crown, hold the scepter, or repeat her solemn vows. Henry VI of England was crowned at the same tender age, in 1422.

_____

The fifth wife of Henry VIII, Queen Catherine Howard, practiced her role in her own execution. When she was informed that she would be beheaded on the following day, the Queen requested that the executioner's ax and block be brought to her cell—and they were.

_____

After a year of entreatment and flattery, the teenage Queen of Sweden finally got her way. In 1645, she got the French philosopher-mathematician-scientist René Descartes—"Cogito, ergo sum"—to help her found an academy of arts and letters and to instruct her privately in philosophy. The Queen, the nineteen-year-old Christina, even sent a warship to fetch the flattered French genius. The project lasted less than five months. A combination of the bitter Scandinavian weather and the working hours—philosophy instruction, for example, occurred in the unheated library of Christina's palace from 5:00 to 6:00 A.M.—led to influenza and Descartes' premature death.

———

ALL THAT GLITTERS

It takes more than two tons of South African rock to produce less than an ounce of gold.

There are more than 1,700 references to gems and precious stones in the King James translation of the Bible.

It took half a year for word to reach the Atlantic coast that gold had been discovered in California. The discovery was made in 1848, but John Augustus Sutter and James Marshall tried to keep it a secret. It wasn't until President Polk, in December 1848, announced the discovery that the gold rush of '49 began.

India has the world's largest stock of privately hoarded gold. Personal holdings are estimated at 5,000 tons, worth approximately $72 billion at a figure of $600 an ounce. Authorized imports are practically nil, but Indians manage to add an estimated 60 to 70 tons of smuggled gold to their hoards each year.

"One of the most beautiful sights is a urine dump at sunset, because as the stuff comes out [in space] and as it hits the exit nozzle, it instantly flashes into 10 million little ice crystals, which go out almost in a hemisphere, because, you know, you're exiting into essentially a perfect vacuum, and so the stuff goes in every direction, and radially out from the spacecraft at relatively high velocity. It's surprising, and it's an incredible stream . . . a spray of sparklers almost. It's really a spectacular sight." —Russell Schweickart, Apollo astronaut

---

Isaac Newton spent considerable time and effort seeking the philosopher's stone, hoping with its help to make gold.

The world's largest diamond—3,106 carats, 1¾ pounds avoirdupois, and valued at $750,000—was literally stumbled upon in Premier Mine #2, near Pretoria, South Africa, in early 1905. It was then sent by ordinary registered mail to England, where King Edward VII exclaimed on seeing it: "I should have kicked it aside as a lump of glass if I had seen it on the road." One hundred and five stones were cut from this diamond, known as the Cullinan. Two of the largest, the 530-carat Star of Africa and the 317-carat Cullinan II, are part of the British crown jewels.

———

Gold is the sixteenth most rare of the chemical elements. If all the gold produced in the world in the past five centuries were melted down, the result could be compressed into a single cube fifty feet on a side.

———

Though it is one of the rarest metals, gold was the first to be discovered.

———

Had the medieval alchemists learned how to make gold out of lead, it would have been a scientific success but an economic failure. The large increase in the gold supply would have decreased its value.

———

Spanish soldiers in Francisco Pizarro's expedition to Peru, in 1532, found emeralds as large as pigeon eggs. In the mistaken belief that true emeralds could not be broken, they pounded their finds with hammers and decided, when the stones shattered, that all they had found was colored glass.

———

Gold is so malleable that a single ounce can be beaten out into a thin film (less than 1/282,000th of an inch) that would cover a hundred square feet, and so ductile that a single ounce can be drawn into a fine wire fifty miles long.

———

"Tissue paper" gets its name from its original use: it was designed for placing between the folds of extremely fine gold-woven fabric, or "gold tissue."

———

When Mansa Musa (1312–37) left his huge African empire of Mali on a pilgrimage to Mecca, he created some unusual problems along the way. Not only was his retinue of 60,000 difficult to supply, but he gave away and spent so much gold in Cairo that the gold standard there was severely depressed, ruining the economy.

———

Neither of the men who started the Gold Rush of '49, Sutter and Marshall, discovered any gold worth mentioning, and both died poor men.

————

The great hall of the Buddhist monastery of Tōdai-ji, in Nara, Japan's first permanent capital, was built in the middle of the eighth century to house an enormous (fifty-three-foot high) cast bronze Buddha. The statue weighs more than a million pounds and is covered with a quarter ton of gold.

————

"Welcome Stranger," weighing about 200 pounds, is the name of the largest gold nugget ever found. It was discovered near Ballarat, Australia, in 1869, by John Deason and Richard Oates. Aside from its value as a unique specimen, its current value as gold alone is about $1,440,000.

————

The English explorer Martin Frobisher created a gold fever in England in 1578 when he returned from Baffin Island with 200 tons of glittering gold ore. Great preparations were made for getting more and more gold, but it turned out that the ore was merely iron pyrite ("fool's gold"). It was eventually crushed and used for road repair.

————

The medieval alchemists sought methods for forming gold out of cheaper metals. They failed and are sneered at in consequence. In the process of searching, however, they discovered the strong acids: sulfuric acid, nitric acid, and hydrochloric acid—substances infinitely more useful to modern industry than gold could possibly be. They get no credit for this.

————

To get at every ounce of gold the earth might yield, miners have dug as deep as 2½ miles.

————

Martha Washington's silver service was the source of the silver that went into the first U.S. coins.

————

Not until after William Hyde Wollaston died was his method for working platinum—that is, making it malleable for commercial use—published. He was so secretive that no one was allowed in his laboratory. Wollaston made a fortune working the glamour metal around 1800. It is heavier, rarer, and more inert than gold.

————

The amount of gold dissolved in the oceans is nearly 9 million tons, about 180 times the total amount of gold dug out of mines in the entire history of humanity. The gold in the oceans is too diffuse to be extractable at a profit.

———

Diamond is the only gemstone composed of just one chemical element, carbon. Although crystal-clear, it is black when reduced to dust. Diamond can be completely consumed by fire at temperatures ranging from 1,400° to 1,607° F., depending on the hardness of the gem. But don't worry about *your* diamonds; such temperatures are seldom achieved in ordinary burning buildings. Only in extensive conflagrations, such as the San Francisco fire of 1906, do temperatures get high enough, up to an estimated 2,200° F.

———

Before the Spanish conquests in South America, the Indians (Incas) had no iron. They had gold in comparatively large quantities, using it not only for decoration but also for everyday objects such as nails, eating utensils, combs, and eyebrow tweezers.

———

The Egyptians were crippling their own economy when they buried quantities of gold and silver with their dead leaders for, presumably, their leaders' use in afterlife. (Paper money did not exist.) Grave robbers, whatever their motives, served to keep the wheels of Egyptian society turning by restoring the gold and silver to circulation.

———

In early Egyptian history, silver was more valued than gold because silver was less often found in nugget form.

———

In order to gain 400 tons of gold a year, the Rand Group of mines in South Africa has to raise and mill over 60 million tons of ore. That much ore, many times the mass of the Great Pyramid at Gizeh, yields as much gold as would form a nine-foot cube.

———

Admiral Sir Cloudesley Shovel, commander-in-chief of the British fleet, was murdered in 1707 by an old woman as he struggled ashore after the loss of his ship on the rocks of the Scilly Islands. She killed him in the belief, current at the time among coastal inhabitants, that a body washed up was a derelict, thus giving her legal possession of the emerald ring on the admiral's finger.

———

AMERICA'S REVOLUTION

An attempt was made to kidnap George Washington while he was commander-in-chief of the army during the American Revolution. The governor of New York, William Tryon, and the mayor of New York City, David Matthews, both Tories, were involved in the plot, as was one of Washington's bodyguards, Thomas Hickey. Hickey was court-martialed and hanged for mutiny, sedition, and treachery, on June 28, 1776.

When the Articles of Confederation were adopted as the governing instrument of the former British colonies after the Revolutionary War, the British colony of Canada was invited to become a member of the Confederation, the only colony outside the original thirteen that was invited to do so. She decided not to become a part of the new nation.

On at least two occasions, in 1744 and 1775, spokesmen of the Iroquois Confederacy of Northeastern America advised English colonists to form a confederacy like theirs. Few are aware of this Indian influence on the U.S. form of government.

During the Revolutionary War, Tories outnumbered the American patriots in New York City, in certain parts of the Carolinas and Georgia, and probably in Philadelphia as well.

About one-quarter (5,400 men) of George Washington's entire army was lost in the Revolutionary War's worst defeat, at Charleston, South Carolina, in May 1780.

When the Continental Congress passed a resolution in 1777 creating the flag of the United States, members said it should have thirteen red and white stripes, but they did not mention whether the stripes should run horizontally or vertically.

Lord North, Prime Minister of England under King George III, put before Parliament in 1775 a number of proposals to conciliate the American colonies. They allowed the colonies to tax themselves to provide for their own civil administration and defense. Parliament approved the proposals, but the news did not reach the colonies until April 24, five days after the Battle of Lexington had ignited the Revolution.

———

When the American Constitutional Convention was held in 1787, its deliberations were kept so secret that the public was not aware for sixty years of what had taken place. The public was merely presented with a *fait accompli* in the form of the finished Constitution, with no idea of how the final draft was arrived at.

———

By 1760, one-third of Britain's ship tonnage was being built in the American colonies. This was due to the abundance of timber that made shipbuilding costs only half of what they were in Europe.

———

One signatory to the Declaration of Independence appended his address: Charles Carroll "of Carrollton," Maryland. He wanted to be sure that the British, if they wanted to hang him, knew full well where to look for him.

———

At the start of the Revolutionary War, the governor of New Jersey was a Tory giving aid and comfort to the British. He was arrested by the Revolutionary Congress of New Jersey and imprisoned. His life was spared because of the reverence the colonists had for his father. He was exchanged for Americans held prisoner by the British and sailed for England. The Tory was William Franklin, a son of Benjamin Franklin.

———

Andrew Jackson, later a U.S. President, was taken prisoner by the British during the American Revolution, when he was only thirteen years old. He had refused to polish the boots of a British officer.

———

The eight British soldiers and one officer responsible for the so-called Boston Massacre of March 5, 1770, actually were defending their own lives. Surrounded by a howling mob of more than a hundred civilians who hurled chunks of ice and rocks at them, the frightened soldiers fired their muskets almost spontaneously, without an order being given. A jury of Massachusetts men agreed it was self-defense, acquitting seven of the redcoats. The two who were found guilty of manslaughter were given suspended sentences.

The Boston Massacre was not, as is commonly supposed, the first instance of bloodshed between American and British forces as a prelude to the Revolutionary War. Two months earlier, a riot had taken place in New York in which British troops had cut down a liberty pole and killed a citizen in subsequent fighting.

Before there was George Washington, there was Artemas Ward. A graduate of Harvard (1748) and a Massachusetts storekeeper, Ward was a member of the first and second provincial congresses of Massachusetts. In April 1775, he took command of the forces besieging Boston, and in May was formally commissioned general and commander-in-chief of Massachusetts troops. He was, in effect, the first commander-in-chief of the American revolutionary army. When Washington was appointed to supreme command, Ward became second-in-command with the rank of major general. He viewed Washington without cordiality and offered his resignation to Congress soon after the fall of Boston, in March 1776. After the withdrawal of Washington's main army to New York, Ward remained in command at Boston, until relieved in March 1777.

The reason Washington's army starved at Valley Forge is that Pennsylvania farmers preferred to sell food to the British for ready cash.

The illegitimate son of an incompetent, bankrupt exile from an aristocratic European family became, only five months after joining George Washington's headquarters staff, in 1777, the general's de facto chief of staff. Though only twenty years of age, this "obscene" child—Alexander Hamilton—issued orders in "His Excellency's name" to men who were his superiors in age, rank, and breeding.

When Lieutenant General Lord Charles Cornwallis surrendered his British army of 7,400 troops (including 2,000 Germans) to the American Continental Army (8,850 Americans, 7,800 French) at Yorktown, on October 17, 1781, virtually ending the Revolutionary War, 7,000 British reinforcements were only a week away. (Cornwallis personally had opposed the British policies that antagonized the North American colonists but led the British forces that tried to put down the Revolution, defeating Washington in 1776 and Gates in 1780. He did not surrender in person, pleading illness. He remained in high esteem at home, and later distinguished himself as British Governor-General of India and Viceroy of Ireland.)

———

When Paul Revere reached Lexington in 1775 to warn the rebel leaders staying there that British troops were on the way, he was almost denied admittance to the parsonage where the rebels were quartered by the Reverend Mr. Clark, who did not recognize him. Fortunately for the future of the American Revolution, John Hancock recognized Revere's voice and admitted him. After Revere told his story, the patriots, including Hancock and Samuel Adams, realized that the enemy's first mission was to capture the American leaders, and they escaped to Concord.

———

John Adams, one of the American Revolution's most devoted patriots, was the lawyer who successfully defended the British captain and eight soldiers who had been charged with murder after the Boston Massacre of 1770. Although Adams was staunchly anti-British, and Boston was loudly clamoring for the execution of the soldiers, his belief in justice led him to accept their defense. He expected his action to end his career, but instead it won the respect of his peers. And mine today.

———

Ethan Allen (1738–89), one of the Green Mountain Boys in the American Revolution, informed the Continental Congress that he was fighting for the independence not of the United States, but of Vermont, which he wished to become a separate nation. Vermont declared its independence in 1779, but this was not recognized by the Continental Congress. When his goal appeared doomed to failure, Allen later in 1779 negotiated with the British in an effort to have Vermont made a part of Canada.

———

Three months after the Battle of Lexington had touched off the American Revolution, the Continental Congress made an attempt to stop the conflict by adopting John Dickinson's Olive Branch Petition, which asked the king to use his authority to end the war. The petition was signed by almost every delegate who would later sign the Declaration of Independence, but King George III refused to accept a petition from a rebel group; thus the American Colonies' final peace effort failed.

———

The British tea tax of three pence per pound that led to the Boston Tea Party of 1773 was actually a lower tax than the colonists had been paying. But they preferred to smuggle in Dutch tea rather than pay any tax to the British, even though British tea would still cost less than the untaxed Dutch tea. John Hancock, one of the most prominent smugglers, had attacked the tax as the forerunner of many more taxes, and the colonists bought his argument.

On June 12, 1775, the British offered a pardon to all colonists who would lay down their arms. There would be only two exceptions to the amnesty: Samuel Adams and John Hancock, if captured, were to be hanged.

Henry Laurens, who had served in the Continental Congress, was captured by the British when abroad in 1780 to negotiate a treaty with the Dutch. Before being exchanged two years later for Lord Cornwallis, Laurens was imprisoned in the Tower of London and charged "rent" for the "privilege."

New Hampshire lumbermen successfully resisted British confiscation, in 1734, of their most valuable trees for masts for the Royal Navy. Twice, in what came to be known as the Sailing-Mast Tree Riot, the townspeople of Exeter, using small-arms fire, beat back forces led by Daniel Dunbar, a British surveyor-general and lieutenant governor of the Colony, who had discovered in local mills pilfered lumber from those trees. Dunbar was unable to prosecute the townspeople because the legislature included lumber owners and the local justices of the peace included mill owners—they naturally all looked with favor on breaking this particular British law.

"July 4" could just as well be celebrated on July 2. It was on the latter date in 1776 that the Second Continental Congress voted independence from England. John Adams, in fact, wrote: "The Second Day of July 1776, will be the most memorable Epocha in the History of America.—I am apt to believe that it will be celebrated, by succeeding Generations, as the great anniversary Festival. It ought to be commemorated, as the Day of Deliverance by solemn Acts of Devotion to God Almighty. It ought to be solemnized with Pomp and Parade, with Shews, Games, Sports, Guns, Bells, Bonfires, and Illuminations from one End of this Continent to the other from this Time forward forever more."

It wasn't until January 19, 1777, that the Continental Congress made public all the names of the men who had affixed their signatures to the Declaration of Independence. One reason for the delay may have been the knowledge that if the war effort failed, the signatories would have sealed their fate as traitors.

At the time he signed the Declaration of Independence, Charles Carroll was prohibited from holding public office in his state of Maryland because he was a Roman Catholic. Catholics in Maryland also could not teach the young or be lawyers. Carroll, the only Catholic to sign the Declaration, was born to great wealth in Annapolis. His career as a public servant—and as a staunch patriot—began in 1773 when he wrote a series of articles denouncing government decrees without legislative action.

On July 4, 1776, George III wrote in his diary, "Nothing of importance happened today." He had no way of knowing what had occurred that day in Philadelphia, Pennsylvania.

The first surgeon general of the United States was appointed in July 1775 and was court-martialed less than three months later for spying for the British. Dr. Benjamin Church was convicted of having "criminal correspondence with the enemy" and was sentenced to life imprisonment.

A number of high-ranking British military officers refused to take up arms against America in the Revolutionary War, and there was a great deal of sympathy for the Americans throughout England.

The American army had to abandon its plan to attack the British at Newport, Rhode Island, in 1778, when over 5,000 militiamen deserted and returned to their homes. Throughout the Revolutionary war, George Washington's soldiers were short-term enlistees at best, and the army was forever on the point of disintegration.

Two of the major combatants of the American Revolutionary War clashed at sea off the eastern coast of India. France, an ally of the United States, sent a squadron of ships under Comte d'Estaing against thirty British ships under Admiral Augustus Keppel. The battle lasted the whole day, on July 27, 1778. Neither side lost a ship, but both fleets had to withdraw to repair damages.

A plan was afoot among George Washington's aides to kidnap King George III's son William, serving as a midshipman in the Royal Navy in British-occupied New York. The year was 1782, months after Yorktown but a year before the formal peace treaty was signed and the British returned New York to the U.S. Prince William would wander around New York seemingly at will, and Washington said that the kidnap plan merited "applause," giving his authority to try "in any manner, and at such time, as your judgment may direct." But when the guard was doubled around William's home, the commander-in-chief called off the scheme.

Although the British troops under Cornwallis surrendered at Yorktown on October 19, 1781, the preliminary articles of peace ending the Revolutionary War were not signed until November 1782, in Paris. Another year went by before the last British troops left New York. It wasn't until December 4, 1783, that George Washington rode triumphantly back into New York, from which he had retreated in 1776.

The first victory of the U.S. colonies over a British fleet was won on land. In the spring of 1776, a powerful fleet of British warships, commanded by Commodore Sir Peter Parker, joined a force of 2,500 seaborne troops under General Sir Henry Clinton to capture Charleston. During the close-in attack, the American patriots fought back valiantly under Colonel William Moultrie, decimating the invaders and the fleet. Commodore Parker sailed north to find safety.

At the end of the American Revolution, Congress was forced to flee Philadelphia—not due to British activity, but because of a mutiny by Pennsylvania troops demanding back pay. The Congressional meeting site was changed to Trenton, New Jersey, and later to Annapolis, Maryland.

The constitutional guarantee of a free press is a wholly American concept, emanating from early conflicts between the British authorities and editors in the American colonies.

In January 1781, more than 1,000 soldiers "resigned" from the small, already sorely depleted American army because they had not been paid.

AMERICAN INDIANS

In the early history of the American colonies, several Indians were seized and taken to England. Once there, the Indians were taught English and put to work making promotion speeches about the wonders and plentitude of the New World.

Many Indians, even though born in the United States, were not considered citizens until an act of Congress granting them citizenship was passed in 1924. Before this law was passed, those who had not been granted citizenship by specific treaties were considered members of "domestic independent nations."

Though she was born a Delaware Indian, Nancy Ward (1738–1822) was made "Beloved Woman" by the Cherokees and sat on their Council of Chiefs after taking command in a successful battle with the Creeks. After she married a white man, in 1760, she used her influence to keep peace with his people, but always managed to put the Cherokees' interests first.

P.T. Barnum signed a group of Indians for his famous nineteenth-century American Museum. Part of their performance was a wedding dance twice a day. The chief demanded a "new, red woollen blanket at a cost of ten dollars for the groom to present to the bride's father." When Barnum discovered that it had to be a new blanket for each performance, he complained, pointing out that the wedding was only make-believe. When the chief insisted that the dance was genuine, Barnum had to cough up an extra $120 a week.

When Columbus returned to Spain from his historic first mission to the New World, he brought back with him six Indians. On his second return, he brought back 500, with the suggestion that they be sold as slaves in Seville. Columbus's scheme was vetoed by Queen Isabella, who ordered that the Indians be returned to Haiti.

Indians of the Northwest Coast of North America had great ceremonial feasts where the host distributed gifts to invited guests. The feast was called a potlatch. Guests accepted gifts with the understanding that in the future they would give the host an even larger gift. This custom was sometimes used to cause the impoverishment of a disliked person, who had to provide a gift he may not have been able to afford. The Kwakiutl Indians of the area had huge potlaches as a challenge to a rival chief. The Kwakiutl chief would burn all his property and belongings in order to prove his great wealth. In one such potlatch, the chief who had been invited attempted to put out the fire with seven canoes and four hundred blankets. But he did not succeed because the host continued to pour oil on the fire until the entire house was nearly burned down.

———

Winston Churchill's mother was one-eighth Iroquois, of the American Indian Confederation, and it was to *that* she ascribed her exuberant energy.

———

The Hopi Indians, on their reservation in Arizona, so zealously guard their privacy against prying tourists that in some of their more conservative communities no cameras are allowed. Old Oraibi, said to be the oldest continuously occupied settlement in the U.S. (dating from 1100), will not admit outsiders at all.

———

Nearly 1,000 French veterans of wars with the Turks were shipped by the Marquis de Tracy to North America in the summer of 1665 to help put down the Iroquois guerrillas.

———

The American paleontologist Edward Cope (1840–97), whose large collection of fossil mammals is at the American Museum of Natural History, in New York, was a Quaker and consequently refused to carry a gun during his U.S. Western expeditions, despite the very real danger from Indians. He once flabbergasted hostile Indians surrounding him by removing his false teeth and putting them back, over and over. The Indians let him go.

———

A socialistic society of 200,000 Indians was organized and run by 150 Jesuits in a Portuguese colony along the Uruguay River between 1620 and 1750. Nearly all agriculture, commerce, and industry were managed by the ruling priests, who also arranged for recreation, sports, dances, choral performances of a thousand voices, and orchestra performances of European music. Every able-bodied person had to work eight hours a day in the trade of his choice. The penal code did not include capital punishment. The Indians were said to have been docile and content, and surprisingly fierce in defending themselves from attackers. The Spanish eventually took over the area and forced the priests and the Indians to leave.

———

The Apache chieftain Geronimo, after surrendering in 1886 and being imprisoned in Florida and Alabama, became a farmer and a member of the Dutch Reformed Church on a military reservation in Oklahoma. He was eventually expelled by the church for gambling.

———

With all their boldness, it is interesting to note that some of the conquistadors who were successful in the New World became so with Indian help. Vasco Nuñez de Balboa, for example, too poor to outfit himself as a proper conquistador, stowed away in a barrel on a ship bound for Panama. There he successfully romanced the daughter of Careta, cacique of Coiba, made friends with Panciaco, son of Comogre, cacique of Comogra, and with these local Indian chief allies became a leader of men and fought his way to the Pacific.

———

Germ warfare was used against the American Indians by the colonials. During Pontiac's rebellion in 1763 and 1764, the great chief and his warriors destroyed many British army forts. In retaliation, General Jeffrey Amherst and Colonel Henry Bouquet decided to transmit smallpox to the Indians by means of two infected blankets and handkerchiefs the British obtained from a hospital.

———

There were no pre-Columbian American Indians with blood type B. The American Indians are type A or type O, and exclusively O all the way from the southern edge of the last glacier to the Horn at the southern tip of South America.

———

A chief of the Omaha Indian tribe, Blackbird, was buried sitting on his favorite horse.

———

An "apartment house" of the Pueblo Indians at what is now Bandelier, New Mexico, rose three stories and had more than 600 rooms.

———

Navajo Indians are far more numerous today than they were in the past. Also, they occupy, more or less exclusively, far more land.

———

The suicide rate among American Indian teen-agers is about ten times the U.S. average.

———

The son of a full-blooded member of the Kaw tribe of Indians served as Vice-President of the United States: Charles Curtis, under President Herbert Hoover. Before 1929, Curtis had been a Representative and a Senator from Kansas.

———

American Indian women sometimes attacked United States troops. Indian males often would give their prisoners of war to the women for torturing.

———

It is now estimated that the Aztec civilization each year sacrificed to their gods 1 percent of the population, or about a quarter of a million people. The dead were eaten by the Aztec masses, whose diet was low in protein. The rich were able to import game from afar, but crop failures regularly deprived the poor of the maize and beans that, in combination, might have supplied adequate protein from vegetarian sources.

———

There were about 50 million Indians living in the Western Hemisphere in 1492.

———

ANCIENT PEOPLES

The natural dye Tyrian purple was so expensive—it was obtained from the anal gland of a small Mediterranean shellfish, and its production was the specialty of the ancient Phoenician city of Tyre—that its use was restricted to royalty. The shellfish were not only small in size but the quantities available were small, too. Only small amounts of dye could be produced, and as a result the price was very high. Before 1856, the only dyes available to mankind for use on textiles were those that could be found in nature.

———

The oldest continuously inhabited city, Damascus, Syria, was inhabited at least as early as 2000 B.C.

———

The rich tin mines of Cornwall on the southwestern extremity of England were dug in the thirteenth century B.C. by Phoenicians in their search for the metal that goes into the making of bronze. In over 3,000 years of mining, some 3 million tons of tin have been removed from the Cornish mines, and they still are not exhausted. (The greatest contribution of the seafaring eastern Mediterraneans—the name "Phoenician" was given by the Greeks to the Canaanites who lived on the seacoast—was an alphabet later adapted by the Greeks.)

———

The Phoenician navigator Hanno was the first to circumnavigate Africa. He accomplished the feat about 500 B.C. He observed that at the southern end of Africa the noonday sun shone in the north. This sounded ridiculous to Herodotus, the Greek historian, who reported the tale; but that very report shows us that Hanno *did* circumnavigate Africa. He would never have been able to imagine the sun shining in the "wrong" part of the sky if he had not seen it.

———

Though Sumeria was a notable culture, in what is now Iraq, modern man did not get the first hint that the Sumerians had even existed until a mere century ago, when the palace of the priest-governor of Gudea was discovered. The Sumerians practically invented civilization in the 5th and 4th millennia B.C.: wheeled transport, astronomy, mathematics, commercial enterprise, large-scale brickwork, and writing. And then the Sumerians, and their language, faded away. They were not killed and did not die out; they may have just stopped thinking of themselves as Sumerians. By 1900 B.C., none remained.

The ancients knew hardly anything about tides, because there are virtually none in the Mediterranean Sea. The first Greek to report tides was the explorer Pytheas, who explored the North Atlantic in 270 B.C. Even so, when Julius Caesar invaded Britain over two centuries later, he lost many ships because he didn't beach them high enough. It didn't occur to him to take tides into account.

The best-known story about Archimedes is that when he discovered the principle of buoyancy in the bathtub, he ran naked through the streets of Syracuse, shouting *"Eureka! Eureka!"* ("I have it! I have it!"). That was not a very astonishing thing for him to have done. The Greeks habitually exercised in the nude, and the sight of a naked male figure meant little to them.

Excavations at Ur in Iraq show that the Flood recorded in the Bible may have been a flood that occurred along the Tigris and Euphrates Rivers in an area about 400 miles long and 100 miles wide. The water rose high enough to submerge whole cities and deposit a layer of clay eight feet deep. To the survivors, it must have seemed that the entire world had been inundated.

Most amazing to the troops of Thutmose I, king of ancient Egypt about 1525 B.C., in their invasion of Syria and Carchemish on the upper Euphrates were the Nile "falling from the sky" and the river that "in flowing north flowed south." The soldiers were sons of the cloudless land of the Nile and thus were fascinated when they encountered rain (the Nile from the sky) and amazed at the direction of the flow of the Euphrates. The Nile flows north, so "north" means "downstream" to the Egyptians, and they naturally saw the Euphrates as flowing "backward."

Early Egypt recorded the names of the architects who built the great pyramids. The first great architect, Imhotep—who lived almost 5,000 years ago—is also the first scientist in history known by name today. China and Sumeria and Babylon did not record the names of their early architects.

————

The oldest man-made building of any kind still existing is the central edifice of the 4,600-year-old mastaba (a tomb for kings) built at Sakkara, Egypt, to honor King Zoser, first ruler of the Third Dynasty. The base of about 400 feet by 350 feet was surmounted by six mastabas of decreasing size, one on top of another, reaching a total height of nearly 200 feet. Smaller structures surrounded the step pyramid, and the whole was surrounded by a high wall made of elaborately designed panels of limestone. The enclosure was 1,800 feet long and 900 feet wide.

————

A city of men was needed to pull the 4,000 oars of the largest ship (420 feet long, 57 feet wide) built by King Ptolemy IV of ancient Egypt; his unusual hobby was the construction of immense ships. Because they were cumbersome and unmaneuverable, the ships usually were useless.

————

On the death of Amenhotep III (ca. 1372 B.C.), under whom Egyptian prosperity reached its zenith, a splendid temple was built in his honor. One of the pair of great statues of Amenhotep that flanked the temple emitted a high note shortly after sunrise. There seems to have been some internal arrangement set up by the priests of Amen to impress the unsophisticated.

————

No secret, now-forgotten preservatives were involved in preparing an Egyptian mummy. Common substances were used—such as beeswax, oil, and salt. The procedure, though, could be complicated and take up to seventy days. To be made waterproof, the body was wrapped in bandages, then smeared with wax. The Persian word for the wax was *mum*. The Arab word was *mumia*. To us, it's now "mummy."

————

In 8000 B.C.—which was about 500 years after the beginnings of agriculture, northeast of the Tigris River—there may not have been more than 8 million humans on earth. It is a little more than the total number of people who today live in just one city, New York.

————

One of the Seven Wonders of the World was the 200-foot- to 600-foot-tall lighthouse on the island of Pharos in Alexandria harbor. (No precise description of the lighthouse has survived and modern estimates of its height vary between the two figures given.) Completed ca. 280 B.C., it had been designed by Sostratus of Cnidus, who also built the immense Doric stoa that overlooked the Cnidian harbor. A wood fire that could be seen at a distance of twenty miles perpetually burned in the lighthouse for the protection of Mediterranean shipping. A large statue of the god of the sea, Poseidon, stood at the apex. The structure was destroyed by an earthquake in the fourteenth century.

The ancient Egyptians believed that forty-two demons were present at the Last Judgment of every human being. The number forty-two represented the districts of Egypt, which meant that at least one demon could claim an individual's soul from personal knowledge of his past life in the district from which he came.

There were no garbage-disposal systems in the early towns of Mesopotamia. Rubbish accumulating in the streets was packed down by the comings and goings of men and animals. As the streets grew higher, the floors of houses had to be raised with additional layers of clay.

Dice have been discovered in the excavations near the site of Nineveh.

Alexander the Great spared one house after he captured Thebes in 335 B.C. The city had refused to surrender, and he ordered it razed to the ground. Because he loved poetry, he spared the house in which Pindar the poet had lived over a century before.

The first person we know to have dated historical events from the time of the birth of Jesus was the Venerable Bede, an English scholar who was writing about 700 A.D.

Although they lived on the coast of the Mediterranean, the Egyptians were not a seagoing people. They were content to cruise "the mother of all rivers," the Nile. Under Snofru, ships as long as 170 feet traveled the Nile. Columbus's oceangoing ships were just about half that size.

The art of mapmaking is older than the art of writing. Many preliterate peoples, including the Eskimos, American Indians, and Marshall Islanders, drew diagrams of areas familiar to them. The oldest known map, now in the Semitic Museum of Harvard, is a Babylonian clay tablet dating from about 2500 B.C.

In the 2,000-year period of history that is covered in the Old Testament, almost every name mentioned is an original; no repetition such as in the form of naming a son for his father is found.

One of the causes of the Maccabean rebellion, of 166 B.C., was the fact that the Seleucid king, Antiochus IV, constructed in Jerusalem a gymnasium—"a place for exercise in the nude." The Jews were deeply shocked at the sight of open nudity.

The lone surviving written record of Mayan history is three codices written in hieroglyphs on bark paper.

A tablet from ancient Assyria, about 2800 B.C., has been found that states: "Our earth is degenerate in these latter days. There are signs that the world is speedily coming to an end. Bribery and corruption are common." More than 2,000 years later, Socrates complained, "Children are now tyrants. . . . They no longer rise when elders enter the room. They contradict their parents, chatter before company, gobble up dainties at the table, cross their legs, and tyrannize over their teachers." And Plato wrote of his students: "What is happening to our young people? They disrespect their elders, they disobey their parents. They ignore the law. They riot in the streets inflamed with wild notions. Their morals are decaying. What is to become of them?"

When the Greek historian Herodotus visited the three great pyramids at Giza, near modern Cairo, about 2,430 years ago, he was—like any other traveler—looking at an ancient tourist attraction. Even then, the pyramids were well over 2,000 years old.

The Minoans of ancient Crete, around 2000 B.C., had surprisingly advanced plumbing. Well-engineered drain systems, supply pipes, and a flush toilet were found in the palace of Knossos when it was excavated in 1899.

Syracuse's leading citizen in the third century B.C. was the greatest scientist and mathematician of ancient times, Archimedes, nine of whose famous treatises on geometry and hydrostatics survive. When the Roman consul Marcellus conquered Syracuse in Sicily, he instructed his men that Archimedes was not to be harmed. But Archimedes was run through by a sword when he begged a Roman soldier not to destroy geometrical figures he had drawn in the sand.

History's first known attempt at creating a nonperson occurred in Egypt. Thutmose III, having been kept from power by the female Pharaoh Hatshepsut, tried to consign her to oblivion by having her statues smashed and her name chiseled from public buildings after her death.

An Egyptian papyrus, which is dated at around 1850 B.C., gives us the earliest record of a method to prevent pregnancy. This contraceptive method consisted of putting into the vagina a concoction of honey, soda, crocodile excrement, and some sort of gummy substance. (It worked—if it made men stay away.)

If Spartan youngsters, inspected at birth, were found to be physically unsound, they were abandoned and allowed to die. Those in good health were taken from their mothers when they reached the age of seven and brought up in barracks to live the "Spartan life."

February originally had twenty-nine days every year. In 8 B.C., the Roman Emperor Augustus renamed the thirty-day month of Sextilis, giving it the name of August to honor himself. He took a day from February so that his month would have as many days as July, which had been named for Julius Caesar.

The Egyptian temples at Abu Simbel that were moved in the 1960s to escape the Nile waters gathering behind the Aswan High Dam were carved into 1,050 sandstone blocks, which were lifted to the top of the cliff and fitted back together. The temples are now as they were for more than 3,000 years, but situated 200 feet higher.

One of the Seven Wonders of the World, the elaborate Temple of Artemis in Ephesus, was destroyed in October 356 B.C.—a case of deliberate arson. When the culprit was captured and asked why he had done the deed, he replied he did it so that his name might live in history. The man was executed, and it was ordered that his name be erased from all records and never be spoken. But he did succeed after all; we know his name: Herostratus.

The first needles were made by Cro-Magnon man about 30,000 years ago. Made of bone, the needles contained eyes for the insertion of some type of thread, probably made of animal sinews. Cro-Magnon man, consequently, wore clothing made of stitched animal pelts.

———————

Though Venus is an elusive planet—by turns it is the morning and the evening star—its path was calculated by the Mayas with an error of only fourteen seconds a year.

———————

The famous Bent Pyramid was the tomb of Snofru (ca. 2780 B.C.), last king of the Third Dynasty of ancient Egypt. Snofru also built the first true pyramid, and his son Cheops was the builder of the Great Pyramid. A true pyramid has unbroken sloping sides. The Bent Pyramid had a rhomboid shape—that is, at a point somewhat above half its height, the angle of inclination decreases sharply, giving it a "bent" look.

———————

The greatest soldier of ancient times, Alexander (356–323 B.C.) was tutored by the greatest thinker, Aristotle.

———————

ANIMAL WORLD

The giraffe's blood pressure is two or three times that of a healthy man and may be the highest in the world. Because the giraffe has such a long neck, ten to twelve feet, its heart needs tremendous force to pump blood through the carotid artery to the brain. The giraffe's heart is huge; it weighs twenty-five pounds, is two feet long, and has walls up to three inches thick.

———

Alligators and old people have something in common, at least auditorily. They can hear notes only up to 4,000 vibrations a second.

———

Scientists have applied electrodes to the pleasure center in a rat's brain. The rat pressed a lever 48,000 times over a full day in order to receive that shock that seemed to him pleasurable, choosing the stimulator instead of having water or food or sex.

———

A species of sponge, called the red sponge, can be pushed through a piece of fabric so that it is broken into thousands of tiny pieces. The animal does not die. Rather, all the pieces reassemble until the sponge is back to its original, whole self and continues with its life.

———

Cattle branding was practiced 4,000 years ago. Old tomb paintings show Egyptians branding their fat, spotted cattle.

———

The formidable-looking black rhinoceros, weighing over a ton, is considered the most easily tamable animal in Africa. Once penned, he becomes so gentle he will eat out of his keeper's hand, and will come on call to have his ears rubbed.

———

The ring-tailed cat, the crayfish, the firefly, the glass snake, the horned toad, and the civet cat have something in common: none is what its name implies. The ring-tailed cat is a raccoonlike animal. The crayfish is a crustacean. The firefly is related to the beetles. The glass snake and the horned toad are lizards. The civet cat is related to the mongoose.

————

Thanks to ovum transplants of livestock, a bull in Texas can be mated with a cow in Scotland and the several progeny, incubated in the womb of rabbits, can be flown to any country on earth—to Australia or Argentina or Kenya, for example—for implantation in cows there.

————

Elephants, lions, and camels roamed Alaska 12,000 years ago.

————

A woodchuck breathes only ten times per hour while hibernating. An active woodchuck breathes 2,100 times an hour.

————

The smallest North American mammal, the shrew, is one of the most vicious. The short-tailed variety can attack animals twice its weight, poison them with a secretion from its salivary glands, and completely devour them—including the bones. Experiments have shown that the glands of a short-tailed shrew can contain enough poison to kill 200 mice.

————

The hippopotamus gives birth underwater and nurses its young in the river as well, although the young hippos do come up periodically for air.

————

The Chinese, during the reign of Kublai Khan, used lions on hunting expeditions. They trained the big cats to pursue and drag down massive animals from wild bulls to bears, and to stay with the kill until the hunters arrived.

————

So aggressive is the horned frog of Argentina that people believe that if the frog bites the lip of a horse, the horse will die. Actually, the frog's mouth contains no poison. It earned its fearsome reputation because it attacks animals many times its size.

————

The vampire bat is not as vicious as its image. It does not puncture the skin of its victim's neck, but, instead, scrapes exposed patches of skin with its teeth until it draws blood. So gentle is the scraping that the sleeping prey does not wake up while the bat is at work.

————

The horse was originally a small animal, incapable of carrying a rider for long periods. When the larger domesticated horse bred by nomadic tribes for warfare first appeared in the Middle East and Europe, it was met with terror.

––––––––

Apes are mentioned in the Bible (1 Kings 10:22), although in biblical times none of the animals we call apes today was known. The ape referred to in the Bible is the Barbary ape, which is not an ape at all by modern definition but a tailless macaque. It was the absence of a tail that made a primate an ape. When animals such as the chimpanzee and the gorilla were discovered, they were called "anthropoid apes" ("manlike apes") to distinguish them from the Barbary ape.

––––––––

The Goliath frog (Rana goliath) of West Africa measures more than 30 inches long (up to a length of 32.08 inches) from nose to toes and weighs about 7 pounds (up to 7 pounds, 4.5 ounces).

––––––––

The fastest dog, the greyhound, can reach speeds of up to 41.7 miles per hour. The breed was known to exist in ancient Egypt 6,000 years ago.

––––––––

Camels roamed the Wild West after a joint army-navy expedition landed with thirty-four camels in Texas to test their usefulness in the American desert—a pet project of Jefferson Davis (who later became President of the Confederacy), Secretary of War in the cabinet of Franklin Pierce, fourteenth President of the United States (1853–57). The project failed, and the camels ended up in a variety of civilian jobs, including racing. (A camel can beat a quarter horse in a short race.)

––––––––

The Egyptians trained baboons to wait on tables.

––––––––

The grizzly bear can run as fast as the average horse.

––––––––

A seeing-eye dog, or any dog trained to guide the blind, cannot tell a red light from a green one. When it leads its master across the street, it watches the traffic flow to tell when it is safe to cross.

––––––––

Thinking that its parents were a camel and a leopard, the Europeans once called the animal a camelopard. Today it's called a giraffe.

––––––––

Horses were not commonly used for farm work until the twelfth century, because the chest harness in use since Roman times was inefficient. The invention of the shoulder harness, the "horse collar," enabled them to pull a much greater weight and to therefore pull farm implements.

———

Bats are the only mammals that are able to fly. The "flying" squirrel can only do what the gliding opossum does—glide for short distances.

———

Chimpanzees have been trained to have recognition vocabularies of 100 to 200 words. They can also distinguish among different grammatical patterns.

———

The cheetah, the world's fastest mammal, runs at a maximum speed of sixty to sixty-three miles per hour. Remarkable also is its rate of acceleration—from a standing start to a speed of forty-five miles per hour in two seconds. However, it can maintain its top speed only for about 300 yards before exhaustion causes it to give up the chase.

———

It is the female lion who does more than 90 percent of the hunting while the male is afraid to risk his life, or simply prefers to rest.

———

A type of lizard, the chuckwalla, escapes pursuers by crawling into a crack in a rock and inflating its body with air so that it is wedged tightly into the crack and can't be pulled out.

———

Contrary to their reputation as cowardly scavengers that feed off the remains of carcasses left by lions, hyenas are active and brave hunters whose main prey is more often healthy, adult wildebeest and zebras than sick or helpless animals. They even will take on a half-ton African buffalo.

———

"The wolf at the door" was once a sad reality. Wolf packs could be found in all the forests of Europe, and in 1420 and 1438 wolves roamed the streets of Paris.

———

The camel originated in North America. Before it became extinct there, groups migrated to Asia and to South America. The Asian group currently includes the single-humped Arabian camel and the two-humped camel of Central Asia. The South American group includes the wild guanaco and vicuña and the domesticated alpaca and llama.

———

The opossum, the only native North American marsupial—carrying her offspring in a pouch—gives birth to babies that weigh only 1/15 of an ounce and are not yet fully developed. The babies of marsupials are not born in the pouch; as blind infants, they must feel their way along the mother's abdomen by instinct to get to it. Then they remain inside the pouch for several months, completing their development.

———

Despite man's fear and hatred of the wolf, it has not been proved that a nonrabid wolf ever attacked a human. For years there has been a reward offered by the Sault Ste. Marie, Ontario, *Star* to anyone who could document an attack by a wolf. The reward has never been claimed.

———

Marco Polo's account of wild sheep in the Pamir Mountains (in Central Asia at the borders of Russia, China, and Afghanistan) with horns six spans long seemed fantastic to his first readers. Other Europeans followed him and saw the sheep for themselves. Today, his description gives him a place in natural history, for this species is called *Ovis poli* in his honor.

———

"Buffalo Bill" Cody claimed killing 4,862 bison, a record, in one season, including 69 in one day alone. (Though popularly known as "buffalo," those were bison that roamed the Western Plains.)

———

The largest African elephant today may reach a total weight of seven tons—the largest land-living mammal alive in the time of man. (Yet it has only about the weight of a newborn blue whale.) The largest land mammal that ever lived was the extinct giant rhinoceros of the Miocene epoch, the baluchitherium. It stood eighteen feet tall at the shoulder, and probably weighed about 13½ tons. (Yet it had only one-tenth the mass of an adult blue whale.)

———

Between the mid-1860s and 1883, the bison population in North America was reduced from an estimated 13 million to a few hundred.

———

An animal's proportions—the shape of its legs and its wings, for example—are determined by its size, and they would be all wrong if that size were changed without an appropriate change in proportions. No insect the size of a man that retained the proportions of ordinary insects could (in the earth's gravitational field) walk, fly, hop, or otherwise progress the smallest fraction of an inch.

———

At birth, a panda is smaller than a mouse and weighs about four ounces.

Because the lemur, a primitive monkey, exists in Madagascar and in a few places in southeast Asia, some romantic people imagine there was once a continent in the Indian Ocean that connected Madagascar and Malaya and that most of it sank, marooning its lemur inhabitants at the two ends that remained above water. (This imaginary continent, which was named, naturally enough, Lemuria, has entered fiction as a kind of second Atlantis.)

Hamadryas baboons, in ancient Egypt, were believed to be companions and oracles of the god Thoth. They were given the honor of being mummified when they died.

The mouth-breeding frog, *Rhinoderma darwinii,* is unique in that its larvae are carried by the male in a large vocal pouch. When the eggs laid by the female are almost ready to hatch, a male frog—not necessarily the father—picks up several at a time and slides them into the pouch. The tadpoles remain in the pouch until they are fully developed frogs. Discovered by Charles Darwin, *Rhinoderma darwinii* is the only amphibian that breeds in this manner.

All other things being roughly equal, a small animal must have a faster metabolism than a large animal if it is to replace the more quickly leaking energy. The metabolic structure of an organism is related to its size. A shrew or a hummingbird must be constantly eating or it will die of starvation in a matter of hours, while a large animal can fast for long periods.

If the eucalyptus tree were to become extinct, the koala would become extinct, too, for it eats nothing but eucalyptus leaves. If the zebra population were to vanish overnight, African lions would decrease drastically in numbers. Bees, and numerous species of plants that depend on bees for cross-pollination would be wiped out as well.

Thirty thousand monkeys were used in the massive three-year effort to classify the various types of polio.

In Russia, dogs have been trained to sniff out ore deposits that contain iron sulfides.

In the first years of this century, by official count more than 100,000 horses were trodding—and polluting—the streets of New York City.

———

A rat can associate mission with assignment for about twenty-five seconds. If the delay between pressing a lever and receiving a bit of food stretches beyond thirty seconds, the animal is stumped.

———

In the days of the great buffalo herds on the plains, the largest recorded group was observed by a Thomas Farnham. Traveling the Santa Fe trail in 1839, he was in the midst of buffalos for three days. It is estimated that this herd of well over a million buffalo covered some 1,350 square miles—a little more than the size of the state of Rhode Island.

———

Although an alligator can close its jaws with a force sufficient to break a person's arm, the muscles that *open* its jaws are so weak that it is possible for a man to hold the mouth of a full-grown alligator shut with only one hand.

———

The digestive juices of crocodiles contain so much hydrochloric acid that they have dissolved iron spearheads and six-inch steel hooks that the crocodiles had swallowed.

———

A Tasmanian marsupial known as the "wolf" is a strange predator. As long as fifty inches with a twenty-five inch tail, it prefers the *blood* of its victims, or their blood-filled tissues such as nasal membranes and liver. It rarely eats muscles, and seldom returns to its kill. This habit leaves carrion for smaller predators, known as Tasmanian "devils."

———

While elephants and short-tailed shrews get by on only two hours of sleep a day, gorillas and cats sleep about fourteen hours. From two hours to fourteen hours seems to be the range of necessary nocturnal bliss.

———

Larger animals generally live longer than smaller animals of the same type. An odd exception is the human being. The human being lives longer than mammals larger than itself, such as gorillas, elephants, and whales. In fact, of all existing mammals, the human being is the longest-lived. No one knows why, but it isn't due to medical advances. Even in ancient times, human beings occasionally lived more than a century; no other mammal ever does.

———

All our domestic animals were domesticated by primitive man. Not one new animal has been added to our livestock in 4,000 years.

The opossum, often called "possum," dates back 45 million years.

Beneath the long, shaggy hair of the musk ox, which inhabits the Arctic tundra, is a dense woolly undercoat. It is such a good insulator that, when the musk ox lies down, its body heat does not melt the snow it lies upon.

The koala, of Australia, is perfectly adapted to one specific tree, the eucalyptus, and doesn't need anything else, not even water. It is one of the few land animals that do not need water to supplement their food.

When racing at top speed, the jack rabbit bounds, or broadjumps, up to fifteen feet.

The okapi can wash its own ears with its fourteen-inch-long tongue. It also uses the tongue to flick flies from its withers, clean its face, and reach the tender shoots of tall shrubs and trees. The okapi has a shape reminiscent of a giraffe. It is smaller and has a shorter neck. It is deep reddish brown with black-and-white zebra-striped legs.

The blubber of a male elephant seal may be only seven inches thick, but it yields as much as 210 gallons of oil. The oil is considered superior to that of the sperm whale for lubricating machinery.

Human beings are not the only animals that abuse their children. The Yerkes Regional Primate Research Center, in Atlanta, Georgia, concludes from studies of mother-infant relationships among the seventeen lowland gorillas at the center that abuse by gorilla mothers seems to be the norm when the animals are caged alone with their babies. By contrast, mothers in groups displayed loving, nurturing behavior toward their infants.

A minute-old cria, or vicuña, can outrun a man. In the Peruvian Andes, Indian shepherds smear infants with vicuña bone marrow so they will grow up to run as fast as the vicuña.

A mature porcupine has some 30,000 quills on its head, back, flanks, and tail; the belly is the only large area without armor. Once a quill enters flesh, it is difficult to remove, and it tends to "travel." A porcupine researcher whose leg was impaled with a quill in a laboratory accident observed that it took exactly thirty hours and thirty minutes for the tip of the quill to emerge on the far side of his leg.

———

The word "orangutan" did not originally refer to an ape; it was the Malay term for the "savage" people of the Sunda Islands and means verbally "man of the woods." European explorers changed the definition of the word so that it now means the animal that was known to the Malays as the *mawas*.

———

Three months after they have been laid, crocodile eggs are ready to be hatched. But the baby crocodiles cannot dig away the sand above them. They peep while still inside their shells, and their mother, who has been guarding them, hears their calls and digs them free.

———

The ancestors of the horse were only about a foot tall 60 million years ago.

———

The burrowing rate of the gopher is equivalent to a man digging a tunnel nearly eighteen inches in diameter and seven miles long in a period of ten hours.

———

Toads and frogs use their eyes to eat with. In swallowing, they close their eyelids, press down with their extremely tough eyeballs, and lower the roof of their mouth against their tongue, forcing the food down and into their stomach.

———

The cat, although not related to the camel or giraffe, shares one striking trait with them. When other animals move, the front leg on one side and the hind leg on the other move together, followed by the other two diagonally opposed legs. The cat, camel, and giraffe move their front and hind legs on one side and then the front and hind legs on the other side.

———

Only New World monkeys (those from Central and South America) can hang by their tails. No Old World (African and Asian) monkeys can, although many have long tails. Another difference: New World monkeys do not have sitting pads of tough skin; Old World monkeys do.

———

ART

A nearly fatal misjudgment marked Pablo Picasso's birth. The midwife, thinking him stillborn, had abandoned him on a table; but his uncle, a cigar-smoking physician, revived him with a blast of needed (albeit smoke-filled) air into his lungs.

———

The most celebrated statue in antiquity—Praxiteles' nude *Aphrodite*, made in the fourth century B.C.—had an almost identical twin. The principal difference: the second *Aphrodite*, which stood in Cos, was clothed. The nude *Aphrodite* stood for seven centuries at the highest point of Cnidus, which was at the tip of a peninsula in the far southwest of Turkey.

———

The idea that the American government should be involved in supporting the arts began with George Washington, who urged Congress in 1789 to use its "best endeavors to improve the education and manners of a people to accelerate the progress of art and science; to patronize works of Genius, to confer rewards for inventions of utility and to cherish institutions favorable to humanity." Succeeding Presidents expressed a similar concern. But it took almost two centuries for a President to translate good intentions into official policy. In 1962, President John F. Kennedy initiated government involvement by appointing August Heckscher as his special consultant in the arts.

———

After painting his most famous work, *Nude Descending a Staircase*, which was the cause of great controversy when it was exhibited at the New York Armory Show in 1913, the French Cubist Marcel Duchamp abandoned painting for "ready-made sculpture," such as found objects. He then abandoned art altogether for chess in the last forty years of his life.

———

47

Charles Willson Peale, American portraitist who seven times painted George Washington from life, also made for him innovative dentures—elks teeth set in lead.

———

Artists consider the basic colors to be red, yellow, and blue, but scientists say they are red, *green,* and blue. No pigment combination of red, green, and blue will produce yellow. Yet, if a beam of red light and green light overlap, the result is yellow. The answer to this riddle lies primarily in the totally different ways colors are achieved with light and with pigments.

———

When he won 100,000 francs in the state lottery, bought in the Crédit Foncier in 1891, Claude Monet became financially independent. He could then spend his life the way he wanted to—and he did—wandering about and painting the French countryside.

———

When Paris's most celebrated beauty, Mme. Virginie Avegno Gautreau, was presented by the realistic painter John Singer Sargent in his masterpiece *Madame X* exactly as she was—shallow, egocentric, immodestly garbed—the public was shocked, Mme. Gautreau became hysterical, and the artist was forced to retreat to London.

———

The world's largest art gallery is the Winter Palace and the neighboring Hermitage in Leningrad, U.S.S.R. One has to walk fifteen miles to visit each of the 322 galleries, which house nearly 3 million works of art and archaeological remains.

———

The earliest works of art are paleolithic animal paintings discovered in prehistoric caves in southern France (Lascaux) and northern Spain (Altamira). The paintings, which are superb, date from 30,000 to 10,000 B.C.

———

If he were not so famous as the inventor of the electric telegraph and the Morse code, Samuel F. B. Morse would be remembered for introducing the daguerreotype process into the United States, from France, and for his notable portrait paintings. He was a founder, in 1825, of the National Academy of Design and its first president. In addition, he was, for forty years, professor of painting and sculpture at the University of the City of New York (now New York University).

———

The *Mona Lisa,* completed by Leonardo da Vinci in 1503, is considered the most valuable painting in the world. In 1962, its value was assessed for insurance purposes at $100 million. The painting, which hangs in the Louvre, apparently portrays the Duchess of Milan. But legend has it that its subject is Moṇa (short for Madonna) Lisa Gherardini, whose husband Francesco del Giocondo of Florence, is said to have disliked the painting and refused to pay da Vinci for it. Francis I, King of France, bought it about ten years later for 492 ounces of gold (now equivalent to about $300,000).

In his "desperate struggle to liberate art from the ballast of the world of objects," the Russian painter Kasimir Malevich in 1913 "took refuge in the form of the square." His picture of a black square on a white ground was one of the first purely "abstract" pictures.

Hans van Meegeren, the forger of paintings supposedly by Vermeer, might never have been caught had he not sold one to the Nazi leader Hermann Goering. The postwar Dutch government, assuming that the painting was a genuine Vermeer, indicted van Meegeren for sending a national treasure out of the country. The artist confessed the fraud, and proved his point by painting another "Vermeer" for a jury of art critics.

The art forger Madame Claude Latour was so skilled that some of her vivid paintings of streets and suburbs of Paris in the style of Maurice Utrillo fooled even Utrillo himself. Utrillo confessed he often wasn't sure which were his and which were Latour's.

In grassy fields above the cliffs at Etretat, Claude Monet would work on five or six paintings at the same time. As the weather changed, he would switch from one canvas to another.

The largest painting in the world is *The Battle of Gettysburg,* painted in 1883 by Paul Philippoteaux and sixteen assistants, who worked for two and a half years. It is 410 feet long, 70 feet high, and weighs 11,792 pounds. In 1964, the painting was bought by Joe King of Winston-Salem, North Carolina.

Cézanne was turned down by the École des Beaux-Arts when he applied for entrance.

In the nineteenth century, the French painter Jean Géricault studied dying men at a hospital, shaved his head, and locked himself in with corpses in the morgue. This was his way of carrying the spirit of social realism to an extreme when he was working on his master-piece, the *Raft of the Medusa*. It had been inspired by a sea disaster in which 149 passengers from a wrecked ship ended up drifting on a raft at sea. His *Raft* drew furious protests from those of the classical school.

––––––––

The Swiss painter Angelica Kauffman (1740–1807) was already famous at the age of eleven. She died at sixty-seven, having painted all her life. Her portraits and historical paintings hang in nearly all the great museums of Europe.

––––––––

Henri Matisse's *Le Bateau* hung in New York's Museum of Modern Art for forty-seven days in 1961 before someone noticed it was upside down. About 116,000 people had passed in front of the painting before the error was noted.

––––––––

As though he didn't have everything else going for him, Leonardo da Vinci was described by people who knew him as "the most beautiful man who ever lived."

––––––––

A fine-quality Persian rug, containing as many as 1 million knots in every three square feet, may last as long as 500 years before it wears out.

––––––––

The record for both the largest and the heaviest mobiles (sculptural objects that move and are usually suspended in midair) belongs to Alexander Calder. His heaviest piece is *Spirale* and weighs 4,000 pounds. The largest weighs only 600 pounds, but is forty-five feet long and seventeen feet high.

––––––––

Five-year-old Arshile Gorky, the future nonobjective painter, stopped talking when his father walked out on the family. He began to speak again only when he cried out in dismay on seeing his tutor leap from a cliff; the tutor had only been pretending, but the stunning sight restored Arshile's speech.

––––––––

The Statue of Liberty was first erected in Paris, where, on July 4, 1884, the government of France officially presented it to the United States. Five months later, the French dismantled the statue and shipped the carefully numbered pieces to New York aboard the warship *Isère*. The statue is the work of the Alsatian sculptor Frédéric

Auguste Bartholdi. (A smaller version was erected on one of the islands [Isle of Swan] in the Seine River in Paris.)

The famous "Athenaeum" portrait of George Washington, which hangs in so many school rooms, was never finished—intentionally. After Gilbert Stuart painted it, in 1796, he did not deliver it to Martha Washington—who had commissioned it—but kept it and copied it repeatedly, in hopes of getting rich. He never finished the background so that he could tell Martha truthfully, whenever she requested the portrait, that it was incomplete.

Vincent van Gogh is known to have sold only one painting.

Fra Filippo Lippi, a Carmelite monk, and one of the master painters of the Renaissance, used as a model for his famous Madonna and Child the nun he ran off with. He also wrote a humorous romance in a racy style.

Picasso chose to stay in his studio on the Rue des Grands-Augustins in Paris during World War II rather than to escape to England, the U.S., or an unoccupied country.

The elegant songwriter Cole Porter was noted for his lavish gift-giving. One Christmas, he gave more lavishly than he himself realized. He bought twenty paintings from a little old lady who lived near his estate. Years later, after fame came to the elderly painter, twenty of Porter's friends discovered they owned original paintings by Grandma Moses.

Two British art historians proved in 1978 that more than a dozen major paintings attributed to the nineteenth-century landscape artist John Constable were, in fact, painted by his son Lionel.

Picasso, when he died in 1973, left in four repositories in the south of France the following: 1,876 paintings, 1,355 sculptures, 2,880 ceramics, more than 11,000 drawings and sketches, and some 27,000 etchings, engravings, and lithographs in various states. His estate was worth—at the official appraisal—1,251,673,200 French francs, or approximately $250 million.

Students were given a month to complete the competitive art examination at the estimable Barcelona Academy of Fine Arts. Picasso, at the age of fifteen, completed the examination in one day and, furthermore, won first place over all adult competitors.

An infamous murderer was caught, brought to justice in Florence, and hanged. Leonardo da Vinci, who already had made a name for himself, drew a sketch of the body and submitted it to the men responsible for commissioning the painting of the dead killer. Leonardo didn't get the assignment—Botticelli did. To this day, Botticelli's portraits of hanged men decorate the tower of the chief magistrate's palace in the former cultural capital of Europe.

In his early days, Picasso kept warm by burning some of his drawings.

Not until he was twenty-seven years old did van Gogh start to draw.

Charles Willson Peale, the patriot painter who did portraits of Washington, Hamilton, John Paul Jones, and other Revolutionary heroes, never saw a painting until he was a grown man. He was a saddlemaker in Annapolis, Maryland, when he one day went to Norfolk for supplies and there saw paintings for the first time. They were so bad that he was sure he could do better. On returning home, he started to paint, made money at it, and decided to make painting his career. He took lessons from John Singleton Copley in Boston and Benjamin West in London. He believed anyone could learn to paint, and he taught painting to his brothers, sisters, sons, daughters, nephews, nieces, and other relatives. Two of his sons (he had seventeen children), Rembrandt and Raphaelle, became famous painters, as did his brother James.

Claude Monet was painting the portrait of a huge oak tree that stood out vividly against a ruddy cliff in the Creuse near his home in Giverny, in 1883, when his work was interrupted by three weeks of bad weather. When Monet returned to the site, the tree was in full bloom, completely enveloped in buds. At the request of Monet, the mayor of the village organized a working party that proceeded to remove every single leaf from the tree. Monet then continued his painting where he had left off.

The genre of art known as Cubism derived its name from a belittling remark made by Matisse in reference to a Braque painting. Matisse said that the landscape looked as though it were wholly made up of little cubes.

Paul Cézanne was fifty-six years old when his first one-man exhibition opened at Vollard's gallery, a shop on the rue Laffitte in Paris, in 1895.

————————

Janet Flanner wrote that Gertrude Stein posed eighty times in 1906 for Picasso's portrait of Stein, after which he wiped the face off, saying he couldn't "see" her anymore, and then finished the likeness in Spain, where he couldn't see her at all. He also said, when friends complained that the portrait didn't look like Stein, that someday Stein would look like the portrait. And she did.

————————

The Dutch painter Peter Paul Rubens preferred to speak Italian rather than Dutch when talking to a cultured person. Even when he wrote letters in Dutch, he signed his name "Pietro Paolo."

————————

In 1930, during the depths of the Depression, Andrew Mellon, the American financier, bought twenty-one paintings from Russia's Hermitage Museum for $7 million. The Russians needed the cash and this American millionaire had lots of it, even in the Depression.

————————

Picasso and the poet Max Jacob, down but not quite out in Paris, shared a bed in turn. Jacob slept at night while Picasso worked, and Picasso slept by day when Jacob worked as a novelty-shop clerk. On arising in the morning, Jacob often would have to walk on a floor carpeted with drawings. Later, Jacob's footprints had to be removed by art experts.

————————

The Steins—Gertrude and her brother Leo—paid the equivalent of $30 for their first Picasso, "Girl with Basket of Flowers," and for three years, from 1906 to 1909, they controlled the Picasso output for the simple reason that no one else wanted a Picasso at the time. When they no longer could afford to buy, the Steins were *given* paintings by Picasso.

————————

As penance for a quarrel with Pope Julius II, Michelangelo, in 1505, began a more than year-long project creating a gigantic bronze portrait of His Holiness. Later, the portrait was melted down for cannon.

————————

Ambroise Vollard (1867–1939), French art dealer, collector, and publisher, made many small but wise investments in the paintings of Van Gogh, Cézanne, Matisse, Picasso, and Rouault when there was no market for these artists destined for worldwide acclaim. He accumulated and held their works for years, then slowly sold them to collectors and dealers, and got rich in the process.

———————

The facade of the Louvre runs two and a half miles.

———————

Both Leonardo da Vinci and Michelangelo were accused of performing dissections on living people in the pursuit of their anatomical studies. For this reason, Pope Leo denied Leonardo permission to study anatomy at the hospital in Rome.

———————

The famous cartoonist Al Hirschfeld has, for three decades, woven the name of his daughter Nina into his caricatures. For Hirschfeld fans, finding the hidden "Nina"s has become a regular sport. The U.S. Air Force uses Nina-searches as an exercise to train bomber pilots to spot targets. A Pentagon consultant has scanned Hirschfeld cartoons, looking for Ninas as part of a $60,000 grant for the study of camouflage techniques.

———————

"I am so rich that I just wiped out a hundred thousand francs," said Picasso, after making a new picture he didn't like disappear from the canvas.

———————

One of the common laborers on the Panama Canal was Paul Gauguin, the French painter and woodcut artist (1848–1903): "I have to dig . . . from five-thirty in the morning to six in the evening, under tropical sun and rain. At night I am devoured by mosquitoes." (About 25,000 workers died during construction.)

———————

The first American to become a professional sculptor was a woman, Patience Lovell Wright. She worked in wax, taking her models from life—including some of the most important people in English and American society. Only one of her works is known to survive: Lord Chatham (William Pitt the Elder), completed in 1779, now in Westminster Abbey.

———————

Paul Emile Chabas's popular painting of a nude, *September Morn*, now in the Metropolitan Museum of Art in New York, was not publicly seen for about two decades. It had created a sensation when it was first exhibited in 1912. It was sold to a Russian and hidden during the Revolution, and not seen again until 1935, when it was discovered in a private collection in Paris.

———————

BETTER TO GIVE

Ernest Hemingway gave to the Shrine of the Virgin in eastern Cuba, where he lived, Nobel Prize money he had won for the novel *The Old Man and the Sea.* "You don't," he said, "ever have a thing until you give it away."

———

Rodin bequeathed all of his work to his country. France paid Rodin's son a small annuity by way of compensation for his lost inheritance.

———

From his own pocket, Superintendent of Finance Robert Morris met the American army's demobilization pay in 1783. He was later thrown into debtors' prison, financially ruined in land speculations.

———

Because he felt such an important tool should be public property, the English chemist John Walker never patented his invention— matches.

———

Pierre and Marie Curie refused to take out a patent on the process of making radium. Radium, they declared, belonged to the world— no one had any right to profit from it.

———

John D. Rockefeller made his first contribution to a philanthropic cause at the age of sixteen, which was in 1855. By the time he died, eighty-two years later, the oil magnate had given away $531,326,842.

———

The German physicist Wilhelm Konrad Roentgen, who discovered X-rays in 1895 and initiated a scientific revolution in doing so, refused to apply for any patents in connection with the discovery or to make any financial gain out of it. But if virtue is its own reward, it is sometimes its only reward, for Roentgen, despite winning a Nobel Prize for his feat, died poor.

––––––––

When he learned, in 1905, that one of his company's batteries was defective, Thomas Alva Edison offered to refund all buyers. From his own pocket he returned $1 million.

––––––––

To help raise funds for the starving poor of Berlin, Albert Einstein in 1930 sold his autograph for $3 a signature and autographed photographs for $5 each.

––––––––

The Swiss philanthropist Henri Dunant devoted so much of his money and his energy to the establishment of the Red Cross that his textile business failed and he was reduced to pauperism. He was a co-winner of the first Nobel Peace Prize, in 1901, and left the honorarium to charities, not to his family.

––––––––

St. Francis, who founded the Franciscan religious order in 1209, had no theological training. He was a layman, born rich. But when he gave away his possessions and embarked on a career of charity and good deeds, his father disowned him.

––––––––

About $330 million was donated by Andrew Carnegie to libraries, research projects, and world peace endeavors.

––––––––

The richest heiress of her time was the Baroness Angela Burdett-Coutts, a friend of Charles Dickens. She gave away most of her huge fortune on whatever she considered worthy causes, not only endowing schools, bishoprics, and scholarships—as others did—but supporting poor peasants in Turkey, building model dwellings in London's East End, paying for a topographical survey of Jerusalem, sending cotton gins to Nigeria, founding charities for the protection of Australian aborigines, providing lifeboats for Brittany and bells for St. Paul's Cathedral and drinking fountains for dogs and—the list seems endless. When Queen Victoria bestowed peerage on her, in 1871, it was one of the extremely rare cases that a woman received this honor not for being mistress to a king but for her accomplishments.

––––––––

In his will, Tadeusz Kościuszko, the Polish patriot who fought in Washington's army in the American Revolution, specified that the

U.S. land tracts he had received be sold and the money therefrom be used to purchase the freedom of black slaves.

————

Gerrit Smith, a trader of Dutch descent, made available 120,000 acres of Adirondack wilderness to runaway slaves—a noble experiment with the help of his son, who was a professional reformer active in the Underground Railroad.

————

BOTTOM LINE

The use of Social Security number 078-05-1120 declined sharply in 1977, Social Security officials said—with a sigh of relief. This is the number a wallet manufacturer used forty years ago on a specimen card that he inserted in each wallet to demonstrate how cards of this size would fit. (It was his secretary's number.) Although the card was marked "specimen," countless purchasers of these wallets believed it was the number assigned to them, and tens of thousands of Social Security deductions were credited to 078-05-1120. It took twenty years to straighten out most of the mess. Today, things are more or less under control, but Social Security officials estimate that some confusion will continue for many more years. (As for that secretary, she was given a new number. Otherwise, among the payments to her account would have been millions of dollars in retirement benefits.)

————

Cyrus McCormick's reaper was considered worthless by his creditors when he went bankrupt after the Panic of 1837. Although he lost his farm, and everything he owned was put up for sale, no one considered the reaper a marketable item, and he got to keep it.

————

President Carter's "lean and tight" budget of $500 billion for the fiscal year 1979 equals the spending of $690,000 a day since the birth of Christ. To dispose of this amount of money in a year, the government has to spend $951,000 a minute, $57 million an hour, or $1.37 billion a day, including holidays and Sundays.

————

In 1900, the U.S. Treasury showed a surplus of nearly $47 million in income over expenditures. (The last time the Federal Budget was balanced was in 1969.)

————

At the age of 12, Andrew Carnegie worked as a millhand for $1.20 a week. Half a century later, he sold his steel company for nearly $500 million.

————

In the last half century, the U.S. federal budget has multiplied over 150 times, to $500 billion. Interest on the federal debt costs taxpayers more than $936 million a *week*.

———

Found on the site of the Sumerian city of Ur on the Euphrates were literally tens of thousands of clay tablets covered with inscriptions. It was hoped they would reveal important political and cultural information—and in a way they did: they were records of bookkeeping items and business transactions.

———

The gold reserve of the U.S. Treasury was saved in 1895 when J.P. Morgan and the Rothschilds loaned $65 million worth of gold to the United States government.

———

The system of writing checks predates the use of coinage. Fully a millennium before the world's first coins were struck, checks inscribed on clay tablets were used as currency in ancient Babylonia.

———

In 1969, a seat on the New York Stock Exchange went for a whopping $515,000; in October 1977, the same seat sold for a thirty-four-year low of $35,000—rampant deflation in an era of rampant inflation.

———

Sixty years after World War I, monetary debts owed by nations to the U.S. arising from "the war to end all wars" totaled nearly $26 billion, including interest. Great Britain owed more than $11 billion, France more than $8 billion, and Italy more than $2 billion.

———

Not a single bank existed anywhere in the thirteen colonies before the American Revolution. Anyone needing money had to borrow from an individual.

———

In 1878, Thomas Alva Edison announced that he would try to invent a practical electric light bulb. Such was the faith of the world in this young man (he was only thirty-one) that, on the bare announcement, illuminating-gas stocks tumbled in value in New York and London.

———

Money made from the slave trade by northern "Yankee" merchants was used to build the mills and factories that produced the war materials that enabled the North to defeat the South in the United States Civil War. Many of "the best" New England families made their fortunes off slavetrading.

———

For its investment of $400,000 in the Broadway production *My Fair Lady*, the Columbia Broadcasting System has earned more than $40 million.

———

Benjamin Franklin made the post office a financial success when he served as a deputy postmaster general for the colonies for twenty-one years, 1753–74. He had solicited the position.

———

As early as 1522, there was concern about business monopolies. In that year, the Imperial Diet of Nuremberg looked into the effect that monopolies had on the standard of living. The Imperial Diet was particularly concerned about the pepper monopoly controlled by the King of Portugal.

———

The registrar of the U.S. Treasury, L. E. Chittenden, suffered years of physical pain after signing in just two days 12,500 bonds in 1863 for immediate shipment to England. As it turned out, the bonds were not used.

———

Millions of dollars are pumped into the treasury of the state of Oklahoma by more than a dozen oil wells that rise on the grounds of the capitol in Oklahoma City.

———

In the 1880s, big industry began to set up trusts to monopolize production and distribution. The first big trust was Rockefeller's Standard Oil Corporation, in 1882. The first international trust was Nobel's Dynamite Trust, in 1886.

———

Andrew Carnegie, one of the richest Americans ever, practically became allergic to money as he grew richer and older. He was offended, he said, just by the sight and touch of it, and never carried any. Because he had no money with him with which to pay the fare, Carnegie was once put off a London tram.

———

To finance the Civil War, a 3 percent income tax on all incomes over $800 was enacted by the federal government in 1864. It was the first time an income tax was enacted in the United States. The law was discontinued in 1872. The U.S. Supreme Court declared the law unconstitutional in 1894. Not until 1913, with the adoption of the Sixteenth Amendment, did the income tax become law.

———

About 5,000 Americans have a net individual worth of $10 million or more, according to the 1970 U.S. Census.

———

Women as well as men ran farms in colonial America, and some women made a fortune at it. Indigo, a blue dye, was a leading source of South Carolina's prosperity. It was introduced into the colony by twenty-one-year-old Eliza Lucas Pinckney while running her father's farm. Seeds from her first successful crop, in 1744, were distributed to other farmers, and three years later South Carolina exported almost 100,000 pounds of indigo to England.

———

Western Union Telegraph Company had the opportunity—for $100,000—to buy the rights to the invention of the telephone, but declined. By 1881, five years after he had invented the telephone, Alexander Graham Bell had sold off almost all of the shares of stock he held in the company he had formed, never realizing how profitable they would be.

———

Klondike gold wasn't the only way to strike it rich in Dawson in the Yukon Territory of Canada in 1898. Entrepreneurs selling milk for $16 a gallon, eggs for $3 a dozen, butter for $3 a pound, and onions for $1.50 apiece struck it rich, too. For comparison, a good meal in San Francisco cost 25¢.

———

Although he is famous for inventing the cotton gin, in 1793, Eli Whitney made no money from his invention because he did not have a valid patent on it.

———

The first goal in life of Joseph P. Kennedy (1888–1969) was to become a millionaire. President John F. Kennedy's father reached the goal by the time he was thirty—and kept right on going, becoming one of the U.S.'s wealthiest men.

———

At the height of inflation in Germany in the early 1920s, one American dollar was the equal of 4.2 trillion (4,200,000,000,000) German marks.

———

In only thirteen years since 1851 has the U.S. Post Office taken in more money than it has spent. Congress has made up the difference in the deficit years.

———

America's first millionaire was Elias Hasket Derby, a merchant with the nickname "King." While other men of Salem, Mass., made their fortunes by commanding sailing ships that plied their trade around the world, Derby never went to sea at all. He knew all about ships and what was going on in the world, and used this information to accumulate his fortune. Information is still power.

When Cyrus McCormick invented his reaper in 1831, he invented along with it a concept that would become even more widespread and have more of an influence on the life of the average American than the reaper: the installment plan, a revolutionary idea for selling the machine to farmers.

Paul Revere, the American silversmith and patriot, designed paper money for the Commonwealth of Massachusetts, which issued the money in defiance of English law even before independence was declared. The notes were handsome but soon depreciated. Some of them subsequently were used as wallpaper in barbershops.

The longest jury trial ever in the U.S. federal courts began on June 20, 1977, and ended on July 10, 1978. It took the judge almost an hour to read the verdicts on forty-nine separate questions. During this antitrust action, by SCM Corporation against Xerox, it is estimated that both sides spent well in excess of $60 million in attorneys' fees.

Thomas Alva Edison's first attempt at marketing an invention was an offer of a new stock ticker he had devised to the president of a large Wall Street firm. Edison wanted to ask $5,000, but he was only twenty-three and completely inexperienced, and his nerve failed him. He asked the president to make an offer, and the president offered $40,000. Edison learned the lesson of not asking too little, and that was probably more valuable to him than this particular sum.

With no ready cash to do business, the town of Tenino, Washington, issued wooden money in 1932. There were denominations of 25 cents, 50 cents, and $1, printed on three-ply Sitka spruce wood—but no wooden nickels.

Henry Ford shocked his fellow capitalists by more than doubling the daily wage of most of his workers in 1914, eleven years after he had established his first automobile factory. He knew what he was doing. The buying power of his workers was increased, and their raised consumption stimulated buying elsewhere. Ford called it the "wage motive."

––––––––

The federal government keeps billions of dollars—much of it taxes collected by the Internal Revenue Service—in bank accounts that draw no interest. Banks turn around and invest much of these deposits in U.S. Treasury bills, on which the government frequently pays more than 9 percent interest. Incredibly, the government is paying the banks to borrow back its own money.

––––––––

When Jacob A. Riis published his classic book *How the Other Half Lives,* in 1890, the fortunes of about 1 percent of the U.S. population totaled more than the possessions of the remaining 99 percent. The pattern hasn't changed much. Today, the fortunes of about 8 percent of the U.S. population total more than the possessions of the remaining 92 percent.

––––––––

Despite inflation, the use of very large denomination bills has declined sharply. The $500, $1,000, $5,000, and $10,000 bills are no longer being issued by the U.S. The largest denomination being issued is the $100 bill. As the larger denomination bills reach the Federal Reserve Bank, they are removed from circulation.

––––––––

The largest part of the $15 million needed to buy Louisiana from Napoleon was lent to the U.S. by English, Dutch, and French bankers.

––––––––

The builders of the Carpenters Company of Philadelphia, in the eighteenth century, were paid for their work after the structure was finished. An independent assessment determined the payment on the basis of both the labor consumed and the quality of the workmanship.

––––––––

It cost $4,000 per inch to build an interstate highway project on the fringe of New York City in the late 1970s—over $250 million per mile.

––––––––

New York City's newest subway line cost $100,000 a foot to build— more than $500 million each mile.

––––––––

If things are too simple to construct, patents do no good. For example, in 1816 the Scottish physicist David Brewster invented the kaleidoscope. He patented it and sold it at a rate of thousands a day. However, many other people began to construct kaleidoscopes, and it became impossible to sue them all. Brewster made virtually no money out of his invention after the first few days.

The *Mayflower* was originally scheduled to sail for Virginia, but its destination was changed when word reached the Pilgrims that they would not be welcomed. The non-Pilgrims among the passengers were so upset with the decision to change course that they became mutinous. The Pilgrims forestalled an uprising when the ship dropped anchor off Massachusetts, in 1620, and persuaded most of the men to sign the Mayflower Compact providing for a government under law.

After twenty years as a faithful unpaid servant of the Duke of Windsor (formerly Edward VIII), Walter Monckton was rewarded with a cigarette case on which his name was engraved—misspelled.

The first plans for a tunnel connecting England and France were made in 1802, during Napoleon's reign. The plans developed slowly because of technical difficulties. By 1880, the British opposed the idea because they thought such a tunnel would make them vulnerable to attack. In the age of air traffic, a tunnel is now too expensive.

Henry Ford and Thomas Edison tried to produce rubber in the U.S. Edison tested seventy plant varieties for rubber-bearing qualities, in a laboratory on the Cherry Hill plantation near Way Station, Georgia, in 1929. The project was abandoned because of meager results, Edison's advanced age, and the Depression. (Goldenrod yielded some rubber in a process of chemical reduction.)

As early as 1655, the Dutch used lotteries to raise money for the relief of New York's poor.

The first "transcontinental" railroad was completed fourteen years before the historic "golden spike" linked the east and west coasts of the U.S. The lesser known "first" was completed in 1855 across the Panamanian isthmus—at forty-eight miles, the narrowest point on the American landmass.

Until there was a pay raise in 1814, U.S. Congressmen were paid $6 per diem when Congress was in session.

The *Mayflower* was not alone when it set sail from Southampton for the New World in 1620. Her companion for 300 nautical miles was the *Speedwell,* which twice developed trouble. The first time, repairs were made at Dartmouth. The second time, it turned back to Plymouth, where it was abandoned. *Speedwell* indeed. The *Mayflower* went it alone on September 16.

In the 1910s, there were about 300 auto companies in business in the United States. Today, just a small number of companies (primarily General Motors, Ford, Chrysler, and American Motors) put out "the American dream."

One of the most tenacious myths is the one of extreme human longevity. There are periodic reports that certain regions—the Balkans, the Caucasus, the Andes, and most recently the village of Vilcabamba in Ecuador—produce people who reach an age of 120 to 130, or even longer. Not one of the reports holds up under close examination. (For example, not one of the people of Vilcabamba who claims to be over 100 can be older than 96.) Many people *do* live to 100 and beyond—there are around 15,000 centenarians in the U.S. alone—but the oldest human reliably on record lived "only" to the age of 113 years and 214 days. She was Mrs. Delina Filkins, née Ecker, who was born in Stark, Herkimer County, New York, on May 4, 1815, and died in Richfield Springs, New York, on December 4, 1928.

One of the most resourceful counterfeiters was Mary Butterworth, a well-to-do American (1686–1775). She mass-produced eight kinds of monetary bills, in her kitchen, and distributed them through her large and well-organized gang—mainly respectable people of her community, Rehoboth, Massachusetts, including the justice of the county court and the town clerk. After Mary Butterworth and others were arrested, in 1723, their guilt was obvious, yet they all were acquitted. The reason was that she had devised a way of forging without copper plates, so that the court was left without hard evidence.

Except for the oil sheikdoms, Bermuda has the highest per capita income in the world.

The Fourth Crusade, launched by Pope Innocent III in 1202, supposedly to liberate the Holy Sepulcher, was the most profitable business transaction in Venetian history. Not only were the Venetians to receive about $3 million (85,000 silver marks of Cologne), but also half the spoils of all conquests made on land or sea. The Venetians and other Crusaders first conquered Dalmatia, which had recently rebelled against Venice. They sacked Constantinople in 1204 and sailed away with cargoes of silks, statues, gold, precious gems, and sacred relics.

CATASTROPHES

Probably the most intense earthquake in the history of the United States occurred December 16, 1811, and in two further shocks five and seven weeks later. It centered on New Madrid, Missouri, about 50 miles south of the confluence of the Mississippi and Ohio Rivers. One million square miles were shaken, a much greater area than that affected by the California quake of 1906. Chimneys were knocked down in Cincinnati, 400 miles away. Shocks were felt 500 miles away in New Orleans and in Boston, 1,100 miles distant. The naturalist James Audubon wrote from Kentucky that "the earth waved like a field of corn before the breeze." The course of the Mississippi was changed, some islands disappeared, and new lakes and creeks were created.

———

So far in the twentieth century, two objects have struck the earth with enough force to destroy a whole city. Each object, one in 1908 and one in 1947, struck isolated regions of Siberia. Not one human being was hurt either time. Pure luck.

———

An avalanche that is on the point of happening can be set off by the air vibration that accompanies a loud noise. For example, in December 1916, during World War I, Austrian troops stationed in the Alps started an avalanche when they began firing their cannon. Several thousand soldiers were buried.

———

A fully loaded supertanker traveling at its normal speed of sixteen knots needs at least twenty minutes in order to stop. In the absence of lateral leeway, a collision would be inevitable if an immobile object suddenly loomed up as much as three miles away.

———

The first hydrogen bomb, tested in 1952, was as powerful as the total of all the bombs dropped on Germany and Japan during World War II, including the atomic bombs on Hiroshima and Nagasaki.

———

In the famous Courrières coal mine disaster in northern France in 1906, which killed more than 1,000 miners, surviving miners thought they had been trapped for four or five days—it was for three weeks!

If the contemplated canal for Central America had crossed the nation of Nicaragua as originally planned, Lake Nicaragua would have been part of the canal and that would have consumed half the distance and reduced the construction to be accomplished. Strong Congressional sentiment for the Nicaraguan route vanished because there was an active volcano within a hundred miles of the proposed route. (Another volcano, about 1,600 miles away, Mount Pelée on the western tip of the French Caribbean island of Martinique, had exploded suddenly in 1902. The eruption destroyed the nearby port town of Saint-Pierre and killed 30,000 people.)

There have been at least fifty-four major floods in Florence since 1333. Italy's irrigation laws—devised with the assistance of Charles Perkins Marsh, President Lincoln's minister to the kingdom of Italy and the author of the seminal book *Man and Nature, or Physical Geography as Modified by Human Action*—were never adequately enforced, and the floods have not lessened. Marsh's ideas led to the enactment of conservation policies in the U.S.

Because there was a shortage of labor and a rise in wages after the Black Death killed much of England's population, in 1348–49, the nation adopted the Statute of Labourers, fixing rates of pay and preventing wage rises. Discontent built up over the years and finally exploded when the poll tax was increased. In 1381, a revolt of the peasants erupted. Led by Wat Tyler, the rebels seized Canterbury and marched to London. There, after a fruitless attempt to see King Richard II, they seized the Tower of London, killed the Archbishop of Canterbury, and burned and pillaged public buildings. The next day they met the King at Smithfield. Tyler exchanged blows with the mayor of London and was mortally wounded. The rebellion was put down ruthlessly.

In the seventeenth century, and principally during the period of the Thirty Years War (1618–48), about 60 million people died in Europe from smallpox.

About the year 1500 B.C., a volcanic eruption occurred on the island of Santorini in the Aegean Sea that was greater than any recorded in modern times, five times greater than Krakatoa, a volcanic island between Java and Sumatra that erupted in 1883. The chamber and mountain of the volcano collapsed, forming a caldera, a giant crater, 2,500 feet deep and thirty-two square miles in area. The eruption threw six cubic miles of ash into the sky. The virtual destruction of the island may be the source of the Atlantis legend.

———

In 1946, people and houses in Hawaii were swept out to sea by a tsunami, a catastrophic ocean wave caused by underwater movements generated by earthquakes, that had originated five hours earlier in the Aleutians, 2,300 miles away.

———

In one of the greatest natural catastrophes of the twentieth century to date, upwards of half a million people died when a tropical cyclone swept in from the Bay of Bengal and struck East Pakistan, in November 1970.

———

The sinking in 1912 of the *Titanic* with a loss of 1,513 lives is not, as most people seem to believe, the greatest sea disaster of all time. Far from it! It was dwarfed by the sinking thirty-three years later of the German vessel *Wilhelm Gustloff*, torpedoed in the Baltic Sea by the Russian submarine S-13. Close to 8,000 people drowned, most of them women and children—more than five times the number of victims that went down with the *Titanic*.

———

The most damaging earthquake in U.S. history, on April 18, 1906, lasted forty-seven seconds. The subsequent fire razed San Francisco. More than 500 people died or were missing and property damage was about $250–300 million.

———

As the Great Chicago Fire of 1871 was killing 300 people, an even deadlier fire was underway 200 miles to the north. It devastated Peshtigo, Wisconsin, killing 600 people; but somehow it never got the same attention.

———

When the volcanic island of Krakatoa exploded in 1883, tidal waves between 50 and 100 feet swept over towns and settlements along adjacent coasts, killing more than 36,000 people. Dust from the explosion spread over the greater part of the globe's surface. Where a cone 1,400 feet above sea level once existed, there now is a gulf more than 1,000 feet deep.

———

The earthquake that wrecked Tangshan, China, on July 28, 1976, killed about one-quarter of a million people. The quake originated directly under the city, and the night shift of 10,000 coal miners was underground when the quake struck, at 3:43 A.M. Some of the workers were not rescued until two weeks later. Four hundred and twenty years earlier, China had suffered recorded history's worst quake. In January 1556, an estimated 830,000 people were killed in the provinces of Shensi, Shansi, and Honan.

CHILDREN

Not until January 1978 had a child been born on every one of the world's seven continents. The last of the seven was Antarctica—with the birth of Emilio Marco Palma, on an Argentine military base.

———

So they would have a fashionably flat skull, infants in the Chinook Indian tribe were strapped between boards, from head to toe, until they were about a year old.

———

At the turn of the century, nearly 2 million children helped to turn the wheels of U.S. commerce and industry. Some worked in chemical vats at 2:00 in the morning—without a stitch of clothes on.

———

Though they were only five and three years old, Susan and Deborah Tripp, two sisters in the U.S. in 1829, weighed 205 and 124 pounds, respectively.

———

In 1852, police estimated that 10,000 abandoned, orphaned, and runaway children were roaming the streets of New York City.

———

Two gallons of beer were included in the weekly ration for each child in the children's hospital in Norwich, England, in 1632.

———

In the first nine months of 1975, according to the findings of the Council on Children, Media, and Merchandising, a child watching weekend daytime TV on the three major networks could have seen 3,832 commercials for cereals (many of them the heavily sugared kinds) and 1,627 for candy and chewing gum. But he would have seen only two advertisements for meat and poultry and one each for vegetables and cheese.

———

Hans Christian Andersen's fairy tales were greeted by bad reviews: ". . . quite unsuitable for children . . . positively harmful for the mind . . ."

———

So that their children might acquire proper manners and learn proper French, French trappers and rivermen exploring North America set up a "little Paris" in St. Genevieve, Missouri, in the 1760s. At the school for social manners, it was hoped the children seeking good breeding would acquire at least "the two elements of true politeness—grace and self-denial."

In the early seventeenth century, more than 1,000 children were kidnapped in Europe and shipped to America as "indentured" servants.

The mothers of Franklin Delano Roosevelt and Frank Lloyd Wright were convinced of their sons' future preeminence. Mrs. Wright was sure her baby would be a boy, and that he would become an architect. Before Frank was born, Mrs. Wright placed about a dozen wood engravings of old English cathedrals on the walls of the room that was to be the nursery. Mrs. Roosevelt, so sure her only child would be a great man, saved and marked for posterity his baby clothes and his scholastic workbooks.

When he was already President of the U.S. and his mother was past eighty years of age, Franklin Roosevelt (1882–1945) remarked that he had never in his whole life gone out of doors without his mother calling after him, "Franklin! Are you sure you're dressed warmly enough?"

CITIES

All of Reykjavik, the capital of Iceland, is heated by underground hot springs. Reykjavik is probably the cleanest capital city in the world.

———

The city with the most blacks is New York, with 1,666,636, as of the 1970 census. The second largest "black city" is Kinshasa, Zaire, with a population of 1,623,760.

———

New York City's administrative code still requires that hitching posts be located in front of City Hall so that reporters can tie their horses.

———

At the time of the U.S. War of Independence, Philadelphia was second only to London as the largest English-speaking city in the world.

———

Before today's skyscrapers, London's skyline was largely the creation of a single genius, Sir Christopher Wren (1632–1723), who had had only six months of architectural training in Paris. Wren was a celebrated mathematician, but today is remembered as an architect. Among the fifty-two London churches he created from 1670 to 1711 was the great St. Paul's Cathedral.

———

Tiny Juneau, Alaska—whose population in the most recent U.S. Census was recorded as being in excess of 6,000—has the distinction of being the largest city in the United States in terms of area. In 1970, it merged with Douglas, which is situated on an island across the Gastineau Channel, and now 3,108 square miles lie within the city limits.

———

About 35,000 people work in the 110-story-tall twin towers of the World Trade Center in downtown New York, and about 80,000 more visit on business every day.

———

There are more dentists in Ann Arbor, Michigan, proportionately, than in any other city in the United States. Ann Arbor also has proportionately more burglaries than any other city. No connection has been established between the two.

———

When Pierre L'Enfant's plans for "Federal City" were lost, Benjamin Banneker, a Maryland free black, remembered in detail—and in so doing may in part have created—the gridiron arrangement of streets cut by diagonal avenues radiating from the Capitol and the White House. The capital then was laid out by Andrew Ellicott.

———

About 24 percent of the total ground area of Los Angeles is said to be committed to automobiles.

———

From the tenth to the fifteenth centuries, when Paris and London were ramshackle towns, with streets of mud and hovels of wood, there was a queen city in the East that was rich in gold, filled with works of art, bursting with gorgeous churches, busy with commerce, the wonder and the admiration of all who saw it. The city was the capital of the Roman Empire of the Middle Ages—Constantinople. (Indeed, there were many glamorous cities in the non-Western world.)

———

Central Park in the heart of Manhattan, in New York City, is so beautifully designed and its features so finely accentuated that it would seem that nature herself had been the designer. Not so. The 840 acres were a marshy area littered with filth and shanties when Frederick Law Olmsted and Calvert Vaux, in 1857, began shaping a park that now serves as the model for other public areas in the U.S.

———

So many empty mine chambers—called voids—underlie Scranton, Pennsylvania, that the secretary of mines for Pennsylvania suggested in 1970 it would be "more economical" to abandon the city than to fill the voids.

———

Baghdad was once the greatest city of the world. It had a population of 2 million, and was larger even than Babylon in its prime. Baghdad's most glamorous and legendary period began in 786 A.D., when Harun al-Rashid, or "Aaron the Just," ascended the throne.

———

The underground of Paris is unique. A system of pipes, 600 miles long, furnishes compressed air to homes and businesses—it serves many purposes, but it was built originally to operate clocks and elevators.

La Paz, Bolivia, which is about 12,000 feet above sea level, is nearly a fireproof city, and the fire engines—ordered out of civic pride—gather dust in their firehouses. At that altitude, the amount of oxygen in the atmosphere barely supports fire.

Mexico City, known as Tenochtitlán when it was invaded by Cortez in 1519, was a flower-covered, whitewashed city five times as large as London of the same period.

New York City has 570 miles of shoreline.

The largest city in the New World in 1650 was Potosí in Bolivia. Huge silver deposits were discovered there in 1546, and by 1650 Potosí had reached a population of 160,000. Potosí is also one of the highest cities of the world: 13,780 feet. Its population has dropped to about 60,000 because of various natural and man-made disasters and the discovery of competitive mines in Peru and Mexico.

Special oil lanterns for lighting public places began to appear in European cities in the last third of the seventeenth century. The King of Naples tried to introduce street lights, but succeeded only when holy shrines were set up at convenient street corners and the inhabitants were persuaded to keep lamps burning below them. This was the only regular illumination Naples had from the 1750s to 1806, when actual street lamps appeared.

It wasn't too long ago—1977 to be exact—that Cairo, a city of 8 million people, had only 208,000 telephones and no telephone book. The phone system was said to have been practically worthless during the work day. Cairo businessmen often flew to Athens to place calls from hotels there.

COLD FACTS

The coldest temperature recorded in the northern hemisphere was not within the Arctic regions. A temperature of −71° C. (−96° F.) was recorded in January 1964, in the village of Oymyakon in eastern Siberia. It is 320 kilometers south of the Arctic Circle.

———

Africa, the warmest of the continents, has thirteen square kilometers of glaciers on three of its highest mountain peaks. Only Australia, of all the continents, has no glaciers, because it is relatively unmountainous. (Nearby New Guinea and New Zealand have glaciers.)

———

The first mention of an iceberg in world literature did not come till 800 A.D. An account of the travels of the Irish monk St. Brendan in the North Atlantic, three centuries before, appeared about then and mentioned his having sighted a "floating crystal castle." What else could that have been?

———

The ice from spring-fed Rockland Lake, in New York State, was considered of such superior quality that as late as 1924 it was harvested for sale in New York City. The operation—a victim of mechanical refrigeration—was then halted by the Knickerbocker Ice Company. When the harvesting of natural ice was a major industry in the state, the company employed as many as 4,000 men to cut, store, and ship the ice from this single lake.

———

The African climate is not always warm. The Nile has frozen over at least twice, in 829 A.D. and in 1010.

———

The most recent ice age reached its peak in 16,000 B.C., and it wasn't till 8000 B.C. that the ice began its final retreat. In 6000 B.C., the Great Lakes were clear, and for the first time in 25,000 years Canada began to lose its ice cover. It was not until 3000 B.C. that the ice retreated to its present location; by then human beings were establishing cities all over the Middle East.

———

The Antarctic ice is forced out over the Ross Sea—a large inlet into Antarctica—in a layer hundreds of feet thick. It is called the Ross Ice Shelf, and its area is about equal to that of France.

———

At the height of the various ice ages of the last million years, as much as 30 percent of all the land on the planet was covered with a thick layer of ice.

———

The Korean women—called *ama*—who harvest shellfish by diving without diving gear into the sea, subject themselves daily to a greater cold stress than any other people.

———

Russia's Winter Palace was an abode of death during construction. Thousands of men would work in rooms heated to 86° F. and on leaving for the day enter outdoor freezes down to 20° below zero. The Marquis de Custine observed, in 1839, that "a considerable number died each day, but, as the victims were instantly replaced by other champions who filled their places, to perish in their turn in this inglorious fashion, the losses were not apparent. . . . Nevertheless, the sovereign was called 'Father' by men sacrificed in such great numbers under his eyes."

———

After the most recent North American glacier ended its southward advance about 11,000 years ago, it took more than 4,000 years for the mile-deep ice mass to melt from the present site of Hartford, Connecticut, to that of St. Johnsbury, Vermont, a distance of 190 miles.

———

The Eskimo make and use wooden "eyeglasses" with only narrow slits for eyepieces, to protect their eyes from glare reflected by ice and snow.

———

Small flat icebergs have been fitted with sails and piloted more than 2,400 miles from the Antarctic to Valparaiso, Chile, and to Cakkaiub, Peru.

———

High altitude and continuous darkness in winter combine to make the interior of Antarctica the coldest place on earth. The lowest temperature ever recorded was −126.9° F. (−88.3 C.), at 11,500 feet above sea level, at the Russian station of Vostok on August 24, 1960.

———

The temperature can become so cold in eastern Siberia that the moisture in a person's breath can freeze in the air and fall to the earth with soft crackling or whispering sounds.

During the last ice age, 23,000 years ago, there were giant icebergs in the ocean as far south as Mexico City.

Some 16,000 icebergs form in the Arctic each year, about 90 percent of them forming from glaciers on the west coast of Greenland. They are dangerous only if they drift farther south than Newfoundland, and an average of 400 do so each year. The record southerly penetration of an iceberg came on June 2, 1934, when one was sighted in mid-Atlantic at the latitude of northern Florida.

An iceberg larger than Belgium was observed in the South Pacific in 1956. It was 208 miles long and 60 miles wide—the largest ever seen.

About 3.9 million square miles of the earth's land surface (about 10 percent of the whole) is under a permanent ice cover. Eighty percent of all the world's ice is in Antarctica; 12 percent more is in Greenland. The remaining 8 percent is distributed among various polar islands and mountain peaks.

The cities of Paris and Vancouver are at 49° North Latitude. At the same latitude south of the equator is an island in the Indian Ocean called either Kerguelen, after its discoverer, or Desolation Island, after its characteristics. It is semipolar, frigid, tempest-ridden, with snowfields and glaciers, reflecting the enormous effect of the Antarctic icebox on the southern half of the planet.

A catastrophic temperature drop is not needed to get an ice age under way. The drop need only be enough to allow a little more snow to fall during a slightly colder winter than can be melted by a succeeding, slightly cooler summer.

An iceberg contains more heat than a match. The total heat energy of the iceberg (i.e., the total kinetic energy of all its molecules) is greater than the heat energy of the match. It's the temperature of the match that is greater.

The Indians of Tierra del Fuego, at the southern tip of South America, near Antarctica, wore no clothes to protect themselves from the sleet-filled air and icy waters.

––––––––

It is not surprising that nine-tenths of an iceberg is under water. The surprising thing is that one-tenth of the iceberg is above water. Ice floats because water expands when it freezes—and there are very few other substances that expand when they freeze. Contraction on freezing is almost universal.

––––––––

Not until the "unsinkable" steamship *Titanic* struck an iceberg in the North Atlantic and quickly went to the bottom, in 1912, did federal authorities order all steamships to provide enough lifeboats for all passengers. (There has not been a single ship collision with an iceberg in the regions guarded by cutters of the International Ice Patrol, which was established—in the wake of the *Titanic* disaster—by the American and British governments to warn of errant icebergs that drift toward the steamer lanes.)

––––––––

The hardness of ice is similar to that of concrete.

––––––––

The American explorer Richard Byrd, the first man to fly over the North and South Poles, once spent five months alone in Antarctica.

––––––––

During most of the history of the third planet from the Sun (our Earth), the North and South Poles have been free of ice.

––––––––

The terrain of Antarctica, nearly one and a half times as big as the United States, is amazingly varied. The South Pole itself is flat, snow-covered ice. Elsewhere, there are jagged mountains, an ice-covered lake whose depths register 80° F., and a smoking volcano.

––––––––

Mountains, lakes—some more than a hundred miles long—and deep troughs have been found, by airborne radar, to be entombed under Antarctic ice.

––––––––

Endolithic organisms, meaning those such as mollusks or coral that live within rocks, have been found in ancient frozen rocks dug out in Antarctica. The organisms are said to be as much alive as the petunia in the window of a florist shop.

––––––––

Water freezes faster if it is cooled rapidly from a relatively warm temperature than if it is cooled at the same rate from a lower temperature.

———

COMMUNICATIONS

The Leyland liner *Californian,* bound in April 1912 from London to Boston, with room for forty-seven passengers but carrying none at the time, was close enough to receive wireless messages from the foundering *Titanic* and to help in a rescue. But the *Californian's* radio operator was not on duty. He had had no relief, and had to sleep sometime.

Columbus was on the road out of Spain and on his way to Paris for financial backing in early 1492, when a messenger overtook him with news that the Spanish King Ferdinand had changed his mind and would finance a westward voyage to India.

Not until November 18, 1951, had anyone in the United States seen both the Atlantic and Pacific Oceans "live" and simultaneously. To demonstrate the power of television, Edward R. Murrow's first "See It Now" telecast, on that day, spanned the continent on a split screen.

Public relations methods were used to sell to Englishmen the idea of settling in the American colonies. In 1605, George Waymouth, commander of a trading voyage to the Maine coast, returned to Dartmouth with a valuable cargo of furs and five captive Indian maids. The girls learned the English language and adopted English dress and habits, including a taste for beer. They made numerous public appearances extolling their native land as a veritable paradise. They were a sensation.

As Apollo 11 approached the moon, the onboard computer "panicked," repeatedly stating that it could not handle the data. The astronauts took over the landing procedure.

Based on the rate at which knowledge is growing, it can be speculated that by the time today's child reaches fifty years of age, 97 percent of everything known in the world at that time will have been learned since his birth.

––––––––

Fiber-optic wires can now conduct 800 million pieces of information in one second. These glass wires are lighter, cheaper, and far more efficient than copper cables, and are rapidly replacing them.

––––––––

It took five months to get word back to Queen Isabella about the voyage of Columbus, two weeks for Europe to hear about Lincoln's assassination, and only 1.3 seconds to get the word from Neil Armstrong that man can walk on the moon.

––––––––

Because radio waves travel at 186,000 miles per second and sound waves saunter along at 700 miles per hour, a broadcast voice can be heard sooner 13,000 miles away than it can be heard at the back of the room in which it originated.

––––––––

The "hot line" between Moscow and Washington—it is a direct teletypewriter cable—is leased from commercial companies.

––––––––

In the early 1900s, Adolf Hitler regularly had lessons in mass psychology and speaking under the tutorship of a man named Erik Jan Hanussen, one of the most renowned seers and astrologers in Europe. He taught Hitler the tricks of elocution and use of body language.

––––––––

There were 7,433 licensed commercial radio stations in the United States on January 31, 1978. (The first commercial radio station in the United States, KDKA Pittsburgh, began broadcasting in November 1920.)

––––––––

Paris's best-known monument, the Eiffel Tower, was saved from demolition in 1909 because there was an antenna, of great importance to French radio telegraphy, mounted at the top of the nearly 1,000-foot-high structure.

––––––––

In the mid-19th century, the French semaphore system stretched over 3,000 miles, through 556 separate stations. Atop 556 hills, wooden towers with movable arms signaled messages in code. Official messages could be sent across France quickly.

––––––––

During the "blackout" of July 13–14, 1977, when electric power to New York City failed during the early evening and was not restored until the next afternoon, a record eighty million telephone calls were made. On an average business day, thirty-six million calls are made in the city.

COMPOUNDS
AND ELEMENTS

The most common compound in the universe (a compound is something with a molecule made up of more than one kind of matter) is water. Its molecule is made up of two hydrogen atoms and one oxygen atom. Hydrogen is the most common atom in the universe, and oxygen is the third most common, so water has to be the number-one compound. The second most common atom? Helium—and it forms no compounds.

———

There are only eighty-one stable chemical elements. The last of these to be discovered, rhenium, was found in 1925. Since then, fifteen additional elements have been discovered—all radioactive.

———

If a substance is burned and all the products of its burning—smoke, ash, soot, gas—are captured and weighed, the products together will weigh a little more than did the original substance because they have combined with oxygen.

———

Coal and diamonds are made of the same chemical element—carbon.

———

Only one of the eighty-one stable chemical elements is named after a human being. It is gadolinium, which is named for a Finnish chemist, Johan Gadolin, who first studied the minerals from which no less than fourteen elements, including gadolinium, were isolated.

———

The least dense solid is solid hydrogen, which is only one-tenth as dense as ice.

———

Organic compounds are those that contain carbon. Inorganic compounds may contain any of the other 104 elements, but *not* carbon. In any comparison with carbon and all the others, carbon wins. There are thousands of times as many organic compounds as inorganic compounds.

———

An example of a long chemical term, the name of an amino-acid compound, contains some 3,600 letters, which would consume three pages of this book if they were reproduced.

————

A brick wall and a plate-glass window are made from the same principal ingredient: sand!

————

CREEPY CRAWLY

Massed opposing armies fight each other along a front. The fighting continues for days, and hundreds die. This is not trench warfare among men. The armies are the weaver ants of African forests. The ants are so fierce that when the battle is resolved and the boundaries of the opposing colonies have been fixed, a "no-ant's-land" exists between them where ants from each side do not dare to enter.

The female salamander inseminates herself. At mating time, the male deposits a conical mass of jellylike substance containing the sperm. The female draws the jelly into herself, and in so doing fertilizes her eggs.

The reproductive cycle of some worms is in phase with the moon. The sex organs of adult palolo worms mature once a year at about the same time of day, on a day when the moon is in its last quarter. The organs split off with the worm's tail section, which swims to the surface and sheds the eggs and sperm into the water. The head and upper half of the body remain in their coral reef and develop new reproductive organs.

There are one-celled creatures that have the properties of both plants and animals. An example is the flagellate *Euglena*, which propels itself rapidly through the water like an animal by means of undulating, snakelike appendages. Also, it contains chlorophyll, a substance as characteristic of plants as blood is of animals.

Bombyx mori, a silkworm moth, has been cultivated for so long that it can no longer exist without human care. Because it has been domesticated, it has lost the ability to fly.

There are some fifty different species of sea snakes, and all of them are poisonous. They thrive in abundance along the coast from the Persian Gulf to Japan and around Australia and Melanesia. Their venom is ten times as virulent as that of the cobra. Humans bitten by them have died within 2½ hours. In 1932, a "continuous mass" of sea snakes ten feet wide and seventy miles long was observed in the Straits of Malacca.

There are more different kinds of insects in existence today than the total of all kinds of all other animals put together.

Some insects, after their head is severed, may live for as much as a year. They react automatically to light, temperature, humidity, chemicals, and other stimuli.

The honey ant of the desert has an unusual method of providing food in times of scarcity. Certain members of the colony are stuffed with liquid food or water until the rear portions of their bodies are enlarged to the size of a pea. When a famine occurs, these ants disgorge their supplies to feed the others.

There are locusts that have an adult life span of only a few weeks or so, after having lived in the ground as grubs for fifteen years.

When a queen bee lays the fertilized eggs that will develop into new queens, only one of the newly laid queens actually survives. The first new queen that emerges from her cell destroys all other queens in their cells and, thereafter, reigns alone.

The male praying mantis often loses his head—literally—after courting the female. The latter is known to decapitate the earnest suitor, and she often completely devours him.

Snails sleep a lot. In addition to several months of winter hibernation, they crawl into their shells to get out of the hot sun, which dries them, or heavy rain, which waterlogs them. Desert snails may even doze for three or four years.

The president of Memorial Sloan-Kettering Cancer Center in New York, which specializes in cancer treatment, has observed that "ants are so much like human beings as to be an embarrassment." Writes Dr. Lewis Thomas: Ants "farm fungi, raise aphids as livestock, launch armies into wars, use chemical sprays to alarm and confuse enemies, capture slaves. The families of weaver ants engage in child labor, holding their larvae like shuttles to spin out the thread that sews the leaves together for their fungus gardens. They exchange information ceaselessly. They do everything but watch television."

Snails produce a colorless, sticky discharge that forms a protective carpet under them as they travel along. The discharge is so effective that snails can crawl along the edge of a razor without cutting themselves.

The original state constitution of Nebraska was reframed and re-adopted in 1875 and is known as the "grasshopper constitution," though there is no clause or article about grasshoppers. The new constitution got its appellation simply because it was drawn up—to remedy some long-standing complaints about the existing constitution—while the state was suffering the results of the preceding year's plague of grasshoppers that was said to have all but eaten Nebraska off the map. Later, the legislature passed a bill authorizing the supervisors of each road district to call out all men from sixteen to sixty years of age to work at exterminating any new plague.

There is an average of 50,000 spiders per acre in green areas. Essential to the balance of nature, spiders annually destroy a hundred times their number in insects.

Cockroaches have quite a capacity for survival. If the head of one is removed carefully, so as to prevent it from bleeding to death, the cockroach can survive for several weeks. When it dies, it is from starvation.

Trinervitermes, a species of termite that is native to the African savanna, builds mounds that are only about twelve inches high. However, the termites bore shafts deep into the ground for access to water. Holes have been found below these termite mounds that go more than 130 feet into the earth.

The cecidomyian gall midge, a type of fly, can reproduce by laying eggs or by parthenogenesis (reproduction without fertilization by males). In the latter process, the female never becomes an adult. It reproduces while still a larva or pupa, and its offspring develop within the body of the mother, not in a uterus but within her tissues. In order to grow, the offspring eat the mother from the inside, and when they emerge, all that remains of the mother is a shell. Within two days, the children's own children begin to develop and devour their parents in turn.

————

If they lived on the ground, ants in the flood regions of the Amazon and its tributaries would drown by the millions every year, for the water level rises often by several yards. The ants live in the "upper stories" of the forest, building their nests in trees, and are secure from flood.

————

Louis Pasteur saved France's silkworm industry. When the industry, in southern France, was dealt a staggering blow by a disease that was killing the silkworms, the call went out for Pasteur—no one but Pasteur. Pasteur's solution, on locating a tiny parasite infesting silkworms and the mulberry leaves that were fed to them, was drastic, but rational: Destroy all infested worms and infected food. It was done. It worked. The silk industry was saved.

————

DE GUSTIBUS

Chocolate was once considered a temptation of the devil. In Central American mountain villages during the eighteenth century, no one under the age of sixty was permitted to drink it, and churchgoers who defied the rule were threatened with excommunication.

———

Vinegar was the strongest acid known to the ancients.

———

During President Rutherford B. Hayes's term in office (1877–1881), he forbade all wines and spirits in the White House. His wife became known as Lemonade Lucy. Unknown to the President and his wife, a steward alleviated the guests' deprivation by spiking the Roman punch, a sherbetlike concoction made with lemon juice, sugar, and egg whites. It was served at mid-meal as a palate refresher, and the Roman punch course became known as "the Life-Saving Station." The Hayeses never caught on.

———

President Grover Cleveland hated fancy food, but he retained the French chef that his predecessor, Chester Arthur, had hired. Cleveland once wrote, "I must go to dinner. I wish it was to eat a pickled herring, Swiss cheese and a chop at Louis's instead of the French stuff I shall find."

———

Andrew Jackson, two weeks before the end of his second term as President, gave a public reception. An enormous cheese weighing 1,400 pounds had been presented by the dairymen of New York, and the public was invited to help itself. In two hours, the gigantic cheese, four feet in diameter and two feet thick, was demolished.

———

Tea, the tax on which was one of the factors leading to the American Revolution, was not introduced into the colonies until 1714. Even then, tea—along with coffee—was not the most popular of beverages. Chocolate was the preferred nonalcoholic drink, with rum in New England and beer in the middle colonies the beverages of choice.

———

During the seventeenth and eighteenth centuries in America, Indians and blacks developed cooking into an art, but most colonial families existed on a monotonous diet of corn meal, salt meat, and beverages such as grog, cider, and molasses beer, with the result that scurvy and other diseases from dietary deficiency were constant threats.

Carbonated beverages became popular in 1832 after John Mathews invented an apparatus for charging water with carbon dioxide gas. It is believed that the first carbonated soft drink was made in Philadelphia in 1807 when Dr. Philip Syng Physick (the "father of American surgery") asked a chemist to prepare carbonated water for a patient. Flavor was added to make the drink more palatable.

Despite their frequent appearance in major Renaissance paintings, oranges were not eaten at the Last Supper, simply because they were not available. Returning Crusaders reported seeing oranges in the "holy lands," which must have influenced Titian, Botticelli, and other artists. But that was more than 1,000 years after the Crucifixion. During that time, citrus fruits had been introduced to the Mediterranean countries from China.

The Arabs are known to have drunk coffee as of 850 A.D. It took Europe almost seven centuries to make its acquaintance. Although Mocha, a town in southwestern Arabia, had become an active port for coffee export by 1450, coffee did not appear in Europe until 1517. By 1580, Turkish coffee was imported in bulk to Italy, through Venice; by 1643, coffee was popular in Paris; in 1632, the first coffee shop opened in London, followed by the first coffee house in Oxford in 1650. Vienna, which was to become so famous for its coffee houses, did not catch up until 1683.

Most healthy adults can go without eating anything for a month or longer. But they must drink at least two quarts of water a day.

The Romans were so fond of eating dormice that the upper classes raised them domestically. The rodents were kept in specially designed cages and were fed a mixture of nuts.

Because of the junk food offered by tourists, a herd of mountain sheep in Alberta, the Canadian province, has been in danger of being killed off. The herd neglects the normal grass diet in favor of the candy and other junk food proffered. The animals are losing weight, and the females may not be producing enough high-quality milk.

When we sit down to dinner each evening, our menu includes a great deal more water than the glassful we consume as a beverage. Many foods contain a surprising percentage of water by weight, e.g., cucumber, 96%; watermelon, 92%; milk, 87%; apple, 84%; potato, 78%; steak, 74%; cheese, 40%; bread, 35%.

When tea was first introduced in the American colonies, many housewives, in their ignorance, served the tea leaves with sugar or syrup after throwing away the water in which they had been boiled.

Lead poisoning has been blamed for contributing to the fall of the Roman Empire. Women became infertile by drinking wine from vessels whose lead had dissolved in the wine, and the Roman upper classes died out within a couple of centuries. Paradoxically, the Romans used lead as a sweetening agent and as a cure for diarrhea. It added up to massive self-inflicted poisoning.

The modern dinner plate is a fairly recent development. Until the fifteenth century, it was customary to eat on a thick slice of stale bread, called a "trencher," that soaked up the juice.

Because Napoleon believed that armies marched on their stomachs, he offered a prize in 1795 for practical ways of preserving food. The prize was won by a French inventor, Nicolas Appert. What he devised was canning. It was the beginning of the enormous canned-food industry of today.

Milk is generally not healthy for adult Orientals or for adult people of black African origin, because they tend to lack enzymes needed to digest the natural sugar in milk.

The major crop of Ceylon was coffee until the entire crop of 1869 was destroyed by a blight. The Ceylonese decided to plant tea, and today tea is the Indian Ocean island's major crop. (Ceylon has also changed its name, to Sri Lanka.)

By the eighteenth century, apple pie had become so popular a dessert in America that Yale College served it every night at supper, and did so for more than a century.

The annual harvest of an entire coffee tree is required for a single pound of ground coffee. Every tree bears up to six pounds of beans, which are reduced to a pound after the beans are roasted and ground.

––––––––

Much has been said about the value of Incan gold, but one of the great legacies of the Incas was food plants. The potato, the pumpkin, and the pineapple came from South America and spread through the world. Coca, the source of cocaine, and cinchona, the source of quinine, are also gifts of Peruvian civilization to mankind.

––––––––

A jeroboam (a bottle holding about four quarts) of Château Lafite 1864 wine was purchased in 1978 by John Grisanti, wine connoisseur and restauranteur, at the tenth annual Heublein Rare Wine Auction, for $18,000. Grisanti then donated the wine to a charity feast, at $1,500 per person, to benefit St. Jude's Hospital in Memphis, Tennessee. Each of the thirty attendees got a taste of the only known 1864 Lafite, and the hospital netted $34,000 for the evening.

––––––––

Humans, if they are very sensitive, can detect sweetness in a solution of 1 part of sugar to 200 parts of water. Some moths and butterflies can detect sweetness when the ratio is 1 to 300,000.

––––––––

The founding fathers of the United States encouraged the making and the drinking of beer and ale as temperance beverages, preferable to hard liquor. To aid the establishment and growth of breweries in America, James Madison urged the first Congress to place a heavy duty on imported beer.

––––––––

Honey was used as a synonym for anything pleasant ("land of milk and honey") in ancient and medieval times because it was about the only sweetener then available to the West. Sugar didn't reach Europe in quantity until the twelfth century, when returning Crusaders brought it with them from the East.

––––––––

At the St. Louis World's Fair in 1904, Richard Blechynden, an Englishman, had a tea concession. On a very hot day, none of the fairgoers were interested in hot tea. In a desperate attempt for business, Blechynden served the tea cold—and invented iced tea.

––––––––

Americans who chew gum are partly responsible for the development of Mayan studies. Workers who go into the jungle to collect chicle, the sap of the sapodilla tree from which chewing gum is made, have stumbled on numerous vegetation-covered ruins and returned to alert the archaeologists.

Nearly 28,000 different ways to lose weight have been tried, according to U.S. government data. The oldest is fasting, "the ultimate diet."

The Manhattan cocktail—whiskey and sweet vermouth—was invented by Jennie Jerome, the beautiful New Yorker who was the toast of the town until she went to England as the wife of Lord Randolph Churchill, in 1874, and gave birth to Winston.

Potatoes were first imported by Europe in the 1500s on Spanish ships returning from Peru. While becoming fashionable in some circles, the vegetable was slow to catch on. Potatoes were banned in Burgundy in 1610 because, it was said, "frequent use caused leprosy." Potatoes were taken to England from Colombia, not Virginia as generally believed, by Sir Francis Drake, in 1565.

After muckraking the meat-packing industry in his explosive eyewitness novel *The Jungle,* the Pulitzer Prize-winning Upton Sinclair ate a diet of only rice and fruit for many years. (Lots of his readers became vegetarian, too—at least for a while.)

English gin was the drink of the poor; the rich drank port and brandy in incredible quantities. Five or six bottles a man were par for an evening. Dr. Samuel Johnson (1709–84), the leading British literary scholar and critic of his time, once drank thirty-six glasses of port without moving from his seat. This was remarkable in more ways than one.

While Europeans in the sixteenth century did not live by bread alone, it can be said they almost lived by grain alone. Beer and ale, both derived from grain, were consumed in vast quantities. Dutch soldiers on campaign in 1582 got two gallons a day. Queen Elizabeth's men got only one.

Americans today consume nearly the same number of calories—about 3,400 a day—as Americans in 1910 did, but the weight of the average American has increased substantially due to lack of exercise.

A highway fifty-five feet wide and six feet thick that's built entirely of grain and stretches around the world at the equator—that's how much the world's annual consumption of grain comes to: 1.2 billion metric tons.

———

The passion for gin that swept over England in the eighteenth century nearly ruined health, morals, sanity, and even the little respect poor people had for the laws of the rich. From 1714 to 1733, English consumption rose from 2 million to 5 million gallons of gin a year, and it receded only when strict laws began to limit sales.

———

Kernels of popcorn were found in the graves of pre-Columbian Indians.

———

To celebrate, in 537 A.D., the dedication of the new church Hagia Sophia—the supreme product of Byzantine art—Emperor Justinian held a banquet that caused the slaughtering of over 10,000 sheep, oxen, swine, poultry, and deer.

———

A plague of drunkenness settled over Europe to match the plague of Black Death in the mid-1300s, and remained after the disease was gone. The theory at the time was that strong drink acted as a preventive against contagion. It didn't, but it made the drinker less concerned, which was something.

———

The tale of "manna from heaven" eaten by the Hebrews in the desert may have been inspired by the sweet secretion produced by insects that are parasites of the tamarisk plant. The secretion is periodic in its appearance, and Bedouins still gather it every June. It preserves well, and therefore is convenient for nomads.

———

To make a one-pound comb of honey, bees must collect nectar from about two million flowers.

———

DISCOVERIES

In 1900, three scientists, the Dutchman Hugo de Vries, the German Carl Correns, and the Austrian Erich von Tschermak, "discovered" the laws of genetics independently. Each one, in searching through previous work on the subject, discovered that Gregor Mendel had made the discovery thirty-three years earlier. Each one published a paper in which he gave the credit to Mendel, a remarkable display of scientific honesty in triplicate.

———

Until the twelfth century, when returning Crusaders brought knowledge of them, windmills were probably unknown in Europe. They thereafter became familiar landmarks in Holland, England, France, and Germany.

———

It was while he was examining urine, seeking the philosopher's stone (the magic elixir needed to change baser metals into gold), that the German chemist Hennig Brand discovered phosphorus.

———

Five years before fleeing to America in 1938 from fascist Italy, Enrico Fermi barely missed making the world-shaking discovery of the phenomenon of fission. He later said that "we did not have enough imagination to think that a different process of disintegration might occur in uranium than in any other element. Moreover, *we did not know enough chemistry* to separate the products of uranium disintegration from one another, and we believed we had about four of them, while actually their number was closer to fifty." If Fermi had been successful, it is likely that the Axis would have had an insurmountable head start in nuclear chemistry.

———

It sometimes pays to relax. When James Watt was trying to work out an improvement on the Newcomen steam engine that would make it truly practical, the deepest concentration didn't help. One Sunday afternoon in 1764, he took a peaceful, relaxed walk, and the key notion popped into his head. Chance favors the prepared mind.

———

The most remarkable of all the seventeenth-century microscopists was Antonie van Leeuwenhoek, who held the position of janitor at the Delft City Hall for all of his adult life (it was a sinecure). Building his own microscopes, he was the first to describe spermatozoa—reporting the discovery rather nervously, fearing it might be considered obscene. He was the first to describe structure that could only be bacteria. No one else was to see bacteria again for over a century, that is, until microscopes were devised that could magnify as well and as clearly as Leeuwenhoek's tiny lenses.

When the time's ripe for a discovery, it's ripe. For decades, organic chemists had been trying to explain certain puzzling facts about organic chemicals. Finally, in September 1874, a twenty-two-year-old Dutch chemist, Jacobus H. van't Hoff, suggested that a carbon atom had four bonds arranged in such a way as to point to the apices of an imaginary tetrahedron (a three-sided pyramid). It explained everything. Two months later, a twenty-seven-year-old French chemist, Joseph A. Le Bel, published a paper containing precisely the same suggestion. The two men had worked independently.

The *Quiz Kids*, an early question-and-answer radio program on which bright children panelists were asked hard questions and received prizes for correct answers, was the forum for the first public announcement of the discovery of element 95, americium, and element 96, curium. The news was scheduled to be released at a meeting of the American Chemical Society, but on the program, in 1944, the chemist and physicist and future Nobel Prize winner Glenn Theodore Seaborg was asked if there were any new elements. Seaborg and co-workers had just witnessed the birth of the two new elements, in the cyclotron in the Radiation Laboratory of the University of California at Berkeley, and Seaborg, an adult guest on the program, issued the news in response to the question.

The nineteenth-century Scottish botanist Robert Brown could merely report on the "Brownian," or erratic, motion of pollen in water observed under the microscope; he had no explanation for it. Today, it is known that the Brownian motion was a visible effect of the fact that water is composed of particles. Brown's was the first evidence for atomism—the concept that the universe is composed of indestructible material particles—that was an observation rather than a deduction.

To work out a mathematical relationship of the "Doppler effect," relating the pitch to the relative motion of source and observer, the Austrian scientist Christian Johann Doppler placed trumpeters on a railroad flat car and musicians with a sense of absolute pitch near the tracks. A locomotive engine pulled the flat car back and forth at different speeds for two days. The musicians on the ground "recorded" the trumpet notes as the train approached and as it receded. Doppler's equations held up.

———

The key "bits" of information that Charles Darwin and Alfred Russel Wallace needed to work out the theory of evolution by natural selection were found in an English clergyman's tome published in 1801, eleven years before Darwin's birth. The clergyman was Thomas Robert Malthus, and his work containing the skeleton key was *An Essay on the Principle of Population.*

———

The Italian Giovanni Girolamo Saccheri (1667–1733), a professor of mathematics at the University of Pisa and a Jesuit priest, found himself faced after much work with the possibility that one could build up a thoroughly self-consistent geometry that was based on at least one axiom that directly contradicted a Euclidean axiom. The result would be a "non-Euclidean" geometry that might seem against common sense, but it would be internally self-consistent and therefore mathematically valid. Saccheri hovered on the brink of mathematical immortality—and backed away. When his gradual development of acute geometry went on without any contradictions to the point where he could take it no longer, he argued himself into imagining he had found an inconsistency, though in fact he hadn't. With great relief, he concluded he had proved Euclid's fifth.

———

Linus Pauling pointed out the dangers of carbon-14 (a radioactive atom that is part of all living tissue) in detailed form in a paper in *Science* in 1958. This may well have been one of the deciding factors a few years later in the elimination of atmospheric testing of nuclear bombs in the test-ban treaty signed by the United States, Great Britain, and the Soviet Union. I personally had mentioned those same dangers (in far less detail) in an article I had written in 1955—my proudest scientific accomplishment. Pauling, of course, deserves full credit (I had been airing a casual idea), but he was gracious enough to admit he might well have read my article and been inspired by it.

———

The most important industrial chemical is sulfuric acid. This chemical was discovered, about 1300, by someone who may have been a Spaniard. In order that his writings be given credence, he wrote of his discoveries under the name of Geber, who was an Arabic alchemist who had lived five centuries before. He was entirely too successful, for his real name is not known. This greatest of the medieval alchemists is known only as the "False Geber."

How to manufacture porcelain, or "china," was a mystery known only to the Chinese until around 1700. Although imitation porcelain was made earlier in Italy, it was Johann Friedrich Böttger, of Saxony, who made true porcelain (the Dresden china) for the first time in the Western world.

Until the 1830s, rubber was not a very useful material. It grew stiff and hard in cold weather and soft and sticky in warm weather. Charles Goodyear, no chemist, a business failure, and once imprisoned for debt, decided to recoup his fortunes by finding a way to improve rubber. He first experimented by adding sulfur and failed. But one day he spilled his mixture on the stove by accident and found when he picked up the hot rubber-sulfur mixture that he had something that was dry and flexible at all temperatures. He patented this discovery of "vulcanized rubber" in 1844. It was the first important advance in what is now called "polymer chemistry." Goodyear's process was too simple, however, and many people infringed on the patent. When he died in 1860, Goodyear was more in debt than ever. He owed hundreds of thousands of dollars.

For years, the German chemist Friedrich August Kekule von Stradonitz tried to figure out how the atoms were arranged in the molecule of a very important chemical, benzene. No arrangement seemed to explain benzene's properties. In 1865, he was on a horse-drawn bus and fell into a semi-doze in which (according to his own account) he saw atoms whirling in a dance; suddenly, the tail end of one chain attached itself to the head end and formed a spinning ring. The "benzene ring" is just about the best-known and most commonly used structure in the symbolic formulas of organic chemistry.

The first synthetic dye was produced by William Henry Perkin, an eighteen-year-old English schoolboy, in 1856. His teacher had mentioned how valuable it would be to have someone figure out how to make synthetic quinine, and Perkin decided to try in his home laboratory. He failed, but he noticed a purple tint in the mess he produced, left school, opened a factory—and became a millionaire.

Scientific discoveries are where you find them. The English astronomer James Bradley was puzzled over certain shifts in star positions in the course of the year. In 1728, he was on a pleasure sail on the Thames River and noted that the pennant on top of the mast changed direction according to the relative motion of ship and wind and not according to the direction of the wind alone. In a flash, he found he understood the important principle of "the aberration of light."

The German chemist Christian F. Schönbein was experimenting with a mixture of nitric acid and sulfuric acid in the kitchen of his house in 1845. Frau Schönbein strictly forbade such experiments in the home, but she was out at the time. Schönbein accidentally spilled some of the acid and, in a panic, he seized the first thing at hand, his wife's cotton apron, sopped up the mixture, then hung it over the stove to dry before his wife came home. When the apron dried, it suddenly burned, and so rapidly that it seemed simply to disappear. The astonished Schönbein investigated and found he had formed what is now called "nitrocellulose" or "guncotton." This was the beginning of the replacement of gunpowder on the battlefield, where it reigned supreme for 500 years.

In 1847, the Italian chemist Ascanio Sobrero produced nitroglycerine for the first time. But when he heated a drop of it, there was a shattering explosion. Realizing, in horror, its possible application to warfare, Sobrero stopped all research in that direction. The trouble was that other scientists didn't.

In 1842, the German physician Julius Robert von Mayer published his arguments in favor of the theory of the conservation of energy. That same year, another physician, the American Crawford W. Long, performed the first operations using anesthesia. Five years later, another German, Hermann von Helmholtz, advanced the theory of the conservation of energy, and another American, William T. G. Morton, performed operations using anesthesia. The history books give Helmholtz and Morton the credit for those advances and the earlier workers are forgotten. The race is not always to the swift.

Cyprus was one of the world's important mining centers in ancient times, but for reasons still unknown the Romans halted operations there and sealed the tunnels. Many of the tunnels were found and reopened in this century, thanks to clever detective work by an American mining engineer, D. A. Gunther. In the New York Public Library, he had happened to find an ancient account of the mines. Years of ingenious search in Cyprus led him to the tunnels, which he found complete with usable support timbers and oil lamps. Cyprus became an important mining center again.

———

Long before William Hunt invented the safety pin in 1849, a kind of safety pin made of gold was used by the Etruscans, in the seventh century B.C.

———

While fighting with the French underground during World War II, Jacques-Yves Cousteau invented the aqualung, the self-contained device that supplies air under pressure for underwater divers.

———

The first person born in the American colonies to be knighted by the British crown had once been an illiterate shepherd boy in Maine. William Phips, one of twenty-six children, found a fortune in gold, silver, and jewels on the Spanish Main, which led to the knighting. He became the royal governor of Massachusetts.

———

When Galileo wrote his masterpiece, Dialogue on the Two Chief World Systems, he made no mention that his longtime friend Kepler had modified and improved the Copernican theory beyond measure.

———

The first human beings to arrive on Iceland were Irish explorers, in 795 A.D. They established a colony, but it didn't last. By the time the Vikings arrived eighty years later and established a permanent settlement, the Irish were gone.

———

The first man ever to set foot on the continent of Antarctica was an American sealer, John Davis. He did this on February 7, 1821, but the fact was not known till 1955, when the log of his ship was discovered and studied.

———

ECCENTRICITIES

The Winchester House, near San Jose, California, is perhaps the most bizarre house ever built. Mrs. Sara Winchester was convinced that if she stopped adding rooms to her house, she would die. So every day for thirty-eight years construction went on. The house contains 2,000 doors and 10,000 windows, many of which open onto blank walls, and stairways that lead nowhere. The eight-story house has forty-eight fireplaces and miles of secret passages and hallways. When Mrs. Winchester died, in 1922, at the age of eighty-five, her mansion contained 160 rooms and covered over six acres of ground.

Isaac Newton's only recorded utterance while he was a member of Parliament was a request to open the window.

Dr. James Barry, a woman posing as a man, became a general in the army of Queen Victoria. Barry entered the medical corps, served forty years as a surgeon, and rose to the rank of inspector-general of hospitals. Only after Barry's death in 1865 was "his" true sex discovered.

One of the most picturesque Mississippi River gamblers was George Devol. A formidable fighter, Devol was good with his fists, but his principal weapon was his head. If doctors who examined him are to be believed, his skull above the forehead was more than an inch thick. In 1867, he had a friendly butting contest with Billy Carroll, a circus performer known both as "The Great Butter" and "The Man with the Hard Head" and whose act consisted of smashing barrels and heavy doors with his head. George Devol knocked him out. His talent came in handy, during his forty years as a professional gambler, whenever he needed to butt his way through crowds of irate suckers whom he had cheated.

The use of fingerprints for identification purposes was first worked out by the English anthropologist Francis Galton, a first cousin of

Charles Darwin. Galton was a fiend for statistics. He tried to use statistical methods to work out the distribution of good looks in England and to determine what percentage of prayers were answered.

Thomas Alva Edison suffered early from deafness and taught his wife-to-be Morse code while he was courting her. When she was able both to send and receive messages, Edison proposed to her by tapping out the message in her hand. She answered in the same way. After they were married, they often "spoke" to each other in Morse code. When they attended a play, Mrs. Edison kept her hand on her husband's knee and telegraphed the actor's words to him so he could appreciate it.

When Jacques Necker, a former French finance minister, became a widower, he had his late wife's body placed in a stone basin filled with alcohol and entombed in a mausoleum to which he alone had a key. He paid regular visits to the corpse until his own death in 1804, when he joined her in the basin. The mausoleum was opened in 1817 to receive the coffin of their daughter. It has remained closed ever since.

No matter where she went—and she went as far afield as the Crimea, in 1854—the "Lady of the Lamp," the English hospital administrator and reformer Florence Nightingale, carried a pet owl in a pocket.

John Johnston, born in 1823, was famed as a killer of many Crow Indians. He said he was getting his revenge for the murder of his wife and unborn child at the hands of Crows. He attained infamy, however, for his practice of eating the livers of the Indians he killed. Liver-Eating Johnston, as he was called, lived to be seventy-six years old.

William Randolph Hearst's mother claimed that every time he felt badly, he went out and bought something. Once, he bought, sight unseen, a tenth-century Spanish cloister in Segovia for $40,000. In order to move it, the entire cloister had to be dismantled, stone by stone; twenty-one miles of railway to connect with the nearest line had to be built; and a sawmill to cut wood for the 10,700 crates in which the stones would be packed had to be constructed.

Henry Ford was convinced that the soybean was a promising raw material. He was sure it could be converted into products with commercial value. Ford once appeared at a convention with his entire attire, except for his shoes, having been produced from soybeans.

During World War II, a guest at the White House was Soviet Minister V. M. Molotov. His visit was not publicized, and he was officially listed as "Mr. Brown." The White House servant who unpacked Molotov's bag found a chunk of black bread, a roll of sausage—and a pistol.

The French social philosopher Charles Fourier (1782–1837) had some "strange" ideas. He condemned existing institutions and proposed a kind of utopian socialism. He said that if the natural passions of man were properly channeled, they would result in social harmony. The organization set up to achieve this would consist of 1,620 people who would live in community buildings, and work would be divided among these people according to their natural inclination. Basically, his idea was an agricultural society systematically arranged. Fourier waited every day for ten years for somebody willing to put up the money, but no one did. He died disappointed but not disillusioned. The doctrine of Fourierism spread to America under the auspices of Prosper Considerant, Albert Brisbane, and Horace Greeley. Brook Farm, in Massachusetts, was Fourierist for a time. The most successful Fourierist community in the New World was at Red Bank, New Jersey.

"The Prince of U.S. Cranks" became lieutenant governor of Minnesota at the age of twenty-eight and later a U.S. Congressman, a state senator, and the candidate of the Populist Party for Vice-President. Ignatius Donnelly was a radical political reformer (he sharply opposed political corruption and corporate monopolies) as well as a pseudo-scientist. He got his nickname from the press for asserting that Atlantis had existed, that Francis Bacon wrote the plays of Shakespeare (there was a cipher message in the plays that revealed the "fact"), and that the Earth had been catastrophically tortured by a visiting comet. Donnelly's novel Caesar's Column, predicting fascism in the twentieth century, was a best seller (a million copies).

An early American Zionist named Mordecai Manuel Noah tried to establish a Jewish homeland—"Ararat"—on Grand Island, forty-eight square miles of white-oak forest, a mile and a half south of Niagara Falls and just north of Buffalo. A dedication ceremony took place at St. Paul's Episcopal Church in Buffalo—there being no synagogue or even Jewish residents in Buffalo at the time (1825)—and Noah declared himself appointed "Governor and Judge of Israel." He believed that in all probability the American Indians were descendants of the lost tribes of Israel, and he urged they be informed of their lineage and reunited with the Jewish race. A few days after the dedication, Noah left Buffalo for good, leaving no one to put his plan into effect.

———

A "burlesque" one-ship blockade of the British Isles was staged in 1814 by a U.S. captain, Thomas Boyle, an outstanding privateer in the War of 1812, with eighty prizes to his credit. He had an unusual sense of humor and superb audacity. Though he employed solely his own vessel, Boyle said his "force" was "adequate to maintain strictly, vigorously, and effectually the said blockade," which he instituted in response to the "paper blockades" of the American coast that the British had pompously declared.

———

Robert Moses, the planner largely responsible for many of New York's bridges, tunnels, and parkways, never learned to drive an automobile.

———

ENERGY

There's enough energy in ten minutes of one hurricane to match the nuclear stockpiles of the world.

———

An electron and a positron attract each other in two ways: the electromagnetic attraction of their opposite electric charges, and the gravitational attraction of their two masses. The electromagnetic attraction is 4,200,000,000,000,000,000,000,000,000,000,000,-000,000,000 times as strong as the gravitational. (Of the four known forces—gravitation, weak interaction, electromagnetic interaction, strong interaction—the gravitational force is by far the weakest.)

———

The daily average yield of an oil well at full production in Alaska's Prudhoe Bay field is 10,000 barrels; it is only 11 barrels in the Lower Forty-eight states.

———

The world's smallest electric motor weighs one half-millionth of a pound and is smaller than the head of a pin. Built by a Californian, William McLellan, the motor measures a sixty-fourth of an inch on all sides. It has thirteen parts and generates one-millionth of a horsepower. It can be seen in operation only through a microscope. McLellan built the motor using a toothpick, a microscope, and a watchmaker's lathe.

———

Internal combustion engines lose efficiency at the rate of more than 2 percent for every 1,000 feet of altitude. At Lake Titicaca, at 12,500 feet in the Andes, motor cars and powered boats lose about 30 percent of their rated horsepower.

———

Release of energy is always at the expense of disappearance of mass. In ordinary chemical reactions, energy is released in such low quantities that the mass loss is insignificant. Six hundred seventy thousand gallons of gasoline must be burned to bring about the loss of one gram.

———

As each additional person walks into a cocktail party, it is the equivalent to turning on another 120-watt electric bulb. A human being, living on 2,500 calories a day, is delivering (in the form of heat, eventually) about 104 calories per hour, which is equal to 120 watts.

Heat, light, electricity, magnetism, motion, sound, chemical bonds, nuclear forces—they all represent forms of energy, and all are different forms of essentially the same thing, for one form can be turned freely into another. Electricity moving through a wire can produce light, and a paddle rotating rapidly in water can produce heat. Magnetism can be turned into electricity, chemical explosions into motions, nuclear reactions into sounds, and so on.

The first published description and picture of a "solar motor" appeared in 1615. Lenses concentrated the sun's rays on airtight black metal boxes partly filled with water. As the heated air expanded, it forced the water from the boxes into conduits, and the water reappeared in a small indoor fountain in the next room.

A single lightning bolt may give off 3,750 million kilowatts of electrical energy. About 75 percent of this energy is dissipated as heat, raising the temperature of the surrounding air to around 27,000° F. and causing rapid air expansion which leads to sound waves—thunder—that can be heard up to eighteen miles away.

One pound of *anything*, when it is completely converted into energy, in keeping with Einstein's mathematical equation $E = mc^2$, will produce 11,400 million kilowatt-hours of energy.

The streets of a city, London, were lit by gaslights (instead of torches) for the first time in 1807. Coal gas was used for the purpose.

If one gram (one-twenty-eighth of an ounce) of matter could be converted into its equivalent of pure energy and the energy used with perfect efficiency to keep a 1,000-watt light bulb glowing, there would be enough energy to keep it lit for 2,850 years, or from the time of Homer to the present.

The useful life of a nuclear plant is, on the average, only forty years. But the plant will have to be "mothballed" for a century before certain radioactive materials decay sufficiently to permit economical direct dismantling.

————

The energy contained in a breaking ocean wave is immense. Measurements made with wave dynamometers have shown some waves striking with a force equal to a pressure of 6,000 pounds per square foot. The energy content of a four-foot swell moving along a hundred-mile front would supply power to a city the size of Seattle for almost twenty-four hours.

————

A quarter of the horses in the U.S. died of a vast virus epidemic in 1872. American life and industry were crippled literally because of the diminished horsepower.

————

If harnessed, the energy liberated by an average hurricane could supply the electrical energy used in the U.S. during half a year. The amount of energy would be equivalent to exploding ten atomic bombs every second.

————

During World War II, German chemists developed a successful process for making gasoline out of coal. Also, toward and after the end of the war, many truck engines were converted to run on the fumes from plain firewood. (When you ran out of "gas," you collected some wood along the road, chopped it up, and resumed the trip.)

————

The Earth receives only one-half of one-billionth of the sun's radiant energy. But in just a few days it gets as much heat and light as could be produced by burning *all* the oil, coal, and wood on the planet.

————

The idea of utilizing the energy implicit in inanimate nature as a substitute for slave muscle did not arise until the seventeenth century, and then only in regions, such as Great Britain and Holland, where slave labor did not exist and non-slave labor was getting more expensive.

————

The total quantity of energy in the universe is constant; energy cannot be created, and it cannot be destroyed. One form of energy can be converted into another, or transported from one place to another. But that is as much as can be done. When energy is used, it doesn't disappear; it merely goes elsewhere or is changed into another form.

————

A volcano has greater power than does the greatest hurricane, tsunami (a seismic seawave), or earthquake.

———

Before Benjamin Franklin's time, people thought there were two kinds of electricity. Franklin felt there was only one kind, with two appearances, one representing an excess of the electrical fluid and one a deficit. There was no way of telling which was which, so he guessed. He had a fifty-fifty chance of being right. As it turned out, he was wrong. To this day, electrical engineers prepare their diagrams with the electricity flowing in the wrong direction, following Franklin's guess. It doesn't matter in practice; the electrical devices work just the same. (If everyone goes into the door marked "exit" and out the door marked "entrance," they are going the wrong way, but there's no holdup in the traffic.)

———

As recently as 1964, the United States was still the world's number-one producer of oil. It was overtaken the next year by the Middle East, and by 1970 the Middle East was producing a third more oil than the United States.

———

A lightning bolt generates temperatures five times hotter than the 6000°C. found at the surface of the sun.

———

About 1 million windmills dotted the U.S. landscape in the early 1930s, a time when 40 million people lived on farms and before the rural electrification program was inaugurated.

———

EXPLORATIONS

The first Spanish vessels to reach the New World were commanded by the Italian Cristoforo Colombo. The first English vessels to reach the New World were commanded by the Italian Giovanni Caboto (John Cabot). The first French vessels to reach the New World were commanded by the Italian Giovanni da Verrazano. No Italian vessels explored the New World.

Ferdinand Magellan was Portuguese but sailed on his unprecedented round-the-world expedition under the flag of Spain, Portugal's chief competitor in exploration. He had served as page at the court of John II, the Portuguese King who turned down Columbus's request for financing a voyage west to India. Magellan also had been on Portuguese expeditions to the East Indies and had fought in Morocco, where he was wounded in action and permanently lamed. He was accused of trading with the Moroccans—tantamount to treason—denied a pension, and dismissed in 1517 from the armed forces. Bitter at this treatment, Magellan joined the Spanish service.

Columbus visited England in 1477, and it was probably there that he first heard that lands lay far to the west, across the Great Ocean Sea. Columbus visited Iceland in the 1480s.

The greatest ocean voyagers of all times were the Polynesians. With primitive ships and without compasses, the Polynesians in the centuries before 1000 A.D. located the tiny islands spread over 14 million square kilometers of the Pacific Ocean, from New Zealand to Hawaii and Easter Island, and colonized nearly all of them. The exact starting point of these migrations is not known, and is still a matter of controversy.

In 1642, the Dutch explorer Abel Janszoon Tasman sailed south from the East Indies in search of a possible continent in the area. In the course of a ten-month exploration he sailed all around Australia but never spotted any part of it. He did find a much smaller body of land to the southeast of Australia. It is çalled Tasmania in his honor. (Tasman saw the Australian shore in a later voyage.)

When the Norwegian explorer Roald Amundsen left Norway in June 1910 on what was announced as another voyage to the Arctic, no one knew that he really intended to turn south and sail for the Antarctic in an attempt to beat the English Captain Robert Scott to the South Pole. He beat Scott by thirty-four days, arriving on December 14, 1911.

The explorer Edmund Hillary was the first man to reach the top of the highest bit of land anywhere on the face of the globe, Mount Everest, and he was a leader of the first expedition that crossed by land the entire Antarctic continent from sea to sea.

Captain James Cook's public orders in 1768 were to observe from Tahiti the transit of Venus. Once he reached Tahiti, though, he opened sealed instructions, which told him: "Whereas there is reason to imagine that a Continent or Land of great extent, may be found to . . . the Southward of the Track of any former Navigators . . . you are to proceed to the southward in order to make discovery of the Continent above mentioned." He found it: Australia.

In 1615, the English explorer William Baffin penetrated to within 800 miles of the North Pole. For the next 250 years, no one else got nearer.

Juan Sebastian del Cano, a Spanish navigator, deserves the title of the world's first circumnavigator. When his skipper, Ferdinand Magellan, was killed in a squabble with natives in the Philippines, Cano assumed command of the Magellan expedition and sailed the *Victoria* across the Indian Ocean, around the southern tip of Africa, and back to Spain, arriving September 8, 1522, three years after setting sail. Cano died four years later on a second expedition to the far Pacific.

The Russian Cossacks were known for their skill not only as horsemen but also as explorers and even sailors. The Cossacks spearheaded exploration and colonization of Siberia. They explored the waterways of Siberia north to the Arctic. The Cossack Semyon Dezhnev, with ninety men in open boats, sailed around the eastern part of Asia in 1648.

What a difference success makes. It took Columbus (1451–1506) eight years of supplication before Ferdinand and Isabella of Spain supplied him with three ships and 90 men. The king's minister of the budget, Luis de Santangel, had persuaded the crown and loaned it the money for sponsorship. (It was to the minister that Columbus— who was never known by that name in his lifetime—sent the first reports of the finds of the first voyage.) When Columbus returned from his historic mission, he was made (as agreed in advance) "Admiral of the Ocean Sea" and governor-general of all new lands he had discovered or would discover. The monarchs then provided a fleet of seventeen ships and 1,500 men for his second trip, in October 1493. In all, Columbus made four voyages to the New World.

Only two of Columbus's three ships returned to Spain from the first voyage to the New World. Columbus had commanded the *Santa Maria* when the fleet discovered islands in the Bahamas and later Hispaniola. On Christmas Eve, 1492, a cabin boy was at the helm of the *Santa Maria* when the ship was wrecked on the north coast of Hispaniola. Leaving some men there to found a colony, Columbus raced through winter seas to Spain on the *Niña* to announce his discovery, beating by a few hours the *Pinta* skippered by Martin Alonso Pinzón, who had been censured by Columbus for treasonable conduct for abandoning the expedition in the Antilles for nearly two months. Pinzón's younger brother, Francisco Martin Pinzón, was master of the *Pinta,* and his brother Vicente Yanez Pinzón was commander of the *Niña.*

"Plunder or perish" might well have been Hernando Cortez's motto. On arrival in what today is Veracruz, he ordered his ships destroyed, thereby forcing his men, especially those keen on returning immediately to Spain, to carry on the war against the Indians.

FASHIONS

In order to "become a gentleman" in English polite society, Mohandas K. Gandhi (in his late teens) spent hours practicing the arranging of his tie and hair and taking lessons in dance and music.

There are odor technicians in the perfume trade with the olfactory skill to distinguish 19,000 different odors at twenty levels of intensity each.

During the Renaissance, laws were passed that prescribed which fashions could not be worn by the lower classes, so as to keep social distinctions intact. Queen Elizabeth of England would not allow the ruff to be worn by commoners; and in Florence, women of the lower class were not allowed to use buttons of certain shapes and materials.

The Padaung people of Burma believe that a long neck is beautiful. When a woman is young, she has a brass ring fastened around her neck. Over the years, rings are added until the neck becomes elongated and beauty is achieved. She also wears brass rings around her legs, and daily carries around about twenty pounds of brass.

Among the classical heritage rediscovered during the Renaissance was the handkerchief. It had been used by the Romans, who ordinarily wore two handkerchiefs: one on the left wrist and one tucked in at the waist or around the neck. In the fifteenth century, the handkerchief was for a time allowed only to the nobility; special laws were made to enforce this.

In fourteenth-century France, Philip the Fair forbade dukes, counts, barons, and their wives to own more than four garments; unmarried women could own only one dress, unless they were heiresses who had inherited castles. His edicts did not mention shoes, however, and they became a symbol of elegance. Named after its inventor, the *poulaine* was a shoe whose tip was as long as two feet for princes and noblemen, one foot for rich people of lower degree, and only half a foot for common people. Such shoes proved a hazard among the French Crusaders at the battle of Nicopolis (1396) when they had to cut off tips in order to be able to run away.

———

Until the Middle Ages, underwater divers near the Mediterranean coastline collected golden strands from the pen shell, which used the strands to hold itself in place. Called byssus, the strands were woven into a luxury textile, a "cloth of gold," and made into ladies' gloves so fine that a pair could be packed into an empty walnut shell. Examples of this lost art exist today in some museums, and the cloth retains its color and softness.

———

During the Renaissance, blond hair became so much *de rigueur* in Venice that a brunette was not to be seen except among the working classes. Venetian women spent hours dyeing and burnishing their hair until they achieved the harsh metallic glitter that was considered a necessity.

———

In 1809, President James Madison's wife, Dolley, who loved elegant gowns and gracious entertaining, spent $2,000 on import duties alone for one shipment of fashions from France.

———

Decreeing that the masses (peasants excepted) must be beardless was one way that Peter the Great, in 1698, sought to westernize Russia. Fashion had already banished the beard from the rest of Europe. Some Russians chose to flee the country rather than to have a shaven face. Peter imposed a stiff tax on beards; the men too poor to pay reluctantly cut and shaved their beards.

———

Seventy-three percent of Americans are willing to wear clothes until the clothes wear out. The poll conducted by Louis Harris and Associates also revealed: 92 percent are willing to eliminate annual model changes in automobiles; 57 percent are willing to see a national policy that would make it cheaper to live in multiple-unit apartments than in single-family homes; 82 percent would back steps to reduce sharply the amount of advertising urging people to buy more products; 91 percent are willing to eat more vegetables and less meat for protein.

———

Toward the end of the fifteenth century, men's shoes had a square tip, like a duck's beak, a fashion launched by Charles VIII of France to hide the imperfection of one of his feet, which had six toes.

―――――――

Although wool is one of man's oldest fabrics—Babylonians used woolen clothes as early as 4000 B.C.—it was unknown in America until 1540 when Coronado's expedition brought a few Spanish sheep to southwestern North America. British sheep were imported in 1609 by the colonists at Jamestown, and wool became, with flax, the basis of homemade linsey-woolsey (rough linen and wool) frontier garments.

―――――――

The high-fashion costume of men in the latter part of the sixteenth century consisted of a doublet and hose. Slashing became fashionable, and the clothes were cut into thousands of strips with a different color of fabric underneath. The Germans got carried away with this fashion and wore huge, baggy, slashed breeches. They used at least twenty yards of fabric, which fell in loose strips from the hips to the knees.

―――――――

In 1829, when Mrs. Lydia Child wrote *The Frugal Housewife,* hair care was a lot different from what it is now. New England rum was considered to be excellent for cleaning the hair and keeping it healthy; brandy was supposed to strengthen the roots.

―――――――

Dolley Madison set the style for lavish hospitality and elegant dress in the White House. With her bright-colored dresses, fondness for rubies and emeralds, beaded slippers, and jeweled snuffboxes, she went completely against her early Quaker upbringing. This transformation took place when she married James Madison, and the only sign of her plain past was the gray gown and white apron of a good Quaker housewife that she wore in the morning at home.

―――――――

The custom of being clean-shaven is said to date back to Alexander the Great, who had a scanty beard in any case and set the fashion. A century later, shaving entered the Roman world in the West, and the Eastern world abandoned the custom.

―――――――

Railroad conductors and mailmen in the United States refused to wear uniforms until after the Civil War. In 1844, policemen in New York City staged a strike against their proposed blue uniforms. The reason for their opposition was that they considered uniforms to be symbols of servitude, as maids and butlers wore them in the old country.

———

Using chemicals to get "high" isn't as new as one may think. Nitrous oxide was discovered in 1800. When inhaled, it was found to give a giddy, intoxicated feeling and to release the emotions. People laughed inanely, so it was called "laughing gas." For a while, parties were organized at which people sat around inhaling its fumes.

———

The era of the Middle Ages has been referred to as "1,000 years without a bath." Bathing was rare in Europe at that time, largely because the Christian Church considered it a sin to expose the body, even to oneself. It was not until 1641 that soap was manufactured in England. Religion had become less oppressive, but government harassment in the form of restrictions and taxes on the soapmaking industry caused the soap business to develop slowly.

———

People are marrying younger today than they did before the turn of the century. In the United States, in 1890, the average age of men at their first marriage was twenty-six years, compared with twenty-three today. For women, the corresponding figures are twenty-two then and just under twenty-one now.

———

Dinner guests in medieval England were expected to bring their own knives to table—hosts did not provide them. The fork did not appear until the sixteenth century, and fork-and-knife pairs were not in general use in England until the seventeenth century.

———

A conventional sign of virginity in Tudor England was a high exposed bosom and a sleeve full to the wrists.

———

Ladies in Europe took to wearing lightning rods on their hats and trailing a ground wire—a fad that began after Benjamin Franklin published instructions on how to make them, in his almanac, *Poor Richard Improved,* in 1753.

———

In 1418, women's headgear was so tall that the doorways of the royal castle of Vincennes, France, had to be raised, on the orders of the queen, to allow the ladies of the court to pass through without ducking.

———

FINE FEATHERED FRIENDS

The bearded vulture, or lammergeier, is noted for its habit of carrying off large bones and dropping them onto rocks from heights up to 200 feet, smashing them in order to feed on the marrow inside. It is the only bird of prey to do this.

————

Many songbirds learn to sing by listening to adult birds of the same species. If separated from the adults, they develop unintelligible warbles rather than normal song patterns. But if taught the song of another species, a bird often can pass the foreign language on to its offspring. In one experiment, a male bullfinch raised by a female canary learned the canary's song to perfection. When it was later mated to a female bullfinch, its children and later its grandchildren could sing like a canary.

————

The largest bird colony in the world is located on the islands off the coast of Peru. Ten million Peruvian boobies and cormorants reside there. Their diet—anchovies—produces the world's finest fertilizer, guano. Because of the value of their droppings, the birds were placed under strict protection by the Incas.

————

Arctic terns found in North America and the Arctic migrate each year as far south as Antarctica and back, a round trip of over 18,000 miles. Theirs is probably the longest migratory flight.

————

The great auk, or garefowl, was once common in the rocky ocean areas off Canada, Iceland, Greenland, and northern Europe. Similar to a penguin and also a nonflying bird, the auk was popular among collectors for its eggs and skins. The last of the auks was captured and slaughtered in June 1844, off the coast of Iceland. It is one of the few extinct creatures whose moment of extinction was documented with certainty, and the first native North American species to become extinct through the efforts of man.

————

The ruby-throated hummingbird beats its wings at the incredibly rapid speed of fifty to seventy times a second. If a 170-pound man expended energy at the rate of the hummingbird, he would have to eat 285 pounds of hamburger or twice his weight in potatoes each day in order to maintain his weight. He would have to evaporate 100 pounds of perspiration per hour to keep his skin temperature below the boiling point of water.

———

Birds played a role in aerial warfare during World War I. Because of their acute hearing, parrots were kept on the Eiffel Tower to warn of approaching aircraft long before the planes were heard or seen by human spotters.

———

A little more than a century ago, there was an account of a flock of passenger pigeons in a column 500 yards wide that took three hours to pass over the observer: about a billion birds in all. Today, the passenger pigeon is extinct.

———

The female pigeon cannot lay eggs if she is alone. In order for her ovaries to function, she must be able to see another pigeon. If no other pigeon is available, her own reflection in a mirror will suffice.

———

The largest egg ever laid by any creature we know of was that of the extinct aepyornis of Madagascar. The egg was 9.5 inches wide and 13 inches long. It had a volume of 2.35 gallons.

———

The chick of the mallee fowl never knows either of its parents. As soon as it burrows out of the mound in which its mother built her nest, the chick is able to fly and is left entirely on its own. No mother mallee has ever been seen with a brood.

———

Thomas Edison had a collection of 5,000 birds.

———

In the 1840s, pigeons would carry European news from ships approaching the U.S. to newspapers along the Atlantic coast, from Halifax to the U.S. capital. The limit on how much news a pigeon could carry was one reason for the demise of the medium.

———

A woodpecker uses its beak for obtaining food, chiseling out nests from trees, and as a means of communication. Other birds sing in order to attract a mate or stake out their territory, but the woodpecker beats on a dry, resonant branch with its beak. By the duration and rhythm of the drumming, the woodpecker makes claim to his territory, attracts females, and identifies his own species and other species.

———

For protection against predators, the silvery-cheeked hornbill chooses a hollow tree for a nest and seals herself in until her chicks are grown. Only a very narrow opening is left when the entrance hole is closed with a mixture of mud, bark, and material regurgitated by the male. He feeds her and the chicks ten to twenty times a day over a three-month period. The female keeps the nest clean, throwing out dirt and old feathers, and defecating neatly through the opening. When the young are grown, she breaks down the wall with her bill and everyone emerges, the mother so fat that for a few days she can scarcely fly.

———

With few exceptions, birds do not sing while on the ground. They sing during flight or while sitting on an object off the ground. Exceptions include the turnstone, which is a shorebird, and some American field sparrows.

———

The tallest bird of all time was the moa, a flightless inhabitant of New Zealand that became extinct 400 years ago. It grew to be eleven feet tall. Its drumstick was a yard long.

———

The yolk of a bird's egg is connected to the shell by albumen "ropes." During incubation, these ropes break, and the mother bird must rotate her eggs to keep the yolks in the center while the chicks are forming.

———

The African eagle, swooping at better than a hundred miles per hour, can brake to a halt in twenty feet.

———

The albatross has the largest wingspread, anywhere from 10 to 12 feet, of all creatures flying today. This bird has adapted so well to life in the winds of the Atlantic Ocean that once the young albatross leaves the island of its birth it may not touch any land again for two years. Because of its tapering wing design, it excels at gliding and

flying. It eats mainly fish, floating carrion, and refuse, and can "land" on the water.

A well-intentioned philanthropist, Eugene Scheifflin, instituted a project in the 1890s to bring to America all the birds mentioned by Shakespeare. Unfortunately, Hotspur talks about the starling in *Henry IV, Part I;* starlings were therefore let loose in New York's Central Park. The noisy nuisances now number in the millions from Alaska to Mexico, and they will be with us for as long as the plays of Shakespeare. Maybe longer.

Migrating geese fly in a V formation to save energy. A goose's wings churn the air and leave an air current behind. In the flying wedge, each bird is in position to get a lift from the current left by the bird ahead. It is easier going for all, except the leader. During a migration, geese are apt to take turns in the lead position.

To survive, every bird must eat at least half its own weight in food each day. Young birds need even more. A young robin, for example, eats as much as fourteen feet of earthworms a day.

The largest bird egg in the world today is that of the ostrich. Ostrich eggs are from six to eight inches long. Because of their size and the thickness of their shells, they take forty minutes to hard-boil.

The ancient Vikings navigated by depending on the instincts of birds. They took on board a number of ravens, and released them one by one as they sailed to the west. If the raven flew back along the course from which it had come, the Viking ships continued due west. But when a raven flew a different way, the ships would change course and follow its flight path to search for new lands.

The breeding ground of the emperor penguin is inland in Antarctica, some fifty to eighty miles from the coast. The emperor penguin walks there, and the female lays her egg and walks back to the sea. The male stays behind, incubating the single egg between his feet and his abdomen, during the depth of an Antarctic winter in temperatures that go as low as −60° C. and in gales at speeds of up to ninety-five miles per hour. Only when the female returns and takes over can the male return to the sea. Four months elapse between leaving the sea and returning; during that time, the male does not eat.

In the old days, first-class birds for use in falconry were sold to European kings for thousands of dollars a bird.

———

A newborn turkey chick has to be taught to eat, or it will starve. Breeders spread feed underfoot, hoping the little ones will peck at it and get the idea. Turkeys tend to look up with their mouths open during rainstorms. Lots of them drown as a result.

———

A parrot's beak can close with a force of 350 pounds per square inch.

———

FINNY FACTS

Certain kinds of European eels lay their eggs in the Sargasso Sea, on the edge of the Gulf of Mexico, thousands of miles from their home rivers. To reach the spawning grounds, they leave the European streams, using any kind of waterway they can find, or even traveling short distances by land when obstacles such as dams force them to do so. When they reach the ocean, they set out on a compass course for their destination 3,000 to 6,000 miles away. The adult eel does not return from the spawning ground but, carried by the Gulf Stream, the newly spawned larvae return to Europe, a journey of about three years' duration.

———

The tail propulsion of dolphins is superior in efficiency to that of ship propellors; they use less energy to achieve a given speed.

———

When they die, some fish spectacularly change colors. The dying mullet, for example, flashes patches of red, ocher, and green. In Roman days, the host at a posh banquet would have a still-living mullet brought in a vase to table. When the water was removed from the vase, guests would watch the fish change colors as it gasped out its life. Pale in death, the mullet would be returned to the kitchen.

———

A starfish can be cut into sizable chunks and each piece will grow into a completely whole starfish.

———

Black sea bass, when young, are preponderantly female. At the age of five years or so, many switch sex and become functional males.

———

The cod lays vast numbers of eggs, but fewer than five eggs out of a million hatch and mature.

———

The whale shark, which may grow to be forty-five feet long and weigh fifty tons, is harmless. It eats very small animals, which it strains from the sea water.

———

Not all fish live only in the water. Walking catfish, mudskippers, and flying fish, among many species, can live on land.

———

Sharks are ovoviviparous—that is, they bring forth living young instead of eggs. But there is no mammalian placenta.

———

In a reversal of normal biological roles, the male pipefish carries fertilized eggs in a pouch in its stomach, where they are deposited by the female. The eggs incubate for seventeen to twenty-one days and then emerge from a slit in the pouch.

———

The Nile catfish swims upside down, and therefore has developed a light back and a dark belly, the reverse of the usual fish color scheme.

———

Oysters shipped 1,000 miles inland, from the Connecticut shore to Illinois, open their shells in Illinois at the times of high tides at their ancestral beds. After a couple of weeks, they alter their schedule and open their shells when it would be high tide in their new domicile.

———

The giant squid continues to grow as long as it lives. Some specimens reach 50 feet from the tip of the tentacles to the end of the tail.

———

There are fish that use sounds for defense and as part of their reproductive process. Although most fish do not have vocal cords, many are able to make sounds, usually by vibrating their swim bladder or rubbing parts of their skeleton together. They produce such noises as squeaks, whistles, coughs, and snapping or grinding noises.

———

The head of the adult sperm whale represents a quarter of the animal's length and a third of its total weight.

———

The electric eel is one of the most dangerous electric fish, with an average discharge of 400 volts. More than half its body is given over to electrical production.

———

The globefish staves off predators by gulping a large quantity of water, till it becomes simply too large to be swallowed by its enemies.

———

The paddlefish, a living fossil, has existed virtually unchanged in the Mississippi River for 230 million years, although it now weighs no more than one-third of its ancient weight. The only other part of the world in which the paddlefish is found is China.

———

Tuna swim at a steady rate of nine miles per hour for an indefinite period of time—and they never stop moving. Estimates indicate that a fifteen-year-old tuna must have traveled one million miles in its lifetime.

———

We are sure that whales and dolphins had land-living ancestors, but we don't know what they were like, and we don't know how whales and dolphins evolved.

———

The largest animal that ever lived is alive right now. It is the blue whale, which can weigh nearly 200 tons—almost twice as much as the largest dinosaur on record. (The largest accurately measured blue whale had a length of 110 feet, 2½ inches.)

———

The oyster is usually ambisexual. It begins life as a male, then becomes a female, then changes back to being a male, then back to being a female; it may go back and forth many times.

———

It is the male seahorse, not the female, that carries the embryo of the species. The female fills the male's brood pouch with eggs, which remain in the swollen sac for the gestation period of eight to ten days.

———

The archerfish catches prey, such as insects that hover over the surface of the water, by firing volleys of water from beneath the surface. Compressing the covers of its gills, the fish forces the water through a small tube formed by its palate and tongue. Its aim is so accurate that the water knocks the victims down.

———

The blue whale can go up to half a year without eating—it is maintained by its blubber.

———

The chambered nautilus (immortalized in poetry by Oliver Wendell Holmes), from whose ancestors the squid and the octopus evolved, has been roaming the world's oceans for 450 million years, antedating the dinosaurs.

———

Sharks can be dangerous even before they are born. One scientist, Stewart Springer, was bitten by a sand tiger shark embryo while he was examining its pregnant mother.

———

So light-shy—and so ingenious—are some sea urchins that they pick up pebbles and hold them up to cast shadows when caught in flashlight beams.

———

The female anglerfish is six times larger than her mate. The male anchors himself to the top of her head and stays there for the rest of his life. They literally become one. Their digestive and circulatory systems are merged. Except for two very large generative organs and a few fins, nothing remains of the male.

———

The Portuguese man-of-war is not one animal but a colony. It is made up of many modified animals of the same species, perhaps several hundred in number. They live together and divide their work. A lone animal of one type forms a float. Several other animals provide the tentacles for fishing. A third variety digests the food caught by the second, and a fourth has the job of reproducing.

———

The U.S. Fish and Wildlife Service restocks lakes by cascading newborn trout from an aircraft skimming the water at low speed.

———

Of interest to computer manufacturers has been the way the eye in the tail of the crayfish functions. It is a pigment-cup (ocellus) kind of eye, and the crayfish uses it, or turns it on, when it wants to back into a dark crevice.

———

Lake Baikal, in Siberia, is the only lake in the world that is deep enough to have deep-sea fish.

———

Amid the lethal tentacles of the Portuguese man-of-war (and apparently oblivious to the dangerous nematocysts, its minute stinging organs) are fish who seem content to live there. They feed on whatever comes their way.

———

A plaice, a large European flounder, can lie on a checkerboard and reproduce on its upper surface the same pattern of squares, for camouflage.

———

Over 500 varieties of fish are able to generate appreciable amounts of electricity. Torpedo rays can produce current up to 50 amperes at 60 volts. The organs that generate electricity contain tubes filled with flat, disc-shaped cells, similar to the plates in a car battery.

———

One species of Antarctic fish is the only fish known to have white blood. It has no red pigment in its blood. Normally, the lack of hemoglobin would mean death because oxygen could not be carried to the body cells without it. However, the white-blooded fish appears to enjoy good health.

———

Sea otters live where there are very strong currents. A family of otters will spend every night resting in a kelp bed. To prevent themselves from floating away from one another, they twist themselves around in the seaweed until they are tied in. The kelp bed may be carried away by the current during the night, but the otter family will still be together.

———

Fish can be susceptible to seasickness. Artificial "storm waves" made in a glass bowl, in a scientific study, resulted in seasick goldfish.

———

The blackswallower, a deep-sea fish, is able to swallow prey larger than itself. It accomplishes this by moving its heart out of the way and pushing its gills aside. Movable teeth in its throat help get the meals down, and its stomach stretches far enough to accommodate fish twice its size.

———

Dolphins can, and do, crush barracudas with one snap of their jaws and kill sharks by merely ramming them with their snout. However, dolphins have never been known to attack humans. This is considered evidence of their intelligence.

———

Because its eyeball is fixed, the whale must move its huge body to shift its line of sight.

———

Dolphins do not breath automatically, as humans do, and so they do not sleep as humans do. If they became unconscious, they would sink to the bottom of the sea. Without the oxygen they need to take in periodically, they would die.

———

A shrimp has more than a hundred pairs of chromosomes in each cell nucleus. Man has only twenty-three. (It once was thought man had twenty-four.)

———

The skin corrugations that dolphins develop while accelerating and while swimming at their maximum speed are thought to make it possible for them, by reducing water resistance, to sustain speeds that are about ten times more than they "should" achieve with their muscle power.

———

Polyp, fish, worm, plant, crab, mollusk, and plankton in symbiotic relationship (the habitual living together of organisms of different species) make up a coral reef.

———

FLUID FACTS

The Amazon River is so wide that from its mouth pours one-fifth of all the moving fresh water on Earth. In addition to being the widest river, the Amazon also has the distinction of being probably the longest (estimates vary up to 4,200 miles), covering the largest area (2,772,000 square miles), and having the greatest discharge (7,200,000 cubic feet per second). The area drained by it is almost as great as the area of the entire United States.

———

Lake Balkhash, in the southern Russian desert near the U.S.S.R.'s border with China, is about 360 miles long; the water at its western end is fresh, but the water in its eastern end is salty. The two halves are separated by a sandbar. The western is fed by the Li River. The other half is shrinking due to evaporation, and the concentration of minerals contributes to the salinity.

———

When you suck water into a straw, you are creating a partial vacuum in your mouth and allowing air pressure on the water reservoir to push that water up the straw to fill that partial vacuum. Air pressure is only so great, however, and it can only serve to push water to a height of thirty-three feet. If you had a straw longer than that, neither you nor any suction device could draw the water higher. Mercury, which is much denser than water, is pushed thirty inches high by the average pressure of the atmosphere at sea level. As air pressure changes slightly, with weather, the height of the mercury changes slightly—and this is the principle of the barometer.

———

The Chicago River used to flow into Lake Michigan. Through engineering ingenuity, the river is now formed by water flowing in from the lake.

———

The Amazon River has 1,100 tributary streams.

———

The Salto Alto (Angel Falls) in Venezuela is the highest waterfall known. It is more than twenty times higher than Niagara.

If all the water vapor in the Earth's atmosphere were condensed to liquid water at the same time, there would be enough water to cover the United States (including Alaska and Hawaii) with a layer of water twenty-five feet deep.

There have been violent conflicts in the competition for water rights. It is appropriate that the word "rivalry" comes from the Latin *rivus*, a "stream."

The bottom of the Arctic Ocean—depths of 2.8 miles have been recorded—is nearly 9 miles closer to the center of the Earth than the bottom of the world's deepest trench, Mindanao, which is 6.8 miles below sea level. Sea level at the latitude of Mindanao is almost 13 miles above the polar sea level, making the greatest depth of the trench still about 6.1 miles above the polar sea level.

Only about 1.6 percent of the water on Earth is fresh. Most of it is locked—unusable for living things—in the snow and the ice at the poles and on the peaks of the highest mountains.

Depending on the shape of the shore, the rise and fall of tides can make a difference of sixty feet in a funnel-shaped bay like the Bay of Fundy or only a few inches in a nearly landlocked sea like the Mediterranean. Because the land masses get in the way of tides and break up what would otherwise be an orderly progression of the water-hills, the connection of the water-hills and the moon went unnoticed until early modern times.

A sizable oak tree, during the typical growing season, gives off 28,000 gallons of moisture.

Human beings can neither smell nor taste a substance that is not soluble. On a dry tongue, sugar has no taste. In a dry nose, the smell of a flower would not be noticed. Anything to be smelled must float in the air.

The largest landlocked body of water in the world is the Caspian Sea. It receives the Volga River (the longest in Europe) and has an area of 154,000 square miles. It has no outlet, so it collects salt and is two-fifths as salty as the oceans. Its level—and thus its area—has been fluctuating over the centuries. In recent years it has been shrinking, but current engineering plans may make it rise soon, artificially, by making water flow from the Vychegda and Pechora Rivers into the Volga—a gigantic feat.

———

Perfectly still water can be lowered to temperatures several degrees lower than the freezing point (32°F., 0°C.)—and remain liquid.

———

The sponge filters morsels of food out of the seawater that passes through its pores. Before it can obtain enough food to gain an ounce of body weight, a sponge must filter a ton of water.

———

The deepest part of the oceans is farther below sea level than the highest land is above it. The Mariana Trench, a great fissure in the floor of the Pacific Ocean, reaches a depth of 36,198 feet at its lowest measured point, just off the Philippines. Mount Everest, considered to be the world's highest mountain, which dominates the Himalayan chain on the Nepal-Tibet border, is "only" 29,028 feet high.

———

Nearly three centuries passed between discovery by Hernando de Soto of the lower Mississippi River, in 1541, and by Henry Rowe Schoolcraft—leading a government research party—of the giant river's source.

———

If the 23 million cubic kilometers of ice in the world melted at the same time, the volume of the oceans would increase only 1.7 percent, but this would be enough for the sea level to rise about 180 feet. The Empire State Building would be in water to nearly the twentieth floor.

———

The level of the sea fell 400 feet during the first Ice Age. Much of the Earth's water had been absorbed by ice caps.

———

The deepest lake in the world—it is nearly a mile deep in places—is Lake Baikal, in Siberia. Though Lake Superior covers a greater area—32,000 square miles to Baikal's 13,000—it contains less water. Lake Baikal represents the largest single volume of fresh water in the world.

———

Water is the only substance on Earth present (in quantity) in solid, liquid, and gaseous forms. There is an ocean full of water. There are polar caps of miles-deep ice. There is water vapor making up a major, if variable, part of the atmosphere.

———

A scientist at Michigan State University has calculated that the production of a single hen egg requires about 120 gallons of water, a loaf of bread requires 300 gallons, and a pound of beef, 3,500.

———

The $200-million cleaning up of England's "Father Thames" has resulted in a startling ecological turnaround. The British magazine *Water* noted that it marked "the first time in the world that an industrial river once so polluted as to be recognized as lifeless has been restored to something approaching a natural state." In 1978, wildfowl and waders returned in profusion, and salmon can be found today in the inner reaches of the Thames for the first time in more than a century.

———

A single drop of water is composed of so many molecules—about 1.7 quintillion (1,700,000,000,000,000,000)—that, if it were "diluted" by all the water in all the oceans, a pint of that ocean water would contain about twenty-four of these molecules.

———

The Amazon River pushes so much water into the Atlantic that, more than a hundred miles at sea, off the mouth of the river, one can dip fresh water out of the ocean and drink it.

———

Luckily, the water that composes a wave does not advance with it across the sea. If it did, navigation would be practically impossible. Each water particle in the wave describes a circular orbit, returning very nearly to its original position.

———

The Tonle Sap, a major river of Cambodia, is most exceptional. It flows north for roughly half the year and south for the rest of the year. This happens because it diverts some of the rainy-season floodwaters of the Mekong River to fill the great lake in the center of Cambodia. The flow reverses to drain the lake in the dry season.

———

The wave that is generally accepted by oceanographers as being the highest ever was sighted from the *U.S.S. Ramapo* in the Pacific Ocean on February 6–7, 1933, during a sixty-eight-knot (seventy-eight-mile-per-hour) hurricane. The wave was calculated to be 112 feet from trough to crest.

———

Each time the tide rises, every one of us loses a fraction of an ounce in weight; sorry, but the weight is regained as the tide falls. We are affected by these tidal waves, just as the ocean is, because of the water and salt content of our bodies. The land and the air are affected as well by the tides. Every time the water rises in a ten-foot tide, the continents rise about six inches and the atmosphere bulges many miles.

———

Every year, the Yellow River in China carries to the sea enough loess, a yellow loamy deposit blown from the deserts, to build a wall three feet high and three feet thick that would stretch twenty-three times around the planet.

———

The Gulf Stream's warm blue waters are so clearly defined, even as far north as Newfoundland where they meet the Labrador Current, that the bow of a ship entering the stream may momentarily be 20° F. warmer than the stern, which is still in the Labrador Current. Truly "a river in the ocean."

———

Until life forms were found, in 1860, clinging to a cable that had lain at the depth of a mile in the Mediterranean, it had been assumed that ocean life was confined to the surface layer and that the depths, with their cold, darkness, and enormous pressures, were barren of life. We now know that life can be found even at the bottommost foot of the deepest abyss.

———

The longest river in North America has no single name. A drop of water starting in southwestern Montana flows through a river named the Missouri for 2,466 miles. When it passes the city of St. Louis, it flows on for 1,294 more miles, but the river is now called the Mississippi. The combined length of the river from Montana to the Gulf of Mexico is 3,760 miles, but the only name we can give it is the Missouri-Mississippi. (The only rivers longer than that are the Amazon in South America and the Nile in Africa.)

———

If the oceans were divided up among all the people of Earth, every single man, woman, and child would get the equivalent of 110 billion gallons, which is the equivalent of a tenth of a cubic mile of ocean water. If each person were given only fresh water, which makes up only 1.6 percent of the water on the planet, each would still get 40 million gallons.

———

Though the 4,157-mile-long Nile was all-important to Egypt, European and American explorers, and not Egyptians, were the first to trace the Nile all the way to its sources. In 1857, the Englishman John Hanning Speke reached a great equatorial lake that he named Lake Victoria, for his Queen. Many rivers flowed into the lake from the mountains of Kenya, near the central East Africa coast, but the Nile issued from Victoria.

———

The boiling point of water varies according to air pressure. At sea level, water boils at 212° F. (100° C.), but water under pressure boils at higher temperatures. At a pressure equivalent to that exerted by a column of water 500 feet high, water will have to reach a temperature of 394° F. before it boils. The principle of increasing the pressure to increase the boiling point and thereby make for faster cooking is the basis for the pressure cooker.

———

Without the Antarctic waters, Earth's oceans would support only a comparatively limited amount of life; Earth's land surface would be the poorer for it as well. It is the cold waters of the ocean off the southern continent that tend to fertilize the rest of the world. The waters are rich in oxygen and, being heavy with cold, seep northward at the bottom of the ocean, aerating it. When these cold waters well upward for any reason, they bring up minerals too; where the welling occurs, the ocean teems with life.

———

FOSSILS

Sometime between the fourth century B.C. and the present, the coastline around Possulooli and the Bay of Naples sank beneath the Mediterranean, and then rose. Evidence for this is found in the marble columns of the ruined Temple of Serapis, which were pitted by the rock-boring mollusk *Lithodromus lithophagus*. Shells of the long-dead mussels are still in place. Only while the area was submerged could these mollusks have bored into the columns and excavated deep pits for themselves. Below sea level a mile away, the same species today follows tradition and bores into rock and hard mud.

———

The roof on Philadelphia's Independence Hall and many of the three-foot shingles on historic American homes were made of white cedar that had been buried under water for up to 1,000 years. By the 1800s, the New Jersey cedar swamps had been depleted of living white cedar trees. It was then discovered that a layer of fallen cedar trunks covered the swamp bottom to a depth of twelve feet. These ancient submerged logs were mined and made into light, durable white-cedar shakes.

———

Some dinosaurs were as small as hens.

———

The Cardiff giant, a ten-foot tall, 3,000-pound "petrified human being," was "discovered" when a well was being dug on a farm in rural New York State in 1869. The giant, which was accepted by doctors and archaeologists as an authentic fossil, turned out to have been carved from a block of Iowa gypsum a year earlier and buried at the site of the future "well." The giant was sold and resold at ever increasing value, a one-eighth share finally reaching $25,000. When he was unable to buy the original, the showman P. T. Barnum had a copy made and exhibited it successfully.

———

Ninety-nine percent of all forms of life that have existed on Earth are now extinct.

————

Wood has an immortality all its own. Log palisades that protected the prehistoric lake-dwellers of northern Italy have been found intact, as have pilings buried under Venice for 1,000 years. White cedar trees buried in the swamps of Virginia for an estimated 3,000 years have been dug up and sawed into boards that may last another 1,000 years.

————

For reasons unknown, the prehistoric horse vanished in America about 30,000 years ago. The horses of the West today are descended directly from wild horses of central Asia, out of horses imported by Europeans.

————

The stegosaurus was a dinosaur with a head so small that the nerve knot in the middle of the back was larger than its brain.

————

In 1938, a coelacanth was found off the coast of Madagascar. Until that time, this primitive fish, an ancestor of the air-breathing amphibians, was believed to have become extinct more than 60 million years earlier.

————

When zoologists examined a platypus for the first time, some suspected a hoax, thinking that parts of different animals had been sewn together. The platypus has the fur of an otter, the tail of a beaver, the bill and feet of a duck, and the venomous spurs of a fighting gamecock. Although the platypus is a mammal, it lays eggs and does not have nipples (milk oozes out of pore openings in the abdomen). Because of its reptile-like characteristics, it is assumed now to have descended from a link between reptiles and mammals of 150 million years ago—a living fossil.

————

Because the chalky shells of certain marine animals have a composition that depends upon the temperature of the water in which they were formed, a "time thermometer" can fathom when a fossil lived, what the water temperature was, how long the fossil lived, and in what season it died—even though it was tens of millions of years ago.

————

The touring Peter the Great shipped back to Russia the Dutchman Frederich Ruysch's collection of 1,300 fluid-preserved examples of natural history—fossils, rocks, plants of many varieties—and embryonic stages of humans and animals. By the time the collection arrived in St. Petersburg, the sailors had drunk the brandy in which many specimens had been preserved.

Because the huge skeletons that were built up out of fossilized remnants were clearly reptilian in nature, they were called "terrible lizards," which in Greek is *dinosauria,* by the nineteenth-century zoologist Sir Richard Owen. But the ancient giant reptiles are more closely related to alligators than to lizards, and should have been named *dinocrocodilia.*

The tyrannosaur approached the practical limits for bipedality. The full length of its body, from snout to tail tip, was probably fifty feet. Its four-foot-long head was carried some nineteen feet above the ground. Its thighs were enormous, but its forelegs were tiny, not much longer than a man's, and far too short to be of any use. They couldn't even reach the mouth.

Tyrannosaurus rex was the largest carnivorous reptile of the dinosaur period. But it was not the largest of all dinosaurs; this distinction belonged to the herbivorous sauropods, of which the largest, *Brachiosaurus,* weighed as much as fifty tons.

Dinosaurs were mostly vegetarians, despite their enormous size and decidedly carnivorous appearance. One exception was the mammoth *Tyrannosaurus rex,* which apparently ate other dinosaurs. The food making up a single bite for a tyrannosaur, it was speculated, would feed a human family of four for an entire month.

FOUNDING FATHERS

In 1804, during President Thomas Jefferson's first administration, there was a plot by the Federalists of New York and New England to secede from the United States. The plan was to run Vice-President Aaron Burr for the governorship of New York State. Once elected, Burr would lead an insurrection of the secession states and he would become president of the new nation. Alexander Hamilton, the U.S. Treasurer, refused to join the group and instead used his influence to ruin Burr's election chances. Burr's fury at Hamilton's interference led to the famous duel in which Burr mortally shot Hamilton.

Paul Revere, the greatest silversmith of colonial America, was a failure at his second trade, copperplate engraving. His artistry on copper was poor, and he worked at engraving only when he was financially hard put.

At his death, at the age of ninety-five years and two months, in November 1832, the last surviving signer of the Declaration of Independence was the nation's wealthiest man. Charles Carroll, of Maryland, a Revolutionary War patriot, Irish-American Catholic, squire, lawyer, and businessman, had "dabbled" in canals and railroads. At the age of ninety-two, he broke the ground in Baltimore for work on the first passenger and freight railroad in the U.S.

Although the Declaration of Independence was adopted in July 1776, it was not until printer Mary Katherine Goddard distributed her first edition of the Declaration—when commissioned by Congress in January 1777—that all of the signers were publicly identified.

Not until 1826 were fireworks used to celebrate the Fourth of July. Coincidentally, it was the very day that two of the founding fathers died, but their demise did not interfere with the national celebration of the fiftieth anniversary of the Declaration of Independence. It took four days for the news of John Adams's death to reach Washington and two days for the capital to learn of Thomas Jefferson's death.

British ships in the English Channel fired a salute of twenty guns when word reached them that the country's erstwhile great adversary, President George Washington, had died in the States.

The first U.S. Chief Justice, John Jay, bought slaves in order to free them.

"You replace Mr. Franklin," said Comte de Vergennes on Thomas Jefferson's arrival as envoy to France. "I succeed him," Mr. Jefferson replied; "no one could replace him."

Presidents George Washington and John Adams had to employ protection money—paying off certain pirates in the Mediterranean Sea with a couple of million dollars—while Congress debated the creation of a U.S. navy.

James Madison was the "Father of the Constitution." But it was against Madison, serving as Secretary of State under Jefferson, that the historic first case was brought in which the Supreme Court asserted a right to declare unconstitutional an act of Congress. The landmark decision, *Marbury v. Madison,* established the vital doctrine of judicial review.

Alexander Hamilton, a major mover in the call for the Constitutional Convention, wanted to make the nation "the united state of America," doing without individual states altogether.

Thirteen years after Thomas Jefferson successfully urged the U.S. to abandon British currency and adopt decimal currency, the French revolutionaries designed and instituted the metric system, which Jefferson no doubt would have preferred and whose adoption *then* would have saved the U.S. much economic disarray today.

When George Washington first visited Massachusetts as U.S. President, he had accepted an advance invitation to dine with Governor John Hancock, fully expecting that Hancock would call on him first. But when Washington arrived in Boston, Hancock was not among the welcomers, sending word that gout made it impossible for him to move from his house. Washington realized that Hancock, a strong states' rights advocate, was trying to establish the principle that when a President visited a state, he did so only as a guest of the governor. Washington canceled the dinner engagement. Hancock got the message, literally and figuratively, sent emissaries, and came to call.

In 1826, Thomas Jefferson, then eighty-three years old, was flat broke and in debt for $107,000. He convinced the Virginia state legislature to allow him to sell lottery tickets, and the winner would get Jefferson's land. The lottery was not successful. When Jefferson died, he left many unpaid debts.

Thomas Jefferson apparently did not love his mother. In his diary, he made exactly one reference to her. "March 31st—My mother died about 8 o'clock this morning. In the 57th year of her age." When he once was told by a servant that his mother's house had burned down, Jefferson's first question was, "What about my books?" Jefferson did not invite his mother to live in his home. (According to one story, she was "crazy" and thrice tried to burn down her house before finally succeeding.)

One of the most popular men during Europe's Age of Enlightenment—probably the most popular in France—was an American, Benjamin Franklin. His portrait was to be seen everywhere in Paris, in store windows and in many private houses. His image appeared on medals, medallions, rings, watches, snuffboxes, and bracelets. John Adams said that Franklin's reputation "was more universal than that of Leibniz or Newton, Frederick or Voltaire, and his character more beloved and esteemed than any or all of them."

George Washington had to borrow £500 to pay off his debts and another £100 for the expenses of the trip to his inauguration in New York, in 1789. Washington, one of the richest men of his time, was "land-poor." He borrowed the money from Richard Conway of Alexandria, Virginia, and said that "short crops and other causes not entirely within my control" were the reasons.

Thomas Jefferson chose not to attend ceremonies marking the death of George Washington in 1799, nor did he write a note of condolence to Washington's widow. This enmity stemmed from the last year of Washington's second term as U.S. President, when he suspected Jefferson of being responsible for scurrilous attacks in the press on him. Jefferson denied responsibility and Washington accepted his word, but there was a chill between them thereafter.

————

President Thomas Jefferson told Congress that the Louisiana Purchase he had effected was unconstitutional, but he urged that the agreement with Napoleon be ratified, casting behind them "metaphysical subtleties."

————

George Washington refused to publish his recollections or to let those men who knew him reach the printed page. "Any memoirs of my life," he said in 1784, "would rather hurt my feelings than tickle my pride whilst I lived. I had rather glide gently down the stream of life, leaving it to posterity to think and say what they please of me, than by any act of mine to have vanity or ostentation imputed to me. . . . I do not think vanity is a trait of my character."

————

The first English settlement in what became New England was founded thirteen years before the arrival of the Pilgrims. In 1607, a settlement was established at Popham Beach, Maine. After a year, its inhabitants found the climate too harsh, and departed.

————

Thomas Paine, whose best-selling forty-seven-page book *Common Sense* hastened the Declaration of Independence, designed the first long bridge that could cross a river without a supporting prop in the middle.

————

Thomas Jefferson was a smuggler of sorts. He went into northern Italy, in 1787, to see the machines used there for cleaning rice seed, and was able to filch and bring back to the U.S. samples of rice that he gave to planters in Georgia and South Carolina. He also picked up information about the olive tree.

————

George Washington was not born on "Washington's Birthday," February 22. He was born on February 11, 1732, according to the Julian calendar then used in Great Britain and the colonies. In 1752, they switched to the Gregorian calendar (which we use today) and dropped eleven days. Washington shifted his birthday by eleven days—as did many of his contemporaries—in order to keep the "real" day.

————

The President's Cabinet is not mentioned in the Constitution. But George Washington found that he had to consult regularly with the

Secretary of State and other heads of major departments, and the Cabinet developed from this practice of the first President.

Thomas Jefferson did important scientific work. He experimented with new varieties of grain and studied and classified fossils at a time when the investigation of these objects was in its infancy. On the other hand, he refused to believe meteorites fell from the sky. When scientists in Connecticut reported witnessing such falls, Jefferson is reported to have stated: "I would rather believe that two Yankee professors would lie than that stones fall from the sky."

James Oglethorpe, English general and philanthropist, established the colony of Georgia as a refuge for the rehabilitation of men freed from English debtors' prisons. His liberal, humanitarian ideals failed when few debtors came to the new colony and many of those reverted to their old ways. Oglethorpe himself ran into debt after spending his fortune to develop the colony. He was recalled to England and court-martialed in 1743, but the charges were dropped.

A former U.S. Vice-President, Aaron Burr, was charged with treason—for trying, it was said, to separate the Western lands from the U.S. and establish his own rule in the early 1800s. He was acquitted, but his image remained tarnished.

Apparently, Mason Locke Weems could tell a lie. It was Weems (1759–1825), clergyman, author, and promoter, who concocted that famous cherry-tree story in his book *Life of George Washington: With Curious Anecdotes, Equally Honourable to Himself and Exemplary to His Young Countrymen.*

George Washington seldom slept more than three or four consecutive hours in any day during the Revolutionary War.

Signing a memorial to Congress for the abolition of slavery was the last public act of Benjamin Franklin.

Thomas Jefferson was so upset with the Continental Congress's editing of his original Declaration of Independence that for years afterward he sent copies of both the original and the final versions to friends and asked their opinions as to which version they preferred.

The epitaph over Thomas Jefferson's grave reads: "Here was buried Thomas Jefferson, author of the Declaration of American Independence, of the statute of Virginia for religious freedom, and father of the University of Virginia." There is no mention that Jefferson was the U.S.'s third President, serving two terms. Jefferson wrote the epitaph himself.

Ben Franklin wanted the turkey, not the eagle, to be the U.S. national symbol. He considered the eagle "a bird of bad moral character" because it lives "by sharping and robbing."

The British erected in London's Trafalgar Square a statue of the U.S. President, George Washington, whose armies overthrew British rule in the colonies.

Throughout the secret discussions of the delegates meeting to prepare the new U.S. Constitution, the founding fathers held a distrust of the common man and democratic rule—in the opinion of the political analyst Richard Hofstadter. George Washington, who was the presiding officer, exhorted the delegates not to produce a document of which they themselves could not approve simply in order "to please the people." Alexander Hamilton charged that the "turbulent and changing" masses "seldom judge or determine right," and he advised setting up a permanent governmental body that would "check the imprudence of democracy."

Four of the most prominent American politicians did not attend the Constitutional Convention of 1787, which was called for the purpose of amending the Articles of Confederation, the supreme law of the land at the time. The four were Thomas Jefferson, who was the U.S. minister to France; John Adams, minister to England; Samuel Adams, who had not been elected a delegate; and Patrick Henry, who refused to attend. Henry feared the convention would devise a strong central government that would interfere with the rights of the states and of the people.

Collectors have paid as much as $16,000 for the signature of Button Gwinnett. Gwinnett was born in England of a Welsh family and became a rich rice merchant in Georgia, and eventually chief executive of the state. A year after signing the Declaration of Independence—his signature is the first one on the upper left of the parchment—Gwinnett was killed in a duel. Because he died so young (forty-four), his signature is one of the rarest of American holographs.

———

In addition to silversmithing, Paul Revere practiced dentistry in colonial Boston. He learned the craft from a surgeon dentist and advertised himself as being prepared to fix loose false teeth and to clean teeth.

———

GENIUS

Sir Isaac Newton (1642–1727), the English mathematician and natural philosopher who is considered by many to be the greatest scientist who ever lived, did practically all his scientific work prior to becoming master of the mint in 1699. Though he did reform the English coinage system, which was no mean feat in itself, Newton's scientific efforts and accomplishments were practically nil in his last twenty-five years.

Benjamin Franklin invented the rocking chair.

The assembly-line process, with its division of labor and standardized parts—exploited so successfully by Henry Ford—was pioneered by Eli Whitney over a hundred years earlier. Whitney, more famous for his invention of the cotton gin, applied these techniques in fulfilling a U.S. government contract for muskets in 1798.

When Alfred Nobel's nitroglycerine factory blew up in 1864, killing his brother, the Swedish government refused to allow the factory to be rebuilt. Nobel, who had invented dynamite, came to be looked upon as a mad scientist viciously manufacturing destruction. He fought that reputation all his life, finally winning out posthumously with the establishment of the Nobel Prizes in his will.

Antoine Laurent Lavoisier (1743–94) did more for chemistry than any man, before or since. He was one of the first to introduce effective quantitative methods in the study of chemical reactions. He explained combustion. He clearly described the role of oxygen in the respiration of animals and plants. His classification of substances is the basis of the modern distinction between chemical elements and compounds and is the basis of chemical nomenclature. But Lavoisier failed to do the one thing he most wanted to do: discover a new element.

Albert Einstein's famous letter of August 2, 1939—it was prepared by the nuclear physicist Leo Szilard—advised President Franklin Roosevelt on the probability that a nuclear chain reaction could be set up in a large mass of uranium, "by which vast amounts of power and large quantities of new radiumlike elements would be generated." If this phenomenon occurred, construction of atomic bombs would be possible. The letter noted that "it is conceivable—though much less certain—that extremely powerful bombs of a new type, carried by boat and exploded in a port, might very well destroy the whole port, together with some of the surrounding territory. However, such bombs might very well prove to be too heavy for transportation by air."

The seventeenth-century French mathematician, physicist, philosopher, and stylist Blaise Pascal built a calculating machine and a slide rule in his childhood, laid the foundation for the modern theory of probabilities, invented the mathematical triangle that bears his name, discovered the properties of the cycloid, and advanced differential calculus. But his best-known remarks had nothing to do with science. He was the man who said that if Cleopatra's nose had been differently shaped—aquiline, for instance—or if Cromwell's bladder had not been obstructed and he had lived longer, the history of the world would have been altered.

The English scientist Isaac Newton and the German mathematician Gottfried W. Leibniz, working independently, both discovered calculus, the branch of mathematics that studies continuously changing quantities.

Though he had never seen a clock, Benjamin Banneker (1731–1806) was able to make a clock, in 1754, that ran accurately for a score of years. Banneker was a mathematician, astronomer, surveyor of the District of Columbia, and almanac publisher.

The eccentric English chemist and physicist Henry Cavendish (1731–1810) had no appropriate instruments for the purpose, so he measured the strength of an electrical current in a direct way. He shocked himself with the current of the charge and estimated the pain. (He managed to live to be nearly eighty.)

John A. Roebling (1806–69), America's pioneer bridge builder and designer, died before his greatest achievement, the Brooklyn Bridge, was completed in 1883. Injured while visiting the bridge site before construction began, in 1869, he developed tetanus and died. His son Washington (1837–1926), a talented engineer in his own right, took over his father's project and saw it through, but at great personal sacrifice. Washington was stricken in 1873 by the "bends" while working in pressurized concrete chambers many feet under the river. He was so weak and ill thereafter that for a decade he had to direct the construction of the bridge from a window of his Brooklyn house. He was aided by his wife, who acted as liaison.

———

Isaac Newton dropped out of school when he was a teenager, at his mother's behest. She hoped he would become a successful farmer.

———

As a reward for snatching a boy from the path of an oncoming railroad locomotive, the teenage Thomas Edison was offered telegraphy lessons by the boy's grateful father. Edison quickly became one of the best and fastest telegraphers in the U.S.

———

When the French physicist Guillaume Amontons (1663–1705) went deaf at an early age, he considered it a blessing. It permitted him, he said, to concentrate on his scientific work. He made a thermometer that was somewhat more accurate than Galileo's, showed that each gas changes in volume by the same amount for a given change in temperature, gained a vision of a kind of absolute zero, designed barometers that could be used at sea, and invented an early type of semaphore.

———

John Shaw Billings (1838–1913), who started out as a surgeon, was responsible for a wide range of accomplishments. During his amazing career, he served in the U.S. Civil War as medical inspector of the Army of the Potomac, was in charge of the surgeon general's library in Washington (which he later expanded and catalogued), designed plans for the construction of Johns Hopkins Hospital, wrote essays on hospital administration and training that have become classics, united the various free circulating libraries of New York City, and supervised compilation of the U.S. censuses in 1880 and 1890. It was at Billings's suggestion that punch-card machinery was developed—the beginnings of computer technology.

———

Burial in Westminster Abbey was a great honor, but it was the only great honor granted to Charles Darwin by the ultrarespectable government of Great Britain under Queen Victoria. When Darwin received the Copley medal of the Royal Society, in 1865, it was for his achievements as a biologist and naturalist and not for his historic theory of evolution.

Henry David Thoreau (1817–62), the American author and naturalist who spent more than two years in close harmony with nature, leading a near-solitary life free of materialistic pursuits, built his hermitage cabin on the shore of Walden Pond near Concord, Massachusetts. The cabin was only 500 yards from the railroad tracks connecting Fitchburg and Boston.

The suggestion of a moratorium on invention was put forward in 1933 by Sir James Alfred Ewing, an eminent British engineer. The moratorium would have allowed for assimilation and integration of the existing mass of inventions and for evaluation of further proposals.

Albert Einstein was offered the presidency of Israel. He refused the opportunity, having no head, he said, for human problems.

Freud never learned to read a railway timetable. He almost always had to be accompanied on a journey.

Thomas Edison's first patented invention was a voting machine, designed in the 1860s and completely uninteresting to the customers for whom it was intended. It took many years before it was considered acceptable by American politicians.

The story of Newton and the apple is one legend that's true. Newton described it himself. He saw an apple fall from a tree to the ground at a time when the crescent moon was in the evening sky. He pondered on whether the moon was held in the grip of the same force the apple was—the rest is history. However, there is one part of the legend that *isn't* true. When it fell, the apple did not hit Newton on the head.

Louis Pasteur, whose work on wine, vinegar, and beer led to pasteurization, had an obsessive fear of dirt and infection. He refused to shake hands, and he carefully wiped plate and glass before dining.

Gregor Johann Mendel, an Austrian monk who founded the science of genetics, went unappreciated in a variety of ways. He wanted to be a college teacher, but thrice failed to pass the necessary examinations. (His University of Vienna examiner wrote that he lacked "insight and the requisite clarity of knowledge.") When Mendel sent the result of his classic pioneering experiments in genetics to a Swiss botanist, it was returned with brief and cold comments. When he published his work, it went unnoticed, and as a result Mendel gave up his scientific labors. The importance of his work wasn't understood until 1900, sixteen years after his death.

———

Claude Bernard dropped out of school because it was his ambition to be a great writer. At the age of twenty-one, he wrote a five-act tragedy called *Arthur of Brittany* and brought it to a well-known Parisian critic. The critic read the play and strongly advised young Claude to return to school at once and forget all about writing. Claude did—and became one of the greatest biologists in history, virtually founding "experimental physiology." When he died in 1878, he was given a state funeral, the first scientist upon whom France had bestowed this honor.

———

Albert Einstein's last words will never be known. He spoke them in German, and the attending nurse did not understand German.

———

Rudolf Virchow (1821–1902), the German scientist who was the first to engage in cancer research on a scientific basis, was dead set against the germ theory of disease advanced by Pasteur. Rather than be forced to admit he was wrong on this point and Pasteur right, Virchow—who had practically founded the science of pathology and made important advances in anthropology—quit science altogether and went into politics.

———

So given to detail was the English chemist James Smithson (whose generosity led to the founding of the Smithsonian Institution in Washington, D.C.) that he even analyzed a tear he observed gliding down a lady's cheek. He managed to catch half of the drop on a crystal vessel and submitted it to reagents, detecting what was then called microcosmic salt, with "muriate of soda" and three or four more saline substances held in solution.

———

George Perkins Marsh, of Woodstock, Vermont, may have been the world's first ecologist. He correctly predicted that invention of the silk hat would cause the formation of many small lakes and bogs in the U.S.; the reason: there would be a reduced demand for beaver furs, and beavers in large enough quantities would again set about their business of reshaping the geography. Marsh was a polymath. He spoke twenty languages, and his fields of study and activity included art, architecture, literature, anthropology, law, politics, diplomacy, philology, geography, and education. He served Lincoln as minister to Italy. While there, he completed his groundbreaking classic, *Man and Nature, or Physical Geography as Modified by Human Action.*

Einstein, who said he refused to make a profit out of science—"My laurel is not for sale"—declared that had he known the Germans would not succeed in developing an atomic bomb, he would have done nothing for its development in the U.S.

Their mothers' fierce and single-minded ambition for them drove Dmitri Mendeleev, William Thomson, and Ernest Rutherford into lives of science. (Mendeleev developed the concept of the periodic law of classification of elements. Thomson [Baron Kelvin] contributed to thermodynamics and coordinated various theories of heat. Rutherford won a Nobel Prize for chemistry, for his research in radioactivity.)

Thomas Edison, "the wizard of Menlo Park," established an "invention factory," the first industrial research laboratory, with the hope of producing a new invention every ten days. In one four-year period he obtained 300 patents, or one every five days. In all, he patented nearly 1300 inventions. (His favorite accomplishment: the phonograph.)

Ernest Rutherford (1871–1937), a New Zealand scientist working at the Cavendish Laboratory at Cambridge, England, in the 1890s, became the first man to split the atom, thus establishing the new science of nuclear physics. He gathered around him a group of brilliant nuclear physicists. Their work led to release of nuclear energy and eventually to the atomic bomb. Among his pupils were fourteen future Nobel Prize winners.

More than once, the English physicist William Crookes (1832–1919) fogged photographic plates during the running of his Crookes tube, even though those plates were enclosed in their containers. He missed the connection, however. A decade later, Wilhelm Roentgen (1845–1923) used a Crookes tube and discovered X-rays that had the ability to pass through solid material. This initiated the Second Scientific Revolution and won Roentgen a Nobel Prize.

The French mathematician Pierre Bouguer (1698–1758), who was among the first to measure the intensity of light, became a professor of the Hydrographic School in Paris at the age of fifteen. He is said to have taught mathematics to his instructors when he was ten.

Alexander Graham Bell was working to improve the telegraph when he invented the telephone.

One of the most famous experiments in the history of physics was a failure. Albert Abraham Michelson and Edward Williams Morley tried to measure the change in the speed of light when it traveled with and when it traveled against the motion of the Earth. All their efforts failed; they could find no change. Attempts to explain the failure ended with Einstein's theory of relativity, which showed that the speed of light in a vacuum never varied. (Every scientist wishes he could have such a failure.)

On the eve of World War I, the chemist Chaim Weizmann—a fiery Zionist working in England—discovered a way to put a particular strain of bacterium to work synthesizing the compound acetone in the course of its fermentation of grain. Acetone supplied the essentials for the manufacture of cordite, and thus guaranteed Britain a war-long supply of explosives. It was partly in response to Weizmann's achievement that the British government was induced, in 1917, to put forth the Balfour Declaration agreeing to the reestablishment of a Jewish national state in Palestine. (Weizmann's process also had peacetime application. It was the forerunner of the deliberate use of microorganisms for a wide variety of syntheses. Such compounds as penicillin and vitamin B_{12} were produced by microorganisms cultivated for the purpose.)

Television is the indirect offspring of a ray of sunlight. Noticing that his instruments malfunctioned in sunbeams, Joseph May, working in a cable station off the coast of Ireland in 1861, finally traced the disturbance to selenium resistors whose current varied with the amount of light they received. A mosaic of such cells was soon fashioned into an image collector for transmission.

One man—Isaac Newton—presented the world in 1665 with three fundamental discoveries: the method of calculus, which is the basis for much of modern mathematics; the spectral composition of light along with the fundamentals of optics; and the law of universal gravitation and the basic laws of mechanics. Newton was then twenty-three years old.

The roots of Einstein's intellectual development of relativity grew, he said, from his wonder at what light waves would look like to him if he moved as fast as they did.

In 1813, an almost uneducated boy of sixteen named Joseph Henry (1797–1878) was vacationing near Albany. He chased a rabbit under a church building, found some of the floorboards missing, and decided to explore the church. On a bookshelf, he found a volume called *Lectures on Experimental Philosophy*, leafed through it, and grew fascinated. The owner of the book let young Joseph keep it, and the boy went back to school to learn more. He became the greatest scientist in nineteenth-century America, heading the nation's scientific mobilization during the Civil War. Henry invented the first electromagnetic telegraph, the basis of the commercial telegraph system. He instituted the weather-report system and was the first secretary and director of the newly founded Smithsonian Institution. When Henry died, President Rutherford B. Hayes attended the funeral.

Thomas Alva Edison made only one purely scientific discovery: the "Edison effect." It involves the flow of electricity across a vacuum. He patented the effect, but could think of no use for it, and went on to other things. The Edison effect, however, turned out to be the basis of the whole electronics industry—radio, television, and all.

Newton, when asked how he managed to make all those important discoveries, replied, *"Nocte dieque incubando"* ("By thinking about it night and day").

One of the fundamental laws of physics, the law of conservation of parity, said that if you perform an experiment and then perform exactly the same experiment but reverse left and right, the same result should be obtained. Chien-Shiung Wu, an experimental physicist with a laboratory at Columbia University, was able to announce in 1957 the overthrow of parity. For the first time in the history of physics, an experiment had been conceived and carried out to upset a basic law.

The first person to work out the manner in which a telescope handled light according to strict scientific principles was the German astronomer Johann Kepler. His eyesight was so bad, however, that it was useless for him to try to use a telescope himself.

———

The one relationship involving the electric current that almost every high-school student learns is Ohm's Law—the flow of current is equal to the voltage divided by the resistance. The man who worked this out, in 1827, was a German high-school teacher, Georg Simon Ohm. He hoped to get a university professorship as a result of discovering the relationship. Not only did he not get the university appointment, but the finding produced such opposition from some other scientists that Ohm was forced to resign his high-school position. In the then class-conscious Germany it was unthinkable for a high-school teacher to seek a university position.

———

Thomas Young, who worked out the wave theory of light in 1803, was an infant prodigy. He could read at two and had worked his way twice through the Bible at four. During his youth, he studied a dozen languages, and could play a variety of musical instruments. At Cambridge, he was called Phenomenon Young. In addition to his theory of light, he was the first to make progress in deciphering the Egyptian hieroglyphics.

———

Asaph Hall, the discoverer of the satellites of Mars, had an unusual career. He had been a carpenter without formal education and was mostly self-taught, picking up bits as he went along. He became interested in astronomy in 1857 and took a job as an assistant at Harvard College Observatory at a salary of $3 a week. Only six years later, he became a professor—fourteen years before his discovery in 1877.

———

Thomas Edison, who bordered on the totally deaf, did not think of the phonograph in terms of music and entertainment. He was interested in the business and educational potential of his invention—dictation, recordings for the blind, oral histories, the preservation of languages, the teaching of elocution, and clocks that could tell time aloud. He envisioned other uses, too, for another of his epochal inventions, the motion picture. "Americans require a restful quiet in the moving-picture theater," he was quoted in 1926 in *The New York Times*, "and for them talking . . . on the screen destroys the illusion. Devices for projecting the film actor's speech can be prefaced, but the idea is not practical."

On every October 19 for the rest of his life, Robert Goddard (1882–1945) recollected the October 19 in 1899 when he, then a seventeen-year-old high-school sophomore, climbed a cherry tree and experienced a kind of epiphanal vision that launched his interest in rocket technology and space exploration. His vision was of a vehicle that would transport human beings to the planet Mars. Twenty-seven years later, Goddard launched a rocket from his Aunt Effie's farm in Massachusetts.

"The cow must go"—a Henry Ford dictum in 1921. Always the iconoclast, the industrialist proposed that milk be made synthetically. His regard of dairy cows as inefficient and unsanitary animals may have stemmed from unpleasant experiences on his father's farm, where milking had been an exasperating and disagreeable labor.

Charles Dickens believed that a good night's sleep was possible only if the bed was aligned from north to south. In this manner, he thought, the magnetic currents would flow straight through the recumbent body.

We all learned that Thomas Alva Edison invented the electric light, in 1879, by using a carbon filament in an evacuated bulb (one from which the air had been pumped). Actually, the English inventor Joseph Wilson Swan produced such an electric light at about the same time. In fact, Swan was using a carbon filament two decades before Edison, but couldn't get light bulbs in which the vacuum was good enough. Eventually, in 1883, Edison and Swan formed a joint company in Great Britain.

It could have been the Gray System, rather than the Bell System—but Elisha Gray's description of his invention arrived in the U.S. Patent Office *a few hours* after Alexander Graham Bell's. Bell noted that "it is a strange fact that important inventions are often made almost simultaneously by different persons in different parts of the world." (There were about 600 lawsuits over the Bell telephone patents.)

The newly unified Kingdom of Italy apparently expelled all but one Jesuit in 1870—Pietro Angelo Secchi, whose importance as an astronomer outweighed the fact of his membership in the order. Secchi employed photography, and was the first to make color drawings of Mars and to show the yellow desert areas and the darker areas.

The German mathematician Johann Karl Friedrich Gauss (1777–1855) proposed that long, ten-mile-wide strips of trees delineating the Pythagorean theorem be planted in the Siberian steppes so that watchers from other worlds might see that people on Earth were bright enough to know geometry, and, who knows, they might even respond with cyclic quadrilaterals. For the same purpose, the Austrian Joseph Johann von Littrow suggested, in 1840, that immense fires set in geometrical patterns in the Sahara could be seen from other planets.

Albert Einstein published a triple thunderbolt of three historic papers in 1905, but it took him four more years to land a professorship (and a poorly paying one at that), at the University of Zurich. He was a clerk in a Swiss patent office while revolutionizing physics.

There was some intention in 1912 of giving a Nobel Prize jointly to Thomas Alva Edison and the electrical engineer Nikola Tesla. Both were well deserving of the honor. Tesla, who was eccentric, loathed Edison because he believed he had been cheated by Edison in a financial transaction. Tesla refused to be associated with Edison in the honor, and the physics prize instead was awarded to a Swedish inventor of lesser merit.

The German mathematician Gottlob Frege prepared a colossal two-volume book systematizing the entire structure of mathematics. The first volume appeared in 1893. The second was about to appear in 1903, when the young Bertrand Russell, the English mathematician, asked Frege how his mathematical system would solve a particular conundrum. It couldn't, and Frege was forced to publish a final note to the second volume admitting that the very foundation of his reasoning was shattered and his two volumes were useless as a total synthesis.

Thomas Alva Edison was one of a fair number of geniuses who did poorly in school. (Einstein, Newton, and Pasteur were three others.) In fact, Edison's mother, a schoolteacher, was so offended with the bad reports young Tom was getting at school that she took him out of school altogether and taught him herself.

During World War I, Albert Schweitzer, famous later as a theologian, musician, and medical missionary, made a living by giving organ recitals and lectures in Europe after being deported from Africa. As an enemy alien of German nationality living at his own hospital in French Gabon, Dr. Schweitzer was then imprisoned in France. He was freed in an exchange of prisoners and earned money to pay his hospital's debts by his concerts and theological lectures. (He had been a church organist as a youth and had earned a degree in theology in addition to his Ph.D. and M.D.) He returned to Africa in 1924. In 1952, he was awarded the Nobel Peace Prize.

———

Thomas Edison, though still in possession of his sight, found Braille preferable to visual reading.

———

The American physicist Henry Augustus Rowland (1848–1901) was well known for his modesty. Once, when he testified at a trial as an expert witness, a lawyer asked him who the greatest living American physicist was. Rowland answered, "I myself am." Afterward, when a friend asked him in amazement how he could give such an uncharacteristically conceited answer, Rowland replied, "I couldn't help myself. I was under oath."

———

Some historians of science claim that the handsomest of the great scientists was the English chemist Humphry Davy. His lectures on science during the years of the Napoleonic wars were extremely successful, society women flocking to them as much to see him as to hear his excellent talks. He discovered seven new elements and nitrous oxide (a gas), and he invented the miner's lamp. He seems also to have been a talented poet, according to the estimate of such established poets as Wordsworth and Coleridge.

———

Charles Darwin's theory of evolution owes much to his grandfather, Dr. Erasmus Darwin, who was one of England's outstanding physicians and the author of a poem called *Zoonomia*, which was written both as a medical textbook on the subject of disease and an explanation of life. Erasmus Darwin's theories on the subject of man's origin were widely translated in the early nineteenth century.

———

Robert Hooke (1635–1703) was considered the greatest mechanic of his age, and one of the most eminent microscopists. He was a most ingenious and capable experimenter in almost every field of science. It was Hooke's discovery of what is now called the hairspring that made small and accurate timepieces possible and, by eliminating the bulky pendulum, led ultimately to wristwatches and ship's chronometers. He coined the word "cells" in discovering the porous structure of cork, and made some of the most beautiful drawings of microscopic observations ever made, particularly of insects, feathers, and fish scales. When London was destroyed by the Great Fire of 1666, Hooke found himself busily engaged in rebuilding projects and never returned to his microscopy.

Christian Heinrich Heinecken, who lived only four years, from February 6, 1721, to June 22, 1725, became famous as "the Child of Lübeck" (Germany). When he was about 2½ years old, he was versed in the history of the Old and the New Testament. He had learned French and Latin by the time he was three. The only person on record who comes close to this precocity is Kim Ung-Yong of Seoul, born on March 7, 1963, who at the age of four composed (and published) poetry and spoke Korean, English, German, and Japanese. When he was four years and eight months old, he performed integral calculus on a live television program in Tokyo, *The World Surprise Show.* IQs in this range are not measurable, but his is estimated to be around 210. Among known personalities with an estimated IQ of about 200—usually early achievers—were Emanuel Swedenborg (1688–1772), Johann Wolfgang von Goethe (1749–1832), and John Stuart Mill (1806–73).

The longest delay on record in awarding a Nobel Prize was in the case of the American physician Francis Peyton Rous. In 1911, he discovered a virus that caused a particular variety of cancer. It was not until 1966, fifty-five years later, that the work was finally judged important enough for a Nobel Prize. Rous was still alive—eighty-seven years old—and still working. He died at the age of ninety-one, working nearly to the end.

One of the premier scientific theorists of the century, perhaps an equal of Einstein, is a man who cannot raise his head without great efforts and whose slurred monotone is comprehensible to just a few intimates. Stephen Hawking, of Cambridge University, is a victim of a rare, wasting disease of the nervous system and muscles. Because he cannot write his intricate equations, Hawking must remember them as they flash into his mind. This is comparable to Mozart's having composed an entire symphony in his head. Hawking's special province is the physics of black holes.

Alexander Graham Bell was also interested in eugenics, and deve oped a more prolific breed of sheep.

Scientists require powers of concentration, but even that can be carried too far. In 1807, the mathematician Johann Karl Friedrich Gauss was caught up in a problem while his wife lay sick upstairs. When the doctor told him his wife was dying, Gauss waved him away and, never looking up from his problem, muttered, "Tell her to wait a moment till I'm through."

The botanist George Washington Carver, who is best known for his pioneer work with peanuts, developed 536 dyes when experimenting with plant leaves, fruits, stems, and roots. Forty-nine separate dyes were derived from the scuppernong grape alone.

The youngest Nobel Prize winner was twenty-five-year old William Lawrence Bragg who, with his father, shared the award for physics in 1915 for work they had done on the determination of crystal structure by X-ray diffraction.

It was said in 1928, when Congress awarded Thomas Alva Edison a gold medal, that the inventions of "the wizard of Menlo Park" were worth $25 billion to humanity.

The physiologist Otto Loewi was working on the mechanism of nerve action, in particular on the chemicals produced by nerve endings. One night in 1921 he woke at three o'clock with the perfect experiment in mind, but in the morning couldn't read what he had jotted down in the dark. The next night he again woke at three with the clear thought once more in mind. But this time, he went straight to the laboratory and began work. Within two hours, he had proved his theory. The consequences of his findings became important enough so that in 1936 Loewi shared in the Nobel Prize for physiology or medicine.

Among the designs left by Leonardo da Vinci almost 500 years ago—with notes written backward to be read with a mirror—were the parachute, life jacket, water pump, swim fins, well digger, paddle-wheel boat, horseless carriage, sprocket chain, steam gun, water turbine, lens-grinding machine, shrapnel, machine gun, airplane, helicopter, submarine, and mass production.

Benjamin Franklin developed the first pair of bifocal spectacles. He had owned two pairs of spectacles, one for reading and the other for "greater distances." He had the lenses of both pairs cut horizontally in half. He assembled the near and far lenses so the top halves of the spectacles contained the distance (least convex) lenses and the bottom halves contained the reading (most convex) lenses. Franklin noted that "by this means, as I wear my spectacles constantly, I have only to move my eyes up or down, as I want to see distinctly far or near, the proper glasses being always ready."

A long career of being always right made it impossible for Thomas Edison to endure being wrong. Committed thoroughly to the use of direct electrical current, Edison unscrupulously fought the use of alternating current. He lobbied New York State into adopting a.c. for its newly devised electric chair (and a.c. is indeed more efficient in electrocution than direct current), and then he pointed with great horror to the electric chair as an example of the deadly nature of a.c.

Joseph Priestley is immortal in the history of chemistry as the discoverer of oxygen, in 1774. Lost in that glory is the fact that he also discovered soda water and that he gave the name "rubber" to that soft, bouncy stuff because it could be used to rub out pencil marks.

Nearly five centuries ago, Leonardo da Vinci had notions, later proved correct, about fossils, about the circulation of the blood, about the Earth *not* being the center of the universe, about falling bodies, and about anatomy. His close observation and his amazing skill at drawing were such that his pictures of waves and bubbles in water could be improved on only by the slow-motion camera. But his genius went for naught. He kept these ideas to himself, writing them in code in voluminous notebooks, so that his contemporaries knew little of his ideas and remained uninfluenced by them. Most of these writings remained unpublished until the nineteenth century. Two lost works were found in 1965 in the National Library of Spain in Madrid.

The cars on the freeways today would be electrics if Thomas Alva Edison had had his way. At the turn of the century, he worked on an improved battery to power an electric car that would be quiet, light, clean, and odorless. By 1909, his new battery was on the market, but it was too late. Ford's internal-combustion engine had become king of the road.

———

William Thomson (who became Baron Kelvin) entered the University of Glasgow at the age of eleven, and finished second in his class in mathematics. His first paper on mathematics was written while he was still in his teens but was read to the Royal Society of Edinburgh by an elderly professor. It didn't seem proper to have it read by a schoolboy just because the schoolboy wrote it.

———

Dr. Alexis Carrel immigrated to Canada from France in 1904, with the intention of becoming a cattle rancher. Eight years later he was awarded the Nobel Prize in medicine and physiology for his work on blood-vessel suturing. Carrel, who had received a medical degree at the University of Lyon, decided shortly after reaching Canada that the call of science was not to be ignored, and he joined the Rockefeller Institute for Medical Research in New York.

———

Nicholas Copernicus, the Polish astronomer (1473–1543), had his hand in many pies. He founded the system on which modern astronomy is based, holding that "the sun is the center of our universe." He worked on currency reform, coining the notion that the appearance of debased currency drives good money into hiding. (It's today called "Gresham's law," for an English economist who was incorrectly thought to have originated the idea.) He was a canon at Frombork and was involved in diplomatic negotiations between the Poles and the Teutonic Knights of Prussia.

———

Jean-François Champollion, the French linguist who decoded the hieroglyphics of the Rosetta Stone, had, in 1801, at the age of eleven mastered Latin, Greek, and Hebrew. Two years later, he had also learned Arabic, Syrian, Chaldean, and Coptic, the Greek-based language of the early Egyptian Christians. In 1822, Champollion published the paper that made him famous, "In Regard to the Alphabet of Phonetic Hieroglyphics"—the basis of decoding the story of the ancient Egyptians.

———

Margaret Mead's first foray into observation of human behavior occurred before she was a teenager. As a young person of eight or nine years, she recorded the patterns of speech of her younger sisters.

———

When Darwin visited Madagascar during his voyage on the *Beagle*, he was intrigued by a large waxy white orchid with a nectar spur almost a foot long. How could such a flower be pollinated? He did not have the opportunity to find out by observation, but he guessed—correctly—by an insect with a foot-long proboscis. His theory was ridiculed. Twenty years later, a nocturnal moth was collected that had a wingspread of only 5½ inches but a proboscis a foot long. In honor of the fact that its existence had been predicted, it was named *Xanthopan morganii praedicta.*

The 19th-century mathematician Janos Bolyai, who generally shares the credit for having discovered non-Euclidean geometry, specialized in the violin and the dueling sword, in the true tradition of the Hungarian aristocrat. He once fenced with 13 swordsmen, one after the other, vanquishing them all and playing the violin between bouts. Bolyai gave up work in mathematics when he felt embarrassment and humiliation at the disclosure that a little earlier Karl Friedrich Gauss (1777–1835), the famous German mathematician and astronomer, had had the same ideas about non-Euclidean geometry but hadn't published.

Benjamin Franklin was cautious in performing his famous kite experiment in which he charged a Leyden jar with electricity drawn from the clouds. The first two men who tried to repeat the experiment were electrocuted.

Alexander Graham Bell, inventor of the telephone and teacher of the deaf, was a speed demon. His hydrofoil boat set a world water speed record in 1919, when Bell was seventy-two, by topping seventy miles per hour.

George Washington Carver, whose research on such common crops as the peanut led the South away from its perilous one-crop economy (cotton), was illiterate until the age of twenty.

Michael Faraday, the self-educated son of a blacksmith, was hired by the great chemist Humphry Davy as a bottle washer. With time, Faraday became a still greater scientist than Davy, and the last years of Davy's life were embittered by jealousy.

In preparing his "periodic table," the Russian chemist Dmitri Ivanovich Mendeleev lined up the chemical elements in rows and columns so that such properties as atomic weights, melting points, and so on showed regular increases or decreases. To maintain that regularity, he had to leave gaps, and, in 1869 he asserted that the gaps contained elements that were yet to be discovered. He predicted the properties of three of those undiscovered elements, using the periodic table as his guide. Within a dozen years, these three elements (which were eventually named scandium, gallium, and germanium) were discovered, and their properties jibed in every particular with those predicted by Mendeleev.

————

Paper was invented in China about 105 A.D., by Ts'ai Lun, a eunuch—the only eunuch of importance in the history of technology. According to the official history of the Han dynasty (third century A.D.), Ts'ai Lun was given an aristocratic title after he presented Emperor Ho Ti with samples of paper. In 751 A.D., Chinese papermakers were captured by the Arabs at Samarkand, and by 794 A.D. several state-owned paper mills operated in Baghdad. The Arabs were manufacturing paper in Spain around 1150. It was not until 1590 that the first English paper mill was founded, at Dartford.

————

Charles Darwin spent fourteen years working on his theory of evolution, refusing to publish because he kept trying to incorporate more and more evidence (knowing that his conclusions would be very controversial). Another naturalist, Alfred Russel Wallace, sick in Borneo, passed the time by working up a theory of evolution (in three days) that, without his knowing it, was identical with Darwin's—and sent it to Darwin for a critique. Darwin was thunderstruck, and agreed to publish a paper on the subject, jointly with Wallace, in 1858. The next year, Darwin published his famous *The Origin of Species,* which revolutionized biology. It was only one-fifth as long as he was planning, and for the rest of his life Darwin referred to it, disparagingly, as an "abstract".

————

One of the early proponents of the theory of conservation of energy was James Prescott Joule, an English brewer. Because he was not a professional scientist, he couldn't get his paper on the subject published in a learned journal. He therefore presented his paper in the form of a public lecture in Manchester and arranged to have it printed in full in a Manchester newspaper on which his brother was music critic. Before long, scientists were forced to recognize, reluctantly, that Joule had made a great discovery.

————

Jean Bernard Léon Foucault (1819–68) was an utter failure as a physician. He couldn't stand the sight of blood. So he took up physics as his lifework. He invented the gyroscope.

———

Charles Darwin was introduced to Charles Lyell's theory of uniformitarianism by someone who felt Lyell was ridiculous and thought Darwin would get a good laugh. Darwin didn't laugh; he was converted to uniformitarianism in geology and to a clear realization of the antiquity of the Earth and of the long ages through which life had had time to develop. Uniformitarianism in geology is a doctrine that says changes in the Earth's surface that occurred in past geologic time are referrable to the same causes as changes now being produced on the Earth's surface.

———

Though England was at war with France at the time, 1806, Napoleon awarded to the English chemist Humphry Davy a prize established for the best work of the year in electricity. Davy accepted it, declaring that the governments might be at war but the scientists were not.

———

DeWitt Clinton (1769–1828), who sponsored the Erie Canal as canal commissioner, served as a New York state senator, lieutenant governor of New York State, and mayor of New York City *simultaneously*, in 1811.

———

Though Nathaniel Bowditch left school at the age of ten, his quick, retentive mind, unquenchable thirst for knowledge, and disciplined study habits enabled him to teach himself algebra, Latin, French, German, Spanish, and Italian. Choosing a life on the sea, he worked up to captain and applied his formidable knowledge of mathematics to navigation. Finding thousands of errors in the best available book on the subject, J. H. Moore's *Practical Navigator*, Bowditch brought out a corrected version in 1799, and his own book, *The New American Practical Navigator,* in 1802. When he died in 1838, ships of all countries flew their flags at half-mast in appreciation of his contributions to their safety on the high seas.

———

Frederic Tudor (1783–1864), who did more than anyone to make ice an American institution (he became known as "the ice king"), was a man of many talents. He tried raising saltwater fish in a pond in

Massachusetts. He built what is thought to be the first amusement park in North America. He brought the first steam locomotive to New England. He experimented with raising cotton and tobacco at Nahant. He made paper from white pine. He operated a graphite mine. He designed a hull of a ship. He made a siphon for pumping water from the holds of vessels. He dug for coal at Martha's Vineyard. In 1833, he sent a cargo of ice to Calcutta.

As a boy in Scotland, Alexander Graham Bell made a talking doll that said "Mama."

Charles Babbage (1792–1871), who thought out the basic principles that guide modern computers, invented the skeleton key and the locomotive "cow-catcher."

John Dalton (1766–1844), the English scientist, was the first to advance a quantitative atomic theory and the first to prepare a table of atomic weights, but he was a rather clumsy and slipshod experimenter because—of all things! for a chemist!—he was colorblind. Colorblindness, specifically the inability to distinguish between red and green, is now called daltonism.

Paul Charles Morphy (1837–84), an American chess master, was acknowledged at age twenty-one to be the greatest chess player in the world. His astounding memory allowed him to achieve amazing successes while blindfolded. For example, in a set of eight games of chess played simultaneously against eight opponents, Morphy not only had to memorize the positions of 256 chessmen but also had to revise his mental images of them after every move. At the same time, he had to plan eight separate attack and defense postures. The result: He won six games, tied one, and lost one.

A year before he earned his degree in electrical engineering from Columbia University, Edwin Howard Armstrong (1890–1954) made the first of his seminal inventions—the feedback circuit that raised the sensitivity of radio receivers and opened the way to practical long-distance reception. He went on to devise, during World War I, the superheterodyne circuit, which remains the basis of nearly all radio receivers to this day. And from 1925 to 1933, he developed workable frequency modulation (FM) radio. Armstrong became a millionaire, but he ruined his health and squandered his fortune through a series of legal battles concerning patent infringements. Embittered, he committed suicide in 1954. His widow continued the suits, and the majority were either won or settled in his favor.

Lewis Carroll, by his own account, wrote 98,721 letters in the last thirty-seven years of his life.

Freud cast aside his most promising protégé, Victor Tausk, out of jealousy over both Tausk's original insights and his paramour. Tausk committed suicide. When he learned of Tausk's death, Freud said, "I do not really miss him; I had long taken him to be useless, indeed a threat to the future."

When Einstein published his equations of general relativity, he failed to notice that his theory predicted an expanding universe. A Russian mathematician, Alexander Friedmann, found that Einstein had made a schoolboy error in algebra that caused him to overlook a solution to his own equations. In effect, Einstein had divided by zero at one point in his calculations—a no-no in mathematics.

GLORY
THAT WAS ROME

At its zenith, about 200–250 A.D., the land area of the Roman Empire was roughly the size of the U.S. today. The population was in excess of 100 million, with the city of Rome itself having a population of about 1 million. The empire was knit together by 180,000 miles of roads.

The Circus Maximus in Rome, after its rebuilding by Julius Caesar, could hold 150,000 persons. It was enlarged again in the early empire to admit an additional 100,000.

Veteran Roman soldiers, called *triarii*, carried a normal marching load weighing eighty-eight pounds. It included a bronze helmet and breastplate, a deep rectangular shield made from leather-coated wood trimmed with iron, a long thrusting spear, and a two-foot stabbing sword. The *triarii* were spared the first onslaught of battle. They were held in reserve to strike the decisive blow.

Because of a rapidly increasing population, the ancient Romans built tenement houses. They were made cheaply, of a kind of concrete, and usually had three stories.

To provide for quick action in times of emergency, the Roman republic 500 years before Christ provided for a temporary king, so to speak. The senate could appoint someone to supreme control over Rome for a specified period of time, someone whose word, while he was in office, was law. For that reason, he was called a dictator, from a Latin word meaning "I have spoken." Usually, he was to hold office for six months. In 458 B.C. (according to legend), the Roman general Cincinnatus was appointed "dictator" to meet the threat of an advancing army. He marched off to war, defeated the army, returned, and resigned instantly. Cincinnatus had been dictator for sixteen days.

The Romans were the supreme heating engineers of the ancient world, and their heating system was employed everywhere that Roman culture flourished. Hot gases from furnaces were piped under floors (raised on pedestals for that purpose) and guided through tubes in the walls. Modern civilization has rediscovered this method.

Trying to beef up the population of Rome, Julius Caesar offered rewards to Romans who had many children. Childless women were forbidden to ride in litters or to wear jewelry.

At the height of his power, the Roman gladiator Spartacus, who led a slave revolt in 73 B.C., had 90,000 men under his command and controlled almost all of southern Italy.

Some nineteen centuries ago, the Roman naturalist Pliny the Elder (Caius Plinius Secundus) recognized earthquake warnings that today's geophysicists also keep an eye out for: foreshock, turbidity in wells, and frightened birds. Pliny also listed an anomalous "fog" in an otherwise clear sky, an idea that only now is catching on as a valid signal.

A freak birth was considered an ominous warning by the diviners of ancient Rome. From the Latin *monere* ("to warn"), they got *monstrum* ("divine warning of ill omen"), from which our word "monster" is derived.

Julius Caesar was compelled by increasing traffic congestion to ban all wheeled vehicles in Rome during the hours of daylight.

The Romans' *milia* ("thousands") has come down to us as "mile." A *milia* was the distance covered by 1,000 paces of a marching legionnaire.

The Italian city of Ravenna was once an important port on the coast of the Adriatic Sea. In 402 A.D., Honorius made it the capital of the west Roman Empire. (Earlier, Augustus had made its port, Classis, a major Roman naval station.) Today, Ravenna is some five miles from the sea, and no longer a port. Sand and silt brought down from the plains of Lombardy by the great River Po and washed up by sea currents slowly formed a huge sand bar, burying the harbor and forming new land well beyond it.

AND GREECE TOO

Aristotle, the pupil of Plato and one of Greece's greatest philosophers, was primarily a biologist. However, the biological portion of his work was largely ignored, and his successors were mainly influenced by his theories in physics and astronomy. Centuries later, Aristotle was praised by Darwin as the wellspring from which the modern biologists Linnaeus of Sweden and Cuvier of France took their inspiration. Linnaeus (1707–78) was the originator of modern scientific classification of plants and animals. Cuvier (1769–1832) was a pioneer in the science of comparative anatomy.

If he had not married by the age of thirty, a Spartan of ancient Greece lost his right to vote and was forbidden to attend events in which nude young men and women made merry.

The Greek philosopher Democritus is known today almost entirely as a result of references, often unfriendly, in the works of others. Only fragments of Democritus' seventy-two books have survived the ages. Like all the early rationalists, "the laughing philosopher" had startlingly modern-sounding notions. One: The Milky Way is a vast conglomeration of tiny stars.

A temple of Aphrodite, the Greek goddess of love, was discovered—appropriately—by the American archaeologist Iris C. Love.

Socrates left no writings of his own. All that is known of the Greek philosopher and gadfly of Athens is through the words of others, principally Plato's. (When the oracle at Delphi proclaimed him the wisest of the Greeks, Socrates replied that if he was the wisest, it was only because he alone knew that he knew nothing—Socratic irony at play.)

Concerning oneself with public business was the hobby of every ancient Greek, the most political of people. A Greek who was odd enough to concern himself only with his private business rather than with public business was an *idiotes,* from the Greek word *idios,* meaning "private." The Greek view concerning such a person is obvious—*idiotes* and "idiot" are the same word. (The most seriously retarded person is now called an idiot. He is not capable of connected speech or of guarding himself against the ordinary dangers of life.)

———

The cult of Pythagoreanism, named for and led by the Greek philosopher, forbade the eating of beans and the poking of fire with an iron poker. Pythagoras is the first person known to have called himself a "philosopher" ("lover of wisdom"). He felt that the then customary *sophis* ("wise man") was immodest.

———

Sparta's prestige suffered when it took five years to subdue an insurrection of the city's helots, or slaves. The helots struck after an earthquake shook Sparta to pieces. They fortified themselves in Mount Ithome, beginning in 464 B.C., and surrendered only when they were promised they would not be killed or forced to return to slavery. Sparta kept its promise, allowing the helots to sail to the naval station of Naupactus, founded by Athens on the northern shore of the Gulf of Corinth.

———

Though he is usually considered the founder of botany, Theophrastus, a student of Aristotle, is best known today for a series of satiric character portraits that bear the mark of universality—such as the Boastful Man, the Flatterer, the Grumbler.

———

Though it was only the fifth century B.C., the Greek philosopher Empedocles expressed a dim notion of an evolutionary process. He felt that some creatures, ill-adapted to life, had perished in the past. He also believed the heart was the center of the blood-vessel system.

———

In the second half of the third century B.C., the Greek geographer and explorer Pytheas—he became a geographer and explorer as a result of his enterprise—probably sailed up the northwest coast of Europe, explored the island of Great Britain, sailed northward to "Thule," which was possibly Norway, and penetrated the Baltic Sea as far as the Vistula. His works are the earliest first-hand information we have on northwestern Europe.

———

The early Greeks were not always sure about the direction in which lines should be written. At first, they used lines reading alternately from right to left, then left to right. From about 500 B.C. they adopted what has become the modern Western practice of reading and writing from left to right.

———

Zeno's logical paradox of Achilles and the tortoise, articulated about 425 B.C., could not be expressed in a mathematical formula for twenty-one centuries. Suppose, Zeno had said, that Achilles can run ten times as fast as a tortoise and that the tortoise has a ten-yard head start. It follows, then, he said, that Achilles can never overtake the tortoise; while Achilles covers the ten-yard difference, the tortoise will have moved ahead one yard. When Achilles covers that one yard, the tortoise will have moved on a tenth of a yard. And so on. Our senses, however, clearly show us a fast runner overtaking and passing a slow runner. The Scottish mathematician James Gregory, in the mid-1600s, was to demonstrate the existence of "converging series" in which an infinite number of terms added up to a finite sum. The Achilles and the tortoise paradox involved, without Zeno's knowledge, such a converging series.

———

Because Aristotle rejected Democritus' belief that all matter consisted of tiny particles—they are so small that nothing smaller was conceivable, hence they were indivisible and eternal and unchangeable and indestructible—the atomic theory was doomed through ancient and medieval times.

———

Heraclitus (ca. 535–ca. 475 B.C.) was called "the weeping philosopher" because of his pessimism. He thought so little of the unchangeability of even so glorious an object as the sun that he suggested it was made fresh each morning—every day, there was a different sun. In contrast, Democritus (ca. 460–ca. 357 B.C.) was called "the laughing philosopher," partly for his teachings, but mainly for his cheerful disposition. (He had reason to laugh: most philosophers were poor; Democritus had inherited a vast fortune.)

———

The city of Corinth, in ancient Greece, made prostitution a major industry. Over a thousand women worked as prostitutes at the temple of Aphrodite Porne, and the city became a notorious port of call for sailors.

———

Alcmaeon and Democritus and Hippocrates felt that the brain was the center of intellectual activity. The view was not accepted by Aristotle, however, and thus did not come into its own until modern times. Aristotle considered the brain merely a cooling organ for the blood.

––––––––

In the sixth century B.C., a half-mile tunnel was dug on the Aegean island of Samos under the supervision of the Greek architect Eupalinus. Though the tunnel was started at both ends and worked toward the middle, the two halves met only a couple of feet off center; it was a stunning achievement in those days.

––––––––

Plato had a chance to put his idea of a philosopher king into practice in 367 B.C. when Dionysius II ruled Syracuse. Summoned to be royal adviser, Plato tried to make Dionysius govern according to constitutional principles. But the monarch got tired of philosophy and restraints and dispatched the resident philosopher back to Athens.

––––––––

After the Athenians had driven out the tyrant Hippias in 510 B.C., they tried to work out methods to prevent the establishment of another tyranny. Once a year they set up an opportunity for a vote that was aimed not at electing someone but at exiling someone. Each Athenian could write down the name of a politician he felt was growing too dangerously powerful for the good of the state. If any one man got a vote of more than 6,000, he was forced to remain away from Athens for ten years. It was not a disgraceful exile; his property was not confiscated, his family was not mistreated; when the decade was up, he was welcomed back heartily. He understood he had been sent away to be kept from the temptation of trying to upset the democracy.

––––––––

No matter who disagreed with them, even other philosophers, Aristotle's ideas—whether right or wrong—usually won out. He thought the heavens were perfect and could not change. He thought only the Earth and the regions below the moon could show change and corruption. To Aristotle, comets were part of the Earth's atmosphere and not really heavenly objects.

––––––––

When Eratosthenes, a Greek scholar and astronomer credited with measuring the circumference and the tilt of the Earth and the size and distance away of the sun and moon, needed to know merely the distance from Alexandria to Syene, men were engaged who were trained to walk in uniform steps and count them. (The distance was about 500 miles.)

———

Solon's first step as Athenian archon, or lawgiver, around 600 B.C., was to cancel all debts, to forbid the enslavement of debtors, to set free those who had been enslaved, and to buy back at public expense those who had been sold outside Athenian territory.

———

GOOD OLD DAYS

There was no soap in the ancient Mediterranean world. Olive oil was used not only for cooking but for washing the body.

Slavery was a universal institution throughout ancient times. It was not even questioned in the Old Testament or in the New Testament.

The umbrella, that pedestrian implement, originated in ancient Egypt, where it was used by the royal family and nobles as a symbol of rank in a theocratic hierarchy. Practical use came later.

Two hundred years ago: For kissing his wife in public on a Sunday after just returning from a three-year voyage, a Boston ship captain was made to sit two hours in stocks for "lewd and unseemly behavior."

In photography's pioneer days, sitting for a portrait called for extreme patience. Making a daguerreotype in 1837 required a fifteen-minute exposure. The subject's head was put in a clamp to hold it still.

Venice in the eighteenth century was a society gone mad. Gambling went on day and night; on one evening in 1762, the Abbé Grioni bet all his clothes on the turn of the wheel, lost, and returned naked to his monastery. Nuns wearing pearls and low-cut gowns fought among themselves for the honor of serving as mistress to a visiting papal nuncio. It was considered a disgrace for a married patrician woman not to have a *cicisbèo,* a combination of lover and gentleman-in-waiting.

Many Americans in the eighteenth century could read but did not know how to write. While religious and political ideals dictated that all children should learn a smattering of history and to read the Bible (and many did), writing was not considered essential. In addition, writing was time-consuming and expensive to learn, given the high cost of paper and ink, and the difficulty of keeping a quill pen in repair.

The commonly held notion of colonial American family life—that many generations lived together and shared farm and household chores—is far from the truth. Few people lived long enough to see their children grown, let alone their grandchildren. Data compiled in 1790 by Dr. Benjamin Rush, the prominent physician, indicate that of a hundred people born in a given year in Philadelphia more than one-third died before the age of six and only one-quarter lived beyond the age of twenty-six.

The first Cadillac, which was produced in 1903, cost less than the original Model T Ford. Their prices, respectively, were $750 and $875.

As late as 1890, nearly 75 percent of Americans had to fetch their mail from a post office. A community had to have at least 10,000 people to be eligible for home delivery, and most people lived in towns or on farms.

The Puritans, considering buttons a vanity, used hooks and eyes.

The bathhouse in the late medieval town became the habitat for loose women and lecherous men as family life deteriorated. The medieval word for bathhouse, "stew," has come down in English as a synonym for brothel.

Dueling was so popular among wealthy gentlemen in Ireland during the eighteenth century that travelers could always find a special set of dueling pistols at an inn—in readiness for those who had forgotten their own.

In 1868, during the early days of the Kansas Pacific Railroad, Kansas Pacific engineers stopped trains so as to allow passengers the opportunity to leave the cars and shoot at passing buffalo.

If he left it alone for even a minute, some inquisitive person would try to run away with Henry Ford's early gasoline motorcar. Finally, Ford had to chain the vehicle to a lamp post whenever he left it anywhere.

———

In the Middle Ages, the brothels were under the protection of the community and the prostitutes formed guilds in German cities. In Hamburg today, a multi-story brothel exists with the approval of authorities.

———

One-third of all the automobiles in New York City, Boston, and Chicago in 1900 were electric cars, with batteries rather than gasoline engines.

———

In order to populate the frontier, the United States Congress in 1862 passed the Homestead Act. It offered free 160-acre farms to all homesteaders who would live on them and farm the wilderness. What is little known is that only the poorest-quality land was given away free. Good farms that size cost about $1,000 at that time.

———

Life expectancy at birth for Americans was 34.5 years for males and 36.5 years for females when George Washington became President in 1789.

———

The average married woman in seventeenth-century America gave birth to thirteen children.

———

The Abbaye of Toulouse, in medieval France, was a municipal brothel whose revenues supported the University of Toulouse. It bore a royal charter and flourished until a prostitutes' strike and attacks by angry mobs caused its decline.

———

Marco Polo reported a strict sense of justice in India. If a man would not pay his debt, the creditor would draw a circle around the debtor. If the debtor should try to step out of the circle, he would be liable to punishment by death.

———

In colonial America, the manufacture of clothing at home was a time-consuming, never-ending task. Because it took nearly a year and a half to create linen from flax, a man's shirt often wore out by the time a woman could complete a new one.

———

In 1853, the city council of Cincinnati, Ohio, ordered a steam-driven fire engine and hired men to run it. When the new engine answered its first alarm, 250 angry volunteers turned out to give the city firemen a beating. But the fire chief had known what to expect. He had a small army of strongmen with him, and they fought off the volunteers while the hired firemen did their job. The new engine was a big success in Cincinnati, and soon other cities were using a steam-driven engine.

———

In 1909, Annette Kellerman, the Australian swimming star, appeared on a Boston beach wearing a figure-fitting jersey bathing suit with sleeves shortened almost to her shoulders and trousers ending two inches above her knees. She was arrested for indecent exposure.

———

During most of the Middle Ages, few people, including kings and emperors, were able to read or write. The clergy were virtually the only ones who possessed these skills.

———

Around 1500, Nuremberg in Germany had fourteen public baths with low admission prices, special hours set aside for city employees, and free admission once a week for prostitutes and for children accompanied by their parents. The possibilities of infection—physical and moral—soon led to their closing.

———

In colonial days it was legal to smoke tobacco in Massachusetts only when the smoker was traveling and had reached a location that was five miles away from any town. Although earlier regulations of this nature were enacted on moral grounds, the 1646 law was based on the danger of fire. A year later, Connecticut passed a law forbidding social smoking and limiting the use of tobacco to once a day, and then only when the smoker was alone in his own house.

———

During Prohibition in the U.S., there were more than 200,000 illegal "speakeasies." In New York City alone, an estimated 32,000 speakeasies replaced about 15,000 saloons. Prohibition encouraged hypocrisy and disrespect for the law. Politicians, including President Warren G. Harding, paid lip service to Prohibition in public, and drank freely at home. The expression was that "Congress votes dry and drinks wet."

———

Human skulls have been used as drinking cups throughout history. Cro-Magnon man scraped away muscles and flesh and hacked off and smoothed the lower portion of the skull. (It is not known whether these skulls belonged to revered ancestors or hated enemies.) In the Middle Ages, the skulls of saints were used as drinking cups on ceremonial occasions. Lord Byron served wine to his visitors in New-stead Abbey in a human skull that he had found in the cloisters there. Today, human skulls are still used ceremonially in parts of Africa.

The "pony express" could cover in just a day and a night what would normally have been a ten-day journey. Using the most powerful horses, the riders wore wide belts with many bells that announced their approach to the horse post houses at twenty-five-mile intervals along the route. A fresh horse would be saddled and waiting for the rider, who would press on—toward the palace of Genghis Khan at Chand. It was the middle of the twelfth century.

No one went hungry or unclothed under the benevolent dictatorship of the Inca empire.

When Theodore Roosevelt was police commissioner of New York City, he attempted to prohibit the selling of liquor on Sunday. One such measure, which was passed in April of 1896, stipulated that hotels could continue to serve liquor. A hotel was defined as a structure with ten bedrooms and with facilities for serving food. A local furniture store offered to furnish the ten rooms of any hotel for $81.20. One of the new hotels on the Bowery had stable stalls for rooms and a sign posted in the bar that stated "Sleeping in This Hotel Positively Prohibited." By December of 1896, approximately 2,000 new hotels had appeared in New York City.

About 25 percent of all male Americans between the ages of ten and fifteen were "gainfully employed" at the turn of the century. By 1970, so few in that age bracket were employed that the U.S. Census Bureau did not bother to make inquiries about them.

Frank James, after a career of robbery and murder in the company of his brother Jesse, settled down to a peaceful life of thirty-two years. He sold souvenirs at the James farm, worked as the doorman of a theater, and fired the starter's gun at Missouri race tracks, where he always was cheered by the crowd.

GREEN WORLD

So dense, so impenetrable is the spruce-treed forest of the vast Canadian Lakes District, lying athwart central Canada, that winter snow stays on top of the trees, like a blanket, and the forest floor stays bare.

A weirdly shaped tree has revolutionized knowledge of early civilization. The bristlecone pines of California are the oldest living things, some 4,000 years old. The rings of the bristlecone have turned out to be more accurate than carbon dating. Using this information, historians have concluded that some European artifacts have to be dated hundreds of years earlier than carbon 14 had indicated. This means that European culture was parallel to cultures of the Middle East and not a later offshoot.

The stems of a type of wild iris—blue-eyed grass—are not strong enough to support more than one blossom at a time. One flower blooms each morning, then dies that night to make room for the next.

Lichens have been detected on bare rock in Antarctica as close as 264 miles from the South Pole. This is the most southerly occurrence of land life (except for Antarctic explorers and their dogs, and perhaps other life forms they bring with them).

One rye-grass plant, grown as a scientific experiment, put out roots totaling 378 miles in a single four-month period.

The typical tree or plant receives about 10 percent of its nutrition from the soil. The rest comes from the atmosphere.

Seeds of the African baobab tree sprout more easily if they are first eaten by a baboon and passed through his digestive tract. Apparently, the baboon's digestive juices erode the tough seed coat, permitting water to penetrate more readily.

In a series of experiments performed by Dorothy Retallack in 1969, it was shown that music affects the growth of plants. Tests on corn, squash, and several flowers showed that rock music stunted the growth of some of the plants and caused others to grow unusually tall at first and produce extremely small leaves. They required more water, yet grew shorter roots. Within several weeks, all the marigolds in one experiment had died, but—only a few feet away—identical flowers listening to classical music were blooming.

When Luther Burbank published his seed catalogue at the turn of the century describing new varieties of plants he had developed by crossbreeding, he was charged with blasphemy and denounced by churches for interfering with nature and bringing forth new creations, a power considered to be God's alone.

The sap of the giant sequoia is nonresinous. The trees, once they have developed a heavy bark, are practically fireproof, which may account for their long life. Even if they are fire-damaged, the high tannin content of the sap has the same healing action that tannic acid has on human flesh when burned.

Plant life could not exist without lightning. Nitrogen is an essential food for plants. The atmosphere is 80 percent nitrogen, but in a form that is insoluble and unusable. It is the intense heat of lightning that forces the nitrogen to combine with oxygen in the air, forming nitrogen oxides that are soluble in water and fall to the earth in rain as dilute nitric acid. This reacts with minerals in the ground to become nitrates on which the plants depend.

The yellow evening primrose opens only at dusk, and so swiftly that it can be seen and *heard*. The buds sound like popping soap bubbles as they burst.

Bamboo may grow three feet in twenty-four hours.

When Eric the Red discovered a new land of eternal ice and snow in 982 A.D., he wanted to encourage his fellow Norsemen to go there. So he named it Greenland. Shortly thereafter, twenty-five ships filled with eager settlers sailed for the place.

One of the great but little-known treasures of New York City is a forty-acre hemlock forest, undisturbed, as far as is known, since the time of the Indians. The grove stands on the banks of the Bronx River, in the New York Botanical Garden.

One variety of bamboo, *Phyllostachys bambusoides,* was recorded to have flowered in the year 999 A.D. in China. Since that time, it has continued to flower and set seed every 120 years. It follows this cycle wherever it lives; plants of the same species flower simultaneously no matter where they have been transplanted.

Scientists from the New York Botanical Garden and the University of North Carolina discovered leaves that have remained green and intact for more than 15 million years. These leaves, from a Chinese elm called zelkova, which is extinct in North America, were found in eastern Oregon—remarkably preserved in volcanic ash. They were described as appearing almost as if they had been pressed in the pages of a book for only a few weeks.

The plant life of the oceans makes up about 85 percent of all the greenery on the planet.

The leaves of the mallow weed, as those of many other plants, follow the movement of the sun's light, turning with it as it moves across the sky. More unusual is the mallow weed's reaction at sundown. As soon as the sun sets, all the mallow weed's leaves turn around and face the east, where the sun will rise in the morning.

A giant sequoia waits 175 to 200 years before it first flowers, the most delayed sexual maturity in all nature. It will bear millions of seeds, but each seed is so small that it takes 3,000 of them to weigh one ounce.

The giant sequoia tree seemingly can last forever, but its wood is practically useless as timber. The tree is so brittle that, when it falls, it often cracks both lengthwise and across into fragments fit only for use in lead pencils.

Once a black-walnut log is ready for milling, it is examined carefully for figured grain. If any is seen, the wood instead is shaved into sheets less than 1/32 of an inch thick. One uniquely beautiful log is said to have been sold in the veneer trade for $20,000 wholesale.

———

In a single growing season, ten small water hyacinths can increase to become more than 600,000 plants, forming a mat an acre in size and weighing 180 tons.

———

Duckweed, or *marimo*, is a now-you-see-it-now-you-don't weed found in Lake Akan in Daisetsuzan National Park in Japan. The weed forms in a ball at the bottom of the lake, rises to rid itself of oxygen, then sinks and rises again—up and down, seemingly forever. "*Marimo* spotting" is a water sport there.

———

Airborne spores of fungi, those mushrooms and puffballs that live in damp, dark places on the ground, have been detected in astronomical numbers in the sky as high as 35,000 feet.

———

One type of mushroom, the *Ganoderma applanatum*, can live for fifty years and grow to a diameter of two feet.

———

In Amsterdam, the first center of bourgeois capitalism, the tulip was so prized in the seventeenth century that one collector exchanged 1,000 pounds of cheese, four oxen, eight pigs, twelve sheep, a bed, and a suit of clothes for a single bulb of the Viceroy species. It was the tulip—not sugar or oil or spices—that caused the first boom and slump in capitalistic economy. When the bottom fell out of the tulip market in 1637, the Dutch economy was shaken badly.

———

Plants, like animals, can exist as male and female—a fact detected in the late sixteenth century by the Italian botanist Prospero Alpini when he studied the date palm. It was sexual differences among plants that Carolus Linnaeus used a century and a half later as the basis for his classification of the plant kingdom.

———

During the thousands of years since Florida rose from the sea, hurricanes have torn loose vegetation, including tree branches, from Cuba, swirled them high over the Gulf Stream, and deposited them battered but alive at random over the southeastern part of the U.S. Thus West Indian mahogany, gumbo limbo, poisonwood, and co-

coplum, all native to the tropics, are found growing on the U.S. mainland.

The transplanted Australian eucalyptus tree is an ecological godsend at the fringe of the Algerian Sahara in North Africa. Growing to the incredible height of 300 feet, which is as tall as the tallest sequoias and redwoods in the American West, the eucalypti form a barrier to the encroachment of sand dunes that would otherwise result in the desertification of arable land in a 900-mile belt of the Sahara.

Luther Burbank, who had no formal education beyond high school, was inspired by Charles Darwin's *Variation of Animals and Plants under Domestication* to pursue a career as a plant breeder. Using his keen memory and powers of observation to detect changes in his breeding stock, Burbank developed more than 800 new plant varieties.

The first botanical garden in the United States was planted by John Bartram (1699–1777) and exists today as part of the Philadelphia park system. In 1728, Bartram, a pioneer American botanist, purchased land along the banks of the Schuylkill River near Philadelphia and established his garden there.

In 1855, Richard Deakin published *Flora of the Colosseum,* a copiously illustrated catalog that recorded 420 varieties of plants growing in the ruined Roman amphitheater. Among the plants that grew there were rosemary, thyme, sage, cyclamen, daisies, hyacinths, violets, strawberries, marigolds, and larkspur. Trees—fig, cherry, pear, and elm—flourished on lofty ledges.

The giant water lily *Victoria regia* has leaves so large and buoyant that one can support the weight of a young child, like a raft. The leaves grow as large as eight feet across.

In 1792, when Thomas Jefferson was Secretary of State, he had the honor of having a plant named for him, the *Jeffersonia diphylla.* The citation stated that "in botany and zoology, the information of this gentleman is equalled by few persons in the United States."

By running a temperature as much as 25° F. warmer than its surroundings, the feverish skunk cabbage melts its way to the surface of snow.

Though most of the eighty-eight constellations were named by an agricultural society, not one was named for a member of the plant kingdom. (Thirty-six represent mammals.)

––––––––

The tiny discs of chlorophyll in plant cells move about within those cells to adjust for different light and heat conditions. When the sunshine is too strong, they can turn edge on. On a gray day, they may roll to turn broadside to make the most of the available light.

––––––––

The chrysanthemum requires an uninterrupted period of approximately thirteen hours of darkness of an autumn night before it will flower. Commercial flower growers, in order to delay the blossoming for a more profitable market, illuminate the plants briefly at night to break up the dark period.

––––––––

"Flower clocks" provided a unique and decorative means of telling time in the formal gardens of nineteenth-century Europe. A series of flower beds was laid out to form a clock face, with each bed representing a daytime hour. The beds were planted with flowers known to open or close at the prescribed hours. On a sunny day, the time on a flower clock could be determined to within a half-hour.

––––––––

HALLS OF IVY

The worst college campus riot prior to this century erupted at medieval Oxford—the "town and gown" battle of 1354. Originating in a tavern quarrel, the violence lasted for three days, involved dozens of townsmen and students, and ended with several dead and many injured.

————

Heavyweight boxing champion Gene Tunney lectured on Shakespeare at Yale University.

————

Oxford University was founded because a king quarreled with a saint. Henry II, feuding with Archbishop Thomas Becket and incensed with the King of France for defending Becket, ordered English students home from the University of Paris. Most of the returnees settled at Oxford and started a university of their own.

————

At the close of the fifteenth century, the University of Paris could boast fifty colleges and 20,000 students.

————

Howard University was named after its founder, Oliver O. Howard, a white Union general who was dedicated to the cause of black betterment. General Howard founded the university in 1867 and served as its president from 1869 to 1874.

————

Because physical vitality was considered as precious a legacy as intelligence and because the health and usefulness of "our housed-up businessmen" had to be preserved, Yale University at the turn of the century added dancing (jigging, clogging, soft-shoeing) to the curriculum.

————

As early as 1826, Amherst College in Massachusetts and Bowdoin in Maine had each graduated a black man. The first black woman to earn a B.A. was graduated from Oberlin College in Ohio in 1862.

————

In 1881, Booker T. Washington founded Tuskegee Institute so that black students—"because better jobs were not available to them"—could learn bricklaying and prepare for domestic service and simple factory jobs. By 1927, Tuskegee had added a college department, and now gives the highest academic degrees.

―――――

The University of Alaska stretches across four time zones, from the community college in Kitchikan—near Alaska's southeastern border with British Columbia—to a tiny "learning center" on remote Adak in the Aleutian Islands. Those two points are about as distant from each other as London and Moscow.

―――――

Harvard president Edward Everett, taking a firm stand on principle, said that if the white students chose to withdraw because Harvard had accepted a black student, "all the income of the college will be devoted to his education." The student, Beverly G. Williams, died—in 1847—before he could enroll.

―――――

A special ruling by the Crown (the monarch was head of the Church of England and Cambridge was a church school) was necessary before Newton could become Lucasian Professor of Mathematics at Cambridge. The ruling: Newton did not have to become a church member to assume the position. He delivered about eight lectures a year; they were deemed rather poor.

―――――

Elihu Yale, after whom one of America's greatest universities was named, never set foot in the U.S. after he was three years old and moved with his parents to England. The college's ambassador, Cotton Mather, persuaded Yale, then the retired governor of the East India Company, to donate some religious books, a portrait of George I, and £200 to the fledgling Connecticut institution known as Collegiate School of Connecticut. A subsequent shipment of goods raised £562 for the college. Yale died a rich man, but not a penny of his estate went overseas to the school that had changed its name to Yale College in 1718.

―――――

To have his application for medical school even considered, a Japanese student pays about $100,000 in "voluntary gifts" and "voluntary presents" to the faculty members on the admissions committee. (Bribery in Japan is unheard-of, but mutual gift-giving has been obligatory since time immemorial.)

―――――

In the late 1400s, the African kingdom of Songhay was larger than western Europe. It had a public-school system and was particularly proud of its savants. Timbuktu's university was famous throughout Africa and Europe, and its medical center near the Niger attracted the ill from all over.

———

John Dalton (1766–1844), who first worked out the modern atomic theory, received a doctor's degree from Oxford in 1832 and was presented to the British King, William IV. For the occasion he had to wear a scarlet robe. Dalton, because he was a Quaker, could not wear scarlet. Nor could he offend the King. Dalton found a way out. He happened to be totally colorblind. When the scarlet cloak was brought to him, he simply stated that as best as he could tell the cloak was gray. (Dalton was also a pioneer in meteorology, keeping careful daily records of the weather for fifty-seven years, from the age of twenty-one till the day he died. These records, preserved for a century, were destroyed during World War II in the Nazi bombing of Manchester.)

———

Ellen Swallow Richards (1842–1911) was the first woman in the United States to be graduated from a scientific school. In 1873, she received a B.S. degree from the Massachusetts Institute of Technology. She was also the first woman to be elected to the American Institute of Mining and Metallurgical Engineers. A leading figure in the study of nutrition and hygiene, she became the first president of the American Home Economics Association, in 1908.

———

Georges "Tiger" Clemenceau (1841–1929), twice premier of France, spent four years in the United States as a young man. He worked as a journalist, taught French at a ladies' college in Stamford, Connecticut, and married one of the students. They separated after seven years.

———

INNOVATIONS

"If I had been technically trained, I would have quit," said King Gillette after spending eight frustrating years striving to invent and introduce his safety razor.

Henry Bessemer, with a suggestion on perforation from his fiancée, developed an improved method for stamping deeds that was adopted without compensation to Bessemer by the British revenue office, in the 1830s. The government had been losing thousands in revenue because stamps then in use could be removed from documents and used again. Bessemer, after going on to create a significant steel-making process and to make a worldwide name for himself in industrial circles, reminded the British government of its misdeed of more than four decades earlier. He still was not paid, though his method of stamping deeds was still being used, but the justice of the complaint was acknowledged and Bessemer was knighted.

In 1620, Cornelius van Drebbel, a Dutch inventor working in England, built a wood-frame leather-skinned submarine that traveled fifteen feet below the surface of the Thames. It was propelled by twelve rowers. According to reports, King James I was an eager passenger. Drebbel's method of renewing the air in the submerged craft allowed the vessel to remain underwater for up to fifteen hours.

The British engineer Charles Algernon Parsons thought up an excellent way of publicizing his newly devised steam turbine. He waited for Queen Victoria's Diamond Jubilee in 1897, at which time there was a stately review of the British navy. Parsons's turbine-powered ship, *Turbinia*, going thirty-five knots with scarcely any vibration or noise, suddenly skimmed past the navy. It was an effective demonstration, and the navies of the world at once began bidding for turbine engines.

186

The cigarette lighter was invented before the match. In 1816, a German chemist, J. W. Dobereiner, devised a way of automatically igniting a jet of hydrogen. The only problem was that it required powdered platinum to act as a catalyst, so it wasn't very practical.

The electric automobile self-starter, which was perfected in 1911 by Charles F. Kettering, made it possible for women to drive without the companion previously needed for cranking the engine.

In the summer of 1902, a printer in Brooklyn, New York, was having trouble with color printing because the hot, humid weather was causing the paper on the presses to change size enough to cause distortions of printing. Willis Haviland Carrier, a young engineer trying to solve the problem, found that air retained less moisture at lower temperatures. He designed a machine that blew air over chilled pipes and stabilized the amount of moisture. The printing improved, and Carrier's concept became the basis of the home air conditioner.

In 1852, the American inventor Elisha Graves Otis devised the first elevator that would not crash if something happened to it. In 1854, he tested such an elevator and its safety guard in New York City. He had the elevator raised to a considerable height and then had the cable cut completely through. The elevator descended slowly and without harm to the one passenger—Otis himself.

When, in 1891, Whitcomb L. Judson, a Chicago inventor, patented what would later become the zipper, he had in mind something to save people the trouble of buttoning and unbuttoning their shoes every day. He called his invention the "Clasp Locker and Unlocker for Shoes."

Thomas Jefferson invented a wooden forerunner of the modern mold-board plow in the late 1700s.

When William Beebe undertook to explore the ocean depths in a thick-walled vessel suspended from a surface ship, it was his notion to make it a cylinder. A friend pointed out that a spherical shape would be stronger. Beebe adopted the better idea. The friend was President Franklin Roosevelt.

A contrivance as simple as the envelope did not come into use until 1839. Up until then, people usually folded their letters both ways, sealed them with wax, and wrote the address on the back.

Thirty-two thousand patents were granted to Americans between 1836, the year that the Patent Office was established, and 1860. In just the next thirty years, another 450,000 patents were granted. Between 1890 and 1955, 2.5 million more patents were granted. The U.S. registers twice as many patents as does Great Britain or France and four times as many as Germany.

Francis Bacon in 1605 developed a biliteral cipher, using only the letters a and b in five-letter combinations, each representing a letter of the alphabet. This code illustrates the principle that only two signs are required to transmit information in code. It is the same principle that in the late 1600s Gottfried Leibniz developed into the binary system, which underlies the digital computer of today: 0 and 1 (corresponding to the absence or the presence of a current) can be combined to express any number.

An artificial hand, with fingers moved by cogwheels and levers, was designed in 1551 by a Frenchman, Ambroise Paré. It even enabled a handless cavalryman to grasp the reins of his horse.

Jean Eugene Robert Houdin (1805–1871), the founder of modern magic, was an inventor of many complicated toys and automata. His first profitable gadget was an alarm clock; a bell would peal to rouse the sleeper and a lighted candle would come out of a box. It was for his application of electricity to clocks in general that Houdin was decorated in Paris, in 1855. (Harry Houdini assumed his name from Houdin's.)

The first object we can call a photograph was produced in 1822 by the French inventor Joseph Nicéphore Niepce. The process wasn't really practical, though. It required an exposure of as long as eight hours. Niepce became bankrupt, and in 1829 went into partnership with the French artist Louis Jacques Mandé Daguerre, who was also working on the process. Daguerre improved it to such an extent that he usually is considered the inventor of photography.

When he realized that his career would be thwarted in class-ridden Britain, Samuel Slater memorized details of the textile machinery in

Richard Arkwright's modern factory. He disguised himself as a farm laborer and sailed for America. Working from memory, Slater created the industrial age in the New World, building in Pawtucket, Rhode Island, in 1793, the first factory in the U.S. based on the advanced new machinery. He later built other factories in New England. As the father of the industrialization of his adopted country, Slater gave the U.S. even greater opportunity for true independence.

––––––

The first punchcards for giving instructions to machines—the fore-runners of today's computer cards—were used in the textile mills of France in the early eighteenth century. A loom designed by Basile Bouchon in 1725 used holes punched in a roll of paper to weave designs into silk fabric. When the paper was pressed against a row of needles, the needles lining up with the holes stayed in place, while the others moved on.

––––––

Tired of pounding pavements looking for a job, Humphrey O'Sullivan of Boston sat down one day and invented the rubber heel.

––––––

In the early 1860s, a New York firm offered a prize of $10,000 for a satisfactory substitute for ivory in the manufacture of billiard balls. The prize was won by an American inventor, John Wesley Hyatt, who devised for the purpose what came to be known as celluloid. It was the first synthetic plastic.

––––––

In the early 1700s, the French physicist René de Réaumur discovered the concept of making paper from wood after watching wasps chewing wood, turning it to pulp with their saliva, and spreading it on their nests, where it dried into "paper" when exposed to air. But the idea was not put into practical use until 1852, when the first wood-grinding machine for pulverizing wet wood (invented by a German weaver, Frederic Keller) was employed in the production of the first newsprint.

––––––

The inventor of dynamite, Alfred Nobel, also invented plywood and worked out detailed plans for prefabricating plywood houses that could be easily transported to the construction site for quick erection.

––––––

Rubber tires were invented long before automobiles. The first rubber tires were devised by Robert William Thomson, a Scottish engineer, in 1845. They were, at first, just strips of rubber that were fitted around wheels. The first major application was to bicycles.

––––––

Although a writing machine had been patented in England as early as 1714, the first practical typewriter was built by an American, William Burt, in 1829. The chief use for the early machines, which produced embossed writing, was for the blind.

———

Norman Thomas, six-time Socialist Party candidate for President of the United States, never polled more than 884,000 popular votes in one election, but his influence on American political and social thought was widely effective. Among the reforms that he early championed and that later were enacted were unemployment compensation and old-age pensions.

———

After an English fleet had mistaken its longitude and run into the Scilly Islands off southwest England in 1707—with a loss of four ships and 2,000 men (including the commanding admiral, Sir Cloudesley Shovel)—the government offered a prize of £20,000 for a method of determining longitude to within half a degree. The prize was won by a Yorkshire instrument maker, John Harrison, whose chronometer introduced the modern era of ship navigation; it "held sway" for 150 years. Possibly because Harrison was a provincial self-taught mechanic and not a gentleman of the Royal Society, Parliament did not authorize payment until King George III stepped in, in 1765, and assured Harrison his reward. By today's standards, the value of the reward would be close to $1 million.

———

The first American submarine was built about 1776. The inventor was David Bushnell (1750–1824), a student at Yale. *American Turtle,* as the submarine was called, was a cask made of oak. It operated satisfactorily as an underwater vessel, but it failed in the task for which it was designed, namely, the destruction of British ships during the Revolutionary War by attaching a time bomb to their hulls. Because Bushnell could not find a satisfactory method of attaching the bombs, he abandoned the submarine and concentrated on building underwater mines.

———

U.S. patent number 6,469, titled "Buoying Vessels over Shoals," in the inventor's description, was "a new and improved manner of combining adjustable buoyant air chambers with a steamboat or other vessel for the purpose of enabling them to pass over bars or through shallow water." The inventor whittled a model twenty inches long, but a life-size version was never built. The inventor—Abraham Lincoln.

———

The first great oceanographer was the American Matthew Fontaine Maury. A native Virginian, he sided with the Confederacy during the Civil War, and emigrated to Mexico for a while after the Confederacy had been defeated. He returned to Virginia in 1868 and was forgiven. Although he had actively tried for four years to destroy the United States through his invention of an electric torpedo and in his role as head of coastal defenses for the Confederacy, there now stands Maury Hall at the U.S. Naval Academy at Annapolis.

———

INTO THE AIR

The first "airmail" letter in the U.S. was written by President George Washington, who gave it to the Frenchman Jean Pierre Blanchard to carry with him on the first balloon flight in America. With Washington as a witness, the balloonist ascended from a prison yard in Philadelphia, then capital of the U.S.; he landed forty-six miles away in Gloucester County, New Jersey. The letter identified the balloonist as a guest of the young republic.

———

Twenty-one of the first twenty-three U.S. astronauts who flew on space missions were either an only child or were firstborn sons.

———

Somewhere out there in space, amid the junk, is the Hasselblad camera dropped during a space walk by the U.S. astronaut Michael Collins. It will orbit the Earth for an indefinite period.

———

In the forty-one years between 1859 and 1900, no one flew farther in a balloon than the 804 miles covered in the U.S. in July 1859 by a former pianomaker named John Wise. In 1873, he tried for a new record. Packing aboard the gondola an assistant, a navigator, and a correspondent from the sponsoring newspaper, and slinging a lifeboat beneath the gondola, Wise set off for Europe, convinced that a steady west-to-east wind would lead to a successful flight. They crashed in New Canaan, Connecticut. Six years later, trying for still another long-distance flight, Wise crashed and drowned in Lake Michigan.

———

The most disastrous crash in the first seventy-five years of aviation history occurred when two jumbo jets collided *on the ground*, in Tenerife, the Canary Islands, on March 27, 1977. One plane accelerating on a runway during takeoff ran into another that was taxiing between holding areas, waiting its turn to fly. Five hundred seventy-nine people were killed.

———

When the Wright brothers offered to the United States Army their airplane that launched powered flight in 1903, Army officials were so skeptical of the Wrights' claim that they refused to see a flight demonstration until 1908. Record-breaking flights by Orville Wright in the U.S. and by Wilbur Wright in France brought the brothers worldwide fame. In 1909, the U.S. government accepted the Wright machine for army use.

After the first moon walk, in 1969, Pan American Airlines began accepting reservations for commercial flights to the moon, dates and time unspecified. More than 80,000 requests poured in immediately.

In the year that the Wright brothers first flew, for twelve seconds, it took only twelve minutes for a message to be cabled around the globe.

A boomerang cannot return to the thrower after hitting anything.

"Five, four, three, two, one, lift-off"—the now famous rocketry countdown—was invented by the German director Fritz Lang for his 1928 motion picture *Die Frau im Mond,* or *Woman in the Moon.* (The movie is also known as *By Rocket to the Moon.*)

Less than five years elapsed between the time Wilbur and Orville Wright began the serious study of flight, in 1899, and their historic flight at Kitty Hawk, North Carolina. In 1900, they tried out man-carrying gliders; the following year, they designed and tested some 200 shapes of wings in a homemade wind tunnel (six feet long and sixteen inches square); the next year, they made record-breaking glider flights; in 1903, having designed and built a light-weight twelve-horsepower gasoline engine, they built and flew the first self-propelled plane.

A manned rocket reaches the moon in less time than it took a stagecoach to travel the length of England.

A German inventor placed an engine on an aircraft in 1900 and flew it successfully—three years *before* the Wright brothers. The inventor was Count Ferdinand von Zeppelin, but the aircraft was not heavier than air. Von Zeppelin had invented the dirigible—the Zeppelin.

Exploration of the upper atmosphere isn't completely a new enter-prise. As long ago as 1804, the French chemist and physicist Joseph Louis Gay-Lussac rose in a balloon nearly 4½ miles into the sky in order to obtain air at that height for analysis.

Hot-air balloons are having a commercial comeback. They are, for example, lifting huge loads of timber in the mountains of the Pacific Northwest and swinging freight off and onto ships in Yemen.

The first aerial photograph was made from a balloon during the U.S. Civil War.

Because the Smithsonian Institution would not acknowledge that the Wright brothers had built the first man-carrying heavier-than-air ma-chine capable of powered flight, the Wrights sent their craft to the Science Museum in London. It remained on display there until the Smithsonian admitted its mistake and agreed to house the historic plane.

A thirty-one-year-old airplane mechanic named Douglas Corrigan took off in his monoplane from Floyd Bennett Field in New York, in July 1938, and supposedly headed toward his home in California. The next day he landed in Ireland, saying, "I guess I flew the wrong way." Authorities had denied him permission to make such a solo flight across the Atlantic, because his old crate had no safety equip-ment, no radio, and no direction finders. Corrigan claimed his com-pass had gone out of whack. He became famous, paraded down Broadway, made a movie, and earned the nickname that stuck with him from then on—"Wrong Way" Corrigan.

In 1930, Ellen Church recruited seven other young nurses to work 5,000 feet above the Earth. They were the first airline stewardesses, flying on Boeing's San Francisco–Chicago route, a trip that, in good weather, took 20 hours and made 13 stops.

The first known design for a complete lighter-than-air craft was made, in 1670, by a Jesuit priest, Francesco de Lana-Terzi. The craft, shaped like a rowboat, was intended to "float on the atmosphere," with the aid of four copper spheres from which all air had been pumped. It was an idea that didn't get off the ground.

Astronauts circling the Earth may get to see sixteen sunrises and sixteen sunsets every "day."

Astronauts rarely wear spacesuits. On a mission from eight to eighty days, for instance, suits are worn for only a total of four to twenty hours. Length of time depends on the nature of the mission. *Apollo* and *Skylab* crews began working in their "shirtsleeves" when the National Aeronautics and Space Administration (NASA) gained confidence in the pressurization systems of the spacecrafts. Crews always are suited if there is a potential hazard of spacecraft damage, such as in launch phase or docking with and extracting the lunar module during trans-lunar coast, or in operations such as docking the module during the mission. A suit is worn during all extravehicular activity, such as space walking and moon roving.

The first coast-to-coast airplane flight in the U.S.—from New York City to Pasadena, California, by Galbraith P. Rodgers, in 1911—took forty-nine days. (There were many, many stops, of course.)

The speed of sound—known as Mach 1, after the Austrian physicist and philosopher Ernst Mach—is different at different heights. At sea level, for example, it is 760 miles per hour. Above 36,000 feet Mach 1 is reached at about 660 miles per hour.

After the Wright brothers had flown four times that historic day in 1903 at Kitty Hawk, a gust of wind overturned and wrecked their wooden flyer. They stuffed the pieces and fabric covering into barrels and shipped them back home to their bicycle shop in Dayton, Ohio.

The first freight shipped by air from Chicago was loaded under an armed guard. Handled by National Air Transport, in 1927, the item was a "ten-gallon" Stetson hat to be delivered to Will Rogers, the popular comedian.

Daredevil pilot Hanna Reitsch was the first woman to test a rocket plane, the Messerschmitt Me163, and may be the only person to have "traveled" for in-flight observation in a test model of the V1-V2 rockets. Testing what was the latest vehicle, she inevitably crashed many times (as she did in that Me163); it was said with some exaggeration that there was not a single bone in her body that hadn't been broken at least once. Hanna Reitsch appears in history books as the lone pilot who—in the final days of the siege of Berlin—flew into the Nazi capital to rescue Adolf Hitler at the very last moment. (Hitler insisted on staying behind, and killed himself in his bunker.)

Prior to takeoff, the "engine" was fueled with bananas, apples, hard rolls, and one pint of water. The engine was the pilot himself, twenty-six-year-old Bryan Allen, whose long, powerful legs pedaled a seventy-pound airplane, the *Gossamer Albatross*, the twenty-three miles across the English Channel from England to France in two hours and forty-nine minutes in June 1979. The plane, which flew little more than a few feet above the waves, had a ninety-six-foot-long wing made of Mylar .0005 of an inch thin. Two tiny wheels weighing one ounce each were the landing gear.

In 1978, when the first new class of U.S. astronaut candidates in eleven years was being formed, more than 8,000 persons applied. Thirty-five were chosen by the National Aeronautical and Space Administration for a two-year program of study and training. The group included six women, a few candidates who could not fly an airplane and were not expected to learn, three blacks, and a Japanese-American.

It was only 1 cubic foot of space, but the biology unit in the Viking lander that touched down on Mars in 1976 and examined soil for signs of life contained the following: three automated chemical labs; a computer; ovens for heating samples to 1,100° F.; counters for radioactive tracers; filters; sun lamp; gas chromatograph to identify chemicals; forty thermostats; 22,000 transistors; 18,000 other electronic parts, and forty-three valves.

LAWS

From all levels of government, federal, state, and local, Americans get 150,000 new laws and 2 million new regulations every year.

When John F. Kennedy was assassinated in 1963, it was not a federal felony to kill a President of the United States.

From 1836 to 1896, the Red Flag Act in England required that any self-propelled vehicle be preceded by a man carrying a red flag by day and a red lantern by night. In effect, this limited speed to four miles per hour and retarded development of all self-propelled vehicles, including automobiles.

Town laws in the U.S. Midwest in the 1880s were passed prohibiting the sale of ice-cream sodas on Sunday. In Illinois, ingenious soda fountain owners got around the law by omitting the carbonated water and serving just the scoop of ice cream and the syrup. They called this a "Sunday soda." Later that name was shortened to "Sunday," and then it became "sundae."

"Red tape," the rigid application of regulations and routine, resulting in delay in getting business done, got its name from the color of the tape that was commonly used to tie official papers. The term occurs as early as 1658.

In one of the first law codes in history, handed down by Hammurabi (1792–1750 B.C.), King of Babylonia, the penalty for medical malpractice was to cut off the doctor's hands. Hammurabi's code of laws is one of the greatest of ancient codes. The diorite column on which the laws were carved is now in Paris.

Despite the much publicized de-Nazification procedure in Germany after World War II, about 70 percent of all teachers, judges, lawyers,

197

and police officers remained at, or soon returned to, their posts to provide "administrative continuity." They had been the makers and implementers of the Nazi laws, and they now slavishly implemented the new laws handed down by the victorious Allies.

––––––––

The English philosopher John Locke drafted the constitution for South Carolina.

––––––––

A number of personages on the international governmental scene were approached to suggest a constitutional structure for governments being formed in Latin America. Pierre Samuel du Pont de Nemours, founder of the Compagnie d'Amerique, the first du Pont family venture in the United States, was one of the personages, and he prepared an essay entitled "Republiques Equinoxiales" around 1815, when he was in his mid-seventies. The constitution was to serve as a model for Latin American governments then being formed, and was not intended for a particular republic.

––––––––

Sir Henry Morgan was the captain of ships that sailed the Spanish Main searching for plunder in the seventeenth century. He found it on the high seas and in cities of Cuba, Venezuela, and Panama. Yet, when called a pirate in print, Morgan sued for libel and won. A London jury awarded him £200 for defamation of character.

––––––––

"Neither slavery nor involuntary servitude, unless for the punishment of crime, shall ever be tolerated in this state." Thus read the state of Michigan's constitution in 1850. Inadvertently, it legalized slavery as an appropriate punishment for crime. Not until 1963 was the comma shifted from its position after servitude to a position after slavery, and slavery was once again outlawed in the state.

––––––––

The Massachusetts School Law of 1647 required that towns with fifty or more families establish schools or pay a fine of £5. Several schools were opened as a result of this law. Although the schools were not the first supported by the public, the law forcing their creation was an important milestone in public education.

––––––––

It was only in 1968—43 years after the Scopes "monkey trial"—that the state of Tennessee abolished its anti-evolution law and accepted the doctrine of evolution.

––––––––

City Ordinance No. 352 in Pacific Grove, California, makes it a misdemeanor to kill or threaten a butterfly.

————

Blue Laws became known as such because of the color of the paper on which they were printed. In 1665, Theophilus Eaton, governor of the New Haven Colony, and a friend, clergyman John Davenport, drew up the strict legal code regulating personal conduct that subsequently was called Blue Laws.

————

The United States Refuse Act of 1899 is a long-ignored federal statute. It prohibits all industrial discharges into bodies of water. Every industrial discharge since 1899 has been a crime.

————

Islands garnered by the U.S. in war against Spain at the turn of the century were no longer to be considered foreign territory; on the other hand, the U.S. Supreme Court declared that they were not automatically covered by the Constitution and that it was up to Congress to decide what portions of the Constitution, if any, applied to them. This had been precisely the quarrel between the American colonies and Great Britain that resulted in the founding of the U.S. Seen like this, the Supreme Court in 1901 would have decided in favor of George III.

————

Courts of law in the United States devote more than half their time to cases involving automobiles.

————

LITERARY LIFE

O. Henry, the pseudonym of William Sydney Porter (1862–1910), was serving three years in prison for embezzlement when he began to write short stories. Upon his release, he gained national fame with 300 stories, most of which had a surprise ending.

The *Scientific American* magazine rejected the story by A. I. Root, a beekeeper in Medina, Ohio, on the first motorpowered air flight of the Wright brothers. Root had read a brief account in a Dayton, Ohio, paper, realized its significance, and wrote a full-fledged account. After the *Scientific American* rejection, Root submitted it to the magazine *Gleanings in Bee Culture*, which published the exclusive story.

For putting together in one place, in the first of the great encyclopedias, all the scientific views of the Age of Reason, Denis Diderot made about $12 a week over a period of 20 years. Once the 28-volume *Encyclopedia* was completed, in 1772, he decided to sell his library, out of financial necessity, in order to supply a dowry for his daughter. Catherine II, Empress of Russia, paid $5,000 for the library, but allowed Diderot the use of it during his lifetime.

To gain firsthand experience with "proselytized immigrants" who were traveling west to seek their fortunes, the reporter Robert Louis Stevenson rode in an "immigrant car"—an old railroad coach, springless, rattling, poorly ventilated, with double rows of narrow backless benches bunched close together—completely across the U.S., from Castle Garden (now Battery Park on the southern tip of Manhattan), New York, to the West Coast.

Gustave Flaubert's masterpiece, *Madame Bovary*, a brutal and realistic love story with a theme of adultery, was condemned as pornography when it was serialized in a periodical in 1856 and

Flaubert was charged with offending public morality and religion. The court censured the book but acquitted the author. Though the novel was selling in the thousands, Flaubert said he wished he had enough money to buy up every copy, "throw them all into the fire and never hear of the book again."

———

Cyrano de Bergerac really lived (from about 1620 to 1655), big nose, dueling, and all. He was a poet, a dramatist, and a science-fiction writer. He wrote of voyages to the moon and to the sun and was the first person in history to suggest (in 1650) the one method that could carry us into space—rockets.

———

When D. W. Griffith made his masterpiece, *Birth of a Nation*, he used the book *The Clansman* by Thomas Dixon as the basis for the script. He agreed to pay Dixon $10,000 for the rights, but ran out of money and could pay only $2,500 for the original option. For the balance, he offered Dixon 25 percent interest in the picture. Dixon reluctantly agreed. Dixon's proceeds became the largest sum any author ever received for a motion-picture story—several million dollars.

———

D. H. Lawrence, one of the most original and controversial writers of the twentieth century, had a fancy for removing his clothes and climbing mulberry trees.

———

Emily Dickinson, whose poetry thrills millions today, fantasized about the earth and sky and heaven itself, but left her home state, Massachusetts, exactly once, and that was to visit her father in Washington where he was a Representative. She became such a recluse that she would not stay in the same room with her guests but would speak with them from an adjoining room.

———

Samuel Langhorne Clemens was not the first American author to use the name Mark Twain. The name, a steamboat pilot's term, was first used as a pen name by another Mississippi River pilot, Isaiah Sellers, who wrote newspaper articles. Clemens later adopted the name and made it famous.

———

Thomas Hardy, the English author of the novels *Far from the Madding Crowd, The Return of the Native, The Mayor of Casterbridge,* and *Tess of the D'Urbervilles,* was stung by the storm of protests from critics and clergy when they read his novel *Jude the Obscure.* He turned from fiction and wrote only verse—eleven volumes of it!—in the remaining thirty-two years of his life.

———

Murasaki Shikibu (about 978–1026) is known as the author of the oldest full-length novel in the world, *The Tale of Genji*. What is less well known is the fact that *many* great women writers flourished in Japan at that time, as Murasaki Shikibu recorded in her own diaries. *Genji* just happens to be the only work of merit that survived. (After the eleventh century, Buddhism reduced women's status drastically.)

———

When the Portuguese historian João de Barros (1496–1570) wrote *Décadas da Ásia,* his monumental history of the Portuguese Empire, King John III was so pleased that he gave him an area of about 130,000 square miles—the whole state of Maranhão in Brazil.

———

Not until Queen Elizabeth had been dead for five years was the scene in Shakespeare's *Richard II* in which the king is deposed included in a printed text. In the Tudor lexicon, there was no greater sin than to attempt to depose an anointed king. Three printings of the play in Elizabeth's reign did not carry the scene.

———

The phrase "a lost generation," used by Ernest Hemingway in *The Sun Also Rises* (1926), originated with a garage owner in the French Midi. In conversation with Hemingway's friend Gertrude Stein, the man had referred to his young mechanics as "*une génération perdue.*"

———

Vergil's quest for perfection nearly cost posterity his twelve-book Latin classic, the *Aeneid,* a national epic and a literary masterpiece. Generally accepted as the greatest of the Roman poets, Vergil left the instruction that when he died the manuscript should be burned because he had not had time to polish it. The Roman emperor Augustus—at whose request Vergil may have initiated work on the *Aeneid*—stepped in and countermanded Vergil's request. He had others apply what little polish was needed, and ordered the work published.

———

After writing the runaway best seller *Uncle Tom's Cabin,* Harriet Beecher Stowe was bombarded with hate mail. Out of one package that she received fell the ear of a slave.

———

Bertrand Russell is best known and most esteemed for his achievements in mathematics and philosophy—his co-authored *Principia Mathematica* is a classic work on the logic of mathematics—but he won his lone Nobel Prize, in 1950, for literature.

Though his mathematical genius dominated Western scientific thought for well over two centuries, Sir Isaac Newton considered his finest work to be his interpretation of the biblical Book of Daniel. He devoted several million words in manuscript to the book—all of it disregarded by posterity.

The poems and plays of the greatest writer in English literature have been attributed to more than twenty persons. William Shakespeare would have been startled by the names of those who are supposed to have done his writing for him—including Francis Bacon, Sir Walter Raleigh, and, yes, Queen Elizabeth.

René Descartes was writing a book on the universe, in which he accepted the views of Copernicus. But when he heard that Galileo had been condemned for believing with Copernicus that the sun was the center of the universe and that the planets revolved around the sun, the Jesuit-educated French philosopher decided to abandon the work.

Though he was not blind but had failing eyesight, Aldous Huxley learned Braille so that he might rest his pained eyes without having to give up reading, which he so enjoyed. One of the compensations, Huxley said, was the pleasure of reading in bed in the dark, with book and hands snugly under the bedclothes.

The Greek playwright Aeschylus, according to some sources, was killed by a tortoise. The animal, it is said, was dropped from the claws of an eagle flying overhead, which mistook Aeschylus' bald head for a rock.

Theodore Dreiser's novel *Sister Carrie*, which is now considered an American classic, was an immediate success in London when it was published at the turn of the century. But in the U.S. it was published by Doubleday, Page and Company without enthusiasm and virtually suppressed because the wife of the publisher so disproved of the realistic story of the deterioration of a man caused by an immoral girl. Dreiser had been a successful journalist, and he suddenly now found himself *persona non grata* in magazine publishing as well; no editor would buy his articles. He suffered a nervous breakdown, had thoughts of suicide, and could not write another novel for eleven years.

———

Mikhail Yurevich Lermontov, the Russian poet and novelist, first won attention with his poem protesting and lamenting Pushkin's death in a senseless duel. Years later, Lermontov himself was killed in a yet more senseless duel, brought on by his caustic wit.

———

When the French literary critic Sainte-Beuve (1804–69) was challenged to a duel by a journalist a century ago, and thus, according to custom, was permitted the choice of weapons, he told his opponent, "I choose spelling—you're dead."

———

After his Pacific overture, opening Japan to U.S. trading, Matthew C. Perry unsuccessfully requested Nathaniel Hawthorne's help in writing his memoirs—and rejected Herman Melville's help.

———

Charles Lamb's sister Mary spent her adulthood at times in a straitjacket, at other times entertaining the literati. She suffered predictable psychotic attacks; during one of these attacks she slew her mother.

———

Herman Melville "caught on" as a major literary figure only long after his death in 1891. He had become so disillusioned by the commercial failure of *Moby Dick* (1851) and other novels that he gave up the pen and became a clerk—an obscure one at that—in the customhouse in New York. His *Billy Budd* wasn't even published until 1924.

———

There is an O. Henry Bar in Tegucigalpa, the capital of Honduras, where the famous American writer lived for a few months in 1897 while a fugitive from justice, under indictment for embezzling bank funds in Texas. The bar's specialty is a drink called Lost Blend, after one of O. Henry's stories.

———

The History of the Conquest of Mexico and *The History of the Conquest of Peru*—the standard authorities on the two greatest achievements of the Spanish conquistadores in the New World—were written by a blind man, William Hickling Prescott, with the aid of secretaries who read to him.

———

Johann Wolfgang von Goethe, Germany's foremost literary figure, was also a fire chief, a foreign minister, a theater director and actor, a lawyer, a painter, a mining commissioner, a notorious ladies' man, and a scientist. His discovery, in 1784, of the rudimentary inter-maxillary bone in man was important to Darwin's theory of evolution less than a century later.

"Take this script," Rudyard Kipling said to the nurse who had cared for his firstborn child, "and someday if you are in need of money you may be able to sell it at a handsome price." Years later, when the nurse was actually in want, she sold the manuscript—of the first *Jungle Book*—and lived in comfort for the rest of her life.

Maxim Gorky, labeled by the *Soviet Encyclopedia* as "the father of Soviet literature . . . the founder of the literature of Socialist Realism," wrote one of his most influential novels, the propagandistic *Mother,* while in a vacation place in the "capitalistic" Adirondacks, twelve miles from Elizabethtown, in New York State.

After reading Lord Tennyson's poetic-licensed noted line "Every moment dies a man/Every moment one is born," the accuracy-crazed Charles Babbage wrote the poet: "It must be manifest that if this were true, the population of the world would be at a standstill." Babbage's recommended change: "Every moment dies a man/Every moment 1 1/16 is born."

After the first episodes of *The Confessions of Felix Krull, Confidence Man,* the novelist Thomas Mann broke off the writing, published it as a short narrative, and did not return to the subject for thirty-two years. When he picked up exactly where he had left off, not a word was altered in the preceding fragments, and the whole, a novel, is as well balanced as all his other works.

Only seven poems by Emily Dickinson, one of America's greatest poets, were published during her lifetime. After her death in 1886, over 1,000 poems were discovered in a bureau. These were sub-sequently published, but often after word and punctuation changes by overzealous editors. A definitive edition of her works did not appear until the 1950s.

The aloof French author Michel de Montaigne (he was also a mag-istrate and was mayor of Bordeaux from 1581 to 1585) answered the rhetorical question "Would you, if you had to choose, burn your children or your books?" by declaring he would burn his children.

————

Émile Zola received a zero in French literature and failed German and rhetoric at the Lycée St. Louis.

————

A post-Civil War novel by Augusta Jane Evans, *St. Elmo,* was so popular that many towns in the U.S. were named for it—in Alabama, Tennessee, Georgia, California, Colorado, Illinois, Kentucky, Louisiana, Mississippi, Missouri, New York, Texas, and Virginia. Ms. Evans was a staunch antifeminist. In all her novels, she never was more than a hack writer. She was so shallow, moralistic, and pompous that *The New York Times* regularly poked fun at her and once published a parody of *St. Elmo,* "St. Twelmo."

————

Six popular books of science fiction for high school students published under the pseudonym Paul French were written by—Isaac Asimov. Years later they were republished under my own name.

————

Noah Webster, most famous for his dictionary, was also the first epidemiologist in the United States. Webster published a collection of papers on bilious fevers in 1796, and a two-volume work called *A Brief History of Epidemic and Pestilential Diseases,* in 1799.

————

He was a former U.S. Army general, a former U.S. President, a former alcoholic, and the first President to visit China—and now he was spending the last years of his life fighting cancer of the throat and writing his memoirs. The book, which was published by Mark Twain, was hailed as approaching Caesar's style in clarity and terseness and outshining him in modesty, and it brought wealth to the family of the author—U.S. Grant. (It brought also a lot of money to Mark Twain, who lost it in ill-judged business ventures.)

————

Herbert R. Mayes's book *Alger: A Biography Without a Hero* was assumed by critics to be the gospel truth about Horatio Alger, and it became a source book on the "rags-to-riches" novelist. A well-known publisher and writer himself, Mayes later revealed his work was intended merely to be a spoof on Alger. It was practically all fictional: "The Alger project was taken with malice aforethought."

————

John Milton wanted to reform politics with poetry. When he realized that this was impossible, he gave up his long-held dream of being a superlative poet and chose instead to devote himself almost exclusively to writing revolutionary manifestoes, in prose, which he did for more than a score of years. (After the Restoration, he returned to poetry and wrote *Paradise Lost*.)

In what has been described as "three or four bursts of puritanical zeal," Sappho's poetry was nearly destroyed in the twelfth century. The poems were very erotic and about lesbianism, and there was a reaction against their influence on young women. As it was, only two poems and a handful of fragments were known until the discovery of the Oxyrhynchus Papyri in the sands of Egypt in the Nile Valley between 1897 and 1906, which yielded about one-twentieth of what Sappho apparently had written twenty-five centuries ago.

Franz Kafka longed for and finally, in July 1908, obtained a job in a semi-government office, the Workers' Accident Insurance Institute for the province of Bohemia, in Prague. He studied the prevention of accidents and the appeals in respect of the classification of trades under the various degrees of risk. Kafka's biographer, Max Brod, believes that "whole chapters of the novels *The Trial* and *The Castle* derive their outer covers, their realistic wrappings, from the atmosphere Kafka breathed" in the institute.

While still in his mid-teens, Arthur Rimbaud revolutionized French poetry. His poems had a hallucinatory, dream-world quality. Then, at the age of nineteen, he abandoned his writing career and became a traveling salesman. (He smuggled guns into the Ethiopian jungle, and lived there with his African harem. He died at age thirty-seven, in Marseilles, following amputation of a gangrenous leg.)

After spending fruitless years looking for a story that would match his "strong sense of man's double being," Robert Louis Stevenson dreamed the plot of *Dr. Jekyll and Mr. Hyde*.

After living for seven unforgettable weeks among the stockyard workers in Chicago, Upton Sinclair published his novel *The Jungle*, in 1906, to "frighten the country by a picture of what its industrial masters were doing to their victims." (He had observed that poisoned bread and dead rats were swept together into the meat-conveyor belt and came out in sausages, and that men who fell into open vats went out into the world as Anderson's Pure Leaf Lard.) Sinclair wanted economic and social reform, and his novel indeed played a large part in bringing about a government investigation of conditions in the Chicago stockyards, and thus contributed to pure-food legislation.

Rudyard Kipling spent five of the happiest years of his life in Brattleboro, Vermont, in the 1890s. So that he could get outdoor exercise in the winter, he invented snow golf, painting his golf balls red so they could be located in the snow.

The science-fiction writer Arthur C. Clarke may have lost out on millions of dollars in royalties when he wrote an article about radio communication via a satellite in the sky before first taking out a U.S. patent.

Mark Twain secured a patent in 1873 for a self-pasting scrapbook. A series of blank pages was coated with gum.

It wasn't until the Restoration, which began nearly half a century after Shakespeare's death, that anyone began to write about the bard. Biographically, it was too late; Shakespeare's colleagues and acquaintances were dead, and the conditions under which he had worked were completely different. In addition, the world's most distinguished playwright left no words about himself.

Samuel Beckett, the playwright, was stabbed by a pimp with no specific motive and was found lying in a Paris street by the pianist Suzanne Deschevaux-Dumesnil. She visited him in the hospital, decided to live with him, and twenty-four years later they were married.

The novelist Jerzy Kosinski was flying to Los Angeles from Paris, with a short stopover in New York. All his luggage was accidentally unloaded in New York, and he had to get off the plane to go through customs. That night, because of the luggage mixup, he missed his visit with the actress Sharon Tate and other friends, and thus was not present when Charles Manson and his disciples paid their murderous visit to the Tate house.

Lord Tennyson, for several nights following the funeral of his father, slept in his father's bed. He hoped he would see his father's ghost, but "no ghost came."

Charles Dickens so completely believed in Mesmerism (a system of treatment through hypnotism) that he considered himself a doctor in the method of transferring the healing rays called "animal magnetism" from himself to sick people. Like other Mesmerisers, he never realized that his success was purely psychological.

The French novel *La Disparition* ("The Disappearance"), written in 1969, does not contain the letter *e*, which in French, as in English, is the most commonly used letter. Thirty years earlier Ernest Vincent Wright, a California musician, had written a 50,000-word novel, *Gadsby*, without using a word with the letter *e*, -ither. James Thurber wrote a story about a weird country where no one was allowed to use the letter "o."

Shakespeare probably never saw a practicing Jew. He no doubt saw Jews who had been baptized into the Christian faith to avoid persecution and expulsion. During the Middle Ages, Jews were expelled from England, and the law that kept them out had not been altered by the time the Bard created Shylock.

Because of his spindly arms and legs, the satirist Alexander Pope was described as a "crazy little carcass" of a man. To keep his miniature body erect, he wore stiff canvas. To swell his pin-sized legs to something approaching normal, he wore three pairs of stockings.

A poem became so popular that it helped to save the U.S. frigate *Constitution*—"*Old Ironsides*"—from the scrapyard in 1833. It prompted millions of school children to contribute pennies to save the ship. The twenty-one-year-old author of the poem was Oliver Wendell Holmes. The *Constitution* was made of wood. She was launched in 1797 and put to sea in 1798 in the undeclared war with France. She participated in the Tripolitan War and the War of 1812. After being rebuilt in 1833 and 1877, she was stored at the Boston Navy Yard, where she is on display.

For the first six years of his life, the greatest lyric poet of modern Germany, Rainer Maria Rilke (1875–1926), was treated by his mother like a girl; he was called "Sophie" and kept in girls' dresses. In his mother's fancy, he was replacing a sister who had died before Rainer was born. (As though to make up for these feminizing years, his father enrolled him in a military academy at the tender age of eleven.) The future U.S. General Douglas MacArthur was dressed in skirts by his mother until he was eight; and, though entirely "macho," he remained dependent on her for much of his life.

———

Ben Jonson, the brilliant English dramatist and poet (1572–1637), was working as an actor and playwright in 1598 when he killed another actor in a duel. He was tried, and successfully defended himself by claiming the right of clergy, namely, that he could read and write.

———

The spectacle of a public execution, witnessed in Paris, so horrified Leo Tolstoy that he said, "Never again under any circumstances will I take service under any form of government whatsoever."

———

The fear that he might conceal a joke in it was one reason that Benjamin Franklin was not entrusted by his peers with the assignment of writing the Declaration of Independence.

———

According to scholars, Shakespeare's last two plays, *Henry VIII* and *Two Noble Kinsmen,* were written in collaboration with John Fletcher, another English dramatist of the period.

———

Henry Wadsworth Longfellow, who introduced much foreign literature to readers in the U.S., wrote his epic poem *The Song of Hiawatha* in the meter of the Finnish epic *Kalevala* (a compilation of folk verses dealing with the deeds of three semidivine brothers of gigantic stature).

———

Sir Thomas Mallory wrote the important prose romance *Morte d'Arthur* while serving time in prison on a rape charge (around 1470).

———

At his trial in Jerusalem, Adolf Eichmann asserted that he had not read *Mein Kampf.* Neither had other big Nazis. Too boring, some of them said.

———

Not all the bad guys in Harriet Beecher Stowe's mild abolitionist tract about U.S. slavery, *Uncle Tom's Cabin,* are Southerners. The villains, in fact, are Northern renegades. Simon Legree, the wicked slave driver, was from Vermont.

———

According to those who knew them both, William Woollcott, who manufactured mucilage, had a finer wit than his famous brother,

Alexander, of "the Round Table," whose rapier pen caused many things to become unstuck.

The great French poet François Villon led a life of thievery and murder that several times could have ended on the gallows. No one knows where, or when—or how—he did die.

Edward Taylor, now generally recognized as the finest poet of colonial America, did not allow any of his poetry to be printed while he lived, and he tried to prevent his heirs from publishing his poems after his death. However, 400 manuscript pages were given by his descendants to Yale University in 1883, and finally, in 1939, 210 years after Taylor's death, a selection of his poems was published to wide critical acclaim.

The young reporter on the Seattle *Times* turned in to the city editor a story of a poor husband who had found the body of his wife in the municipal morgue. The reporter quoted the anguished cry of the husband to be, "My God, it's her!" The editor changed it to "My God, it is she!" The reporter, E. B. White, decided then and there to move on to where there was a better understanding of people and a proper feeling for the finer usages of the English tongue. White became a mess boy on a ship bound for Alaska commanded by an old whaling captain and—reported White's friend James Thurber— "manned by a crew who knew that a man says 'It's her' when he finds her dead."

He didn't care much about his studies, and indeed never finished high school. Because he spent more time reading and gossiping with friends than sticking to his job, he was not continued as the community postmaster. "I will be damned," he said after losing the job, "if I propose to be at the beck and call of every itinerant scoundrel who has two cents to invest in a postage stamp." In 1949, he was awarded the Nobel Prize for literature—William Faulkner.

The English poet Thomas Gray (1716–71) was offered the laureateship in 1757 but refused it. He spent most of his life in seclusion in Cambridge, a shy and melancholy man; peace for study and meditation were all he wanted out of life. His "Elegy Written in a Country Churchyard," finished in 1751, is probably the most quoted poem in English.

Six months after compiling and writing his monumental *Dictionary of the English Language* (1755), Samuel Johnson was arrested for debt. He owed five pounds and eighteen shillings. A gift from the successful novelist Samuel Richardson saved Johnson from Marshalsea Prison, which could have been a fate worse than death for a sick, tired man who had already suffered a nervous breakdown.

The great French satirist Voltaire contributed one enormous service to science. He had one of his mistresses write a French translation of Newton's masterpiece, *Principia Mathematica,* and then he himself wrote a commentary. The gracefulness of Voltaire's writing helped to popularize Newton's views throughout France.

"Please, God, let me be the humble poet of the American landscape," wrote William Cullen Bryant (after reading Wordsworth), and he was, writing at the age of seventeen the classic *Thanatopsis*.

Sir Walter Scott wrote prolifically and achieved fame and success. Unfortunately, he invested much of his newly gained wealth in publishing companies that failed in the depression of 1826. Scott assumed a staggering debt of £130,000. He devoted the rest of his life to writing, in order to pay off this debt. As time passed, his wife, son, and grandson died, and he had several strokes; but every last creditor was paid in full.

One of the most popular and important playwrights in the Elizabethan age was Thomas Watson. Not a single one of his dramas exists today.

A masterpiece—*The Rubáiyát of Omar Khayyám*—was published anonymously, in 1859. The poem by an eleventh-century Persian poet was paraphrased by the English dilettante and scholar Edward FitzGerald, who spent most of his life in seclusion. *The Rubáiyát* became one of the most popular English poems.

"I'm sorry, Mr. Kipling, but you just don't know how to use the English language. This isn't a kindergarten for amateur writers." And thus Rudyard Kipling—who had already written one of the best short stories in the history of literature,"The Man Who Would Be King"— was fired as a reporter by the San Francisco *Examiner*.

The author of the best-known document in the U.S., and perhaps in the world, published only one book. Thomas Jefferson's answers to a set of twenty-three questions about the American continent, circulated in 1780 by the French emissary François Marbois, appeared as *Notes on the State of Virginia*.

So sharp was Voltaire's tongue that no one is on record as having beaten him in an argument. He was imprisoned now and then in the Bastille for his lampoons and satires, and he went off for three years to England for his own well-being. When Voltaire died, on the eve of the French Revolution, which his writings had done much to bring about, the Age of Reason died with him.

The world might never have known about the adventures of Daniel Boone if Boone had not met John Filson, a schoolmaster. Boone told his stories to Filson, who wrote them down in what he pretended were Boone's own words. Filson's book was published in 1784. Within a few years, it was reprinted in London and translated into German and French. Boone became a hero to Europeans. They idealized him as a man who had turned away from civilization and found happiness in living close to nature. In America, James Fenimore Cooper later immortalized him as "Leatherstocking," the beloved hero of five frontier novels.

Because "it would be superfluous, as I have already conferred this order on myself," George Bernard Shaw rejected the offer of England's prestigious Order of Merit.

Henry Wheeler Shaw was thrown out of Hamilton College in 1833 for removing the clapper from the chapel bell. He became a drifter and jack-of-all-trades until after he was fifty years old, when he took the pen name of Josh Billings and began writing humorous pieces with deliberately bad spelling. He said, "man haz az much rite tew spell a word az it iz pronounsed as he haz tew pronounse it the way it ain't spelt." People in those days laughed themselves silly over this kind of thing, and Josh Billings became a tremendous success, leaving behind such timeless sayings as (spelling corrected): "The wheel that squeaks the loudest is the one that gets the grease."

The Swedish chemist Karl Wilhelm Scheele discovered oxygen two years before Joseph Priestley, but the latter gets the credit because his results were published at once, while Scheele's were delayed. Publish or perish, 1700s-style!

Kipling got his geography scrambled in "The Road to Mandalay." There is no bay between Burma and China. And as you go up the Irrawaddy "from Rangoon to Mandalay," the sun "comes up like thunder" out of—Thailand.

———

The New Yorker magazine receives upward of 250,000 unsolicited items every year—stories, cartoon ideas, jokes. Each is read by at least two people. Though only 110 to 120 stories are published annually (of the 15,000 manuscripts received), *The New Yorker* publishes more fiction than any other magazine in the U.S.

———

When Thomas Jefferson wrote the Declaration of Independence, the fact of his authorship was known only to the Continental Congress and a few of his friends. The identity of the writer of the most famous document of the American Revolution was not generally known until it was published in a newspaper in 1784.

———

William Shakespeare's average annual income from writing plays was less than £20—about £8 per play. (In a score of years he wrote thirty-seven plays.) Yet Shakespeare made about twice as much from playwriting as Ben Jonson, the only playwright of the period better known at that time than the Bard.

———

Walt Whitman was dismissed from his clerical post in the Indian Bureau of the Department of the Interior when the Secretary of the Interior, James Harlan, read a portion of Whitman's *Leaves of Grass* and deemed it "pernicious poetry."

———

Cotton Mather, the Puritan minister whose writings on sorcery helped set off the Salem witch hunt, was so esteemed as one of the premier scientists of the colonies that he was elected a Fellow of the Royal Society of England after he had written many books on medicine, physics, astronomy, and biology.

———

One of the most learned men of his time was the Swiss naturalist Konrad von Gesner (1516–65). He wrote the *Universal Library* in which he summarized all books known in Hebrew, Greek, and Latin. Between 1551 and 1558, he wrote exhaustive volumes designed to describe all known animals. He was still working feverishly when, in 1565, a plague struck his native town of Zurich. He served as a doctor and would not abandon his patients—and he died of the plague.

———

Mercy Otis Warren, poet, playwright, historian, and political satirist, wrote a three-volume history of the American Revolution that took nearly thirty years to complete. Her lifelong friend John Adams was offended by her portrayal of him and complained that "History is not the Province of Ladies." The breach between them lasted for seven years and was ended through a mutual exchange of locks of hair, which Abigail Adams then had made into jewelry to symbolize the renewed friendship.

———

Historians related the heart-warming story of Abdul Kassem Ismael (938–95 A.D.), the scholarly grand vizier of Persia, and his library of 117,000 volumes. On his many travels as a warrior and statesman, he never parted with his beloved books. They were carried about by 400 camels—trained to walk in a fixed order so that the books on their backs could be maintained in alphabetical order. The camel-driver librarians could put their hands instantly on any book their master asked for. Because of his friendly disposition, Abdul Kassem Ismael was nicknamed Saheb, "the pal."

———

For amusement, it was agreed by four friends holidaying in Switzerland that each would write a ghost story. Percy B. Shelley, George Byron, and Dr. John William Polidori never finished theirs. Only eighteen-year-old Mary Wollstonecraft Godwin did. She published it anonymously two years later, in 1818, with a preface by her husband, Shelley. Mary Shelley's novel about Dr. Victor Frankenstein and his monstrous creation became a classic.

———

If Marco Polo had not been captured by the Genoese and imprisoned for a year, the tales of his historic twenty-two-year adventure in the Far and Middle East (at the end of the thirteenth century) might never have been collected and written down. When he returned to Venice after his odyssey, he became a "gentleman commander" of a war vessel striving to hold off Genoese traders. In a battle off Curzold Island, his galley was captured and Marco was hauled off to Genoa and jailed. There he met a writer named Rustichello, who—hearing Marco's yarns—insisted they be written down.

———

Because the author of *Revelation of St. John* knew that he could be punished for referring in a hostile manner to the Roman Emperor, he referred to the "beast" by the number 666 rather than by his name, Nero. The number 666 has come to represent for occultists the ominous number for beasts, or demons, that need exorcising. Coincidentally, the paperback publisher of the best-selling book *The Exorcist* is situated in New York City's "666" building; its emblem—a bantam—is also coincidental; it is not meant to be the traditional sacrificial rooster to appease the gods, author whimsy aside.

After retiring in 1751 as farmer-general and as chamberlain to the queen, Claude Adrien Helvetius, the French philosopher and one of the Encyclopedists, wrote *Essays of the Mind,* holding that all men are born with equal ability and that educational influences create distinctions. "Truth is a torch," he said, "that gleams through the fog without dispelling it." Voltaire read the book and exhorted Helvetius: "[It] is dictated by the soundest reason. You had better get out of France as quickly as you can." *Essays of the Mind* was considered a godless book and was condemned by the Pope and the parlement of Paris. Helvetius's book had a great influence on Jeremy Bentham and James Mill, the philosophers.

Around 1910, future President Herbert Hoover and his wife, Lou H. Hoover, translated into English a classic of science, *De re metallica,* which in 1556 had summarized all the practical knowledge gained by the miners of Saxon. Through this book, which had excellent illustrations of mining equipment, its author, Georgius Agricola (née Georg Bauer), earned his title of father of mineralogy.

Washington Irving got his idea for Rip Van Winkle from the story of the Cretan poet and sage Epimenides, who lived around 600 B.C. While hunting for sheep at his father's behest, Epimenides lay down in a cave and took a nap—of fifty-seven years, as it turned out. On awakening, he began looking for sheep again. When he came home, he found his younger brother had become an old man.

Jean Victor Poncelet served as a lieutenant of engineers in Napoleon's army and was badly wounded and left for dead on the Russian battlefield. He somehow managed to live, was captured by the Russians, and marched through four months of winter to prison. While incarcerated for a year and a half, he meditated on geometry. His subsequent book on projective geometry is considered to be the foundation of modern geometry.

———

Though he devoted his life to collaborating with Karl Marx and to organizing revolutionary movements, the German socialist Friedrich Engels was simultaneously receiving more than adequate income from, as it was then labeled, "the sweat of the laboring classes" in the Engels family business in the English factory city of Manchester. It was not simply fortuitous that Engels's first major book was about the conditions of the working class in England.

———

Opium was so easy for schoolgirls to get during the 1880s that Jane Addams and other undergraduates at Rockford Female Seminary near Chicago imitated the *Confessions of an English Opium Eater.* All were disappointed at not seeing the weird visions of its author, Thomas De Quincey.

———

Karl Marx wrote to Friedrich Engels, "I do not trust any Russian. As soon as a Russian worms his way in, all hell breaks loose."

———

Copernicus's revolutionary book arguing that heavenly bodies move around the sun ignited the scientific revolution, but it was a financial flop. Published, finally, in 1543, it was overpriced and was allowed to go out of print. A second edition was not printed until 1566; a third, not until 1617.

———

The English poet and critic Leigh Hunt was "imprisoned," or isolated from society, for two years for referring in his journal the *Examiner,* in 1812, to the unpopular Prince Regent (later George IV) as "this Adonis in loveliness . . . a corpulent man of fifty." Hunt's health was frail, and he was confined to two rooms in the infirmary of the Surrey jail. His wife was allowed to spend most of his term there with him, and he decorated the walls of his "cells" with a trellis of roses. Other visitors were allowed as well, and Byron held a dinner party for them. Hunt continued to write and edit his journal, which was a power in its day, and for refusing to recant he came to be regarded as a martyr in the cause of liberty. If he had recanted, he would have been freed.

———

It was not until 1870, when Howard Bronson's play *Saratoga* was produced, that the United States had its first professional dramatist.

Until then, and for the next twenty years as well, no other author made his living exclusively from playwriting.

———

Lord Byron (1788–1824), the dark, handsome English romantic poet, was born with a clubfoot about which much has been written. But was it his right foot or his left? Scholars today are not sure; literature on the handicap is foggy.

———

MAN'S INHUMANITY

The Ming Emperor Hung Wu (1368—98) has been called the harshest and most unreasonable tyrant in all of Chinese history. He had so many people executed that, midway through his reign, government officials got into the custom of saying their last goodbyes to their families if they were required at a morning audience and of exchanging congratulations with fellow officials if they survived until evening.

The Metropolitan Opera House became a showplace for the finest productions during the enlightened leadership of Otto H. Kahn, the main stockholder. He was a man of superb musical taste and great wealth. He poured more than $2 million of his private fortune into the Metropolitan. Ironically, for almost fifteen years Mr. Kahn could not be a box holder in his own opera house because the Metropolitan had an anti-Semitic policy, and Mr. Kahn was a Jew. When he was at last permitted to have a box, he showed his contempt by never sitting in it. He made it available for distinguished foreign visitors.

Adolf Hitler kept a framed photograph of Henry Ford on his desk and Ford kept one of Hitler on *his* desk in Dearborn, Michigan. Hitler had used in *Mein Kampf* some of Ford's anti-Semitic views, and he always welcomed Ford's substantial contributions to the Nazi movement.

When the U.S., in 1916, protested the shipping by conquering German troops of Belgian laborers for slave labor in German factories, the German press insisted that deportation was prompted by "true humanitarianism, protecting thousands of able-bodied workmen from going to ruin by remaining unemployed."

The English promised land in the colony of Nova Scotia to former slaves who joined their side during the American Revolution. When the promise was broken, a former slave, Thomas Peters, who had been a sergeant in the British army, sailed to England and won a concession of land in Sierra Leone in West Africa, for his fellow blacks landless in Nova Scotia.

———

The first person on record to denounce slavery as an evil was Euripides. He wrote in his play *Hecuba,* "That thing of evil, by its nature evil, / Forcing submission from a man to what/ No man should yield to."

———

Because their work was so physically demanding, slave sugar-cane cutters were the South's most costly field hands. At one point, their price became so high on the New Orleans slave market that a Louisiana planter tried to hire Irish and German immigrants instead. This plan backfired when the hired workers went on a strike for double pay right in the middle of the sugar harvest.

———

The first American Jew to serve the U.S. abroad was removed from his post because he was Jewish. Mordecai Manuel Noah was a playwright, a journalist, and a lawyer, born in Philadelphia. In 1813, he was named by President James Madison to be consul to Tunis. Madison's Secretary of State, James Monroe, recalled Noah with the following dispatch: "At the time of your appointment, as Consul at Tunis, it was not known that the religion which you profess [sic] would form any obstacle to the exercise of your consular functions. Recent information, however, on which entire reliance must be placed, proves that it would produce a very unfavorable effect. In consequence of which, the President has deemed it expedient to revoke your commission." In other words, Noah was unwelcome in Tunisia.

———

The belief of the times and of Nathan Hale's family was that the twenty-one-year-old Hale (1755–76), captured on a spying mission during the American Revolution, was betrayed by his Tory cousin Samuel Hale, British Deputy Commissioner of Prisoners. British General Howe himself ordered Hale's execution without a trial. On the eve of the hanging, Hale was allowed to write letters, but they then were destroyed by the jailer, who believed "the rebels should never know they had a man who could die with so much firmness."

———

After a revolt on San Domingo, around 1820, 176 blacks taken prisoner by the French were locked up in a stockade. By the following morning, 173 had committed suicide by self-strangulation.

———

Five years after being involved in the condemning to death of nineteen persons in witchcraft cases in Salem, Massachusetts in 1692, one of the judges, Samuel Sewall, said that the convictions were a mistake. He accepted the "blame and shame" for them, and until his death in 1730 the English-born jurist annually spent a day of repentance in fasting and prayer.

———

Genius is often linked with misery. Galileo lived in exile, wandered from city to city, and ended up in prison. Descartes also lived in exile, had to serve as a soldier, and died in a foreign land. The French anatomist Andreas Vesalius lived a vagabond's life, was accused of heresy, body-snatching, and dissection, and was on the threshold of execution; he was forced to make a pilgrimage to the Holy Land, and he died in a shipwreck. Copernicus did not dare to publish his discoveries. Kepler never received the pension promised by the emperor.

———

Though only a child, Gaius Caesar, son of the famous Roman general Germanicus (15 B.C.–19 A.D.) and his wife, Agrippina, traveled with his parents among the legions of Rome, and was wildly popular. The soldiers nicknamed him Caligula, or "Little Boots," and the sobriquet stuck with him right through the last unbalanced years of his sordid life. Caligula (12–41 A.D.) became Emperor of Rome (37–41 A.D.) and earned a reputation for ruthless cruelty, torture, and execution. He became so hated that he was assassinated by one of his own guards.

———

The French army, unable to defend France against the Prussian invaders in 1871, contented itself with shooting down Parisians in the Commune of Paris, set up at the end of the war in opposition to the government of Adolphe Thiers at Versailles. More than 17,000 people, including women and children, were executed when the army entered Paris after the leftist extremist leadership of the Commune had shot hostages (including the archbishop of Paris) and burned the Tuileries, city hall, and palace of justice.

———

Hypatia, a soaring figure of beauty, eloquence, and learning (around 400 A.D.), was the last recorded member of the great museum of

Alexandria and the only noted woman scholar of ancient times. She taught Neoplatonism and helped to demonstrate Euclid's ideas. She was a pagan. Although Christian bishops were among her pupils, she was the subject of violent antagonism on the part of zealots. She was murdered by rioting fanatic monks, who brutally sliced her body to pieces with oyster shells gathered from the blue Alexandrian harbor.

Major General Curtis LeMay, commander of the U.S. B-29 force in the Marianas during World War II, advised Washington that a forthcoming raid on Tokyo would be "an outstanding show." It was. A one-night firebomb attack in March 1945 leveled densely populated poor sections of the city, and—according to officials and students of the available records—killed (roasting many in their beds) more people than did the U.S. atomic raid on Hiroshima five months later. The Hiroshima toll was about 80,000 people. The historian Lewis Mumford has estimated the Tokyo toll as being upward of 180,000.

From the beginning, the Puritan colonists engaged in the slave trade, first selling captive Indians to the West Indies and then bringing in Negroes from Africa. Cotton Mather, pastor of Boston's North Church, owned both Indian and Negro slaves. In 1641, pious Samuel Maverick proposed the breeding of Negro slaves on Noddles Island, now East Boston.

Jean Marie Collot d'Herbois (1750–96), who was not much of an actor, was booed when performing in Lyons, France. He had his revenge. He returned to Lyons as a powerful judge—appointed by his co-revolutionist Robespierre—and ordered the death of 6,000 citizens.

Governor Willem Kieft of New Netherland in the American colonies is usually given credit for the idea in the 1630s of paying money for proof of killed Indians. The proof: the scalp. The idea caught on. In 1703, the Massachusetts colony offered about $60 a scalp, and Pennsylvania in the mid-1700s offered a bounty of about $134 for the scalp of a male Indian and about $50 for the scalp of a female.

In the "civilized West" a human being has been killed by others every twenty seconds in the last half-century, illegally or legally. This is three times the rate of the century preceding these fifty years.

It has been estimated that the Spaniards killed off 1.5 million Indians within a few years after Columbus had discovered the New World.

———

The total loss in human lives during World War II exceeds anything in the history of wars—55 million to 60 million dead. Over a third of this number were Russians: 10 percent of the Russian population. Between 18 million and 26 million civilians and prisoners were killed in Nazi camps. (The total number of people killed in World War I— terrible as that war was—was not more than about 10 million.)

———

During a reign of persecution in Germany from the thirteenth century to the eighteenth century, at least 100,000 suspected witches were brought to trial and killed. During the reign of Henry III, in the late sixteenth century, over 30,000 executions took place in France, though the Inquisition was waning. The year 1775 marked the last year in which an accused witch suffered the death penalty in Europe.

———

Human beings have been exterminating animals at the average rate of one species a year for the last two centuries. That rate appears to be on the increase, despite the raising of ecological awareness that began in the 1960s.

———

In 1209, in the bloody Crusade against the Albigenses, a French army took the town of Beziers, near the Mediterranean coast. The town was put to the sack, but the question arose as to how to tell which of the town's inhabitants were damned heretics and which were good Christians. Simon IV de Montfort (or perhaps a legate of Pope Innocent III) said he had an easy solution. "Kill them all," he said, "for the Lord will know his own." And so several tens of thousands of men, women, and children were killed.

———

The Ch'in Dynasty (221–207 B.C.) buried alive many scholars in its program to suppress learning and Confucianism.

———

Forty million Americans are murdered, maimed, raped, mugged, or robbed every year.

———

After the bloody victory over the Pequot Indians, in 1637, the Puritans enslaved the surviving women and children and sold some of the male Pequots to Puritans in Bermuda.

———

A skin disease became a capital crime under the rule of France's King Philip V, around 1320, when he accused a particularly helpless minority, the lepers, of conspiring against the government. He put many to death.

————

Thousands of people poured by excursion trains into Palmetto, Georgia, in 1899, to witness a lynching. Slices of the victim's heart were sold as souvenirs.

————

In 1555, Ivan the Terrible ordered the construction of St. Basil's Church in Moscow. He was so pleased with this piece of work by the two architects, Postnik and Barma, that he had them blinded so they would never be able to design anything more beautiful.

————

Vigilantes on the Barbary Coast, around San Francisco, committed at least 7,300 murders—an average of one a night—in a reign of terror between 1860 and 1880.

————

When Thomas Jefferson became President, in 1801, 20 percent of the people in the U.S. were slaves. (There were 5 million people in all.)

————

Three million Russians are estimated to have died in more than a hundred gold-mining labor camps in Arctic Siberia. The camps are considered the very worst component of the entire Soviet concentration-camp system.

————

Christopher Columbus told his Spanish patrons, the king and queen, that the pagan Indians he had met readily embraced Christianity . . . "they are always smiling . . . [their] speech is the sweetest and gentlest in the world . . . they are a loving people, without covetousness . . . weapons they have none . . . it appears that the people are ingenuous and would be good servants."

————

The good people of Salem, Massachusetts, in the late 1600s, tried 150 "witches and wizards."

————

Since records have been kept, upwards of 60 million harp seals have been killed in the Newfoundland herd alone, in the most protracted mass slaughter inflicted by man upon any wild mammal species.

————

"Godfrey's cordial" was a potion that some poor families in England in the nineteenth century mixed to give their children. It was a compound of opium, treacle, and sassafras, originally invented as a medicine; but an overdose was fatal. Parents found that it brought a quick, painless death to unwanted children for whom there was neither space nor food.

Queen Supayalat of Burma was responsible for one of the most atrocious mass murders of the nineteenth century. She ordered a three-day binge at the palace with loud music to cover the work of her executioners, who clubbed to death about a hundred relatives of her husband, King Thibaw. Supayalat's motive was to ensure the throne to her husband, but she did just the opposite, because the British in Burma forced the royal criminals into exile. They are the Thibaw and Supayalat of Kipling's "The Road to Mandalay."

The murder rate in the United States is 200 times greater than in Japan, where no private citizen can buy a handgun legally. In the U.S., which has the world's highest death rate per capita from firearms, a new gun is sold every 13.5 seconds. The extraordinary truth is that almost twice as many Americans were killed on the "home-front" by firearms in the Vietnam war decade of 1963–73 than were killed in Southeast Asia. The figures, respectively, were 84,633 and 46,752.

Basil II of Constantinople in 1014 decided to end once and for all a war that had already lasted forty years. To break the spirit of the hated Bulgarians, he blinded all but 150 of 15,000 prisoners. The "lucky" 150 were blinded in one eye only. Every 100 blind men were guided by a one-eyed leader back to the Bulgarian capital of Ohrid, whose ruler, Samuel, had received word that his army was returning to him. Samuel hastened to meet his men—and found himself staring at thousands of helpless blind men. The sight was fatal. Samuel suffered a stroke on the spot, and died two days later. (Basil II received the surname Bulgaroktonos, meaning "slayer of Bulgarians.")

Charles Richard Drew (1904–50), a pioneer in blood-plasma research, became the first medical director of the American Red Cross blood program. He resigned in protest soon after, when the Armed Forces, yielding to public prejudice, required that blood donations be segregated by race. He was black, and his own donation could have been refused outright or used only to treat black servicemen.

————

During the hundred days of the opening games at the Colosseum in Rome, in 80 A.D., more than 5,000 animals were killed. They included elephants, tigers, lions, elks, hyenas, hippopotamuses, and giraffes.

————

Until recent centuries, imprisonment was not a common punishment. A person was fined or maimed or killed. If he lacked the money to pay a fine, chopping off a hand (of a thief, for example) or a foot and execution were the easiest ways out, especially because little value was placed on poor people then. Mutilation as punishment may seem sadistic and barbaric to us, but in the Middle Ages it was intended as a merciful substitution for execution. Today's substitute is imprisonment, though mutilation, rather than imprisonment, exists in some countries, including Saudi Arabia.

————

Captain Henry Wirz was the only person tried for war crimes after the U.S. Civil War. He was the commander of Andersonville Prison, in Georgia, from March 1864 to April 1865. During his year in charge, more than 13,700 men died at Andersonville. At one time, as many as 33,000 Union men were packed into the prison. Captain Wirz was found guilty, and hanged on November 10, 1865.

————

"To prevent violence," it was at one time customary at certain phases of the moon to chain and flog inmates of England's notorious Bedlam Hospital.

————

Castration does not affect human intelligence. Because a eunuch does not have wives and children to distract him as they might a normal man, he is free to concentrate his intelligence on service to the state. So heavily did Byzantine emperors favor the employment of eunuchs as court officials that men of good family sometimes deliberately had one or more of their sons castrated in order to assure them some good governmental position in the future. The procedure was practiced in Constantinople from the sixth to the eleventh centuries.

————

The Order of the Holy Spirit, formed about 1160 by Guy of Montpellier, specialized in the care of abandoned infants. The order gained the support of the Pope, who was sickened by the great number of dead babies cast into the Tiber River in Rome.

———

In 1973, Detroit had 751 homicides. Northern Ireland, with about an equal population and a hit-and-run war going on between the Irish Republican Army and its adversaries, recorded only 250 homicides. By 1977, the ratio had increased from three to one to almost five to one.

———

Half a billion people—about one of every eight—are suffering chronic malnutrition today.

———

A study of seventy-two factories in Russia in 1881 revealed that some workers were on eighteen-to-twenty-hour shifts and that they often lost most of their wages in fines levied by employers.

———

Knowing nothing of the germ theory or of the danger of fleas, and unable to keep clean in a culture that was already suspicious of cleanliness—considering it unholy—people suffering from the plague of Black Death could do nothing useful. They could, however, find a scapegoat, and for that there were always Jews available. The theory arose that Jews had deliberately poisoned wells in order to destroy Christians. The fact that Jews were dying of the plague on equal terms with Christians was not allowed to interfere with the theory, and Jews were slaughtered without mercy. This did nothing at all, of course, to diminish the scourge.

———

King Henry VIII allowed Sir Thomas More and Anne Boleyn to choose how they would die. The official punishment for treason—the charge against Sir Thomas—was hanging, drawing, and quartering; Sir Thomas chose to be beheaded. Henry's second wife—and the first of two of his wives to be executed— was allowed to be decapitated by a swordsman, specially brought from France, instead of being burned to death.

———

The abolitionist William Lloyd Garrison was collared with a rope and dragged down Court Street in Boston. A spectator, Wendell Phillips, was so appalled by the incident that he converted to abolitionism and became the cause's principal activist.

———

Pope Innocent VIII (1432–92) received a gift of a hundred Moorish slaves, whom he distributed as a gratuity to cardinals and friends.

———

Hernando Cortez, Spanish conqueror of Mexico, introduced branding to North America. He marked his cattle and horses with three crosses. The practice spread throughout the fenceless West, where cattle roamed free.

———

As a follower of the red-shirted revolutionary Giuseppe Garibaldi, Claudio Toscanini, the father to be of Arturo Toscanini, was sentenced with others to be shot. One by one his comrades were placed against a wall and executed. It was then his turn. He was placed against the wall. He was teased. He was taunted. He was finally reprieved, and sentenced to three years' imprisonment.

———

MEDICINE

There is one phobia that is mainly a physical disease and not merely a state of mind. A person who has suffered a certain virus infection that attacks the nervous system cannot swallow. The sight or the sound of water or the attempt to swallow water throws this unfortunate person into a convulsion. The ancient Greeks considered this kind of convulsion to have resulted from a morbid fear of water, and they called the disease hydrophobia—from *hydor*, "water."

———

Ketchup once was sold as a patent medicine. In the 1830s it enjoyed a measure of popularity in the United States as Dr. Miles's Compound Extract of Tomato.

———

Bees have been known to cure rheumatism. A number of sufferers have been given relief through controlled stinging. Several bees are placed in an inverted glass over the aching limbs; they soon sting, irritated by their captivity.

———

The first contraceptive diaphragms—centuries ago—were citrus rinds—half an orange rind, for example.

———

Male embryos, fetuses, and babies have a higher incidence of morbidity than females. Correspondingly, there is a higher rate of language disability among boys than girls.

———

The first successful corneal transplant was performed as early as 1835 by a British army surgeon in India. His pet antelope had only one eye, and it had a badly scarred cornea. He removed a cornea from a newly killed antelope and transplanted it into his pet's eye. The operation was successful, and the pet was able to see.

———

Among twenty-eight major developed nations, the United States ranks twenty-sixth in the percentage of its newborns who are not expected to reach the age of sixty-five. If early death rates for whites only are considered, however, the U.S. moves up to nineteenth place, on a level with Austria and Ireland.

The English physician Edward Jenner, who perfected vaccination in 1798 and conquered the dread disease smallpox, was proposed for election to the College of Physicians in London in 1813. The college wanted to test him in the outdated and useless classics of the ancient medical writers. Jenner refused, being of the opinion that his victory over smallpox was qualification enough. The gentlemen of the college did not agree and Jenner was not elected.

The United States gained control of the Panama Canal because it learned to eradicate a disease. During the construction of the canal, yellow fever was so prevalent that the French builders were forced to offer extremely high wages to induce men to work there. After spending $260 million and losing over 20,000 lives, the French gave up the job in 1904 and turned it over to Americans. The U.S. Army physician in charge, William Crawford Gorgas, learning that the disease was passed on by mosquitoes, was able to eradicate yellow fever in Panama within a year.

Some 2 million persons who enter hospitals in the U.S. each year with one ailment wind up with another. Hospital-related infections are fatal to about 15,000 Americans every year.

There are some 1,400 known kinds of birth defects, but many are so rare that a physician may not see even one of the more unusual in his entire career. A worldwide computer system is now available to provide diagnostic information.

Rattlesnake venom was a popular treatment for epilepsy early in the twentieth century. After hearing about an epileptic who was free of seizures for two years after being bitten by a snake, some doctors hastened to treat their epileptic patients with this venom. Some reported they were successful, but most determined the venom to be valueless. Its use was almost completely abandoned by 1930.

Oliver Wendell Holmes, the philosopher and literary figure, was equally famous as a medical doctor. A professor of anatomy at Harvard, he was noted for introducing into the United States the concept of antiseptic treatment of women during childbirth. By disseminating the information that doctors themselves were responsible for the spread of puerperal (or childbed) fever—and that it could be prevented by the simple expedient of washing hands before delivering a baby—Holmes greatly reduced the death rate among new mothers.

———

Reserpine, a drug widely used since the 1950s to reduce high blood pressure, is actually not new. As one of the most active components of the tropical rauwolfia plant, it has been used for centuries in Africa and India as a cure for mental illness.

———

The Egyptian mummy was a standard drug of European pharmacology until the eighteenth century. Despite criticism within the medical profession, doctors prescribed mummy powder as a cure for internal ailments. Portions of many embalmed Egyptian dead were swallowed before science and common sense rendered the practice obsolete.

———

Before Sigmund Freud (1856–1939) turned to psychoanalysis, he did important work on neurology and was the first to work on the use of cocaine as a local anesthetic. His use of cocaine for minor pains and his high praise for its efficacy led to a wave of cocaine addiction in Europe before the fact that it was addictive became known.

———

The Fourth Lateran Council, in 1215, forbade clerks in holy orders to include surgery in their practice of medicine so they would not spill blood. Surgery was left to men who were neither scholars nor gentlemen. A distinction grew between physicians, who were members of a learned profession, and surgeons, who practiced a menial trade, often doubling as barbers or dentists.

———

Not all scientific discoveries are made in a scientist's flowering youth. The American botanist Benjamin Minge Duggar reached the climax of his life's work when, in 1948, he discovered and introduced the use of the broad-spectrum tetracycline antibiotics—at the age of seventy-six.

———

Victims of disease—people and animals—are buried underground, and yet the soil remains fairly free of disease germs. Germs are destroyed by the bacteria and other microscopic organisms living in the soil.

———

A very small virus, such as the hoof-and-mouth disease virus, contains only about 70,000 atoms, not more than 1/90,000 of the number of atoms in a single human cell. Yet the virus is as alive as we are.

———

Dr. Rene Läennec (1781–1826) rolled a sheet of paper into a tube and placed one end on the chest of a plump female patient whose heart he couldn't listen to by ear in the usual fashion. He listened at the other end of the roll. This workable "stethoscope" was the inspiration for Läennec's invention of the stethoscope while he was with Necker Hospital in Paris.

———

For every ounce of alcohol you drink, it takes an hour to regain full driving faculties, that is, normal, alert, clear-headed reactions. If you have five ounces of alcohol around 8 P.M., you should not drive until at least 1 A.M. the following day.

———

At least one "old wives' tale" was correct. The English physician Edward Jenner established the successful technique of vaccination against smallpox in 1796 when he was guided by the tale that the mild disease of cowpox conferred immunity upon humans.

———

One group of people, and only one, has been found to be totally free of cancer in any of its forms. They are the Hunza in northwest Kashmir, who also are known for their longevity.

———

Included in the good that came out of the violent French Revolution has to be the work with the insane of the French physician Philippe Pinel. Placed in charge of an insane asylum by the revolutionary government ruling France in 1793, Pinel decided it was time for upsetting encrusted tradition there as well. Until Pinel, hospitals for the insane were "snake pits," and the only remedy prescribed for the howling, demented "loonies" was to place them in chains. Pinel advocated considering the inmates as people sick in mind, to be treated with the same consideration as the sick in body, and he struck off the chains. He adopted systematic studies, keeping well-documented case histories of mental ailments.

———

A kidney-transplant surgeon, Dr. James Cerilli, of Ohio State University, cited the motion picture *Coma*, which is about the murder of hospital patients so that their near-priceless organs can be sold, as being at least partially responsible for the sudden and precipitous drop in the donation of organs for transplant. Cities throughout the country reported up to a 60 percent decrease in the number of organs donated in 1978 as compared with the 1977 total B.C.—before *Coma*. "It is not unreasonable to consider the movie a cause," Dr. Cerilli said, "because there is no rational reason for the drop."

Louis Tomkins Wright became the first black doctor to be appointed to the surgical staff of Harlem Hospital in New York, in 1920. While most of the patients were black, the entire medical and nursing staff had been white. Wright later became director of the hospital's department of surgery and president of its medical board. The first black elected to the American College of Surgeons, he developed ingenious orthopedic braces, pioneered in treating skull fractures, and supervised the first use of Aureomycin on human patients.

Not until 1779 and the experiments of the priest-biologist Lazzaro Spallanzani was it shown that semen is necessary for fertilization. Six years later, Spallanzani carried through the artificial insemination of a dog.

Dissections of humans used to be considered cruel, immoral, and sacrilegious, though they fostered the study of anatomy. The first authorized public dissection was in 1375, in Montpellier, France. Authorization was rescinded immediately afterward for reasons of obscenity. Twenty or so years later, one dissection a year was allowed at the University of Bologna. It took the form of a three-day ceremony prior to each Christmas and included a procession and exorcisms.

A man, blind since birth, has been able to "see" with the aid of a miniature TV camera attached to a waistband. The camera transmits images to the man's stomach nerves, which pass the images on to the brain.

The Chinese physician Hua T'o, born sometime between 140 and 150 A.D., was the first doctor known to perform surgery under general anesthetic. The potion used to render his patients unconscious was a mixture of hemp and strong wine called *ma fei san*. Prior to the communist revolution, a national holiday commemorated his birth.

Sigmund Freud turned down a $10,000 fee in 1920 to spend six months in New York treating patients in the morning and lecturing in the afternoon. He had calculated that he would return to Vienna poorer than when he started. So much for medicine!

———

The Reverend Cotton Mather, the Puritan minister, was the first person in North America to advocate the use of variolation (a precursor of inoculation) in the treatment of smallpox. In 1721, he had it applied to a son and several servants, which caused only a mild form of the disease. This breakthrough was the beginning of the eventually successful fight against the disease in America.

———

Opium frequently was used as a painkiller by army doctors during the U.S. Civil War. By the end of the war, according to conservative estimates, 100,000 soldiers were addicted to opium—at a time when the total population of the country was only 40 million. Today in the U.S. there are an estimated 300,000 drug addicts.

———

Penicillin, the first antibiotic, was discovered in 1928 by accident. A shallow glass dish for bacteriological experiments was left uncovered unintentionally by Alexander Fleming in his laboratory in England. An experimenter upstairs was careless with the mold he was using and some drifted in through an open window and landed in Fleming's uncovered staphylococci culture. The following day, the Scottish bacteriologist found in the dish a clear area where the penicillin in the mold had been killing the bacteria.

———

Russia was so thankful for Edward Jenner's discovery of immunization for smallpox in 1796 that the first child to be vaccinated there was named Vaccinov and educated at the expense of the nation.

———

The liquid inside young coconuts can be used as a substitute for blood plasma in an emergency. This property was discovered during World War II. Doctors in Fiji also discovered that surgical incisions heal faster when sewn with sterilized coconut fiber rather than catgut.

———

Florence Nightingale served only two years of her life nursing soldiers. She was so weakened by a fever contracted during her service in the Crimean War that she spent the last fifty years of her life as an invalid.

———

Influenza was so named because the cause of the disease was supposedly the evil "influence" of the stars. This "influence" was believed also to be the cause of plagues and pestilences.

———

Tobacco was once considered a cure for many ailments, including headache, toothache, arthritis, stomach aches, wounds, and bad breath. It was made into a tea and even rolled into pills in order to serve as a medicinal herb. A Spanish doctor, Nicolás Monardes, first described its medicinal potential in a 1577 book called *Joyful News out of the New Found World,* and his views were accepted for more than two centuries.

———

John Locke's political philosophy influenced the emerging American government in many positive ways. He held the doctrine that revolution in some circumstances is not only a right but an obligation, and his policy of checks and balances is followed in the American Constitution. His medical advice was something else again. His *Thoughts on Education,* published in England in 1690, was widely applied by colonial mothers, with disastrous effects on many children. He recommended icy baths for infants and young children (at a time when adults would wash no more than their hands and face for fear of endangering their health) and shoes with thin soles so water could leak in. He cautioned against feeding children meat and fruit, and recommended drinking warm beer instead of water (which was, in fact, often unhealthy).

———

When Galileo was a professor at the University of Padua, the student body included William Harvey, who, after getting his M.D. there in 1602, went on to be the founder of modern physiology. It was Harvey who first demonstrated the function of the heart and the complete circulation of the blood.

———

Though he specialized in hygiene and was one of the first to emphasize the subject as a matter of good health rather than of good manners, the German chemist Max Joseph von Pettenkofer disdained the germ theory of disease. He said he'd show them, and miraculously did—he deliberately swallowed a virulent culture of cholera bacteria. That he did not get the disease remains, a century later, a source of amazement.

———

Not only animals and plants are in a process of evolution. Germs are as well. Diphtheria, for example, had been a mild disease before 1735, when it suddenly assumed a fatal form in an outbreak in Kingston, N.H. Not a single one of the first forty victims recovered.

———

Standard treatment for the plague, in the seventeenth century, was to place upon the carbuncles a live pullet (from which the tail feathers had been plucked), thereby drawing out the venom. When the bird became infected and died, another replaced it. The treatment was repeated until the last bird escaped contagion, at which time it was thought the patient would recover. First introduced in 1603, the live-pullet treatment was still standard in England's great plague of 1665.

In England, from about the fifteenth to the seventeenth centuries, the color red was thought to be helpful to the sick. To bring down the fever, patients were dressed in red nightgowns and surrounded by as many red objects as possible.

In 1777, George Washington had the entire Continental army—then 4,000 men—vaccinated. This action, considered controversial at the time because few American doctors believed in vaccination, may have saved the army as a fighting force.

Abu-Bakr Muhammed ibn-Zakariya al-Razi (ca. 850–ca. 925 A.D.), better known in history as Rhazes, was a famous Arabian doctor. He was a practical man. When he moved to Baghdad, his first job was to pick the most appropriate site for a new hospital; he accomplished this by hanging pieces of meat at various points throughout the city and then choosing the place where the piece of meat was the last one to turn rotten. His encyclopedic works influenced the study of medicine throughout the Middle Ages. He is credited with being the first physician to distinguish between measles and smallpox.

During the Franco-Prussian War (1870–71), vaccination was compulsory in the Prussian army and only 297 died of smallpox; in the French army, where vaccination was not compulsory, 23,400 died of smallpox.

When a comet appeared over Russia in 1664 and the Czar inquired what it portended, he was told there would be a plague in autumn, but one less dangerous to Russia than to other countries. The Czar proceeded to set up a sanitary cordon at his borders and banned foreign—especially English—ships from Russian ports. While this story may be apocryphal, it is interesting to note that Russia escaped the plague at that time.

Every college student knows that the Russian physiologist Ivan Petrovich Pavlov was the first to establish the existence of the conditioned reflex. In 1904, he got the Nobel Prize for physiology or medicine, but it was *not* for the conditioned reflex. It was for earlier work he had done on the autonomic nervous system, which turned out to be not very useful after all.

The technique of diagnosing illness by taking the pulse of an individual was developed in China tens of centuries ago. Fifty-one different types of pulse beats were said to be identified at eleven different locations on the body. Each pulse was linked with a different health problem.

Of the world's 2.5 million physicians, 500,000—or one in five—are Russians.

To convince the community how gravely sick he is, a person among the Gnau of New Guinea will separate himself from everyone else, cover himself with dirt and ashes, take off all of his clothes, refrain from conversation, and do without most food.

The British naval commander Viscount Horatio Nelson never overcame seasickness. (No matter how frequently they are exposed to the motion stimulus, 5 percent of individuals never seem to acquire immunity to seasickness.)

When Columbus returned to Europe, he brought with him not only news of a new world, but a new plague as well. His sailors carried a virulent, deadly variety of syphilis that caused the Barcelona epidemic of 1493, and proceeded to ravage most of Europe.

In the early eighteenth century, there were American slaves who were physicians. They treated not only other slaves and free blacks but whites as well, until restricted by law to serving the black community.

David ———— (his last name has never been publicly revealed) has lived all of his life in a sterile environment. He suffers the rare disease known as severe combined immune deficiency, and his body is unable to fight off even the most common germs. (By living in a germfree life-support system, which is enclosed in a see-through plastic bubble, he has never experienced a sick day, except for his disease, for which doctors say there is still no treatment.) On his seventh birthday, in 1978, he wasn't able to blow out the candles on his cake—they weren't allowed in the bubble, so he was only able to see them. About a hundred people are known to have been born with this blood disorder, and David is the oldest of five survivors. David lives with his family in Houston, and walks out of doors wearing an astronaut's suit with a plastic-bubble helmet.

————

A decade passed between the discovery of penicillin by Alexander Fleming and the development of a purification technique by two British medical researchers that took the "miracle drug" off the shelf and placed it into medical practice, in time for use during World War II. Fleming and the two researchers—Ernst Chain and Howard Florey—shared a Nobel Prize.

————

With the fall of Rome in the fifth century A.D., medical teaching ceased to exist in Europe. However, the Arabs collected, studied, and translated many Greek manuscripts on science and medicine, preserving them for future generations and making useful comments and additions.

————

In 1977, less than 9 percent of physicians in the U.S. were women.

————

Before there was real anesthesia, surgery was as painful as any deliberate torture. Anesthesia was formularized in the mid-1800s. In England, Sir Humphry Davy had investigated the anesthetic properties of laughing gas (nitrous oxide) during the years 1798–1801. Horace Wells, an American dentist, was the first to use laughing gas as an anesthetic in the U.S. (1844).

————

Electrical stimulation of certain areas of the brain can revive long-lost memories.

————

Nearly a century before Edward Jenner in 1796 perfected the vaccination for smallpox, variolation was introduced in England. It deliberately caused a mild case of the disease, which created immunity in the patient. For many years before that time, deliberate infection with material saved from previous mild epidemics had been practiced by the Chinese and the Arabs.

————

Curare, the arrow poison of South American Indians, was once essential to surgeons performing abdominal operations because it was the only drug that could be used as a muscle relaxant. The patient's muscles became much too stiff for safety during the operation, and curare was used to relax them.

————

The ancient world's foremost expert on female complaints, childbirth, and child care was Soranus of Ephesus, who practiced medicine in Alexandria and Rome in the second century A.D. Breastfeeding, Soranus said, was not to begin until the third day; a baby should first be fed on diluted and boiled honey. He showed, too, how a baby should be bathed and dressed, and advised on weaning, teething, and teaching. His writings dominated medical opinion in these fields for almost 1,500 years.

Cataract operations on the eye were performed in India as early as 1000 B.C. In Babylonia at about the same time, the fees of eye surgeons were rigidly fixed by law and were quite generous. A successful operation on a rich freeman cost ten shekels of silver. The same operation on a slave was priced at two shekels. However, the life of the surgeon, though profitable, had its hazards. If the wealthy freeman lost the sight of his eye in the operation, one of the surgeon's hands was cut off. If the slave was blinded, the doctor had to replace him.

Nineteenth-century French agricultural chemist Jean Baptiste Boussingault was correct in theorizing that iodine compounds could be the cure for goiter—but this insight was ignored for over half a century.

The sugar from the urine of a diabetic is identical with grape sugar. Discovery of this fact by the French chemist Michel Eugene Chevreul, in 1815, was the first step in the direction of recognizing diabetes as a disease of sugar metabolism.

Many diseases seem to occur with disproportionate frequency in certain ethnic groups. For example, 43 percent of the persons suffering from Gilles de la Tourette syndrome are Ashkenazi Jews of Eastern European origin. The disease is marked by multiple tics, involuntary movements, and coprolalia, which is an uncontrollable impulse to be foul-mouthed. Sickle-cell anemia is a disease that occurs mainly among blacks.

In the fourteenth and fifteenth centuries, ritualized responses to the plague began to emerge in some societies. In Germany, the Flagellants arose. They attempted to appease the wrath of God by beating one another and themselves profusely.

Monkeys' heads have been successfully transplanted by Dr. Robert J. White, of Case Western Reserve University in Cleveland, Ohio.

———

The first civil malpractice action on record was brought before an English court over six centuries ago. The plaintiff alleged his hand had been maimed by inept treatment, and he sought redress from the accused practitioner. But medieval doctors were organized in "guilds" to safeguard against such threats and to ensure that the fee-for-service principle would be protected from any old-fashioned idealists who might be taking the Hippocratic Oath too literally.

———

Plague is still prevalent in many parts of Asia. In untreated cases, the mortality rate is as high as 90 percent. Modern drugs have reduced it to 5 percent.

———

Mary Mallon, better known as Typhoid Mary, was linked to at least seven typhoid epidemics in New York. When she was finally tracked down by a sanitary engineer, she refused medical help. She was taken into custody in 1907, and released three years later on the condition that she would stop working with food and cooking. But Mary was taken into custody again after an outbreak of typhoid in 1915 at a hospital where she had worked. This time, she was apprehended while preparing gelatin for a friend. She was quarantined by health authorities for twenty-three years, until her death in 1938.

———

According to Herodotus, the Babylonians had few doctors because they left illness to the wisdom of the public. A sick individual was placed in the city square, where passersby who had suffered from the same ailment, or had seen it treated, gave him advice on how to be cured. Pedestrians were forbidden to pass such an individual without inquiring about the complaint and "prescribing" for it if they could.

———

Approximately 3,500 men were practicing medicine at the time of the American Revolution. Only about 400 had a medical degree. Of the much larger number of women who practiced, even a smaller number had had formal training.

———

The use of antibiotics did not begin in this century; early folk medicine included the use of moldy foods or soil for infections. In ancient Egypt, for example, infections were treated with moldy bread.

———

Egypt in the fifth century B.C., according to Herodotus, swarmed with doctors because medicine was in the hands of specialists, each of whom treated a particular part of the body. There were experts in diseases of the eye, the brain, the heart, and so on, but no general practitioners.

———

At the turn of the century, American periodicals carried advertisements for anti-cancer cigar holders and for cures for opium and morphine addiction. Cures, "perfectly safe and reliable," were even offered through the annual catalog of the self-described "cheapest supply house on Earth," Sears, Roebuck. The anti-cancer cigar holder was billed as "the first truly scientific pipe offered to the world," with an offer of $1,000 for "evidence of a tongue burnt by properly smoking a perfect genuine anti-cancer."

———

A study of the common cold, made by two epidemiologists at the University of Michigan, disclosed that the incidence of colds was greater among the better-educated.

———

Dr. Samuel A. Mudd, sentenced to life in prison for splinting the fractured leg of Lincoln's assassin, John Wilkes Booth, became a hero to guards and inmates of his island prison when he stopped a yellow-fever epidemic there, in 1868, after the army doctors had died. President Johnson, Lincoln's successor, pardoned Mudd in early 1869.

———

The bubonic plague that swept through much of the civilized world from 542 to 543 A.D. was reported by a witness, the historian Procopius, to have killed up to 10,000 people a day in Byzantium alone at the height of its virulence. Emperor Justinian caught the disease, but recovered.

———

Lady Mary Wortley Montagu, an Englishwoman, was the wife of an ambassador in Turkey in the early part of the eighteenth century. She contracted smallpox that marred her face, a terrible fate for a lady involved in high society and fashion. As a result of this, she became interested in how the Turks dealt with smallpox. When she found that they inoculated, she proceeded to write a letter to London, in 1721, describing the method. Inoculations against smallpox began to be used in London. In 1798, vaccination, which involved inoculation with the far less dangerous cowpox, was introduced.

———

At the end of the nineteenth century, 50 percent of the hospitalized cases in England died of infections caught in the hospital. Mortality in hospitals was higher than outside because elementary sanitary precautions were ignored.

From 1940 through 1976, 985 new drugs were introduced into U.S. medical practice. Of these, the United States originated 630, or 64 percent of the total, while Switzerland, ranking second, accounted for 7 percent.

Bleeding, usually by the application of leeches, was once so common in medicine that "leech" came to mean physician. George Washington was one of many who died as a result of the pernicious practice.

The South Carolina legislature in 1750 ordered published the medical treatments used by a slave known as Caesar. It also ordered Caesar freed because his cures were thought to be beneficial.

About eight ounces of lamb's blood were injected into the veins of a dying boy, temporarily restoring him, in the first blood transfusion on record. It was performed in 1667 by Jean Baptiste Denis, physician to Louis XIV of France.

A cholera epidemic forced a twenty-day quarantine of New York City in 1892. Sixty years earlier, 2,251 people had died there from that disease. During a twelve-day period in that same year, 1832, more than 6,000 died from cholera in New Orleans. A year after the Civil War, about 200 people died every day at the height of a cholera epidemic in St. Louis.

In 1971, in English mental asylums there was a ratio of thirty-five women to one man. In prisons in England, however, this ratio was the reverse.

Marie Curie, co-discoverer of radium, was the first person known to have died of radiation poisoning. Until her longtime ailment was determined to have been caused by the destruction of her bone marrow, it was not known that radiation was dangerous.

There is a disease—progeria—that causes the entire life cycle of the victim to be compressed into a few tragic years. The person may look, act, and feel like a very old person by the time he is seven or eight, and he dies of "old age" at eleven or twelve.

———

Abraham Lincoln probably had Marfan's syndrome, a hereditary disease of the connective tissue. The disease was first described more than thirty years after Lincoln's death, but it was not linked with the President until 1959, when a doctor in California discovered the disorder in a child who shared an ancestor with Lincoln. Symptoms of the disease include abnormally long limbs, asymmetry between the right and left sides of the body, vision disorders, and cardiac ailments, all of which were found in Lincoln and/or his children.

———

Just after World War II, Dr. Lydia Emery set up practice in Yoncalla, Oregon, which had a population of just under 1,000, and decided to charge $2 for house calls. Thirty years later, she was still making house calls—and still charging only two bucks. (The fee for an office call remained $1.)

———

Men can have hemophilia, but can't pass it on to their children. Women may not even show symptoms of hemophilia, yet can pass on the "royal disease."

———

An apple a day *can* keep the doctor away. A study of 1,300 students at Michigan State University showed that the group that ate apples daily had a lower rate of upper respiratory infections than the student body as a whole. The vitamin C in the apples may account for the result.

———

For lack of another "victim" and/or to prove a point, many medical men have deliberately infected themselves. For example, Dr. Jesse William Lazear (1866–1900), a member of the Yellow Fever Commission in Cuba, allowed himself to be bitten by an infected mosquito. His death from the resulting fever went far to convince the commission that it was on the right path to proof of the mosquito-transmission theory and therefore to effective control of the disease.

———

It's always been tough being a vivisectionist. The French physiologist Claude Bernard also had opposition from his wife and two daughters. Madame Bernard was sincere enough in her anger to contribute large sums to antivivisection societies and to obtain a legal separation. Under Bernard, experimental physiology reached maturity.

———

The scientist Otto Heinrich Warburg, though Jewish, was allowed to work in Nazi Germany. He was working on cancer research, and Hitler feared throat cancer. When Warburg was routinely removed from his post in 1941, Hitler ordered the removal canceled and made it clear that this was an exception.

Physicians in ancient India were skilled in a form of plastic surgery. They created new noses for people whose real noses had been mutilated—a punishment often applied for offenses such as adultery. The physicians cut triangular pieces of skin from the patient's forehead and sewed the graft in place. The patient breathed through reeds placed in his nostrils.

An Austrian doctor, Leopold Auenbrugger, used to watch his father, a vintner, tap wine casts to discover the level of the wine inside them. This gave Auenbrugger the idea of tapping a patient's chest with fingers and listening to the sound thereby produced as a guide to the internal condition of the patient. Auenbrugger published his findings in 1761, but they went unnoticed until they were translated into French in 1808.

Albert Einstein called his brain his laboratory. In science's continuing search for clues to genius, Einstein's brain is being picked apart, gram by gram, and analyzed in a laboratory in Wichita, Kansas. Dr. Thomas Harvey, former chief pathologist, Princeton University, is conducting the study.

Elizabeth Blackwell (1821–1910) was the first American woman physician. She studied privately at first, in 1845, and was finally—after many rejections—admitted to Geneva Medical College, in Geneva, New York. After being graduated she went to Europe to continue her studies, returning to the United States in 1853 with her sister Emily, who was by then also a physician. They trained Union Army nurses during the Civil War. In 1868, Elizabeth helped found the Women's Medical College of the New York Infirmary. In 1869, she moved to England and spent the rest of her life teaching and working to advance medical opportunities there for women.

Twenty thousand plants are listed by the World Health Organization as being used for therapeutic purposes.

William Thomas Green Morton (1819–68), a dentist, induced John Collins Warren (1778–1856), one of America's most prominent surgeons, to conduct the first public demonstration of ether as a general anesthetic, on October 16, 1846, at Massachusetts General Hospital in Boston. The procedure was such an unqualified success that Morton tried to patent ether as his discovery under the name "letheon." Although he had taken the public risks, others had discovered ether's potential before he did, and he was ruined financially by the lawsuits he became involved in.

———

METAL MATTERS

Twenty-three centuries passed between the discovery that iron was subject to magnetic attraction and that another metal, nickel—discovered in 1751—was also attracted by a magnet, though much less strongly.

Though aluminum is the most common metal in the crust of the Earth, it remained completely unknown as a free metal to the ancients. Aluminum does not occur uncombined, but it is an important part of many minerals, including bauxite, mica, feldspar, and the many forms of aluminum oxide (alumina). It wasn't until 1825 that the first piece of aluminum metal (quite impure) was forced out of a compound. Not until 1886 was a good method discovered for extracting the pure metal cheaply and in quantity.

A cathedral in St. Petersburg (now Leningrad) installed a magnificent organ with tin pipes. Came a cold, cold winter and the pipes disintegrated—which is how chemists learned about white tin and gray tin. Ordinary metallic "white tin" is stable only at relatively warm temperatures. In winter cold, there is a tendency for it to turn into a crumbly nonmetallic "gray tin."

The Swedish chemist Georg Brandt's discovery of cobalt, in 1735, marked the first identification of a metal entirely unknown to the ancients.

The first occasion on which humanity "used up" a natural resource was when tin ore was exhausted in the Middle East about 2000 B.C. Because tin was needed to make bronze, the people of the early civilizations had to scour far and wide for it. In their search for tin, the Phoenicians ventured out into the Atlantic and made their way to the island of Britain.

Mercury, which becomes solid at −40° F., is the only metal that is liquid at room temperature. The rare metal cesium, however, almost makes the grade. It melts at 82.4° F., so that on a hot day it would turn liquid. Don't expect to watch that happen: Cesium is so chemically active that it is never seen as a metal except under laboratory conditions.

Ironmakers invested fortunes in "blast furnaces" when Henry Bessemer revealed how steel could be made at a fraction of its previous cost. But they quickly blasted him as a charlatan when the steel they produced was a very poor grade. It turned out Bessemer used phosphorus-free ore, but the ironmakers had used ore that happened to contain phosphorus. The ironmakers wanted nothing more to do with Bessemer, though he had revealed what their problem had been. Bessemer built his own steelworks in Sheffield, in 1860, and grew rich in a very few years.

Stainless steel was discovered by accident. Various experimental alloys were thrown onto scrap heaps. In 1913, someone noticed that a few pieces remained bright and shiny amid the dreary heaps of rust. The pieces were salvaged, analyzed, and the result was stainless steel.

The rare metal gallium melts at 86° F. It is safe to touch; if you hold a piece of it in your hand and wait, it will melt.

A nickel-titanium alloy, 55-Nitinol, can be fashioned at a high temperature into a complex shape, then cooled and crushed beyond recognition. It regains its original shape when it is reheated, "remembering" every curve and angle. A radiotelescope as much as a mile in diameter could be compactly packaged on the ground and sent into space, where it would unfold when solar-heated.

The modern science of mineralogy began with an accident, in 1781. The French mineralogist René Just Hauy accidentally dropped a piece of calcite, and it broke into small fragments. When he bent to sweep it up, he noticed that every fragment had a neat geometrical shape. He discovered that minerals cleave in certain directions and that the cleavage planes meet at fixed angles. This eventually was found to reflect the arrangement of the atoms in the mineral.

Of the seven metals known to the ancients—gold, silver, copper, lead, tin, iron, and mercury—only six are mentioned in the Bible.

There is no mention of mercury. It was the least used. It was what we would today call a "laboratory curiosity."

_____

Shiny metals such as tin or copper turn into black powders when ground fine. Aluminum is the exception.

_____

The densest substance on Earth is the metal osmium, which is one-sixth denser than gold. An ingot of osmium the size of a dollar bill and an inch thick would weigh nearly 13 pounds.

_____

MIGHTY MITES

Bacteria, the tiniest free-living cells, are so small that a single drop of liquid may contain 50 million of them.

Mayflies, after hatching and then spending one to three years developing as naiads, live only one day as adults. During this single day, they molt twice, mate, and lay eggs in water. Because these adults do not have fully developed mouth parts, they do not feed.

The smallest known organism to contain all the chemicals needed for independent life is a bacterium called the pleuropneumonia organism. It would take nearly 2 million of them, side by side and touching, to stretch an inch.

The French physicist René-Antoine de Réaumur (1683–1757) was so impressed by the geometrical perfection of the hexagonal cells of the beehive that he suggested they be adopted as an ideal unit of measurement, superior to any others.

A single-celled animal, the paramecium, divides in two when it is about twenty-two hours old. If a single paramecium began to divide on January 1, and if all its offspring survived, its descendants would fill the volume of one cubic mile by March 7, and their combined volume would be as large as the Earth's by April 12.

The only animals in Antarctica that do not depend on the sea for life are seventy species of mites and primitive insects. The largest Antarctic animal that lives permanently on land is a wingless fly, half a centimeter long. One species of mite has been detected 680 kilometers from the South Pole.

A factory in which 2,000 different machines are operating with twenty-five men on each machine would rightly be considered a complex structure. The smallest bacterium is that complex. In effect, there are 50,000 chemical reactions taking place in each bacterium.

———

Fleas are essential to the health of armadillos and hedgehogs; they provide necessary stimulation of the skin. Deloused armadillos and hedgehogs do not long survive.

———

The migratory locust is kept flying by a bundle of hairs on its head. When these hairs are stimulated by an air current coming from the front, they create a nerve stimulus that keeps the locust's wings beating. The beating, in turn, accelerates the air current; once the locust takes off, it continues to fly for extremely long distances.

———

Maggots were once used to treat osteomyelitis, a serious bone infection. During the U.S. Civil War, it was discovered accidentally that the larvae (maggots) of the blowfly helped heal open wounds by eating away the dead tissue and also by secreting healing substances. The osteomyelitis treatment used laboratory-grown sterile maggots. This method of treatment was discontinued only because analysis proved that urea excreted by the maggots was responsible for the healing process, and the urea could be synthesized inexpensively.

———

A mosquito has forty-seven teeth.

———

Tiny insects called aphids can reproduce parthenogenetically. Female eggs can develop without the fertilizing action of the sperm.

———

Amoebas can be taken apart and new ones created. Cytoplasm from one amoeba, the nucleus of another, and the membranes of a third are combined, and the new creature swims away.

———

A mosquito, engorged on blood, is able to fly carrying a load twice its own weight.

———

Bacteria can reproduce sexually.

———

MILITARY

One of the holders of the first number (258) in the U.S. military draft lottery in 1917 was an Alden C. Flagg. His son, Alden C. Flagg, Jr., of Boston, was a holder of the first number (158) in the U.S. peacetime draft lottery of 1940.

A dwarf eighteen inches high served as a captain of cavalry in the British army. He was Jeffery Hudson and lived from 1619 to 1682. He made his first recorded appearance when he was served inside a pie at the table of the Duke of Buckingham. Later, when he was about thirty years old, he grew to more than twice his earlier adult height—to three feet, nine inches.

One of America's great naval heroes was born John Paul, in Scotland, in 1747. After killing a mutinous crew member in self-defense, he fled to the colonies (to avoid trial) and added Jones to his name. He commanded the *Bon Homme Richard* during the Revolutionary War and won a great battle over the British ship *Serapis*. Jones is also known for his proud statement when he was asked to surrender: "Sir, I have not yet begun to fight."

Americans twice saved from execution Baron Fabian von Schlabrendorff, one of the German officers who had tried to assassinate Hitler. The conspirators had detonated a bomb in Hitler's headquarters on July 20, 1944, but Hitler received only minor wounds. The evidence implicating von Schlabrendorff was in the hands of the president of the German People's Court when a bomb from a raid by a thousand American planes killed the president. Von Schlabrendorff lived to be released from prison by U.S. troops on May 4, 1945, as a Gestapo guard was readying to execute him.

Before he built his financially successful steamboat, Robert Fulton developed a "diving boat" that he thought could be used to sneak up on and place explosive charges against the hulls of enemy vessels. Napoleon encouraged the American inventor, but discontinued his support after Fulton had spent the summer of 1801 unsuccessfully trying to overtake a British ship. Undaunted, Fulton went to the *British,* who authorized an attack on the *French* fleet at Boulogne. The torpedoes didn't work. Back in New York, Fulton actually torpedoed a ship in a demonstration, but the U.S. expressed no interest in pursuing the invention.

———

Baber, the first Mogul emperor of India, marched through the Khyber Pass onto the North Indiañ plain in 1526. The then North Indian ruler, an Afghan king, Sultan Ibrahim, leading an army of 100,000 men, attacked the invaders and lost, despite the nearly ten-to-one odds in manpower in his favor. The reason for Baber's triumph was an ancient Chinese invention that the Sultan had never heard of— gunpowder.

———

The only U.S. Navy man hanged for mutiny was the son of a secretary of war. In 1842, midshipman Philip Spencer was found guilty, along with two enlisted men, of plotting to turn their ship, the U.S.S. *Somers,* to piracy.

———

Spain acquired more new territory in one generation than Rome had conquered in five centuries. She eventually owned all of South America and Central America—from Cape Horn to the Rio Grande— plus much of what is now the United States. (By 1580, Spain had the only permanent European settlements in the New World in addition to outposts in the Philippines.)

———

Joseph Stalin's son Jacob was captured during World War II, but Stalin rejected the German offer of prisoner exchange and Jacob died in a prison camp.

———

"Long Max" and "Big Bertha" were nicknames for two different series of guns used by Germany during World War I. One, the long-range guns, had barrels just over 100 feet in length, and were able to deliver shells weighing 228 pounds for distances up to 76 miles. They were aimed at Paris, but in four bombardments, only one shell, which fell on a church during a Good Friday service, caused serious damage. The other series, howitzers of immense calibre, were named in "honor" of the ample waistline of Frau Bertha Krupp von Bohlen.

———

French archivists claim that the first French soldier who was wounded in the Franco-Prussian War was also the last to be killed, six months later, in 1871.

_____

Two months passed between the U.S. declaration of war on Germany in 1917 and the arrival in Europe of the first skimpy contingents of the American Expeditionary Force. Another four months passed before any American fired a shot at a German. The Americans and the Germans didn't clash in force until the Battle of Belleau Wood on June 6, 1918—the same month and day on which the Allies would invade Europe twenty-six years later in World War II.

_____

Douglas MacArthur's mother used to send fawning letters to his army superiors suggesting that it was time for her son to be promoted to general.

_____

In a rowboat in the St. Lawrence River, in the twilight of September 12, 1759, British General James Wolfe sat and repeated nearly the whole of Gray's "Elegy." He would have preferred being the author of that poem, he said, to the glory of beating the French come the dawn. The next day, Wolfe died at the moment of victory. The best-known line of Gray's poem is "The paths of glory lead but to the grave."

_____

Francisco Pizarro, the nearly illiterate Spanish adventurer, conquered the grand empire of the Incas with a force of no more than 106 foot soldiers and sixty-two downtrodden horses—and gunpowder!

_____

When World War I broke out, Lenin was on a walking tour in the Dolomites. Subsequently, he was imprisoned and might have been shot as a Russian spy by the Austrians if the Socialist mayor of Vienna hadn't believed Lenin was a greater danger to the Russians than he was to the Austrians.

_____

Sauerkraut was renamed "liberty cabbage" by Americans during World War I. In their denunciation of all things German, some A-mericans actually kicked dachshunds.

_____

During the Crusades, the Arabs produced a "Molly Pitcher" who took her fallen husband's place in battle. The wife of an archer who was killed at the Battle of Damascus picked up his bow and immediately joined the conflict. She hit the Crusaders' standardbearer with one arrow and the commander with another, damaging morale and contributing to the Arab victory.

————

Napoleon, if he had conquered Egypt, would have tried to dig a canal at Suez for better access to the wealth of India (which the French had lost to the English in 1763).

————

During World War II, the American air force stationed at Gander, Newfoundland, found that Eskimo hunters who had never before seen a machine were top technicians.

————

The Battle of New Orleans, which made Andrew Jackson a national hero, was fought two weeks after the war (of 1812) had ended and more than a month before news of the war's end had reached Louisiana.

————

During World War II, there was a rumor that the Germans were buying up adrenal glands in Argentine slaughterhouses and that extracts of the glands were enabling Nazi pilots to fly and fight at heights of 40,000 feet. The rumor was untrue, but it spurred American investigation of the adrenals. By 1944, Compound A was synthesized; in 1946, Compound E was.

————

Cavalry captured a fleet during the wars of the French Revolution. General Charles Pichegru, invading Holland in the winter of 1794, found Dutch ships icebound off the coast. He led his Hussars in a charge across the frozen waters and seized the vessels.

————

The German chemist Fritz Haber devised a method for combining the nitrogen of the air into compounds from which explosives and fertilizers could be manufactured. This meant that Germany, during World War I, did not have to depend upon nitrates from Chile for its explosives. Because Great Britain controlled the seas, Germany would have been forced out of the war by 1916 if it hadn't been for the Haber process. Haber also headed Germany's program for development of poison gas. When Hitler came to power, Haber was deprived of his job and forced into exile. He was Jewish.

————

Efforts by German scientists to get top-level Nazi support for development of the atomic bomb were to no avail because Hitler expected a quick victory through conventional weaponry. Construction of the monster bomb would consume a score of years, and by then the Third Reich would own the world.

———

Secretary of State John Hay, who was also a poet, called the Spanish-American War a "splendid little war." The U.S. lost 5,462 men, mostly from disease.

———

In the supreme Roman army—efficient, well trained, and usually well officered—equipment and role were one time determined by wealth. The richest men wore shield, breastplate, greaves (armor for the leg below the knee), and helmet, and carried sword and spear. The less-wealthy men did not wear breastplates. Poor men were equipped with only a helmet. The poorest men had no armor at all, but carried spear and sword.

———

England and Portugal have never been at war with each other. It is probably the longest unbroken peace between nations in the world.

———

When the War Refugee Board urged the U.S. War Department in World War II to bomb the industrial installations and mass-extermination equipment at the Nazi concentration camp at Auschwitz, the plea was rejected because it would be "an unwarranted diversion of planes needed elsewhere."

———

Theodosius II built a triple wall from the Golden Horn of the Sea of Marmara, blocking the landward side of Constantinople by a barrier much stronger than any that had existed. The walls were a generation in the construction, 413–47 A.D. On the far side of the walls was a moat, sixty feet wide and twenty-two feet deep, which the enemy would have to swim or bridge in order simply to reach the first wall. Behind the first wall, which was low, archers crouching in perfect security could pick off the attackers. If the moat was passed and the first wall breached, there were the two additional walls to conquer: the middle wall was twenty-seven feet tall, and the third wall was seventy feet tall; from the third, the defenders could shoot their arrows and catapult their stones. Even now, fifteen centuries later, the ruins are impressive.

———

With both sides willing, the Roman Empire and Persia signed "The Endless Peace" treaty in 533 A.D. They were back at war with each other within seven years.

———

Prisoners were exchanged by the Union and Confederate armies during the U.S. Civil War, until Union General Ulysses S. Grant realized that re-manned enemy forces were impeding the ultimate Union victory. He canceled the program.

The development of long stirrups, enabling the rider to maintain a much steadier seat when riding at full gallop, gave the T'ang cavalry a tremendous military advantage. Beginning in the seventh century, the T'ang managed to extend their control from the whole of central China to much of Manchuria in the northeast and Sinkiang in the northwest.

World War II isn't really over. There has never been a formal peace treaty between Germany and the Soviet Union.

General Douglas MacArthur was relieved of his command in 1951 in a dispute with President Truman. Like his father before him, he had openly critized civilian officials and foreign policy. Although General Arthur MacArthur had risen to highest ranking officer, he never was made chief of staff, and after a policy dispute with President Taft, he retired at 64, a deeply hurt and bitter man.

The parents of Dwight D. Eisenhower, who rose to become one of the few five-star generals in U.S. history, were pacifists.

James Madison was the only President to exercise actively his role as commander-in-chief of U.S. military forces. On August 25, 1814, when British troops were attacking Washington, D.C., during the War of 1812, Madison took command of Commodore Joshua Barney's battery in Bladensburg, Maryland, in an attempt to protect the capital, which lay a few miles to the south.

The Central American country of Costa Rica, which has a population of more than 2 million people, does not have an army.

The British and French armies in World War I did not advance more than three miles at any point on the western front in the whole year of 1915. The three miles cost the French army alone nearly 1.5 million men.

The Mongol army of Kublai Khan tried to invade Japan in 1281 but was foiled by a hurricane that wrecked their fleet. The invaders who had made it to Japan were massacred. The Japanese named that hurricane *kamikaze*, "the divine wind." In World War II, the term was used for a Japanese suicide air force whose fliers crashed their bomb-laden planes into their targets.

————

Immediately after the end of the American Revolution, Congress abolished the United States Army, the Navy, and the Marine Corps, leaving the Congress itself the only national governmental organization. The states feared a standing army.

————

Wars have usually sparked an acceleration in technological skills. In the nineteenth century, for example, demand for accurate small arms encouraged the industrial evolution of interchangeable parts and high-speed lathes, new drilling equipment, hardened metals, and new alloys. World War I gave agriculture the tractor via the tank. World War II gave man nuclear energy via the atomic bomb.

————

In only one battle have elephants been used on both sides. In the Fourth Syrian War, in 217 B.C., Antiochus III of Syria used Asian elephants when he attacked Ptolemy IV's Egyptian army with its smaller elephants of North Africa (which are now extinct). The Asian elephants were the victors, but the Egyptian army went on to win a smashing victory in the engagement at Raphia on the Egyptian border.

————

Nearly 700,000 land mines were dug up from the banks of the Suez Canal by the Egyptians and the Israelis after their brief but bitter war in October 1973.

————

On August 15, 1978, thirty-three years to the day after V-J Day, China and Japan signed a "peace and friendship" treaty, formally ending their part of World War II.

————

In March of 1889, a German naval force shelled a village in Samoa, and by doing so destroyed some American property. Three American warships then entered the Samoan harbor and were prepared to fire on the three German warships found there. Before guns were fired, a hurricane blew up and sank all the ships, American and German. A compulsory armistice was called because of the lack of warships.

————

During the Russo-Japanese War, it took Russia's Baltic fleet seven months to sail the 18,000 miles to the Straits of Tsushima between Korea and Japan. It then took the Japanese only a day and a half in

May 1905 to effect the most complete naval victory in history. In the straits, the Japanese sank or captured eleven Russian battleships, two coast-defense battleships, nine cruisers, and eleven lesser vessels.

———

By the time he was killed, by enemy fire, on the quarterdeck of his flagship *Victory* at Trafalgar on October 21, 1805, Admiral Lord Horatio Nelson (five feet, two inches) had already lost his health to malaria, the sight in one eye while fighting in Corsica, and his right arm in battle at Tenerife.

———

The U.S. military men on the advisory committee on uranium, convening at the direction of President Franklin Roosevelt in the month after the outbreak of World War II in Europe, agreed that nuclear-energy experiments should be done by the universities, not by the federal government. For the purpose of obtaining four tons of graphite and fifty tons of uranium oxide, an appropriation of $6,000 was made.

———

During World War II, construction of ice-ships was considered. Unlike crude icebergs, these ships would be engineered and metal-clad, enormously strong and especially buoyant. According to the British Association for the Advancement of Science, "Had not the atomic bomb been dropped on Japan and the war come to an end, ice-ships would almost certainly have appeared on the oceans of the world."

———

In 1978, the nations of the world spent $800,000 a minute on arms, or an annual total of $400 billion. At the current rate of increase, the figure of $1 trillion per year will be topped by the end of the century.

———

The Japanese kamikaze pilots of World War II were given privileged treatment and considered to be heroes. All volunteers, they underwent rigorous training that prepared them for their suicide missions. If they refused to stay in the corps, they were shot as traitors.

———

In their last attempt at European conquest, the Turks took Crete from the Venetians in 1669 and advanced to the northwest, standing in 1683 on the outskirts of Vienna. The Venetians and Austrians counterattacked successfully. The Turks, defending Athens against naval attack, stored gunpowder in the nearly 2,000-year-old Parthenon. When a Venetian cannonball struck the Parthenon, exploding the gunpowder, the entire center section of one of the most magnificent buildings of all time was destroyed.

By the age of twenty-five, he had been expelled from the army and was disgraced, despondent, without funds, apparently without a future, and suicidal. The man was Napoleon (1769–1821). One year later, he was the youngest general in the French army and began winning victories with ragged troops that were at the point of starvation.

Colonel George Washington of the Virginia Militia was denied a commission in the regular British army in 1754. He resigned his militia commission and became a Virginia planter at Mount Vernon. His resentment of the British over this rejection helped lose George III his colonies.

In September 1942, a Japanese plane flew over Oregon on two occasions and dropped bombs in an attempt to set the forests on fire. The float-equipped plane had been carried across the Pacific by the submarine I-25. It wasn't until many years after World War II that it was revealed that the U.S. mainland had been bombed from the air for the first time. The general public had assumed that the forest fires of '42 were started by firebombs carried in balloons by prevailing winds from Japan to Oregon.

The Crusaders were able to conquer Acre, a coastal town eighty miles north of Jerusalem, in July 1191, only after 100,000 on both sides had been killed.

When Hannibal invaded Italy, in the third century B.C., his military engineers employed fire and vinegar to smash a path through the Alps. The engineers heated immovable rocks with blazing logs, then poured vinegar over the rocks. The rocks split into fragments that could be pushed aside.

During World War II, Japanese soldiers used the remains of crabs so they could read maps at night without attracting attention. Tiny crabs that produce their own biological lights as the result of enzyme action were dried out and ground into a powder. When water was added to the powder held in the soldiers' hands, a faint blue light was produced.

Joseph Wenzel, Count Radetzky de Radetz (1766–1858), served in the Austrian army for seventy-two years, nearly half of this time as a field marshal. Another long military career was that of Sir Thomas Brisbane (1773–1860), who served in the British army for seventy years, many of them as a general; he was also an astronomer—founding observatories in Scotland and Australia—and governor of New South Wales, Australia. (The city of Brisbane in Australia and the Brisbane River bear his name.)

The French general whose name came to mean a strict military disciplinarian—martinet—was killed by gunfire from his own men as he led a charge. General Jean Martinet beat soldiers of Louis XIV into shape by relentless drill, and naturally he became a hated man. (Perhaps his death *was* an accident.)

By making use of the energy of the recoil of a fired bullet to eject the spent cartridge and load the next, Hiram Maxim in 1884 produced the first fully automatic machine gun.

Marie Joseph Paul Yves Roch Gilbert du Motier, Marquis de Lafayette, feared that "no one will know me" when he returned to the United States for a visit at the request of President James Monroe in the 1820s. How wrong he was. America's great friend during the Revolution—he had been at Valley Forge with Washington, was wounded at Brandywine, and helped to negotiate for French aid—was welcomed and acclaimed everywhere. Congress voted him a gift of $200,000 and a township of land.

The Opana radar station of the U.S. 55th Signal Aircraft Warning Service near Hawaii's Kahuku Point picked up incoming aircraft at 136 miles, but the privates on duty there were advised by higher-ups at Information Center not to be concerned—they must be U.S. planes due from the mainland. Radar was a new technology and wasn't entirely trusted yet. The day was December 7, 1941, and the approaching aircraft turned out to be the vanguard of Japan's "wild eagles"—353 carrier-based warplanes that were to sink or heavily damage eighteen U.S. warships in Pearl Harbor and kill 2,403 men.

Though Theodore Roosevelt's famous attack in Cuba in the Spanish-American War is referred to as the charge of the "Rough Riders," the troops were not mounted.

Though the six-year War of Independence ranged and raged over most of the thirteen colonies, George Washington's Continental Army never consisted of more than 22,000 troops at any one time.

———

Early guns took so long to load and fire that bows and arrows—in trained hands—were twelve times more efficient.

———

Several people, including the Secretary of State and the Secretary of the Navy, were killed when the ten-ton gun "Peacemaker" exploded during a firing from the first propeller-driven warship, the U.S.S. *Princeton,* on cruise on the Potomac south of Washington in 1844. The survivors included President John Tyler and his fiancée, Miss Julia Gardiner, who were in a cabin below deck at the time of the accident.

———

The British orders interfering with U.S. commerce that led to the War of 1812 were actually repealed by Great Britain the day before war was declared by the United States. But the U.S. had no way of knowing this because rapid communications methods such as the telegraph had not yet been invented (the first transatlantic cable was not laid until 1866), so it proceeded with the war as planned.

———

Without much knowledge of the deeper aspects of the struggle, 30,000 soldiers from Hesse, Germany, engaged by George III—the Hessians—fought against the Americans in the Revolutionary War. The colonists did not so much dislike the Hessians, recognizing them to be helpless pawns, as they disliked the English king for hiring foreigners to shoot men he considered his subjects.

———

Forty years after Commodore Perry opened Japan in 1854, the half-Westernized island kingdom was militarily and industrially strong enough to defeat giant China in a war and take over Formosa, and ten years later was able to defeat Russia, which led to the virtual annexation of Korea.

———

The Hundred Years War did not end legally; there was never a peace treaty. No English government could bring itself to make peace with France and admit that Crécy and Poitiers and even Agincourt had come to nothing. The English would sign a truce only, and that was all the French got.

———

While being refitted, in 1782, off Spithead, at the eastern end of the channel between Hampshire and the Isle of Wight, the British man-of-war *Royal George* keeled over under the strain caused by the shifting of 108 guns. The commander of the *Royal George*, Admiral Richard Kempenfeldt, and 800 sailors and marines and visitors drowned.

Although the exact figures will never be known, approximately 500,000 soldiers of the German armies are still missing in action from World War II, and 150,000 German civilians are still unaccounted for, nearly all from air raids. The West German Red Cross tracing service, however, has located or answered doubts about more than 1.2 million soldiers missing in action, and closed the books on 208,000 missing German civilians. The agency has reunited many parents and children separated by the war, but it believes about 3,000 children are still alive and "missing."

At the end of the Spanish-American War, in 1898, the United States occupied Cuba. Rioting mobs in the street, along with outbreaks of malaria and yellow fever, created havoc in the country. Lieutenant James Moss was sent with his troops to maintain order; they were successful. The unique thing about Moss's 25th Infantry of only one hundred men was that they were a bicycle corps—they all rode bicycles, they all were black, and they never once used their weapons while in Cuba.

Napoleon hit on the idea of using a semaphore telegraph—visual messages from as far as the eye could see—and gained a huge advantage over his enemies. He could send a message from Paris to Rome in four hours.

When Korea refused to do business with the U.S. in 1871, a month-long war erupted; it ended in a draw. American ships sailed off claiming victory. The Koreans declared they had driven the Americans away.

In a single raid on Britain about 1,000 years ago, the Vikings used a fleet of eighty "dragon ships," each carrying a hundred soldiers.

After the Battle of Waterloo, June 18, 1815, the British commander-in-chief commissioned Captain William Siborne to supervise the making of a model of the famous site. Captain Siborne completed it in 1838 at his own expense when he did not receive the funding he had been promised. On a scale of nine feet to one mile, it measures about eighteen feet square and contains approximately 190,000 figures, each about half an inch high. It is now on display at Whitehall in London.

Despite the antifeminist precepts of Islam, a woman ruled in medieval Egypt and planned the attack against Louis IX (1204–70) and his Crusaders. When the Sultan died during the siege of Cairo, his wife, Shajar-al-Durr, kept his death a secret. Pretending that he was merely ill in the palace, she gave orders in his name and devised the strategy of cutting the Crusader supply lines. The Egyptians won the battle and captured Louis IX, in 1250.

In 1738, Captain Robert Jenkins displayed an ear pickled in brine before a Parliamentary committee in London. He identified the ear as his own, and charged that a Spanish patrol had cut it off while he was sailing in the West Indies. Appalled, the British declared war on Spain—the War of Jenkins's Ear, which expanded into the War of the Austrian Succession.

The British government was advised by Lord Cherwell, Prime Minister Churchill's scientific adviser, that the V-2 rocket was only a propaganda rumor: There was nothing to the stories of a rocket-propelled bomb that the Nazis could send faster than the speed of sound from bases in northern Germany to explode without warning in London and other cities. Hundreds of the V-2—the German abbreviation for *Vergeltungswaffe 2*, literally "reprisal weapon 2"—rocked England until the Allies overran the launching sites.

Five hours after the Japanese had successfully launched a surprise air strike on U.S. bases in Hawaii, in 1941, a message sent through commercial channels was received by the U.S. Army and Navy commanders there. It was from Chief of Staff General George C. Marshall, in Washington, advising the island defense forces they should be on the alert.

The army of the Netherlands is unionized. Overtime pay for KP and for guard duty on the weekend are among the innovations.

Six U.S. Presidents were professional soldiers: Washington, Jackson, William Henry Harrison, Taylor, Grant, and Eisenhower. Five other professional soldiers were nominated for the Presidency. About thirty-five other Presidential and Vice-Presidential candidates served in the military.

———

To terrorize their foes in the fifteenth century, Turks used a gun of hooped iron that had to be pulled by oxen and maneuvered by a hundred men. The gun fired half-ton stone balls.

———

In our century, gas and later the atomic bomb were considered too terrible for use in war. The first weapon arousing such dread was the crossbow. The medieval popes tried to have it banned as inhuman (except against infidels). The medieval kings, however, found it too effective in battle against their fellow-Christians to discard it.

———

The first machine gun was invented during the U.S. Civil War by Richard Jordan Gatling, but it was not adopted till the war was over. It was called the Gatling gun, a phrase that has gone out of fashion. However, the slang term "gat," used for a gun and derived from Gatling's name, survives.

———

The kings of ancient Scythia divided the spoils of victory according to a simple mathematical ratio. Soldiers brought in the heads of the enemies they had killed, and the number determined the individual's share. Those who produced no heads got nothing.

———

The rockets mentioned in "The Star-Spangled Banner" were less effective than bombs. They had a shorter range and were so inaccurate that they had to be abandoned as weapons after the War of 1812. Not until World War II did rockets become important.

———

On the eve of World War II, the U.S. Army ranked, with reserves counted, nineteenth among the world's armed forces. This placed the U.S. after Portugal—but ahead of Bulgaria.

———

When Louis XIV invaded Holland in 1672, the Dutch cut the dikes and allowed the waters of the North Sea to rush in over their land. Amsterdam became an island inaccessible to the powerful French army, which had to retreat from the flood.

———

The American ships firing steadily at the Spanish fleet in Manila Bay, in May 1898, pulled off briefly at one point so that the crews could have a quiet breakfast. On returning to work, they destroyed the enemy.

The famous "Battle of the Thirty" in the fourteenth century: To avoid depletion of the dwindled resources of the two nations, the English and the French each selected thirty champion soldiers to fight under prearranged rules for possession of a fortress. Under Bertrand du Guesclin, Constable of France, the French won.

Germ warfare was used in the fourteenth century, when a band of Tartars surrounded a group of Genoese merchants who had taken refuge in the walled town of Caffa in the Crimea. After three years of fighting, the Tartars finally achieved victory by catapulting into the village, in addition to rocks, the bodies of their own soldiers who had died of bubonic plague. The entire town was infected. After the Tartars departed, the Genoese who survived returned home, where they infected their families and contributed to the spread of the Black Death.

The purpose of the Great Wall of China, the monumental fortification separating China from Mongolia, was not especially to keep out the Huns from the north. The Huns could easily find places along the stretch that they could scale with ladders. But they couldn't get their horses across. Without their horses, they weren't very effective conquerors.

A hundred years before the U.S. Declaration of Independence, a rebellion in Virginia overthrew the British colonial government there. Nathaniel Bacon, Jr., led 500 farmers protesting poor frontier security, taxes, and other conditions against the administration of Governor Berkeley. The group marched on Jamestown and took over the House of Burgesses. The revolt ended after Bacon's sudden death from an attack of dysentery. Bacon's rebellion was the first of many settler-vs.-government skirmishes that would culminate in the American Revolution.

The British government asked Michael Faraday if there was any possibility of preparing quantities of poison gas for use on the battlefield in its Crimean War (1853–56) with Russia and, if it *were* feasible, would he direct the project to perform the task. Faraday's answer was immediate and unequivocal. The project was feasible—and he would have absolutely nothing to do with it.

The first mechanical road vehicle, forerunner of the automobile, was a steam-powered tractor designed in 1769 for pulling cannon. Built by N. J. Cugnot, a captain in the French army, the three-wheeled carriage had a bulky boiler protruding over the front wheel that lead to its description as "a whisky still on a wheelbarrow." Its maximum speed was four miles per hour. Eventually, Cugnot drove the vehicle into a wall, earning himself a jail sentence as the first traffic violator on record.

———

Jean Angot (1480–1551) was a peaceful merchant and shipbuilder in Dieppe, France, until two of his ships were set upon by Portuguese vessels. He became so enraged that he attacked Lisbon with seventeen of his ships. He captured many enemy ships, occupied the harbor, ravaged the surrounding area, and generally blockaded Lisbon until the Portuguese government sued for peace.

———

Christopher Columbus was a naval mercenary in the service of René d'Anjou, King of Naples, in 1472 and 1473.

———

During the War of 1812, much of the action took place at sea. The British had the numbers, 800 naval vessels versus the United States' 16. However, the U.S. had three frigates, the *Constitution,* the *President,* and the *United States,* that were faster and better than any British vessel. Because the battles were duels between single ships, the U.S. won many notable victories.

———

When they would raid Siberia in the months of darkness, the Mongols had an ingenious method for finding their way home in the dark. They would leave at their camp the young foals of their mares. After the raid, the riders would drop the reins, and the mares instinctively carried them straight back to the foals.

———

In 1971—the Vietnam war was on, and it was the third year of Richard Nixon's Presidency—nearly 100,000 men deserted the U.S. armed forces.

———

The Peace of Westphalia, which concluded the Thirty Years War in 1648, left the Holy Roman Empire divided into more than 300 principalities between the Alps and the Baltic. Each had its own government, army, and treasury. Germany remained thus divided, more or less, for two and a quarter centuries.

———

Brigadier General Smedley Butler, a U.S. Marine hero, told the American people via Public Broadcasting Service: "I helped to make Honduras right for the American fruit companies in 1903. I helped to make Mexico and especially Tampico safe for American oil interests in 1914. I helped make Haiti and Cuba a decent place for the National City Bank boys to collect revenues in. I brought life to the Dominican Republic for American sugar in 1916. In China, in 1937, I helped see to it that Standard Oil went its way unmolested. I was rewarded with honors, medals, and promotions. Looking back on it, I feel I might have given Al Capone a few hints. The best he could do was to operate his racket in three city districts. We Marines operated on three continents." General Butler was noted for his violent opinions and flamboyant quarrels. After his retirement from the marines, he campaigned for isolationism prior to World War II.

Giant kelp, a seaweed of the Pacific, is so rich in potash that the Allies' needs in World War I were met by harvesting it, when German supplies were cut off. (Potash is used for fertilizer, for making glass, soaps, and other important potassium compounds.)

When Spain declared war on the U.S. in 1898, the U.S. in turn declared war on Spain but backdated the declaration by three days so it would look more heroic to have declared war first.

The Pentagon, headquarters for the United States Department of Defense, is the world's largest office building—a city in itself. With an area of 6,500,000 square feet the Pentagon has a Main Street lined with shops, restaurants, a bus depot, and a post office. Commercial rental of the office space would come to more than $20 million a day.

Three of Theodore Roosevelt's four sons were killed serving their country in wartime. Quentin was killed in World War I, and Theodore, Jr., and Kermit died serving in World War II.

Until the mid-1800s, the largest ship built in America was the *New Netherland,* in the 1630s. It carried thirty cannons and displaced some 700 tons.

Cheng Ho, court eunuch and great mariner of the Ming Dynasty, led Chinese fleets on seven voyages of conquest and diplomacy, between 1405 and 1433. As a result of Cheng Ho's voyages—as far as West

Africa—thirty-six countries sent tribute to China. But no additional expeditions were organized. The Chinese preferred to let the rest of the world come to them, and eventually they did—to China's regret.

The U.S. warship *George Washington* was captured by forces of the Dey of Algiers in October 1800 and forced to sail under escort to Constantinople. There, the captain and the crew were presented as slaves to the Sultan.

Since the Early Bronze Age, about 5,000 years ago, the seemingly worthless, underpopulated, undercultivated Sinai Peninsula has been the world's most besieged land, the battlefield for at least fifty invading armies on their way to grander prizes in Africa and the Middle East.

Samuel Powhatan Carter (1819–91) was both a major general in the U.S. Army and a rear admiral in the Navy. He organized the first Union troops from Tennessee during the U.S. Civil War, and from 1870 to 1873 he was commandant of midshipmen at the U.S. Naval Academy, which had graduated him in 1846.

MILITARY
SECRETS

Heinrich Albert, the director of German propaganda within the U.S. before the U.S. entered World War I, carelessly left his briefcase on a New York subway train, on July 24, 1915. It was at once picked up by American agents, who were shadowing him, and was found to contain documents relating to plans for sabotaging American plants that served as arsenals for the Allies. The documents were signed by Franz von Papen, a military attaché to the German embassy, and by the ambassador himself.

The Federal Bureau of Investigation captured eight German saboteurs shortly after they had come ashore from a U-boat off eastern Long Island in 1942. Six were executed and two imprisoned. It turns out that one of those imprisoned, the expedition's leader, was an anti-Nazi and had tipped off the FBI. (He was promised that he'd be jailed for only six months. He got, instead, a ninety-year prison term.)

The Spartans used a staff and a coil of paper to keep military messages from being decoded if they fell into the hands of the enemy. Rolled around the staff, the words fitted together and made sense. Unrolled, the paper was covered with gibberish. Each general had a carefully guarded staff of precisely the same diameter around which to roll the paper and read the message.

By the end of World War II, there wasn't a German spy in Great Britain who was not under British control. All either were cooperating with the British while maintaining their German "alliance" or had been caught and "turned around."

The "King's Secret" of Louis XV was a covert diplomatic corps of which the French foreign minister knew nothing. Louis communicated with other governments through secret agents, often contradicting the foreign minister and causing chaos in French diplomacy—one reason for the French disasters during the eighteenth century.

Radio echoes helped to win the Battle of Britain. Using a radio-echo principle—radar—the outnumbered Royal Air Force always seemed to the puzzled Nazi pilots to be lying in wait at the right time and never to be surprised.

The first U.S. Secretary of Defense, James Forrestal, was confined to an upper story of Walter Reed Army Hospital, in Washington, D.C., in 1949, after physicians had diagnosed him as paranoid. He believed that he was being tracked by secret agents of Israel. As he was not properly supervised, the Secretary jumped to his death from a window. It turned out that Israeli agents had indeed been following Forrestal, in their need to know if the U.S. was making secret arrangements with Arab nations.

So that the patent could be kept secret and the knowledge would not be misused, the atomic scientist Leo Szilard assigned to the British Admiralty in 1934 the patent that first outlined the concept of a chain reaction. The patent was not published until after World War II.

During World War II, the Federal Bureau of Investigation secretly established a house of male prostitutes in New York's Greenwich Village. The house was staffed with multilingual agents for the purpose of extracting important shipping information from foreign sailors. The FBI later claimed it had been a very successful operation.

To bemuse Axis agents about the imminence of a cross-Channel Allied invasion of Nazi-held Europe, an actor posed as British Field Marshal Bernard Montgomery and conspicuously visited North Africa.

Bismarck tricked the French into the Franco-Prussian War by altering a telegram from the King of Prussia. He struck out the king's conciliatory words, so that the telegram sounded belligerent. The result was what the Iron Chancellor intended, a French declaration of war, followed by a German victory.

During World War II, the U.S. Navy had a world champion chess player, Reuben Fine, calculate—on the basis of positional probability—where enemy submarines might surface. Dr. Fine says, "It worked out all right."

Novelists sometimes go to great lengths in personally experiencing realistic details to enhance the immediacy in their art. Frederick Forsyth may have topped them all. When his novel *The Dogs of War* appeared in 1974, few readers knew that this tale of a group of mercenaries who overthrow an African government was based on Forsyth's own attempt to do just that—to overthrow, with the help of thirteen men, the government of Equatorial Guinea by kidnapping its President, Francisco Macias Nguema, in 1972, an attempt on which Forsyth had spent $200,000. But—unlike his fictional mercenary, Cat Shannon, in the mythical country of Zangaro—Forsyth failed in Equatorial Guinea when a Spanish co-conspirator did not come through with the ammunition. All of Forsyth's books—which include *The Day of the Jackal* (about an attempt to kill De Gaulle) and *The ODESSA File* (on S.S. leaders still at large)—are so meticulously researched that they often read like how-to manuals rather than novels. His U.S. publishers, The Viking Press and Bantam Books, could not have been too surprised to learn of Forsyth's Equatorial Guinea caper when the London *Times* and *The New York Times* broke the news, in 1978.

The Navajo language was used successfully as a code by the U.S. in World War II.

Mata Hari, the Dutch-Javanese dancer who became the most famous spy of World War I, ordered that a suit be especially tailored for her for the occasion—execution by a French firing squad. She also wore a pair of new white gloves.

During World War I, one of England's greatest novelists, W. Somerset Maugham, worked around the world for British intelligence. He was an agent in the South Pacific, America, and Switzerland. He went to Russia to persuade the Russian government to carry on the war against Germany.

An authentic "lost weapon" is Greek fire, which the Byzantine Empire used on several occasions between the seventh and ninth centuries to defend Constantinople against attacking Muslims. Constantinople might have fallen but for Greek fire, and conceivably the Muslims might have taken over a weak and divided Europe. To this day, we don't know exactly what the "recipe" for Greek fire was. All we know is that it burned all the more fiercely when wet, and that it could be floated toward the enemy's wooden ships.

Ciphers and codes have been used since ancient times, but effective methods for breaking them have developed only in modern times. One of the early cryptanalysts was a French mathematician, Franciscus Vieta (1540–1603). He deciphered the code that Philip II of Spain was using. Philip, who was at war with France at the time, could not understand how his secrets were leaking to the enemy, and he accused the French of sorcery. What's more, he carried his accusation to the Pope.

The Allies learned detailed plans of German fortifications along the coast of France in late 1943—seven months before they invaded Normandy—and of the supersecret rocket bases at Peenemunde and Friedrichshafen. The Allies' secret: They had broken the Japanese code and were able to learn the content of a thirty-page message transmitted to Tokyo by Japanese Ambassador Hiroshi Oshima after he had toured the Germans' defense works.

When the second atomic bomb was dropped on Japan, in 1945, the United States had only one more atomic bomb in reserve. But the second attack convinced Emperor Hirohito to surrender. He had concluded that the first bomb, on Hiroshima, was not a fluke, and that the U.S. could produce more of the terrible weapons.

Secret codes and ciphers are thousands of years old. Many prominent persons throughout history have written in ciphers for diplomatic and military reasons; they include Julius Caesar, Charlemagne, Alfred the Great, Mary Queen of Scots, and Louis XIV.

During the time that the atomic bomb was being hatched by the U.S. at Alamagordo, New Mexico, applicants for routine jobs like janitor were disqualified if they could read. Illiteracy, in other words, was the word of the day. The reason: The authorities didn't want their trash or mislaid plans read.

William Penn, the Quaker pacifist, was the son of a renowned fighting man, Admiral William Penn. The admiral took part in battles under Cromwell against the Dutch and Spaniards, helped capture Jamaica, and was knighted for supporting the Restoration of Charles

II. The admiral never could convince his son that pacifism was wrong, nor did the son's beliefs affect the father.

————

MISCONCEPTIONS

Samuel F. B. Morse did not really invent the telegraph. He managed to get all the necessary information for the invention from the American physicist Joseph Henry, and later denied that Henry had helped him. (Henry easily proved the contrary in a court trial.) Morse was a good promoter, and squeezed $30,000 out of Congress for building the first telegraph line, from Washington to Baltimore, in 1844. He did, however, invent the Morse code.

The Pilgrims did not build log cabins, nor did they wear black hats with a conical crown and a hatband with a silver buckle.

James Watt did not invent the steam engine; Thomas Newcomen did, in 1712. By 1778, more than seventy Newcomen engines were pumping away in the mines of Cornwall alone. When Watt was asked to repair a Newcomen engine, he devised a modified engine that was much more efficient and that could be used to turn wheels. This modified steam engine was so useful that the earlier Newcomen engine was soon forgotten.

The famous painting by Emanuel Leutze titled "Washington Crossing the Delaware" is false in almost every historical detail. Among the misrepresentations are the American flag, which was not adopted until after the event, and the size of the boat, which actually was much larger.

An absurd fiction of history is that when Columbus said the world was round, everybody else thought it was flat. During the debates at the court of Queen Isabella, the true shape of the Earth was never an issue; its size was! The opponents of Columbus said he was underestimating the size, and that he could never sail due west from Europe to the Orient. They were right. Except for the accident of an unknown continent in between, Columbus would either have turned back or been lost at sea.

———

Lloyd's of London, the best-known association of insurance under-writers, does not write life insurance.

———

"The doctrine that the Earth is neither the center of the universe nor immovable, but moves, even with a daily rotation, is absurd, and both philosophically and theologically false, and at the least an error of Faith." This was the wording of the Roman Congregation's decision against Galileo.

———

Albert Einstein, who was awarded the Nobel Prize for physics in 1921, was honored not for his famous theory of relativity published sixteen years earlier, but for his lesser-known work on the photo-electric effect.

———

Most of us learned in school that the Magna Charta was signed in 1215 by King John. But it was not—the monarch could not write his name. He granted the Magna Charta by placing his seal on it.

———

A popular misconception seems to be that filtered cigarettes are less dangerous than unfiltered ones. According to a study conducted by Dr. G.H. Miller at Edinboro State College, Pennsylvania, the opposite would be the case: people who prefer filtered cigarettes are in danger of dying two to almost four years earlier than smokers of filterless cigarettes. Filters prevent the dilution of the smoke by oxygen so that the bloodstream builds up higher levels of carbon monoxide, in the form of carboxyhemoglobin. One of the effects is greater damage to the cardiovascular system, with the danger of strokes and heart attacks. Approximately 50 percent of the deaths studied resulted from heart attacks and about 20 percent from cancer.

———

Until the time of Galileo, an argument used with potent effect was that if the Earth moved, and if it indeed rotated on its axis, the birds would be blown away, clouds would be left behind, and buildings would tumble.

———

President George Washington's often quoted and referred-to Farewell Address was never delivered orally. The address—which was composed with the help of James Madison and Alexander Hamilton—

was merely published, in the Philadelphia *Daily American Advertiser*.

————

St. Patrick (ca. 385-461 A.D.) was not Irish. He was British, probably Welsh, and never saw Ireland until kidnapped by Irish raiders. After his escape, he became a priest and a bishop and returned to Ireland as a missionary. His success made him the patron saint of Ireland.

————

Robert Fulton did not invent the steamship. Seventeen years before Fulton's first ship sailed up the Hudson River, John Fitch maintained a regular steamship schedule on the Delaware River between Philadelphia and Trenton. Financial difficulties and various misfortunes made Fitch's business venture a failure, but it was he who invented the steamship.

————

There are no statistics to indicate the concentration of land ownership in the U.S., and there has never been a land census. Information about size of farms is obtainable from the Department of Agriculture, but nobody knows the identities of the people who own the land, or how much land they own.

————

Henry Hudson cannot be credited with the discovery of the river that bears his name because it was not until September 1609 that he sailed the *Half Moon* into the river. In 1525, the Portuguese Estevan Gomez had entered the "Hudson" at what is now New York Harbor. Later, a letter was found from the Florentine Giovanni da Verrazano relating the details of *his* being there first, in March 1524. (Verrazano's report, however, may have been plagiarized from Gomez's; there is no *proof* that Verrazano ever made such an expedition.)

————

The most exciting cartographic discovery in this century turned out to be a forgery—the infamous Vinland Map, "proof" that the Vikings had explored the New World. An anonymous buyer paid $1 million for three antique items, including the map then thought to be authentic, and donated them to Yale University. Before the Vinland Map was found to be a fake, 10,000 people had paid Yale $15 each for a copy. The map was supposed to have been drawn in the 1430s or 1440s by a monk in Switzerland. Chemical tests showed that the ink used to draw it could not have been made before the 1920s. The other two items, a thirteenth-century narrative of a Central Asian voyage and a fragment of a medical encyclopedia of the same period, were authentic antiques.

————

Charles Darwin rarely used the term "evolution." It was popularized by the English sociologist Herbert Spencer, who also popularized the phrase "survival of the fittest."

Robert Fulton did not call his steamboat *Clermont*, the name by which it is known in history books. The vessel that inaugurated passenger service between New York and Albany in 1807 was registered as the *North River Steam Boat*. Her sailing port was Clermont, New York.

About the first thing any high-school chemistry student learns in lab is how to light his Bunsen burner, a gas burner used to heat solutions of chemicals. The Bunsen burner was not, however, invented by the German chemist Robert W. Bunsen. He merely popularized its use.

The strongest opposition to electoral reform in England in the mid-1850s came not from the rich but from intellectuals opposed in the name of education and intelligence to mass rule.

Englishmen of the sixteenth and seventeenth centuries believed that no one who lay upon feathers could die in peace. Therefore, when death approached, the pillow was withdrawn from under the dying person's head to ease the passing.

Because of the story in Genesis that Eve had been created out of Adam's rib, it was widely believed during the Middle Ages that men had one rib fewer than women.

An ordinary TNT bomb involves *atomic* reaction, and could be called an atomic bomb. What we call an A-bomb involves *nuclear* reactions and should be called a nuclear bomb.

In eighteenth-century London, Jonathan Wild protected his vast criminal activities by joining up with the law. Wild ran an organization of thieves, owned warehouses, depots, and even a ship for illicit trade with the Continent. At the same time, he was an officer of the law who arrested criminals independent of his organization. The authorities were amazed when their trusted representative was nabbed red-handed. Wild's career and execution are chronicled in *The Beggar's Opera*.

As late as the Victorian era, many English parents believed a sucking baby absorbed moral character as it took in milk. Therefore, if the mother could not nurse her own child, selection of the proper wet nurse became of major importance. If the wet nurse were a drunkard or fool, the parents feared their child would become one as well.

When the colonists first arrived in America, some of them believed that the Indians were descended from the ten lost tribes of Israel. In London, in 1650, the Reverend Thomas Thorowgood published a book entitled *Jews in America, or Probabilities that the Americans are of That Race,* in which he pointed out what he saw as similarities between Indians and Jews, such as their customs and their language.

Despite its reputation, the "man-eating" giant clam of the South Pacific Ocean—which grows to more than four feet across and can weigh a quarter-ton—feeds only on microscopic organisms that the tide washes into its maw.

The Cape of Good Hope is *not* the southernmost tip of Africa. About 160 kilometers east of the Cape of Good Hope is Cape Agulhas, which extends 65 kilometers farther south than Hope.

To protect woolens from moths, people for generations have stored them in cedar chests or have built closets lined with cedar. There is no evidence that a cedar chest or closet repels moths.

A person's hair cannot turn white overnight because of some terrible tragedy or frightening experience—or for any other reason.

Contrary to popular belief, the lantern that was hung from the steeple of Boston's Old North Church the night before the American Revolution began was a message *from* Paul Revere, not *to* him. He had the lantern lit as a signal to patriots across the river in Charlestown that he had not yet left Boston to meet with them. The light served as an advance warning that a British expedition was about to set out, but it provided no details; these would be supplied when Revere reached Charlestown.

It is not easy to kiss the "Blarney Stone." Triangular in shape, it is some twenty feet from the top of a castle wall in the Irish village of Blarney. The only way to reach and kiss it is to hang downward in a most dangerous manner.

The almost universal impression of the "prairie provinces" of Canada—Manitoba, Saskatchewan, and Alberta—as an endless expanse of wheat fields could not be more erroneous. The notion derives mostly from the fact that the Trans-Canada Highway and the Canadian Railways cut through the dullest parts of these provinces. Manitoba has more than 100,000 lakes and 400 miles of seacoast on Hudson Bay. At Cypress Hills in Saskatchewan there are mountains 4,500 feet high—just 35 miles north of the U.S. border—and near Prince Albert, in the center of the province, there is a 1500-square-mile forest wilderness of lakes, streams, and hills. The Canadian Rockies belong as much to the western border of Alberta as they do to British Columbia.

Most people whom you ask will say that the Atlantic Ocean (the Caribbean Sea) is at the eastern end of the Panama Canal and that the Pacific Ocean (the Gulf of Panama) is at the western end of the canal. Take a look at a map. If you enter the canal from the Atlantic side, you enter in the western and you leave at the eastern—the Pacific—side.

The family legend that made Betsy Ross famous was first told thirty years after her death. A grandson claimed that she had been visited in June 1776 by a secret committee, which included George Washington, that asked her to design and sew a flag for the new nation. There is no evidence to corroborate the story. Elizabeth Griscom Ross—"Betsy"—was merely the seamstress. The original American flag was designed by Francis Hopkinson of New Jersey. He was a lawyer, author, artist, member of the Second Continental Congress, the first native American composer, and signer of the Declaration of Independence.

Euclid worked out virtually none of the theorems of "Euclidean" geometry. He was a collector of other men's works. His great virtue was that he arranged in so logical an order the geometrical theorems known in his time that they can scarcely be improved on.

The Incas, experts at organization and engineering, did not have wheels, arches, or writing. At the height of their power, before the Spanish conquest in 1532, the Incas ruled the entire area in South America from Quito, Ecuador, to the Rio Maule, Chile. Their empire was centered at Cuzco, Peru.

Benjamin Franklin's invention of the lightning rod in 1753 was the first practical victory of science over a natural phenomenon. Two years later, when Lisbon, Portugal, was destroyed by an earthquake and tidal wave, some ministers in Boston proclaimed it was a punishment for the sacrilege of using lightning rods to avert the wrath of God.

———

In the 1520s a Spanish force of 600 men led by Hernando Cortez with horses and guns overturned an empire of 2 million that had neither horses nor guns. Cortez landed in Mexico, gained allies among the enemies of the Aztecs, and marched on Mexico City, where the local legend of "the pale god from over the sea" overawed Montezuma. Cortez, after having the Aztec emperor murdered, took control of the Aztec Empire with his handful of men.

———

One of the first to speculate on evolution was the French naturalist Georges de Buffon (1707–88). He thought of it as a downhill slide, however. He thought an ape had degraded from a man, a donkey from a horse, and so on.

———

Chester Carlson, the inventor in 1937 of xerography, the dry copying process, could also have been the inventor of another important communication tool if he hadn't given up. Carlson had an idea for what later became the ball-point pen, but he dropped work on the concept long before it was marketed—he thought the pen wouldn't work.

———

Sir Edmund Hillary and Tenzing Norkay deservedly received much praise when they were the first to climb to the summit of Mount Everest. Less known is the fact that they had a roster of twelve climbers, forty Sherpa guides, and 700 porters.

———

Galileo was forced to resign as a teacher at the University of Pisa when he gainsaid Aristotle's long-held thesis that the heavier a stone, the faster it falls. It is now acknowledged that two stones of unequal weight that are dropped from a tower at the same time will strike the ground at the same time.

———

A nonexistent monarch contributed to the opening of Europe's Age of Discovery. In the fifteenth century, Prince Henry the Navigator dispatched his sea captains on voyages to explore the African coast. One of Henry's hopes was that his men would blaze a route around the continent and negotiate an alliance against Islam with the powerful king of Ethiopia known as "Prester John." The Portuguese rounded the Cape of Good Hope and sailed the east coast of Africa, only to find that Prester John did not exist.

The rules of the game of reason say the question is meaningless and requires no answer. The question: "What would happen if an irresistible force met an immovable body?" In a universe where one of the above conditions exists, by definition the other cannot exist.

You won't get a bellyache from eating a green apple, as long as you chew it completely. The stomach doesn't know the difference between ripe and unripe apples.

According to legend, it was the cowboy and the six-gun that won the West. Actually, it was the steel plow, barbed-wire fencing, and the portable windmill that made it possible for pioneers to settle there.

Carolus Linnaeus, the Swedish botanist who was the first to classify most living things, stubbornly fought the idea of evolution. He insisted that all species were created separately, that no new species had been formed since Creation, and that none had become extinct. About a century later, in 1858, the seminal work by Charles Darwin and Alfred Russel Wallace on the theory of evolution appeared in the *Journal of the Linnaean Society*—articles Linnaeus no doubt would have objected to if he had still been alive.

Robert Darwin was strongly opposed to his son Charles going on the five-year around-the-world expedition of the *Beagle*. He saw Charles once again shifting his sights—this time away from the Church—and drifting, he thought, irretrievably into a life of sport and idleness.

Everyone in the Middle Ages believed—as Aristotle had—that the heart was the seat of intelligence.

In order to test whether acquired characteristics could be inherited, the German biologist August Freidrich Weismann cut the tails off twenty-two generations of mice soon after birth and found that each one nevertheless continued to give birth to mice with full-sized tails. No one knows why he bothered. If he'd stopped to think, he'd have realized that more than twenty-two generations of Jewish boys have been circumcised soon after birth, and each newborn Jewish boy comes into the world with a full-sized foreskin.

———

After World War II, England was offered the Volkswagen business as part of reparations, but declined, believing that cars with engines at the back had no future. British occupation authorities, however, placed an order for 20,000 of the "beetles" to help put the VW company back on its feet. By 1959, the company was producing nearly 4,000 cars every day.

———

Contrary to popular belief, there is little scientific evidence that the ages at which parents die have any correlation to the life span of their offspring, according to studies made at Duke University Center for the Study of Aging and Human Development.

———

The most popular exhibit in the 1939–40 New York World's Fair was the General Motors exhibit with its "Futurama" predictions of America in the 1960s: "Federal laws forbid wanton cutting of wooded hillsides. People do not care much for possessions. Two-month paid vacations. Cars are air-conditioned and cost as little as $200. The happiest people live in one-factory villages."

———

A perpetual-motion machine would violate the laws of thermodynamics. Nobody has succeeded in producing one; nobody ever will.

———

Karl Marx expected that his economic ideas in the *Communist Manifesto* and in *Das Kapital* would have their greatest impact on the advanced nations of the West. The nation on which he thought they would have the least influence was Russia. (*Das Kapital* was translated into Russian before English.) They indeed led to modern socialism and communism—in Russia.

———

"While any cabinet headed by Herr Hitler suggests a highly precarious undertaking, the experiment to make him chancellor . . . might be tried out to curb Nazi truculence."—a report in *The New York Times*, January 29, 1933. In Germany and in other countries, many liberals, welcoming the cabinet, reasoned that Hitler had been removed from the street and saddled with the responsibilities of office in a setting that would "severely circumscribe his liberty of action." Most German politicians expected him to hang himself with his own rope and be out of office within six months, with his party discredited.

———

The temperamental captain of the *Beagle*, Robert FitzRoy, studied physiognomy, and nearly rejected Charles Darwin as the ship's naturalist because of the shape of his nose. FitzRoy was not certain that anyone with such a broad, squat nose could have the character and determination to survive a difficult several-year journey.

Prince Henry the Navigator never navigated the seas on exploring expeditions. Henry was given this title because he ran an exploration institute at Sagres, Portugal, where astronomers, geographers, admirals, and shipbuilders pooled their expertise for voyages along the African coast that culminated, long after Henry's death, when Vasco de Gama rounded the Cape of Good Hope and went on to reach India, in 1497.

In and around Zion, a little town in Illinois, on the shore of Lake Michigan about forty miles north of Chicago, there are hundreds, perhaps thousands, of people who believe the Earth is not round. They are the supporters of a theory, proposed in the early 1900s by Wilbur Glenn Voliva, that the Earth is flat. There are also people today who believe the world is hollow and open at the poles. There are some who even believe the Earth is on the inside of a hollow sphere.

Chevalier d'Éon de Beaumont (1728–1810) was a French secret agent whose first mission took him to the Russian court, where he reputedly disguised himself as a woman in order to gain the confidence of the Empress. He served his country more openly in the army and as a diplomat in Russia and England until he became involved in a public quarrel with his superior and refused to accept his own recall or surrender his papers. When he did return to France, the government insisted on his wearing female dress, and he was thereafter known as the Chevalière d'Éon.

MODERN LIVING

Americans spend more time at shopping malls than anywhere outside their homes and jobs. Shoppers can buy anything from diamonds to yogurt there, go to church or college, register to vote, give blood, bet, work, and meditate. In some malls, one can move into a motel room, apartment, or condominium. The Chicago Symphony can be heard at the Woodfield Mall near Schaumberg, Illinois; the Dallas Symphony was on the verge of expiring before a series of successful concerts at North Park Shopping Center revived it. Approximately $60 billion is tied up in American shopping centers, which do about half ($300 billion in 1977) of all retail business. Women meet prospective lovers in shopping malls far more than they do in singles bars.

———

About 1250, the English scholar Roger Bacon pointed out that the year in the Julian calendar, then in use, was a trifle too long; the vernal equinox came earlier and earlier every year. It took only 300 years for the Western world to make the necessary change to the corrective Gregorian calendar now in use. Russia made the change only after the communist revolution.

———

Thanks to the electric light, Americans today, on the average, sleep 1½ hours less each day than Americans of six decades ago. A University of Florida report noted that most adults sleep 7½ hours a day and that about 15 percent sleep less than 6½ hours.

———

Less than a century after Karl Marx died, more than a billion human beings live under governments that consider themselves adherents of his economic theories.

———

In many countries, urine was used as a detergent for washing. (One of urine's major components, ammonia, is used in cleaning products.)

Tooth decay in Britain is so severe that it is expected that four out of ten adults will soon have false teeth. (Consumption of sugar, four pounds per capita in 1845, is now well over a hundred pounds per capita.)

───────

Dorothy Levitt, pioneer motorist, wrote in her book *The Woman and the Car,* in 1906, that lady drivers should carry a hand mirror in the tool chest under the driving seat. It could be used for "repairing" her makeup after a drive, and for holding aloft occasionally to see what traffic was behind her.

───────

MODERN
TECHNOLOGY

The U.S. could have launched a satellite before the Russians launched *Sputnik*. A U.S. Army rocket launched from Cape Canaveral on September 20, 1957, could have achieved orbital speed easily. Due to government orders, the last stage was an empty dummy, so it did not have the fuel and thrust for orbit. It took Wernher von Braun's team only eighty-four days to ready a satellite for Earth orbit once the command to do so was given.

———

A device invented as a primitive steam engine by the Greek engineer Hero, about the time of the birth of Christ, is used today as a rotating lawn sprinkler.

———

The largest light bulb was a foot-long 75,000-watt bulb hand-blown at the Corning Glass Works to celebrate the seventy-fifth anniversary of Thomas Edison's invention of the incandescent lamp.

———

When the first escalator, or "inclined elevator," was installed in the department store Harrod's in London (near the turn of the century), brandy was served to passengers who felt faint.

———

So that its cars will better handle U.S. roads, the British auto maker BL Ltd. (formerly known as British Leyland) has reproduced in its car-testing track near Coventry some of New York City's potholes. Plaster casts were made of the wheel-crackers and used in the design of the test track.

———

The more an organism has to do, the more complex it is and the more genetic information it needs. A bacterium, which is single-celled, has little genetic information. An alga, such as seaweed, has a good deal. With preprogrammed instructions in their computers amounting to a few million bits, the Viking landers that searched for life on Mars had, by analogy, slightly more "genetic information" than a bacterium but significantly less than an alga.

During the building of the Central Pacific portion of the transcontinental railway over the Sierras, three locomotives and forty cars were dismantled and hauled over the mountains on sledges and logs, a feat comparable with the crossing of the ice-clad Alps by Hannibal and his armored elephants.

Scientists have been measuring the speed of light for three centuries, and they have it down to an accuracy of half a foot per second. The speed of light is 186,282.3959 miles per second.

Coal dust sprayed by aircraft over Russian fields absorbs the early spring sunshine. The resulting warmth melts the snow a little sooner.

It is believed that 90 percent of all scientists who have ever lived are alive now, and that as many scientific papers have been published in the years since 1950 as were published in all the centuries before 1950.

They could travel by themselves to their destination. They could move around easily within certain areas. They could work, marry, set up a household. "They" were prisoners in Siberian exile under czarism, and it was indeed a uniquely Russian form of punishment. The effective walls of the "prison": the frozen wastes around them. (One of the men who married in Siberian exile was Lenin. His wife also had been exiled for revolutionary activity.)

Honey is used as a center for golf balls and in antifreeze mixtures.

In order for the film to be processed, the first Kodak hand cameras had to be returned with their exposed film still in the camera. A reloaded camera and prints from the processed film were later sent to the owner. George Eastman devised the Kodak camera in 1888 and founded the Eastman Kodak Company in 1892.

A chip of silicon a quarter-inch square has the capacity of the original 1949 ENIAC computer, which occupied a city block.

Scientists can condense matter to greater densities and temperatures than those at the center of the sun. Fusion-energy research at Lawrence Livermore Laboratory in California uses twenty laser beams to concentrate on targets so tiny that dozens can be gathered on the head of a pin. The system is named SHIVA, after the oldest name for God in the Hindu religion.

When oil was discovered in the United States, in 1859, gasoline was a useless by-product. It remained so until the development of automobiles. In the early days, far more attention was paid to such by-products as cylinder oil and engine oil (both lubricants), kerosene, naphtha for cleaning, petroleum jelly for ointments, and paraffin. The first commercial product made from petroleum was rock oil, sold at $1 a bottle as a cure for cholera, corns, toothache, and neuralgia. In 1870, one company turned 70,000 pounds of paraffin into chewing gum.

In 1920, a Detroit policeman named William L. Potts worked out an electric light system that allowed him to control three street intersections from one tower. He picked the colors red, yellow, and green because railroads used them. These were the first street traffic lights.

In the late 1920s, police in California raided a small laboratory where they thought a scientist, Philo Taylor Farnsworth, was putting together a still for the making of illegal whiskey. They found, instead, that Farnsworth was making a television set. (Development of home television was delayed by World War II.)

Two identical computers, programmed in the same manner, were on board the Viking lander, the vehicle that descended from the Viking spaceship, landed on Mars and processed soil samples there. Before the miniaturized automated laboratory touched down on Mars, however, complications arose because the two computers were giving different signals. Another computer back on Earth administered an intelligence test to the pair and turned off the "dumber" one.

Until the 1850s, shoes were made by hand and most were "straight"—they could be worn on either foot. There were two widths: fat and slim; most Americans wore slim. The concept and production of left and right shoes came in with machines.

Assembly-line methods made it possible for the U.S. shipyards of Henry J. Kaiser during World War II to produce a ship in just four days.

The greatest steady pressure ever recorded in a laboratory is 25.2 million pounds per square inch, which is 700 times the pressure exerted on the Earth's crust by Mount Everest. This pressure, when applied to diamonds, makes them slowly flow like liquid plastic.

Russia built more than 10,000 miles of railroad between 1896 and 1900, the Trans-Siberian driving steadily eastward regardless of the cost. Thirty-two tunnels were smashed through mountains.

As long ago as 1820, a prefabricated house was shipped to Hawaii by pious Bostonians wanting to ease the life of missionaries living on the far-off Pacific island.

Charles M. Schwab, on leave from his job as chairman of the board of Bethlehem Steel, performed great production "miracles" in the last year of World War I. When he was director-general, the U.S. Shipping Board's Emergency Fleet Corporation once launched a hundred vessels on a single day.

When the steamship Great Eastern was launched on the Thames in London, in 1858, she was five times the size of the biggest vessel afloat—693 feet long, with 22,500 tons displacement. The ship was built to carry 4,000 passengers, almost twice as many as the Queen Mary, launched seventy-seven years later. The Great Eastern could carry 15,000 tons of coal, which would allow her to steam around the globe without refueling.

The largest single industry in the Renaissance world was the Venetian shipyards. Fifteen thousand men worked there and a hundred ships could be built or repaired at the same time. This was the backbone of Venice's maritime trade and of her supremacy on the high seas from the end of the fifteenth to the seventeenth centuries.

F. O. Stanley, who with his twin brother F. E. Stanley, invented the steam-powered automobile, drove one of the vehicles to the top of 6,288-foot Mount Washington, New England's highest peak, in two hours and ten minutes, in 1899. Four years later, the first gasoline-driven car managed to get to the summit in a little less than two hours. The following year, F. E. Stanley took a new-model Stanley Steamer up the mountain in twenty-eight minutes.

The highest man-made temperature—70 million degrees Celsius—was generated at Princeton University in a fusion-power experiment in 1978.

A machine has been invented that can read printed English books aloud to the blind, and it can do so at speeds half again as fast as normal speech. Named for its inventor, the Kurzweil Reading Machine uses an electronic camera to scan printed material in virtually any typeface. It feeds these images into a mini-computer that recognizes each letter, groups the letters into words, computes pronunciation and stress, and, with dazzling speed, produces synthetic speech. The machine has an "accent," but it is readily understood by its users.

MONUMENTS
AND PALACES

The Taj Mahal, one of the world's most beautiful buildings, was scheduled to be torn down in the 1830s so that its marble facing could be removed and shipped to London for sale by auction to the landed English gentry. Wrecking machinery was moved into the garden grounds and work about to begin when word came from London not to proceed. The first auction of marble facades of Indian monuments and edifices had been a failure, and it would not be worth it to tear down the two-hundred-year-old mausoleum.

The famous Crystal Palace was the star attraction of the great London International Exhibition of 1851. It was made of 1 million square feet of glass, 33,000 columns, and 2,300 girders, all prefabricated and almost all interchangeable. It contained 100,000 exhibits and was visited by 6 million people during the Exhibition year. The building was removed in 1854 to Sydenham. It was damaged by fire in 1936, and in 1941 its demolition was ordered because it could serve as a visible ground guide for Nazi bombers.

The foundations of the great European cathedrals go down as far as forty or fifty feet. In some instances, they form a mass of stone as great as that of the visible building above the ground.

Egyptians lived an average of only thirty-five years, yet constructed pyramids, each of which took at least twenty years. The average Parisian in the Middle Ages lived only forty-five years, yet the city built the great cathedral of Notre Dame, which took 137 years. The U.S. space program that put men on the moon consumed only one-sixth of an adult lifetime.

The Canal du Midi—also called the Languedoc Canal—which cuts through southern France and connects the Atlantic with the Mediterranean, was built single-handedly, so to speak, by a public official and self-made engineer who financed the canal entirely with his own money when public funds were not made available. This devoted man was Pierre-Paul, Baron Riquet de Bonrepas. He died from overwork, in 1680, while supervising the final tasks. The canal opened the following year and has been in use ever since. The *Encyclopedia Britannica* calls it "the greatest civil engineering project in Europe from Roman times to the nineteenth century."

The Tower of London, for which construction was begun in 1078 by William the Conqueror, once housed a zoo. It also has served as an observatory, a mint, a prison, a royal palace, and (at present) the home of the Crown Jewels.

The great cathedral of St. Sophia at Constantinople (Istanbul) has sustained for 1,600 years what was until very recent times the largest self-supporting dome ever constructed. Moreover, it has done so in an active seismic region.

While Columbus was seeking new worlds to the west, Italian engineers were rebuilding the Kremlin in Moscow.

The height of the 984-foot-tall (usually) Eiffel Tower varies, depending on the temperature, by as much as 6 inches.

NUMBERS
AND STATISTICS

The Swiss mathematician Leonhard Euler was the most prolific mathematician in history. He went blind in 1766, but that didn't stop him, and scarcely slowed him down, for he had a phenomenal memory and could keep in mind computations that would fill several blackboards. He published 800 papers, some of them quite long. At the time of his death he left enough papers in manuscript to keep the printing presses busy for thirty-five years before the last of them was published.

The number of atoms in a pound of iron is nearly five trillion trillion: 4,891,500,000,000,000,000,000,000.

In the 1830s, more than a hundred years before the first generation of modern computers, Charles Babbage, the English mathematician, designed an "analytical engine" that would perform the four major functions of human computing: carrying out arithmetic operations, having a memory, making a choice of computing sequence, and being capable of numerical input and output. Steam-powered, the machine was designed to store a memory of 1,000 fifty-digit numbers; it was to work with punch-card entry; final results were to be printed automatically and set in type. When the machine required further values for calculations in progress, its operator would be summoned by a bell. Lack of money prevented its development.

Manhattan Island from end to end is less than 1 million inches long. One can walk from New York to Boston in less than 1 million steps. The secretary who goes off for eleven days to the mountains had best hurry—she has less than 1 million seconds to enjoy herself.

The Greeks considered the number 6 to be the first "perfect number" because it is the sum of all its divisors except itself. That is, 6 is divisible by 1, 2, or 3, and $1 + 2 + 3 = 6$. In the more than 2,000 years that elapsed between the time the Greeks made their determination and 1952, when computers were first used for this purpose, mathematicians discovered only eleven more perfect numbers. We now know twenty-four. (The highest has 12,003 digits.)

Designers of the U.S. $1 bill apparently had no superstitious fear of thirteen. On its back is a pyramid with thirteen steps. The motto above it, *annuit coeptis,* has thirteen letters. *E pluribus unum,* written on the ribbon in the eagle's beak, also has thirteen letters. There are thirteen stars over the eagle's head, thirteen stripes on the shield, thirteen war arrows in its left talon, and an olive branch with thirteen leaves in its right. But you see, there were thirteen original states, and that made the number lucky.

The modern decimal position system, in which the placing of numerals indicates their value (units, tens, hundreds), was the invention of the Hindus, about 800 A.D. Their invention of the sign for zero greatly simplified arithmetic computation. By comparison, the Roman numeral system containing no zero was awkward. Try adding MXC [1000 + (100 − 10)] to CIV [100 + (5 − 1)]. It's obviously much simpler to add 1,090 and 104.

Three pairs of common English rabbits were let loose in Australia, in the middle of the nineteenth century. Within a decade, the six rabbits had multiplied into millions, menacing the country's agriculture.

Second most numerous of living things—second only to the insects—are mollusks (soft-bodied animals with hard shells).

The royal house of Saudi Arabia may at present have as many as 5,000 princes and an equal number of princesses. King Abdul Aziz Ibn Saud, who ruled from 1932 until his death in 1953, had 300 wives.

If the population of the Earth were to continue to increase at the present rate indefinitely, by 3530 A.D. the total mass of human flesh and blood would equal the mass of the Earth. By 6826 A.D., the total mass of human flesh and blood would equal the mass of the known universe.

Modern archaeologists have not yet agreed on how large a crowd the Colosseum in Rome could hold in its glory days. One authority estimates 50,000, but about 45,000 is the generally accepted figure.

Yugoslavia has two alphabets (Latin and Cyrillic), three major religions (Orthodox, Catholic, and Muslim), four cultures (Latin, German, Slavic, and Oriental), five nationalities (Serbs, Croats, Slovenes, Macedonians, Montenegrins), six republics (Serbia, Croatia, Slovenia, Macedonia, Montenegro, and Bosnia-Herzogovina), and seven neighbors (Italy, Austria, Hungary, Romania, Bulgaria, Greece, and Albania).

It may take many steps, but by adding its reverse to any integer (except perhaps one) a palindromic sum can be attained. That is, the sum is the same from right to left as from left to right. Examples:

38	139	48,017
83	931	71,084
121	1070	119,101
	0701	101,911
	1771	221,012
		210,122
		431,134

From 89 to its palindromic sum—8,813,200,023,188—takes twenty-four steps. (There may be an exception to the conjecture that *every* integer will eventually produce a palindrome. Boris A. Kordemsky, a Russian mathematician, has noted that the number 196 has been carried by computers beyond thousands of steps without yet producing a palindrome.)

The Fibonacci series in mathematics—named for the great thirteenth-century Italian expert on numbers—is the series in which each number equals the sum of the preceding two: 1 plus 1 equals 2, 1 plus 2 equals 3, 2 plus 3 equals 5, 3 plus 5 equals 8, 5 plus 8 equals 13, 21, 34, 55, 89, 144, and so on. The Fibonacci series turns out to be of importance to botanists as well. Leaves on a branch are often placed helically around the stalk; that is, each leaf is a little higher than and to one side of the preceding one. Different plants have characteristic angles of divergence of adjacent leaves. The angle, as Boris A. Kordemsky has noted, is expressed usually by a fraction of

360 degrees. For the linden and elm, the fraction is 1/2; for the beech, 1/3; oak and cherry, 2/5; poplar and pear, 3/8; willow, 5/13, and so on. The same angle is preserved in the arrangement of each tree's branches, buds, and flowers.

––––––

In their encyclopedia, *Elements of Mathematics,* a group of French mathematicians working under the collective pseudonym of Nicholas Bourbaki spent 200 pages just introducing matters relating to the number 1.

––––––

The number of possible ways of playing just the first four moves on each side in a game of chess is 318,979,564,000.

––––––

Using cesium atoms, the clock at the National Bureau of Standards in Washington, D.C., will gain or lose only one second in 300 years.

––––––

Lord Byron's daughter, Augusta Ada Byron, Countess of Lovelace, was an accomplished mathematician and the associate of Charles Babbage, who designed the principles of the first general-purpose digital computer. She is credited with developing the essential ideas of computer programming, which in refined form are still valid today.

––––––

Coffee is the world's second largest item of international commerce. (Petroleum is first.)

––––––

Seven percent of licensed drivers in the U.S. are sixteen- and seventeen-year-olds, and they are responsible for thirty percent of all automobile fatalities.

––––––

Americans' popular image of Europeans may be ten or twenty years out of date. Most 'Europeans have a greater life expectancy than Americans. Four European countries have a higher living standard than the U.S.—Sweden, Switzerland, Norway, Denmark. The gross national product of West Germany and France combined is estimated to be 18 percent larger than the GNP of the U.S.S.R. The GNP of France alone is greater than that of China—higher than the forty-one Latin American countries (including Brazil) combined.

––––––

Twenty-five million of the 162,000,000 telephones in the U.S. have unlisted numbers.

––––––

In the dozen years from 1962 to 1974, the number of dead letters handled by the U.S. Postal Service more than doubled. In 1962, the total was 22,300,000 dead letters; in 1974, there were 44,872,000. At 13 cents per letter in the fiscal year 1976, Americans wasted about $5.5 million on postage. The two major reasons for dead letters: poor or illegible address and no return address.

———

There are more than a hundred distinct ethnic groups in the Soviet Union.

———

You could build a fourteen-story building inside the choir of the medieval cathedral of Beauvais without reaching the roof, which at about 157 feet is the highest of all Gothic vaults.

———

The Cathedral of Notre Dame in Amiens covers 8,500 square yards. When it was completed in the Middle Ages, the entire population of the city, about 10,000, could attend the same service.

———

In the 1970 census, the U.S. had 2,983 men who were already widowers at the age of fourteen and 289 women who—at that same age, fourteen—already had been widowed or divorced.

———

Take fifteen copies of *Isaac Asimov's Book of Facts* and number them "1" to "15." If you tried to line them up in all possible arrangements, and if you made a change a minute, it would take you 2,487,996 years to do it.

———

A prime number is any number that can be divided only by itself and 1. There are an infinite number of primes. Any one of those primes (except for 2 and 3) will become evenly divisible by 6 if you either subtract 1 from it or add 1 to it. For example, the number 17, if 1 is added to it, is evenly divisible by 6; or the number 19, if 1 is subtracted from it, is evenly divisible by 6.

———

Before the computer was used in determining prime numbers, the largest known prime was $2^{127} - 1$. To test such a number on a standard calculator requires many months, and similar amounts of time are needed to check the result. In 1971, the American Mathematical Society received the highest known prime number, $2^{19937} - 1$, a number of 6,002 digits. It was calculated on an IBM computer in 39 minutes, 26.4 seconds.

———

Great mathematical minds have always enjoyed playing with numbers, feeling that there is but a small step from recreational math to creative math. Leibniz, for example, spent much time playing—which in his case meant studying—solitaire, and Einstein devoted considerable shelf space to books on mathematical games.

There are fifty-two cards in an ordinary deck. The number of ways in which they can be arranged is just about 80,660,000,000,000, 000, 000, 000, 000, 000, 000, 000, 000, 000, 000, 000, 000, 000,000,000,000,000. If you had that many decks of cards, each arranged a different way, and if each deck weighed only as much as a single hydrogen atom (the lightest atom), all the decks together would weigh a billion times as much as the sun.

A palindrome is a word or sentence that reads the same backward as it does forward (such as tot and boob). Mathematics, too, has arrangements that could be called palindromes. For example:

$$21978 \times 4 = 87912$$
$$10989 \times 9 = 98901$$

There are more complex examples of reversal, mixing addition and multiplication. For example:

$$9 + 9 = 18 \qquad 81 = 9 \times 9$$
$$24 + 3 = 27 \qquad 72 = 3 \times 24$$
$$47 + 2 = 49 \qquad 94 = 2 \times 47$$
$$497 + 2 = 499 \qquad 994 = 2 \times 497$$

In 1873, the English mathematician William Shanks calculated the value of the mathematical expression *pi* to 707 places. It took him *fifteen years* to do so. In 1949, the first electronic computers calculated it to 2,035 places in *three days*—and found that Shanks had made a mistake and the last hundred or so figures in his calculation were wrong.

When Arabic numerals were invented, they did not win immediate acceptance. In the year 1300, their use was forbidden in European commercial dealings because they could be forged more easily than Roman numerals. (Changing "1979" seems to be simpler than changing "MCMLXXIX.") Arabic numerals were not completely accepted throughout Europe until 1800.

The number 2520 can be divided by 1 and 2 and 3 and 4 and 5 and 6 and 7 and 8 and 9 and 10 (as well as by 12, 14, 15, 18, 20, 21, 24 . . .) without having a fractional leftover.

The number 37, which cannot be wholly divided by any number (except by 1 and itself), has the property that it will wholly divide the following numbers: 111, 222, 333, 444, 555, 666, 777, 888, 999.

There is a way of writing 1 by using all ten digits at once:

$$\frac{148}{296} + \frac{35}{70} = 1$$

And here are four ways of writing 100 by using the ten digits once:

$$70 + 24\frac{9}{18} + 5\frac{3}{6} = 100$$

$$50\frac{1}{2} + 49\frac{38}{76} = 100$$

$$87 + 9\frac{4}{5} + 3\frac{12}{60} = 100$$

$$80\frac{27}{54} + 19\frac{3}{6} = 100$$

There is, of course, a big difference between addition and multiplication, between subtraction and multiplication, between addition and division, and between subtraction and division. But there are exceptions:

$$\frac{13}{4} + \frac{13}{9} = \frac{13}{4} \times \frac{13}{9} = \frac{169}{36}$$

$$\frac{3}{5} - \frac{3}{8} = \frac{3}{5} \times \frac{3}{8} = \frac{9}{40}$$

$$\frac{169}{30} + \frac{13}{15} = \frac{169}{30} \div \frac{13}{15} = \frac{13}{2}$$

$$\frac{121}{28} - \frac{11}{7} = \frac{121}{28} \div \frac{11}{7} = \frac{11}{4}$$

Also, the numbers 19 and .95 give the same result whether you multiply them or deduct the second from the first: 18.05.

$$10 \times 10 \text{ plus } 11 \times 11 \text{ plus } 12 \times 12 = 365$$
$$13 \times 13 \text{ plus } 14 \times 14 = 365$$

The values 10×10 through 14×14 are the only consecutive products that give identical results when arranged as above. By coincidence, the results are the number of days in a year.

————

The largest number that can be written with three digits is $9^{(9^9)}$, that is, $9^{387420489}$. No one knows exactly its value; it's a number that begins with 428124773. . . . It would have 369 million digits—and would take years to read.

————

There are at least two ways of writing "1000" with 8s only:

$$\frac{8 + 8}{8} (8 \times 8 \times 8 - 8) - 8 = 1000$$
$$\frac{8888 - 888}{8} = 1000$$

And here are three of several ways of writing "10" with 9s only:

$$9 + \frac{99}{99} = 10$$
$$\frac{99}{9} - \frac{9}{9} = 10$$
$$\left(9 + \frac{9}{9}\right)\frac{9}{9} = 10$$

————

The number 10 is used as a convenient base to count with, but the Gauls of ancient France, the Mayas of Central America, and other peoples used a base of 20. The Sumerians, the Babylonians, and others after them used a base of 60—convenient because 60 can be evenly divided by 2, 3, 4, 5, 6, 10, 12, 15, 20, and 30. This 60 survives in the divisions of hours into minutes and minutes into seconds, and in the division of the circle into 360 degrees.

————

One of the most famous unsolved problems in mathematics is "Fermat's last theorem," named for the French mathematician Pierre de Fermat (1601–65). He wrote that he had found that a certain equation, $x^n + y^n = z^n$, had no solution in whole numbers, except where $n = 2$. Thus, $3^2 + 4^2 = 5^2$. Fermat went on to say that he didn't have the space in his notation for the simple proof. Mathematicians have been searching for the proof for three centuries, in vain. Modern computers have shown that the equation has no solutions for all values of n up to 2,000, but this is not the general proof we are still looking for.

The abacus was used in the West in medieval times, and then forgotten. Interest in the counting tool was revived when the abacus was brought to France by Lieutenant Jean Victor Poncelet, when he was freed by the Russians after Napoleon's fall.

Fra Luca Pacioli, in 1494, published a huge volume on mathematics that was an important summary of all that was then known on the subject. Pacioli's greatest fame came, however, from the publication of the double-entry bookkeeping system as part of that book. It earned him the title "Father of Bookkeeping."

The method of house numbering using odd numbers on one side of the street and even numbers on the other was instituted in the U.S.

123456787654321 is 11,111,111 multiplied by itself.

There is an infinite number of numbers that have the same value whether added or multiplied. They follow this pattern:
$3 + 1½ = 3 × 1½ = 4½$
$4 + 1⅓ = 4 × 1⅓ = 5⅓$
$5 + 1¼ = 5 × 1¼ = 6¼$
• • •
$1000 + 1\ 1/999 = 1000 × 1\ 1/999 = 1001\ 1/999$
etc.
However, there is only one integer that can be added to itself and multiplied with itself with the same result:
$$2 + 2 = 4 \text{ and } 2 × 2 = 4$$

The Gregorian calendar is the version used today. Pope Gregory XIII corrected the time error in the Julian calendar (used prior to the Gregorian) by eliminating ten days in 1582 and by ordaining that thereafter the years ending in hundreds should not be leap years unless divisible by 400. Most Roman Catholic countries accepted these changes immediately. Protestant countries delayed for a while.

By repeating the number 2 five times, you can write the value of all 10 digits:

$$2 + 2 - 2 - 2/2 = 1$$
$$2 + 2 + 2 - 2 - 2 = 2$$
$$2 + 2 - 2 + 2/2 = 3$$
$$2 \times 2 \times 2 - 2 - 2 = 4$$
$$2 + 2 + 2 - 2/2 = 5$$
$$2 + 2 + 2 + 2 - 2 = 6$$
$$22 \div 2 - 2 - 2 = 7$$
$$2 \times 2 \times 2 + 2 - 2 = 8$$
$$2 \times 2 \times 2 + 2/2 = 9$$
$$2 - 2/2 - 2/2 = 0$$

The total number of different bridge hands possible is roughly 54 octillion: 54,000,000,000,000,000,000,000,000,000.

Because the mathematician John Wallis was an extremely nationalistic Englishman, he used his influence against the adoption by Great Britain of the Gregorian calendar. He argued that acceptance would imply subservience to Rome (and, hence, to foreigners). His view led to a delay in inevitable adoption by half a century.

In 1816, Timothy Dwight, the president of Yale, inveighed against the "alarming and terrible" divorce rate in Connecticut. At that time, about one of every hundred marriages was being legally dissolved. In 1977 alone, about 1.1 million marriages in the United States ended in divorce. In 1977 there were about 2.2 million marriages.

There are 11.5 psychiatrists per 100,000 population in the U.S. In the nation's capital, however, there are 56.1 per 100,000.

A computer program at Dartmouth College on birth-control practices has built into it a 1-in-10 billion chance that a woman will become pregnant though strictly celibate.

The atomic nucleus takes up only about one-quadrillionth (1/1,000,000,000,000,000) of the room in an atom; but about 99.97 percent of all the matter in an atom is squeezed into that tiny nucleus at its center.

While modern man can expect to live out the biblical span of three score and ten years, life expectancy was never so high in the past. The following life expectancies were estimated for the average male at age fifteen, past the age of childhood diseases: Neanderthal, thirty-three years; Bronze Age, forty years; ancient Greece and Rome, thirty-six years; medieval England, forty-nine years; United States at the turn of the century, sixty years. (Estimates were based on examination of skeletons, tombstones, legal documents, and census records. Infectious disease was the most common cause of death.)

The last state to join the union, Hawaii, is the state with the highest average male lifespan—73.60 years. North Dakota has the highest average female lifespan—80.36 years. The District of Columbia has the lowest male lifespan—65.71 years—and it has the lowest for females—75.31 years.

With all the possibilities for variation among the sex cells produced by each parent, it seems quite certain that each one of the estimated sixty billion humans who have lived has been distinctly different from every other one, and that this should continue for the indefinite future. The few exceptions are identical twins, triplets, etc., for they arise from a single fertilized ovum that divides into two or more separate cells that then develop independently.

In India, 34 percent of all rural families and 44 percent of all urban families live in one-room homes. In the four largest cities the figure averages 67 percent. In Calcutta it is 79 percent, and it leaves uncounted the myriad who live and sleep on the pavements and in the streets.

Drilling an oil well five miles deep requires drilling night and day, seven days a week, for as long as 500 days.

In terms of the resources he will use in his lifetime and the pollution he will cause, one citizen of the U.S. is the equivalent of about eighty citizens of India.

The total population of the Earth at the time of Julius Caesar was 150 million. The total population *increase in two years* on Earth today is 150 million.

The English astronomer Edmund Halley prepared the first detailed mortality tables, in 1693. Life and death could now be studied statistically, and the life-insurance business was born.

Three years before the potato famine of 1848, the population of Ireland was 8.25 million. Three years after the famine, it was 6.5 million. About I million people had died, and a million had emigrated. The population of Ireland right now is only a little over half the 1848 figure.

During the next minute, 100 people will die and 240 will be born. The world's population problem increases by 140 people per minute.

The New York Public Library adds nearly a million items to its collections each year.

There are 2,500,000 rivets in the Eiffel Tower.

People who have never married are 7½ times more likely to be hospitalized in a state or community psychiatric facility than those who are married. According to the National Institute of Mental Health, the rate for such admissions in 1975 for Americans fourteen years of age and older was 685.2 per 100,000 unmarrieds, compared with 89.9 per 100,000 marrieds.

In 1978, the Center for Population Research estimated that a million teen-age girls in the U.S., or one in ten between the ages of fifteen and nineteen, become pregnant every year. About 600,000 actually bear children.

OF WIVES
AND MISTRESSES

Stephen Douglas's antagonism toward Abraham Lincoln stemmed partly from the fact that Mary Todd had chosen Lincoln over Douglas as a suitor. Mary Todd met both Douglas and Lincoln at the same time and was courted by both. Her ambition led her to evaluate the two men and she chose Lincoln as the most likely to attain future success and as her own best chance for glory.

―――――――

The love affair of the eighteen-year-old Héloïse (1101–64) with her forty-year-old teacher Abélard (1079–1142) became so well known that it overshadows Héloïse's later accomplishments. After what today would be called a graduate course in medicine, philosophy, and other disciplines, Héloïse practiced and taught medicine for twenty years at the Hermitage of Paraclete near Troyes in France.

―――――――

Peter the Great had his wife's lover executed and his head put into a jar of alcohol. She had to keep it in her bedroom.

―――――――

When the Elector of Hanover became George I of England in 1714, his wife did not become Queen because she had committed adultery. He placed her under house arrest in Ahlden Castle, where she stayed for thirty-two years. Those who knew her fate called her the "Prisoner of Ahlden," and so she remains in history. Ironically, George had arrived in England with his two mistresses. Adultery was a crime only for wives.

―――――――

The Babylonians auctioned off marriageable girls every year. Men had to bid high for the most attractive girls, and their money provided dowries so that the ugly girls, for whom no one would bid, could find husbands. Herodotus considered this the wisest of Babylonian customs.

―――――――

"An utter stranger takes the liberty of addressing you," began a note from Shelley's sister-in-law, Claire Godwin, to George Byron, whom she had not met. "It may seem a strange assertion, but it is no less true that I place my happiness in your hands. . . . I know that you have the reputation of being mad, bad, and dangerous, but nevertheless you hold my destiny. . . ." Byron yielded to the request for assignation. He met Miss Godwin, despised her, loved her—and shucked her.

Marie Budberg (1892–1974) was "the center of London's intellectual, artistic, and social life" for four decades. Born as a Russian aristocrat, she was fluent in five languages, published thirty books, and was a costume designer and an adviser to theater (and, later, movie and television) directors. Her amorous liaisons included Maxim Gorky (with whom she lived for many years) and H. G. Wells. Her home was a salon in the tradition of the eighteenth century.

The Nayar people of South India have had an unusual kind of household. A young woman marries a man whom she almost never sees. Various lovers visit her, and most of her children result from these liaisons. The woman and her children live with her sisters and their children. Their brothers are the male authority figures in the household, although they, too, are rarely present. This life-style is less common today than it was in the past, but it still exists.

Fernande Olivier lived seven years (1904–11) with Picasso and wanted to marry him. However, she was unable to locate her estranged husband and obtain the necessary divorce. In the mid-1940s, she happened to learn that her husband had died just after she had first met Picasso in a corridor of the tenement known as the Bâteau-Lavoir—forty years earlier.

Alexandre Gustave Eiffel, the builder of the Eiffel Tower in Paris, which opened in 1889, created at its peak the highest man-made love nest so that he could carry on his personal trysts. The aerie is open now to all visitors.

Though popularly thought to have been an Egyptian, Cleopatra was a Macedonian, the daughter of Ptolemy XI. She married two of her brothers and was the mistress of both Caesar and Mark Antony.

The British trounced George Washington's depleted army at White Plains, then at Fort Washington, then at Brandywine, then at Germantown, and could have delivered the knockout blow at Valley

Forge in the ferocious winter of 1777–78. But they didn't. They didn't attack because William Howe, the British general in command of George III's forces in the colonies, had found warm comfort in nearby Philadelphia with a certain Mrs. Loring. By spring, the Colonial army was able to wriggle off the hook.

The fourth Mogul Emperor, Jahangir, who ruled from 1605 to 1627, had a harem of 300 royal wives, 5,000 more women, and 1,000 young men for alternate pleasures. Outside the palace, he stabled other kinds of pets: 12,000 elephants, 10,000 oxen, 2,000 camels, 3,000 deer, 4,000 dogs, 100 tame lions, 500 buffalo, and 10,000 carrier pigeons.

After his love affair of two years with Catherine the Great, Gregory Aleksandrovich Potemkin continued to be an important adviser to Catherine. He even helped to choose her subsequent lovers.

The Thracians were a warrior people who lived in what is today Bulgaria, from about 1300 to 500 B.C., when they were reduced to vassals by the Persians. They practiced polygamy. When a man died, his wives argued among themselves as to which one had been his favorite. The wife who was finally decided upon as the favorite won the privilege of being killed and placed next to her husband in his tomb.

In ancient Greece, women counted their age from the date on which they were married, not from the day they were born, signifying that the wedding marked the start of a woman's real life.

By the end of the sixteenth century, there were about 11,600 courtesans in Venice, twelve times the number of patrician wives. The names and addresses of the courtesans were published in a book, copies of which may be seen today in the Library of St. Mark. The courtesans were the only commoners who mixed with ease with the Venetian upper class.

Sally Hemings, the black slave who is thought to have been Thomas Jefferson's mistress for twenty-five years, was a blood relative of Jefferson's wife. She was Martha Jefferson's half sister. Martha's father, John Wayles, had taken Betty Hemings, Sally's mother, as a concubine after the death of his third wife. Betty bore him six children, of whom Sally was one.

ON BOOKS

In 1800, the Congress appropriated $5,000 "for the purchase of such books as may be necessary for the use of Congress at the said city of Washington, and for fitting up a suitable apartment for containing them." Currently, the Library of Congress houses over 72 million pieces of research material, including over 16.5 million books and 31 million manuscripts, and costs over $150 million a year to run.

———

Long before Europeans "invented" movable type of metal, in the fifteenth century, the Tibetans, Chinese, and Koreans were using various other kinds of movable type. The Chinese were motivated primarily by the desire to make Confucian texts more readily available. Later, between 1403 and 1484, the Korean court undertook eight large-scale printing projects with movable type.

———

Columbus had with him on his first voyage to the New World a copy of Marco Polo's book about his thirteenth-century, twenty-two-year odyssey to China and back.

———

A factor in keeping Persian the language of modern Iran (and preventing replacement by Arabic) was the writing of the Book of Kings, in Persian, by the eleventh-century poet Firdausi—a poem of 60,000 verses (seven times the length of Homer's *Iliad*), detailing the history of the Persian kings from legendary beginnings down to Khosru II in the seventh century. It has remained the great national poem of the nation and its preeminent literary work.

———

For some languages, translations of the Bible are the first works, or even the only works, in their literature. The only notable work in Gothic, for instance, is the translation of the Bible by Ulfilas, who was converted to Christianity at Constantinople and in 341 A.D. consecrated a bishop. It is said that Ulfilas even had to invent the alphabet he used.

———

There was a time—the twelfth century—when the most important scientific work was translation. The books of the Arabic scholars, who for centuries had preserved the words of the Greek philosophers by translation and commentary, began to be rendered into Latin.

—————

Chapbooks, the comic books of their time, were named after the chapmen, or peddlers, who sold them. They were cheap in price and crudely illustrated. In 1682, one of the most popular American chapbooks was *Mary Rowlandson's Captivity*, an account of a woman captured by the Indians. It sold 5 million copies. Chapbooks achieved their greatest popularity in the early nineteenth century, but had disappeared by the advent of the U.S. Civil War.

—————

The *Communist Manifesto* of Marx and Engels was ignored in Germany when it was published in 1848, and a Russian translation was suppressed by censors in the 1860s. It remained a rare pamphlet until it was reprinted in 1872.

—————

Twice as many books on religion were published in England as works of fiction in 1870. Sixteen years later, novels far outnumbered religious works.

—————

The first children's book published in the U.S. was written by Puritan preacher John Cotton and printed in Cambridge, Massachusetts, in 1646. Its title was *Spiritual Milk for Boston Babes in Either England Drawn from the Breasts of Both Testaments for Their Souls' Nourishment.*

—————

Some fifty volumes of the writings of Aristotle have survived, many by a fortunate chance. About 80 B.C., the men of a Roman army invading Asia Minor found a number of manuscripts of Aristotle's works in a pit and brought them to their general, Sulla. It turned out that no other copies of many of them existed, and Sulla had them taken to Rome and recopied.

—————

The world's first and "most comprehensive" encyclopedia was three volumes: the *Nuremberg Chronicle*, published in 1493. Its sole author was Hartmann Schedel, a Nuremberg physician who had a passion for collecting books and copying manuscripts. His personal library, in fact, was his best reference source in compiling the *Chronicle*. Though published late in 1493, it did not contain the most momentous news of the preceding year: Columbus's historic voyage.

—————

The art of printing from wooden blocks with the characters in reverse was initiated in Buddhist monasteries in China. The oldest surviving printed book that can be reliably dated is a Buddhist text, the *Diamond Sutra*, made in China in 868 A.D.

By the fifteenth century, manuscript copyists had set up mass-production workshops capable of turning out sizable quantities of books. An order in the year 1437 (found recently at Leyde, the Netherlands) called for 200 copies of the *Psalms of Penitence*, 200 of Cato's *Distichs* in Flemish, and 400 of a small prayer book.

The first European printers were Germans, all from one or more workshops in the cathedral city of Mainz, where the first presses appeared about 1445. By 1480, printing shops had been set up in 110 European towns. By the end of the fifteenth century, fifty years after the first book was printed, at least 35,000 editions had been published and from 15 million to 20 million books printed. (This was at a time when the total population of Europe, after pandemic plagues, was less than 100 million.)

Five hundred years ago, books were so scarce and valuable that the bishop of Winchester, England, whose entire library consisted of seventeen books, had to give a heavy bond, drawn with solemnity, that he would return, uninjured, a Bible from the convent of St. Swithin.

Clement Clarke Moore (1779–1863)—a biblical scholar, professor of Oriental and Greek literature, and compiler of a Greek and Hebrew lexicon—wrote the exquisitely simple and easily remembered "Visit from St. Nicholas": " 'Twas the night before Christmas and all through the house . . . "

The best seller of all American books? The *Guinness Book of World Records*? Dr. Spock's *Common Sense Book of Baby and Child Care*? *The World Almanac & Book of Facts*? None of them comes anywhere near Noah Webster's *Blue-Backed Speller* published in 1783. In revised editions, it is still in print and has sold well over 100 million copies. (Watch out for *Isaac Asimov's Book of Facts*.)

Euclid is the most successful textbook writer of all time. His *Elements*—of around 300 B.C.—has gone through more than 1,000 editions since the invention of printing. The phrase "I studied my Euclid" was for a long time synonymous with "I studied geometry."

———

The first known English book in which the "New World" is mentioned was published in 1509. It was Alexander Barclay's translation of a long didactic poem by the German satirist Sebastian Brant, *Das Narrenschiff*. In English it is *The Shyp of Folys* ("The Ship of Fools").

———

An important step in the history of reference works was made when the German physician and philosopher Johann Georg Krünitz (1728–96) wrote his *Oekonomisch-technologische Encyklopädie*. He wrote it all by himself—242 highly organized volumes. He also wrote 438 other books.

———

The idea for a "nothing book" is not new. When Hermann Boerhaave, a Dutch physician and chemist best known for his *Elementa chemiae*, died in 1738, he left behind a sealed book with the title *The Onliest and Deepest Secrets of the Medical Art*. The book, still sealed, was auctioned for $20,000 in gold. When the new owner broke the seal, he found that 99 of the 100 pages were blank. Only the title page bore this handwritten note by the "author": "Keep your head cool, your feet warm, and you'll make the best doctor poor."

———

The first French translation of Newton's *Principia Mathematica* was done by Gabrielle du Châtelet (1706–49), who was Voltaire's mistress at the time. She also acquainted France with the ideas of Leibniz by writing, in 1740, *Les Institutions de Physique*.

———

General Lew Wallace's Best seller *Ben-Hur*, published in 1880, was the first work of fiction to be blessed by a pope.

———

There are only forty-eight Gutenberg Bibles extant. This figure includes two that were in Germany during World War II; they are missing but presumed by bibliophiles to be safe.

———

Pi, the ratio of the circumference of a circle to its diameter, was computer-calculated to a million decimal places in 1973 by the French mathematicians Jean Guilloud and Martine Bouyer. The value was published as a 400-page book—very important, and yet surely one of the most boring books in the world.

———

Japan's favorite English-language author in the late 1970s was Thomas Hardy, whose nineteenth-century novels, like *Jude the Obscure*, are generally gloomy and naturalistic studies of character and environment.

The first printed editions of the Pentateuch, the first five books of the Old Testament, and the Talmud, the vast compilation of the Oral Law of the Jews, were published in the early sixteenth century by Daniel Bomberg's printing house in the Venetian ghetto, located near San Girolamo. Since then, many important Hebrew texts have been first published in Venice.

America's first best-selling novelist was a woman, Susanna Haswell Rowson. Although it was a melodramatic work with wooden characters and a hackneyed plot, *Charlotte Temple*, published in 1791, appealed to popular tastes. It went through more than 200 editions.

Three of the most influential books ever published came out in Europe in the very same year: 1543. They were Nicholas Copernicus's *The Revolutions of the Heavenly Orbs*, Archimedes' mathematics and physics in English translation from the original Greek, and Andreas Vesalius's anatomical drawings, *De humani corporis fabrica*.

Prior to World War I, fewer than 20 books a year that were published in England dealt with military science. In Germany, almost 700 books a year were being published on the subject.

The art of printing was born at its zenith, for the first printed book, the Gutenberg Bible, is considered by many the most beautiful ever produced. Three hundred copies were printed, nearly 1,300 pages each, forty-two lines in Latin to the page. The Gutenberg Bibles remain among the most valuable books in the world.

It is hard to imagine that an author whose novels have sold over 70 million hardcover copies in twenty-two languages was virtually unknown in America until 1977. He is Karl May, a German writer who lived from 1842 to 1912 and whose spellbinding and inspirational adventure stories are finally appearing in the U.S., after enjoying an ever-increasing popularity around the world. They were accompanied by earlier quotes from Herman Hesse, Albert Einstein, Thomas Mann, Albert Schweitzer, and many other notables in whose lives Karl May seemed to have played an essential role. Most of Karl

May's novels are written in the first person singular—a fictional su-
perhero, who one of May's U.S. editors says is "Jesus Christ and
James Bond in one person."

———

Theodore Roosevelt, twenty-sixth President of the United States
(1901–09), wrote forty books. His first was written during his senior
year at Harvard University—*The Naval War of 1812*. Roosevelt had
a long and varied career. He headed the New York City Police Board
and was a Spanish-American War hero, governor of New York State,
big-game hunter, explorer, and conservationist.

———

Pliny the Elder (23–79 A.D.) was a busy man. He wrote not only a
thirty-one-volume general history of Rome and a twenty-volume history of Roman warfare, but also a thirty-seven-volume natural encyclopedia, an eight-volume Latin grammar, and a six-volume
manual of oratory. In addition, he was, at various times, a general
and admiral, and a governor of the Roman provinces in Africa, Spain,
Germany, and Gaul.

———

A Gutenberg Bible was purchased at auction in 1898 for $15,000
and given to the General Theological Seminary in New York City.
It was locked in a vault until 1978, when it was sold at another
auction for $2 million. (The highest price ever paid for a Gutenberg
Bible was $2.5 million, in 1970.)

———

In another two decades, many of the books published between 1900
and 1940 will be useless. They are self-destructing, principally because of the acid in the paper and the pollutants in the air. Books
made before the turn of the century were principally of rag content,
and are holding up well. Since 1900, the shift in book production
has been to paper of wood content.

———

Charles Darwin believed that the proposed first printing of his book
The Origin of Species would be too large: 1,250 copies. But the
edition was sold out the very first day of publication.

———

Book sales second only to *Uncle Tom's Cabin* in the middle 1800s
were those of Timothy Shay Arthur's *Ten Nights in a Barroom*. The
former was an immediate best-seller and, according to President
Lincoln, the spark that fired the Civil War. About 100,000 copies of
Arthur's temperance work had been bought by 1880. Both books
were dramatized.

———

There are up to 11 million index cards, between the first card for "A" (pseudonym of English writer Matthew Arnold) and the last card for "Zyve, Claire Turner" (editor of radio plays in the 1930s), in the 9,000 separate drawers, or trays, that make up the main catalog of the Research Libraries of the New York Public Library. Nearly 900 trays are needed to hold the "S" cards; even "X" fills the equivalent of two whole trays.

––––––––

Perhaps the world's most prolific playwright was Lope de Vega (1562–1635). He may have written as many as 2,200 plays, of which fewer than 500 survive.

––––––––

The first collection of Aesop's animal fables was put together 200 years after his death, and included many that originated long after the Greek slave from Africa had departed this vale of tears.

––––––––

Freud's major work, by general consensus, was *The Interpretation of Dreams* (1899), for which he was paid $209. Freud himself said of it, "Insight such as this falls to one's lot but once in a lifetime." Nevertheless, eight years were to pass before the entire first printing— 600 copies—had been sold. The work has been reprinted many times in many countries. At least three publishers in the United States, one paperback and two hardcover, are selling it today.

––––––––

Kepler's story "Somnium," published after his death in 1630, is the first piece of authentic science fiction, as opposed to fantasy, because it was the first to try to describe the lunar surface as it really was.

––––––––

Goethe's book *Farbenlehre* ("History of the Theory of Colors") brilliantly but mistakenly argued the case for white light being pure and unmixed. It is now remembered only as the last dying wail against the optical revolution initiated by Newton, who had discovered that sunlight, and white light in general, could be split up by a prism into a rainbow of colors. White light is actually a mixture of colored lights.

––––––––

The first person to labor over the right angles of a particular quadrilateral, in connection with Euclid's fifth postulate, was Omar Khayyám. Omar should be remembered as a great mathematician and astronomer, but his clever quatrains made him more famous as a hedonistic and agnostic poet.

––––––––

A Hungarian mathematician, Farkas Bolyai, published a textbook on mathematics in 1831. He included a twenty-six-page appendix written by his twenty-year-old son, Janos. This appendix proved to be one of the foundations of non-Euclidean geometry; it was a mathematical landmark worth far more than anything else in the book.

———

When Charles Darwin published his pioneer work on human evolution, *The Descent of Man,* in 1871, not a single fossil that was known to be pre-human had been found to support his ideas. Although his theory was later proved to be true, it was formulated entirely without physical evidence and was based almost completely on speculation.

———

Between 1924 and 1932, nearly one hundred British intellectuals wrote a book apiece speculating on the future. Not one book was about the possibility of overpopulation. (The celebrated geneticist J. B. S. Haldane [1892–1964] predicted the U.S. population would level off at 145 million.)

———

In looking at 200 fairy tales by the Brothers Grimm, a rough scoring of the male and female characters reveals a strong dichotomy. There are sixteen wicked mothers or stepmothers and only three wicked fathers or stepfathers. There are twenty-three evil female witches and only two evil male witches. There are thirteen young women who kill or endanger the men who love them, but only one man who harms his bride.

———

It wasn't until 1609, sixty-six years after the book was published, that it was discovered, by Kepler, that a Lutheran minister had added an unauthorized preface to Copernicus's classic. The preface said, in effect, that the Copernican theory was not being advanced as a description of the actual facts but only as a device to facilitate computation of planetary tables. This weakened the book and compromised the reputation of the dead Copernicus. For thirteen years, Copernicus had hesitated to publish his theories, believing that any suggestion that the Earth moved would be considered heretical and might get him into trouble (as, later, Bruno and Galileo got into trouble). Playing it extraordinarily safe, Copernicus carefully dedicated the work to Pope Paul III, but it was not removed until 1835 from the *Index Librorum Prohibitorum*—the list of books officially banned by the Church.

———

Descartes's hundred-page appendix to a book on vortexes and the structure of the solar system proved to be inestimably more important than the book itself. Descartes's appendix combined algebra and geometry, to the great enrichment of both, in explaining that through the use of his coordinate system every point in a plane could be represented by an ordered system of two numbers and every point in space by an ordered system of three numbers.

To get her cookbook published, in 1896, Fannie Farmer had to pay Little, Brown and Company the printing costs of the first 3,000 copies. The publisher refused to take the risk, saying that women would not buy still another collection of recipes. Ironically, her *Boston Cooking School Cook Book* eventually became the most popular cookbook of its time and a "gold mine" through the years for the publisher; millions of copies have been sold in dozens of editions.

The "Athens of the West"—the Moorish capital of Cordoba, in Andalusia, Spain's southernmost region—had in the year 900 A.D. a library of 400,000 books, miles of paved streets, and a population of half a million. To the north, Paris was a bastioned island and London, a stockade built in defense of Viking raiders.

Icelanders read more books per capita than any other people in the world.

There are more than 21 million pages of manuscripts and other documents in the Franklin D. Roosevelt Library, at Hyde Park, New York, the first of the six presidential libraries and museums now open to the public. The others are the Herbert Hoover Library, West Branch, Iowa; the Harry S Truman Library, Independence, Missouri; the Dwight D. Eisenhower Library, Abilene, Kansas; the Lyndon B. Johnson Library, Austin, Texas; and the John F. Kennedy Library, Boston, Massachusetts.

In 1444, Cosimo de' Medici founded the Medici Library in Florence, the first public library in Europe since Roman times. In collecting manuscripts and commissioning new illuminated editions of classic texts, the Medicis spent $15 million between 1434 and 1469. This library, and its 10,000 Greek and Latin manuscripts, played an important role in spreading Italian humanism.

Copies of all the millions of books (over 16.5 million) in the Library of Congress could be reduced page by page to photochromatic microimages and the lot could be stored in six four-drawer filing cabinets.

———

Johann Gutenberg created the world's most famous book—the first printed book, the Gutenberg Bible—but he didn't get to publish it. He had gone into debt to produce the Bible, and was sued for the money. He lost the suit, and was forced to hand over to others his tools and presses, plus the distinction of being the publisher of what is considered by many to be the world's most beautiful book.

———

In his diary entry of August 2, 1882, Lewis Carroll (author and publisher) estimated that even if he sold the entire 2,000-copy first printing of *Alice in Wonderland* he would lose £200. By selling another 2,000 copies, he would make £200. If he sold additional copies, he would then realize a bigger gain, but "that I can hardly hope for." Before his death, in 1898, about 180,000 copies had been sold.

———

Diderot's twenty-eight volume *Encyclopedia,* which included among its contributors the greatest names of the Age of Reason, Rousseau and Voltaire, and exemplified the Age of Enlightenment, began as an assignment to Diderot by a consortium of Parisian publishers to translate a single-volume British encyclopedia into French. Diderot's work took twenty-five years, was suppressed by the state council, and condemned by the Church, yet was quoted by the courts to settle arguments—and elsewhere to stir a revolution. It became the model for all future encyclopedias.

———

Printed books of religious songs were being produced as early as 1476, but at that time each publication had to be run through the press three times: once for the staff lines, once for the note heads and stems, and once for the words. It wasn't until 1525 that a printer worked out a way of printing everything at once.

———

The vast collections of The Research Libraries of the New York Public Library—many millions of books, pamphlets, magazines, and other items—are arranged in the stacks not by author, not by title, not even by subject, but by height. This is done to save space, and is possible only because the stacks are closed to the public, which removes the necessity of having related items physically together.

———

In 1814, when George Byron's poem "The Corsair" was published, 30,000 copies were sold in a single day.

———

THE ORIENT

Emperor Justinian bribed two Persian monks who had lived in China to return there and bring back silkworm eggs by secreting them in hollow bamboo canes. Thus, Constantinople was able to begin silk production, about 550 A.D. From those worms were descended all the silk-producing caterpillars in Europe down to modern times.

So they could be picked out quickly, slaves under the last emperors of China (the Manchus, 1644–1912) wore pigtails.

Among the important devices in naval technology developed by the Chinese are: the stern-post rudder, which appears on a pottery model of a boat dating from the first century A.D.; watertight compartments; and the paddle wheel, descriptions of which date from the fifth century A.D.

The Great Wall of China—2,500 miles long, stretching over more than one-twentieth of the Earth's circumference—was the longest continuous construction project in history. It was built over a period of 1,700 years; enough stone was used to build an eight-foot wall girdling the globe at the equator.

Marco Polo first thought Kublai Khan possessed the secret of the alchemists "because he has the art of producing money." China was using paper money, a medium that hadn't been heard of in Polo's Europe.

Believers in Jainism, a religion practiced in India by about 2 million people, do not believe in killing any living thing, not even an ant. Orthodox Jains do not ride in automobiles, for the tires may kill, and they do not wear shoes, for shoes will kill insects more surely than if one walks barefooted.

Japan did not send an ambassador to another nation until it sent Niimi Masaoki to the U.S. for a few weeks in 1860.

Kublai Khan, grandson of Genghis Khan, and ruling as head of the various Mongol princes over an immense empire, was polite enough to ask Marco Polo's father, Nicolo, and uncle, Maffeo, to send missionaries to teach him and his people Christianity. But the Polos, on their return to Europe, found the papacy in the turmoil of an interregnum, and no missionaries were sent.

The Chinese city of Chinkiang, now 150 miles inland, was once a seaport. Silt of the Yangtze River has built up the land for that distance.

Until 1834, Canton was the only Chinese port allowing any access to foreigners—men only. The Chinese temporarily cut off all trade with Americans when a girl, from Salem, Massachusetts, disguised herself as a boy and sneaked into the trading offices—only to be found out.

A European served as mayor of a Chinese city in the thirteenth century. Marco Polo gained the confidence of Emperor Kublai Khan and was appointed head of the Yang-chau administration. He ran the city for three years.

There were geomancers, literally "earth diviners," in ancient China. They would place on a magnetic stone a metal disc that was inscribed with astronomy and water signs, and from its orientation they would read the "lines of force" stretching across the landscape. Some of the most beautiful Chinese villages and towns were designed by geomancers, who set houses in places needed to concentrate energy or to disperse it.

Astrologers in China, during Marco Polo's visit (1271–95), would tell relatives how the dead person must be taken from the house to ward off bad luck. It wasn't always through the door. The family sometimes would have to break through a wall.

Because the Japanese word for "four" sounds exactly like the word for "death" and because the word for "nine" sounds like the word for "suffering," there are no rooms numbered 4 or 9 in many hospitals and hotels in Japan.

OUR BODIES

"Memory color" means that man tends to see the familiar things as having the same color under a variety of lighting conditions. The owner of a blue automobile is likely to see it as blue in dim light, in bright light, under a yellow streetlamp, or in the glow of a red sunset. Someone not familiar with the car would have difficulty under the same conditions in deciding what the "true" color is. Memory color doesn't always work. When a steak is seen under a blue light, the meat looks putrid regardless of how many steaks the viewer has seen or eaten.

_____

Each square inch of human skin consists of 19 million cells, sixty hairs, ninety oil glands, nineteen feet of blood vessels, 625 sweat glands, and 19,000 sensory cells.

_____

The soft mass of the adult brain is motionless. Though it consumes up to 25 percent of the blood's oxygen supply, it does not grow, divide, or contract.

_____

The pupils of your eyes can give clues to your emotions if the other person can see them. If you are trying to bargain for something you want very much, wear dark glasses, for your pupils may dilate when you show interest and you may end up paying a higher price for the merchandise.

_____

Human reproduction follows lunar time rather than sidereal, or solar, time: Gestation is about 266 days—nine lunar months—and the menstrual period is one lunar month.

_____

Man has tiny bones once meant for a tail and unworkable muscles once meant to move his ears.

_____

Nerve signals may travel through nerve or muscle fibers at speeds as high as 200 miles per hour.

———

Every person has nearly 400,000 radioactive atoms disintegrating into other atoms in his or her body each second. But there's no need to worry about falling apart. Each body cell contains an average of 90 trillion atoms—225 million times that 400,000.

———

Man's three-pound brain is the most complex and orderly arrangement of matter known in the universe.

———

To keep your feet warm, put on a hat. Eighty percent of all body heat escapes through the head.

———

People who live in the high altitudes of the Andes have developed oversized lungs in an extra-large chest in order to live easier with the low air pressure. (In the Andes air pressure is only eight pounds per square inch; at sea level, it is fifteen pounds per square inch.) In addition, their bodies have changed to help meet the problem of cold: Shorter-than-normal arms and legs, the result of countless generations of adaptation, mean that blood needs to circulate shorter distances.

———

Most people by the age of sixty have lost 50 percent of their taste buds and 40 percent of their ability to smell.

———

The largest cell in the human body is the female ovum, or egg cell. It is about 1/180 inch in diameter. The smallest cell in the human body is the male sperm. It takes about 175,000 sperm cells to weigh as much as a single egg cell.

———

The scientist Paul Weiss has estimated that each of us has in his brain about as many cells as there have been seconds in time since our part of the cosmos began to assume its present form—about 1 quadrillion (1,000,000,000,000,000). Further, he estimates that each cell has about 10,000 macromolecules and receives about 10,000 connections from other brain cells as the macromolecules of each develop linkages. Dr. Weiss computes that the brain loses 1,000 cells per day, irretrievably, seemingly at random, which means a loss of 100 billion cross-linkages daily. Yet, amazingly, basic patterns and memories are maintained.

———

The sensitivity of the human eye is so keen that on a clear, moonless night a person standing on a mountain peak can see a match being struck as far as 50 miles away. Much to their amazement, astronauts in orbit around the Earth were able to see the wakes of ships.

———

The lens of the human eye is composed of numerous transparent fibers and is encased in a clear elastic membrane. New fibers are constantly being created. Therefore, the size of the lens increases with age. The lens of an eighty-year-old is more than 50 percent larger than that of a twenty-year-old. However, as the lens grows larger, it becomes less pliable and its ability to focus for near vision is reduced.

———

The human body consists of about 60 trillion cells, and each cell has about 10,000 times as many molecules as the Milky Way has stars.

———

It is a comparatively recent insight that light travels from the object to the eye. Until about 400 years ago, it was thought that there was "something" in the eye that went out and saw the object.

———

Men not only have more blood than women (1.5 gallons versus .875 gallons, on the average)—which you would expect, because men are bigger—but their blood is richer in red cells. Each cubic centimeter of blood in men contains from 4.6 million to 6.2 million red blood cells, compared with 4.2 million to 5.4 million for women.

———

The brain is surrounded by a membrane containing veins and arteries. This membrane is filled with nerves of feeling. However, the brain itself has no feeling; if it is cut into, the person feels no pain.

———

The only part of the human body that has no blood supply is the cornea. It takes its oxygen directly from the air.

———

The heart beats faster during a brisk walk or heated argument than during sexual intercourse.

———

We think we cannot see at night. But given enough time to adjust, the human eye can, for a time, see almost as well as an owl's. Ultimately, as the amount of light decreases, an owl detects shapes after a human no longer can.

———

Arteries got their name (literally "windpipe") when the Greek physician Praxagoras thought they carried air. (In corpses they are usually empty.)

Scientists estimate that they could fill a 1,000-volume encyclopedia with the coded instructions in the DNA of a single human cell if the instructions could be translated into English.

Indians who live high in the Andes Mountains have about 20 percent more blood than inhabitants of lower areas. Their extra blood consists primarily of red corpuscles, which carry the hemoglobin needed to absorb oxygen. The extra oxygen is necessary to survive in the thinner air at great heights. Hemoglobin is increased almost 60 percent by weight at 15,000 feet. The red blood cells are larger than the cells of lowland inhabitants, allowing a greater surface for absorbing oxygen.

Thirty-five percent of all Americans (including children) are overweight. Twenty percent are at least 20 percent over the preferred weight and are counted as obese.

The Fallopian tubes are named for the sixteenth-century Italian anatomist Gabriel Fallopius, who described them but did not learn their function in human fertilization. Their function was not learned for another three centuries—until the mammalian ova, or egg cells, were discovered.

William Harvey (1578–1657) was ridiculed for his theory that blood did not oscillate back and forth in the vessels of the body, as the Greek physician Galen had believed. It moved in one direction, in a closed curve—it circulated. Harvey was called Circulator, which was a cruel pun, for it was the Latin slang for "quack," the name given to peddlers who hawked medicines at the circus. In Harvey's old age, the fact of circulation became generally accepted by physicians; his theory marked the beginning of modern physiology.

If 80 percent of your liver were to be removed, the remaining part would continue to function, and within a few months the liver would have reconstituted itself to its original size.

At sea level there are 2,000 pounds of air pressure on each square foot of your body area.

Seven of the twelve major nerves in the head—the cranial nerves—
were found by the Greek physician Galen in the second century
A.D. For 1,400 years after Galen, physiological research and
neurological knowledge remained more or less static.

Sixty thousand miles of vessels carry blood to every part of the adult
body.

The skin of the human adult body weighs six pounds.

In this era of rampant worldwide inflation, the most inflationary item
may well be the price of a human skeleton. According to a Reuters
report, a well-preserved skeleton went for $190 in 1976; in 1978,
it was selling for $475. Nowadays, a hand or a foot brings $26; a
dental skull, teeth intact, can run to $140, up from $85 in 1975. But
the worth of a *homo sapiens* skeleton cannot compare with that of
a gorilla—$5,700 in the 1979 market!

The hydrochloric acid of the human digestive process is so strong
a corrosive that it easily can eat its way through a cotton handkerchief, and even through the iron of an automobile body. Yet, it does
not endanger the walls of the stomach, which are protected by a film
of sticky mucus.

Among his many achievements, the astronomer Johannes Kepler
chalked up one about man's inner world. It was Kepler who realized
that man's visual apparatus is so constructed that it can produce only
inverted images.

Because regular movements of electric current take place in the heart
and in the brain, there are paper-thin, tiny fields of magnetism around
the torso and around the cranium of every human being. But man
does not possess, as far as is known, an organ that can (as electric
fish can) exert force at a distance.

A group of ductless glands buried in the pancreas, which is an ordinary ducted gland, produces a hormone that controls the manner
in which the body handles its sugar supply. Because the hormone
was produced by little clumps of cells, or "islands," scattered through
the gland, the name "insulin" from the Latin *insula* ("island") came
into being. The islands are called the islands of Langerhans, after
their discoverer, the German pathologist Paul Langerhans.

Scientists estimate that there are 3 million to 4 million genes in each human cell, and yet they have been able to identify one particular gene among those millions, produce an image of that gene, examine it for abnormalities, and determine whether the human being to whom it belongs is missing certain parts of his genetic blueprint. This can even be done long before an individual is born, in a process called amniocentesis, in which cells are taken from the fluid around the fetus and their chromosomes examined to see whether the fetus has an extra chromosome, or missing or rearranged chromosomes. (Such chromosome problems would indicate mongolism, mosaicism, Tay-Sachs disease, neural-tube defects, or other genetic diseases that would make it advisable to abort the fetus.)

The kidney consists of over 1 million little tubes, and the total length of the tubes in both kidneys runs to about forty miles.

The daughters of a mother who is colorblind and a father who has normal vision will have normal vision. The sons will be colorblind, however.

A young French Canadian, Alexis St. Martin, was accidentally shot in the side by a shotgun blast on June 6, 1822, in northern Michigan. A doctor, William Beaumont, who happened to be present, treated him successfully, and St. Martin recovered. He retained an opening nearly an inch across that led directly into his stomach. Beaumont used St. Martin as an experimental subject, studying the behavior of the stomach and its digestive secretions under all sorts of conditions. Beaumont was able to do important pioneer work on digestion, but kept St. Martin so busy that the poor man ran away. Despite the hole in his stomach, St. Martin lived until 1880, to an age of eighty-two, outliving the doctor by twenty-seven years. (William Osler, then dean of American medicine, unsuccessfully tried to buy St. Martin's stomach as an exhibit for the Army Medical Museum in Washington.)

OUR PLANET

Earth's magnetic field has been weakening. It seems to have lost 15 percent of its strength since 1670. At the present rate of decrease, it will reach zero in 2,000 more years. Between the years 3500 and 4500, the magnetic field will not be sufficiently strong to ward off charged radiation from outer space.

The largest desert in the world—the Sahara, the very word, in Arabic, for "desert"—is as large in area as the U.S. The Sahara wasn't always a sahara. Twenty thousand years ago, glaciers covered much of Europe, and cool winds brought moisture to northern Africa. What is now desert was then a pleasant land with rivers and lakes, forests and grasslands.

The driest place on Earth is Calama, in the Atacama Desert in Chile. Not a drop of rain has been seen there.

The fact that the Earth rotates wasn't clearly demonstrated until 1851, when Jean Bernard Léon Foucault set up an experiment in which a pendulum *seemed* to change its plane of swing slowly. Actually, the pendulum continued to vibrate in a single plane; the Earth carrying the observer was slowly rotating beneath it.

The lowest point that a person can get on this planet, unless he descends in a submarine device or a mine shaft, is where the Jordan River enters the Dead Sea—1,290 feet below sea level.

Nearly 94 percent of the volume of the Earth's crust is taken up by oxygen. The "solid" earth is a well-packed set of oxygen anions (negatively charged ions), crowded closely together, with the small cations (positively charged ions) of the other seven elements tucked here and there in the interstices. Even the Rock of Gibraltar is a heap of oxygen and little more.

Erosion of the Earth by river, marine, and ice action in Eurasia, Africa, the Americas, and Australia has been calculated at 350 tons per square mile per year. This corresponds to lowering the surface of the land forty inches every 22,000 years. At this rate (if we ignored other processes acting to raise the surface), all land mass would be worn to sea level in less than 20 million years, which is a very short period in geological terms.

Grains of sand are rounded by the action of the wind, which causes abrasion by blowing the sand particles against each other and surrounding obstacles. Once a grain reaches an almost perfectly spherical shape, it may keep that shape without further wear for millions of years.

To provide a modern person with the necessities—and luxuries—of his or her accustomed life, at least twenty tons of raw materials must be dug from the earth every *year*.

Cape Horn is not the southernmost tip of the South American continent. Cape Horn (in Spanish, *Cabo de Hornos*) is merely the southern tip of the island Hornos in the Tierra del Fuego Archipelago. The South American continent ends almost 150 miles farther north, at Fuerte Bulnes on the Brunswick Peninsula.

An acre of typical farm soil (to a depth of six inches) has a ton of fungi, several tons of bacteria, 200 pounds of protozoa (one-celled animals), 100 pounds of algae, and 100 pounds of yeasts.

Immanuel Kant suggested, in the eighteenth century, that tidal friction slowed the rotation of the Earth. He was correct, but it could not be demonstrated for another century. As the tidal bulge travels about the planet, it scrapes against shallow sea bottoms—especially the Bering Sea and the Irish Sea—and the energy of the Earth's rotation is dissipated in frictional heat enough to slow rotation and lengthen the day by one second every 100,000 years. Over billions of years, the day has, perforce, lengthened a total of many hours.

If you measure a mountain from its base, the tallest is not Mount Everest; it is the island of Hawaii, which is all mountain. Hawaii's topmost peak, Mauna Kea, is 13,784 feet above sea level, but it rises from a sea bottom that is 18,000 feet below sea level. From base to peak, its height is over 31,000 feet. Mount Everest's peak is 29,000 feet above sea level, but it rises only 17,000 feet from a plateau that is itself 12,000 feet high.

———

A force equal to that of a thirty-four-megaton atomic bomb struck northern Arizona when a meteorite impacted there about 27,000 years ago. It carved out the Great Barringer Meteor Crater.

———

Nature's most pervasive force—gravity—is also, paradoxically, its weakest.

———

Almost every bit of helium that exists in the world is a product of natural-gas wells in the United States. (A gas produced by one such well in Arizona is 8 percent helium.)

———

The Swiss-American naturalist Jean Louis Rodolphe Agassiz (1807–1873), who revealed an ice age to the world, has had named in his honor a lake that doesn't exist at present. Lake Agassiz had long ago covered North Dakota, Minnesota, and Manitoba—and Agassiz was able to trace it out.

———

Though the change in direction of Earth's rotation has advanced the December solstice to Sagittarius, the Tropic of Capricorn is used to describe the geographic latitude where the sun appears overhead because two millenia ago the December solstice was located in Capricornus and the reference has stuck. The same is true of the Tropic of Cancer, for the summer solstice is now in Gemini, not in Cancer.

———

One reason there is life on Earth, or that there could be life anywhere in the universe, is that the distant galaxies are moving away from us. As a result of this movement, the light that reaches us is reddened (through the Doppler effect) and loses energy and heat. In a static or a contracting universe, there would eventually be high temperatures everywhere, probably in the millions of degrees, and life could not exist—certainly not life as we know it.

———

Life on the Earth probably developed in an oxygen-free atmosphere. Even today, there are microorganisms that can live only in the absence of oxygen.

———

Because the air at the end of the day is generally dustier than it is at the beginning of the day, the setting sun is redder than the rising sun.

———

Frigid, unattractive Patagonia, the narrowing southern tip of South America, is the only populated continental land area south of 40° South Latitude. By comparison, most of Europe, Asia, and two-thirds of North America are north of 40° North Latitude.

———

An island 100 miles across with an area of over 15,000 square miles sits smack in the mouth of the Amazon River. The island, Marajó, lies right on the equator, and hardly anyone lives there. (Its area is one-third that of New York State.)

———

The surface of the Sahara is strewn in places with milling and grinding stones from the new Stone Age. Biologists and other scientists believe the stones were used to grind wild grainlike grasses that once grew there.

———

Nauru, an eight-square-mile atoll midway between Australia and Hawaii, is an independent nation with a population of less than 9,000 and the highest per-capita wealth in the world. This wealth is based on annual production of 2 million tons of phosphates on which the economies of Australia and New Zealand are heavily dependent. Discovery that a "fossilized" rock from Nauru was being used as a doorstop in Sydney, Australia, and was rich in high-grade phosphates led to the mining of the atoll. The phosphates evolved from eons-old deposits of either decayed marine organisms or bird guano.

———

To go on the lunar day, merely adjust your watch to lose two minutes and five seconds every hour.

———

The last high mountain to have been conquered is the thirteenth-highest mountain. Gosainthan, near Mount Everest, is 4.98 miles (26,291 feet) tall, and finally was climbed, by Chinese, in 1964.

———

Berlin and Warsaw are farther north than parts of Alaska. The southernmost Aleutian island, Amchitka, is at a latitude of about 51.7° North, which is about the latitude of London, which is farther south than Berlin or Warsaw.

———

The Soviet Union is so wide that it encompasses eleven time zones.

———

Chemists know of 105 different types of atoms. Half a dozen types make up 98 percent of the whole Earth; they are iron, oxygen, magnesium, silicon, sulfur, and nickel.

———

The oldest rocks on Earth were discovered by Vic McGregor, of New Zealand, in 1966 and 1967. Working in Greenland, McGregor found rocks that were determined by atomic-dating to be 3.7 billion to 3.9 billion years old.

———

Mount Everest is a foot higher today than it was a century ago, and it may be growing at an accelerating rate.

———

The Soviet Union and the United States are just two miles apart. In the Bering Strait, which lies between Siberia and Alaska, there is an island named Little Diomede, which is part of the United States. Two miles to the west is another island, Big Diomede, which is part of the Soviet Union.

———

North America was called Turtle Island—the emergent shell, shedding water as the land rose from the sea—by the Delaware Indians.

———

The north face of Switzerland's Eiger, "the meanest mountain on Earth," claimed nine victims before it was conquered by four Germans in 1938. It wasn't until 1947 that the second successful ascent was made, this time by two Frenchmen. Then, astonishingly, in one summer, 1952, twenty persons reached the top. After that, the Eiger claimed a new string of nine victims, and it wasn't until 1959 that any other climber achieved the summit.

———

Man in comparison with the animals he once hunted has changed dramatically through the ages. Jacob Bronowski observed that "the ancestor of man that hunted its ancestor two million years ago would at once recognize the Topi antelope today. But he would not recognize the hunter today, black or white, as his own descendant."

———

Nearly 1,000 people live on every square mile of Holland, making it the most densely populated sizable country in the world. (The U.S. has 50 people per square mile; England has 790.)

———

The Philippines consist of 7,100 islands. (The land area is about that of Arizona.)

Half of the world's population lives in just four countries: China, India, the Soviet Union, and the United States. The other half lives in more than 160 countries. (China alone has almost one-quarter of the world's 4 billion people.)

Rarely seen is the longest mountain range in the world. Most of it lies buried beneath the sea. It is the Mid-Atlantic Ridge, which runs 10,000 miles from Iceland toward Antarctica. The tallest mountain is more than five miles high. The tallest point in the range above water is the more than mile-high island of Pico in the Azores.

Man spews nearly a billion tons of pollutants into the Earth's atmospheric envelope every year.

Pesticides used in agriculture and carried out to the ocean follow currents and concentrate as they go along the marine food chain. When twenty whales, born and bred in the East Greenland current from the North Pole, were harpooned for test purposes, six identifiable pesticides, including DDT, were found in the blubber of all of them.

If a set of fine scales is arranged so that one scale is kept dark, and light is allowed to fall on the other, the lighted scale will sink slowly. Light has "weight." The pressure of light on the Earth's surface is calculated as two pounds per square mile.

The spinning of the Earth has an effect on moving objects: it deflects them and causes them to turn slightly to the right in the Northern Hemisphere, while in the Southern Hemisphere they turn to the left. The "Coriolis effect" works equally on a ball and on a ballistic missile.

Earth's magnetic field has flip-flopped, north and south, at least 171 times. The reversals have been confirmed in rocks in many parts of the world and dated by fossils and radioactive isotopes.

The North and South Poles trace a complete circle relative to the stars every 26,000 years.

Though certain valleys in Antarctica are the driest spots on Earth, they have more water than does any place on or above the surface of Mars.

———

There are small ice-free patches of land in Antarctica. Altogether, it comes to an area of 2,900 square miles or 0.06 percent of Antarctica's area. The patches are kept bare by the wind.

———

There are tiny ponds of water in Antarctica, perhaps caused by hot spots in the land beneath. The ponds are small. One of them, San Juan Pond, has enough water to fill six average-sized American living rooms. The only form of life in it is one species of bacterium.

———

There is no native human population in Antarctica, nor are there any large land animals. There are only a few species that are adapted to the Antarctic environment, but individuals of these few species are numberless. In summer, there is microscopic life in the ponds, tiny wingless insects live in patches of moss and lichens, and two types of plants send forth flowers.

———

To view the wonders of the undersea world that no other man had probably seen, Admiral R. J. Galanson, chief of U.S. Naval Materials, peered through the portholes of a U.S. Navy deep-submersible craft nearly half a mile below the surface of the Pacific Ocean. The first thing he saw on the ocean floor was an empty beer can.

———

The Pacific Ocean fills nearly a complete hemisphere of the Earth's surface.

———

In the world's northernmost city, Tromso, Norway, during the period of May 21 through July 23, when the sun is visible round the clock every day, most people act like little kids who never want to go to bed—some even try to fly like butterflies. However, during *morketiden,* the Arctic darkness, when the sun is never seen, many people in Tromso say they lose all energy. A number of ills are attributed to *morketiden.*

———

An ambitious plan for an international map of the world on a uniform scale has been perfected, but only part of the plan has been completed. Designed by the German Albrecht Penck, and presented to several meetings of the International Geographical Congress (in 1891, 1909, 1913), the map would consist of about 1,500 sheets, each covering four degrees of latitude and six degrees of longitude in a modified conic projection, on a scale of 1:1,000,000.

Instruments record some half-million seismic or microseismic disturbances of Earth each year. One hundred thousand are felt, and one thousand cause damage.

Up to 150 tons of meteorite fragments slam into Earth every year. As far as is known, only seven people have been struck by such rocks from space.

PAMPERED PETS

Every year in the U.S. four times the amount of money spent on baby food is spent on pet food, totaling $1.5 billion.

Napoleon suffered from ailurophobia, the fear of cats.

As a young man, Albert Payson Terhune, a parson's son, so much wanted to be a writer that in the pursuit of material he purported to be a leper and entered a Near Eastern leper house. Later, he fought six leading heavyweight boxers. Neither his experience as a leper nor his brief career as a prizefighter brought him into the publishing limelight. Fame and fortune came to him only when he wrote about a subject close at hand, his collie. *Lad, a Dog*, first published in 1919, is still in print.

Until the "pooper-scooper" law was passed in 1978, the 500,000 dogs in New York City deposited 175 tons of fecal matter onto its streets each day. The law requires dog owners to clean up after their dogs, on penalty of fines up to $100. Most dog owners comply, and New York City is much cleaner.

The reproductive system of female cats is similar to that of human females, but cats do not ovulate except during copulation. When the male withdraws his penis, the female cries out in pain because the penis has barbs that are felt only during withdrawal from the vagina. It may be this scraping that causes ovulation to begin.

One of the most famous dogs who ever lived was a homeless Skye terrier named Bobby. As a puppy, he attached himself to an elderly Scottish shepherd named Auld Jock. Jock died in 1858, and for the next fourteen years Bobby guarded his master's grave day and night. He would leave it briefly each day, only to go to the same restaurant where his master used to go. He'd be given food and would eat it near the grave. The citizens of Edinburgh erected a shelter to shield Bobby from the cold winters, and when he died in 1872, he was buried beside Auld Jock.

Betsy, a chimpanzee at the Baltimore zoo, has had sixty-five of her paintings sold—one of them going for $75. Congo, a chimp at the London zoo, is not so "commercial" an artist as Betsy but has made over 400 paintings. If anyone tries to urge Congo to go on with a painting after he considers it finished, the chimp draws lines in all directions that, in effect, cross out and destroy the painting.

The parachute was invented over a century before airplanes were. The first parachute was built by a French balloonist, Jean Pierre François Blanchard. The first parachute jump was made by a dog in a basket, which Blanchard had attached to the parachute and dropped from a balloon, in 1785.

A cat fell from the twentieth floor of a building in Montreal, in 1973, and suffered only a pelvic fracture.

It's generally agreed by the principals that the most important campaign speech each gave centered on the same subject: his dog. In 1944, President Franklin Roosevelt put to shame those Republicans who had accused him of sending an American destroyer to Alaska to pick up his Scottie, Fala. "I am accustomed," he said, "to hearing malicious falsehoods about myself . . . but I think I have a right to resent, to object to libelous statements about my dog." Richard Nixon's "Checkers Speech," when he was the Republican Vice-Presidential candidate in 1952, was designed to defend himself against charges that he was the beneficiary of a secret political fund. " . . . and you know, the kids, like all kids, loved the dog [a gift from a Texas supporter], and I just want to say this, right now, that regardless of what they say about it, we are going to keep it."

POLITICS
AND POLITICIANS

When American public opinion expressed disappointment with President Theodore Roosevelt's inability to get Japan and Russia quickly to sign a peace treaty at Portsmouth, New Hampshire, the President set out to divert the nation's attention. He ordered the Navy's tiny submarine U.S.S. *Plunger* to Long Island, where he boarded it in a gale. By thus becoming the first President to dive beneath the sea in a sub, he was able to make waves that grabbed the headlines away from the peace-making snarl. The treaty was signed later in the year, and T. R. subsequently was awarded the Nobel Peace Prize.

At the Yalta Conference in February 1945, Churchill was an ailing septuagenarian; Roosevelt, very ill, maintained a brittle contact with life; Roosevelt's chief adviser, Harry Hopkins, was dying of cancer. Only Stalin was in good health.

The American Liberty League, dedicated to laissez-faire capitalism, plotted with big business leaders to usurp the power of President Franklin Roosevelt and to take effective control of the Executive with the installation of its own "Secretary of General Affairs." The League asked retired Marine Corps general (and two-time Medal of Honor winner) Smedley Darlington Butler to mobilize and command an army of 500,000 veterans that the league claimed would force F.D.R. into accepting "the popular will." General Butler, instead, reported the plot to the House Un-American Activities Committee. Though the general was a reliable witness, and every word was verified by the Congressional group, the House didn't take the cabal seriously. The league disbanded because, it said, its objectives had been "accomplished." The real reason for disbandment was that the plotters had been unmasked and further agitation would have provoked a serious, high-level investigation.

On the eve of World War II, Winston Churchill was accused by an American Congressman of having served with the Spanish against

336

the United States during the Spanish-American War. Churchill had tried to squelch the persistent rumors that he had been in Cuba during that time. Actually, he had been vacationing in Cuba several years earlier, during the time the Cubans launched an insurrection against the Spaniards, and, as a British officer, he had been permitted out of courtesy to remain as an observer.

Karl Marx was targeted for assassination when he met with two Prussian officers in his house in Cologne in 1848. Marx had friends among the German labor unions, and he was considered a threat to the autocrats. Dressed in his bathrobe, he forced the officers out at the point of a revolver, which, it turned out, was not loaded.

"A democracy—that is a government of all the people, by all the people, for all the people . . . " was written by Thomas Parker in 1850, and repeated by him in subsequent speeches. Some of Parker's sermons and addresses came to the attention of Abraham Lincoln, who is said to have marked with pencil this portion of Parker's speech of July 4, 1858: "Democracy is direct self-government, over all the people, by all the people, for all the people." He used part of it in his Gettysburg Address.

Residential, economic, or educational qualification gave half a million Englishmen more than one vote in England in 1885. A university graduate who also owned a business in the City of London voted three times—once at his home, once for his university, and once in the City.

The influential historian Arnold Toynbee genuinely admired Adolf Hitler—and vice versa. After a private lecture from Hitler, Toynbee wrote, "I cannot think of any academic lecturer to whom I have ever listened who could have spoken continuously for that length of time without ever losing the thread of his argument." But whenever the Nazi leader thought and spoke about Russia, "he genuinely went crazy"—his voice became raucous and its pitch rose to a hoarse shriek.

Seventy-three parties were on the ballot for an election in Italy in 1968. One was Friends of the Moon, which sported exactly one candidate.

When he resigned in 1923 because of illegal behavior in the Teapot Dome Affair, Secretary of the Interior Albert Fall was offered an appointment to the Supreme Court by President Harding. In 1931, Fall was tried and found guilty of conspiracy to defraud the government.

Political candidates on the hustings often absent-mindedly shake hands with their spouse.

Theodore Roosevelt's mother and first wife died on the same day in 1884. He was so bereaved that he left politics for almost two years.

Though President Eisenhower, a Republican, won re-election by a landslide in 1956, Democrats gained control of both Houses of Congress, the first time in 108 years that the party of the incoming President did not have control of at least one House.

Senator Richard M. Nixon, in his denunciation of the Truman Administration, in Boston in 1951: "This Administration has proved that it is utterly incapable of cleaning out the corruption which has completely eroded it and reestablishing the confidence and faith of the people in the morality and honesty of their government employees." The originator of the Watergate tapes also expressed horror at Truman's earthy language.

Daniel Webster, a leading U.S. political figure for thirty-five years in the nineteenth century, was "on the take" from Nicholas Biddle and Biddle's Second Bank of the U.S. Webster once wrote to Biddle to complain that "my retainer has not been renewed, or refreshed as usual."

A Senate debate on Kansas statehood in 1856 climaxed when Representative Preston Brooks of South Carolina cane-whipped into senselessness Senator Charles Sumner of Massachusetts. Sumner had insulted Brooks's uncle, the absent Senator Andrew P. Butler, of South Carolina, during a diatribe against the "harlot slavery" and "rape" of Kansas by "hirelings picked from the drunken spew and vomit of an uneasy civilization." Sumner was so badly injured he could not return to the Senate for three and a half years, and he was in pain for the rest of his life. Brooks resigned after the incident, but was reelected as a hero by his district.

Not until 1969 did a United States Supreme Court Justice (Abe Fortas) have to resign under fire.

For construction of the Sam Rayburn House Office Building, the Congressional bill appropriated $2 million plus "such additional sums as may be necessary." Such additional sums eventually totaled $88 million.

———

A medieval Frenchman established the Parliament of England in its modern form. Simon de Montfort went to England, led a revolt against Henry III, and became master of the realm. To gain support, in 1265, he summoned to Parliament representatives of the boroughs for the first time. His Parliamentary reform survives to this day.

———

Two brothers competed for the Presidential nomination of the Republican convention in 1884—Senator John Sherman of Ohio and General William Tecumseh Sherman. On the first ballot, the senator received thirty votes and the general, two. On the fourth ballot, neither of the Shermans received a vote, but James Gillespie Blaine, of Maine, received enough votes to gain the nomination.

———

In 1920, Eugene Debs was nominated for President of the United States by the Socialist Party while he was serving a prison sentence for sedition during World War I. He has been the only man to run for President from prison. He received nearly a million votes, or 3.5 percent of the total.

———

Should New York City secede either from the Union or from the state of New York? The question has been raised repeatedly. In 1788, it was feared that New York would not join the Union. Some New York City politicians proposed that the city secede from New York State and join New Jersey or Connecticut. In 1804, there was an abortive plot to form a Northern Confederacy, of which New York City would have been a part. In 1861, Mayor Fernando Wood proposed that the city secede from the Union. In 1969, mayoral candidate Norman Mailer proposed that the city secede from New York State and become the fifty-first state.

———

While serving in Congress, Thomas Jefferson introduced a bill that attempted to bar slavery from all future states admitted to the Union, a measure that might later have prevented the Civil War if it had not been defeated—by a single vote.

———

The first American political party to hold a Presidential nominating convention was the Anti-Mason Party, which convened in Baltimore in September 1831. Their candidate in the 1832 election was William Wirt, who was—ironically—a Mason. (His ticket carried only the state of Vermont in the election.)

For a brief while, there was reason to suppose that the Democrats in 1900 might try to counter Republican military glory by nominating for President Admiral George Dewey, the hero of the just-concluded Spanish-American War. But there was an insurmountable barrier: Dewey's wife was Catholic. The South was the core of Democratic power, and strongly Protestant, and that put Dewey completely out of contention.

The first and only Congressman to be jailed for criticizing the President was Matthew Lyon of Vermont, in 1798. He had attacked President John Adams's plainly unconstitutional Sedition Act, which forbade defamation of the government or its officers. The law was repealed during the Jefferson Administration.

Benito Mussolini was originally one of the most vocal critics of Adolf Hitler. Il Duce formed his pre-World War II union with the German dictator only when the free nations of the world censured him for his attack on Ethiopia.

In the early nineteenth century, the English cities of Leeds, Birmingham, and Manchester had a population of nearly 500,000, but no members of Parliament. Old Sarum, a "field and ancient earthwork" without population, had two members by ancient custom. This "rotten borough" system allowed the British establishment to control Parliamentary seats, and rotten boroughs lasted until the Great Reform Act of 1832.

President Theodore Roosevelt, in a highly controversial case, withheld announcement until after the Presidential election of 1908 that the 167 "Brownsville raiders" had been cashiered out of the army by executive order without trial. (In 1906 a group of black soldiers stationed at Fort Brown, Texas, were blamed for a night raid on Brownsville that resulted in the death of a citizen, although no evidence of proof was produced.) A preelection statement, the President felt, would hurt the candidacy of his handpicked successor, Secretary of War William Howard Taft, who indeed went on to win the campaign. Nevertheless, the 1908 election marked a swing by the black vote away from its traditional affinity with the Republican Party. It was a watershed in the development of black power. Recently, as a result of "administrative review," the records of the raiders—now all dead—were cleared of the offense of nearly seventy years earlier.

———

Even before he got there, in 1630, John Winthrop was elected first governor of Massachusetts Bay Colony, in 1629, and was reelected governor eleven additional times. He died in office, in 1649, at the age of sixty-one.

———

In 1954, Vice-President Richard M. Nixon wrote out on a piece of paper a promise to his wife that he would never again seek public office. After showing it to his wife, Mr. Nixon folded the paper and tucked it into his wallet.

———

Victor Berger was elected a United States congressman by the state of Wisconsin in 1920, but the House of Representatives by a vote of 328 to 6 refused to seat him because he was a Socialist who had vigorously opposed U.S. participation in World War I.

———

Threat of a new U.S. Civil War hung over the outcome of the supercharged and highly controversial Presidential election of 1876, "the stolen election." The Democratic candidate was the reform governor of New York, Samuel Jones Tilden. He received a majority of the popular vote, but because of a secret deal lost the election to Rutherford B. Hayes, the Republican candidate, by one vote of a specially created Electoral Commission. In return for getting their candidate into the White House, the Republicans in Congress agreed to make concessions to the South that included the withdrawal of federal troops. Tilden accepted the arrangement, which was the alternative to violence and marked the end of the Reconstruction government and the beginning of the Democrats' hold on the South.

———

The only time in United States history that the President and Vice-President were members of different political parties occurred when Thomas Jefferson, a Republican, became Vice-President under John Adams, a Federalist, in 1797.

———

One Vice-President of the United States—but no President—took the oath of office on foreign soil. William Rufus De Vane King was elected Vice-President in 1852, when Franklin Pierce was elected President. By a special Act of Congress, King was sworn in in Havana, Cuba, by the U.S. consul there, William L. Sharkey. King never got to perform any of the duties of his office, and therefore never presided over the Senate, for he died a month after being sworn in and the first session of the 33rd Congress had not been held. King held another distinction. He was the only Vice-President to have served in both houses of Congress representing a different state in each. He was Representative King from North Carolina from 1811 to 1816, and Senator King from Alabama from 1819 to 1844 and again from 1848 to 1852.

Representatives of several Southern states met in Cleveland in 1838 and openly discussed an invasion of Canada. They framed a constitution for "Free Canada" and made arrangements for the issuance of invasion currency. President Van Buren responded: "This Government recognizes a still higher obligation to repress all attempts on the part of its citizens to disturb the peace of a country where order prevails, or has been re-established." (Later the same year, the President hailed the removal of the Cherokee Indian tribe—by force—to new lands in the West.)

In the first 183 years of the United States, the country had no Vice-President for thirty-seven years and 159 days, almost one-fifth of the time. Seventeen Vice-Presidents did not complete their terms; seven died, two resigned, and eight succeeded to the Presidency.

The House of Representatives and the Senate in 1854 set aside 10 million acres of public lands, in several states, for asylums for the indigent insane. The law was reluctantly vetoed by President Pierce on the constitutional ground that Congress did not have the authority to make such a provision. The veto was sustained.

The Credit Mobilier (1864–72), a trust that plundered the Union Pacific railroad funds, was helped by congressmen, including James Garfield, who received free shares and dividends. When the exposé occurred, Garfield tried to deny his involvement. Despite his pocket-padding at public expense, he was reelected to Congress three more times by his Ohio constituents. The people of America then elected him President.

In its effort to help the U.S. win the hearts and minds of the people of North Vietnam, in 1972, the Committee to Re-elect the President (Richard Nixon) put together thousands of "Democracy Kits" for parachuting into North Vietnam. The kit included a pen-and-pencil set decorated with the Presidential seal and the signature of the President. The sets were similar to those presented to generous political contributors. The kits were never dropped into North Vietnam.

Much has been made in recent years of the instability of Italian governments—at least twenty-nine since World War II. Compared with the Third Republic in France between 1881 and 1914, when there were forty-two different governments, and between World Wars I and II, when there were forty more changes, the Italians look relatively stable.

Richard M. Nixon got his start in national politics indirectly through a newspaper appeal. Republicans in the Twelfth Congressional District of California needed a sacrificial candidate to run in 1946, and Nixon responded to the "help wanted" announcement. He waged a shrewd, tough, and below-the-belt campaign, and defeated the incumbent congressman, Jerry Voorhis, a nationally known New Deal Democrat.

Joseph Stalin studied for the priesthood in a Russian theological seminary in Tiflis, in Georgia, for five years (1894–99). He was a model student until he became aware of the liberal political ideas that permeated the town. He became a Marxist and joined the Social Democrat Party. Because of this, he was expelled by the seminary.

The original Bill of Rights proposed by Congress as an addition to the U. S. Constitution contained twelve, not ten, amendments. The two that failed to be ratified by the states were an amendment to set the size of the House of Representatives and one that would have prevented congressmen and senators from raising their own salaries.

Though Nevada did not have a population large enough to qualify for statehood, President Lincoln rammed through its admission to the Union in order to line up another vote ratifying the thirteenth, or antislavery, amendment to the Constitution.

The idea for the Monroe Doctrine was originally proposed not by James Monroe but by the British secretary for foreign affairs, George Canning, in August 1823. He suggested to the United States that it and England unite in opposing European expansion in the Western Hemisphere. Besides safeguarding America, the policy would help England maintain the balance of power in Europe. John Quincy

Adams, then President Monroe's Secretary of State, disagreed with Canning's suggestion and got Monroe to announce unilaterally, on December 2, 1823, that the U.S. alone would oppose any European attempt to subject to their political systems the nations of the New World.

———

Two British Prime Ministers, Clement Attlee and Winston Churchill, when they were children, had the same governess.

———

William March "Boss" Tweed was so corrupt as the head of Tammany Hall, the organization that controlled New York City politics after the Civil War, that he may have cost the city as much as $200 million through padded and fictitious charges and through tax favors.

———

A president of the Republic of Ireland—Eamon de Valera—was born in New York City, in 1882.

———

Jacob Sechler Coxey, mayor of Massillon, Ohio, and 20,000 unemployed began a march in 1893 to Washington to demand public building programs—mainly railroads—for the unemployed of the nation. Only 600 men had persisted through the length of the march when "Coxey's army" reached Washington, on May 1, 1894, and walked along Pennsylvania Avenue. Before "General" Coxey could make a speech, he was arrested by District police—for walking on the grass. (Coxey lived until 1951, when he died at ninety-seven.)

———

When he wasn't waging wars of revolution, Giuseppe Garibaldi took on a variety of jobs. They included selling spaghetti in Uruguay and making candles in Staten Island, New York.

———

Captain John Smith, was to have been a member of the first governing council of Jamestown in Virginia when the first colonists arrived in 1607. But when the orders from the Virginia Company of London containing his name were opened and read, the colonists immediately voted to deny him the leadership post because he had been mutinous on the voyage from England. He was reappointed when a religious leader interceded.

———

The technocracy movement, popular in California during the Depression, called for placing the government in the hands of scientists and engineers, the end of the profit system, the application of all modern techniques and discoveries to the alleviation of human want, a working-age span from twenty-five years to forty-five years, and a work year of 132 days.

––––––––

The Working Man's Party, the first labor-oriented political party in America, and probably in the world, lasted only two years, 1828–30. It started in Philadelphia and New York. Members demanded a ten-hour working day, abolition of imprisonment for debt, and more public schools. While the party did exert some influence in its time, it failed over doctrine, many members refusing to accept their leaders' radical demands.

––––––––

Winston Churchill failed in his first two attempts to gain admittance to Sandhurst, the British army school, and his father considered using his social connections with the Rothschilds in order to obtain Winston a position in business. However, Winston was tutored for the Sandhurst exam and passed—barely—on his third try. His father was greatly displeased by the marks and wrote a scathing letter predicting his son's future to be that of a "wastrel" leading a futile life.

––––––––

It was in spite of President Andrew Johnson's veto that blacks were given the vote in the District of Columbia, in 1867.

––––––––

Except for five votes in the U.S. Senate, the Panama Canal would have been built in Nicaragua.

––––––––

Although the U.S. Constitution provided for the establishment of embassies abroad, the first ambassadors were not appointed until 1893, more than a century after the nation was founded. Instead of ambassadors, the U.S. had been represented through ministries headed by ministers or through consulates. Ambassadors were considered to be a device of monarchies, and no President until Grover Cleveland was willing to risk being charged with having monarchial pretensions.

––––––––

Because the House of Representatives was more interested in punishing President Andrew Johnson than in buying Alaska, and because American public opinion was not enthusiastic about territorial expansion, the Russians negotiating the sale of Alaska to the U.S. employed well over $100,000 on propaganda. Some of the money was placed directly into the eager hands of a few selected congressmen.

––––––––

Napoleon, after his defeat at Waterloo in 1815 , hoped to find asylum in England, but instead was shipped as a prisoner of war to the British-governed South Atlantic island of St. Helena. It was not until 1840, almost twenty years after his death and after many years of negotiation, that the British released his body to the French, at the request of Louis Philippe, for entombment under the dome of the Hôtel des Invalides in Paris.

PRESIDENTS

In the United States, the presidential candidate usually chooses his vice-presidential running mate on the basis of his vote-getting qualities, particularly in his home state. Yet, through 1976, in eighteen of the twenty-six Presidential elections since the Civil War, vice-presidential candidates on the losing major party ticket did not win in their home states.

Nine of the thirty-nine U.S. Presidents did not attend college: Truman, Cleveland, Andrew Johnson, Lincoln, Fillmore, Taylor, Van Buren, Jackson, and Washington.

Jimmy Carter is the first President to have been born in a hospital. All thirty-eight previous Presidents were born "at home."

While most people are aware of the blood relationships that existed between the Adamses (father and son), the Harrisons (grandfather and grandson), and the Roosevelts (distant cousins), few are aware that President Harry Truman was distantly related to President John Tyler. Truman's paternal grandmother was a direct descendant of Tyler's brother. Tyler, like Truman, was a Vice-President who became President on the death of his predecessor. Aides planned to run the government, but Tyler wanted to be his own man. Truman was equally adamant and attributed the trait to his Tyler blood.

Charles Joseph Bonaparte, a grandson of Napoleon's younger brother, Jerome, served as Secretary of the Navy in President Theodore Roosevelt's cabinet and as T. R.'s attorney general.

Only one President has held a Ph.D. degree—Woodrow Wilson.

Presidents of the U.S. have taken the oath of office aboard a jet airplane in Texas, in a brownstone in New York, in a farmhouse in

Vermont, on the "back porch" of the White House, under the portico of the Capitol, and in the Wall Street district of New York.

———

Not until 1967 was there a Constitutional provision for electing or appointing a new Vice-President when the elected Vice-President had succeeded to the Presidency. The Twenty-fifth Amendment states that whenever there is a vacancy in the office of the Vice-President, the President shall nominate a Vice-President, who shall take the office upon confirmation by a majority vote of both houses of Congress. (The amendment has been used twice already: President Nixon named Gerald Ford to succeed Spiro Agnew in 1973, and President Ford named Nelson A. Rockefeller to fill the second highest office in the nation when Ford succeeded Nixon in 1974.)

———

The middle initial in Harry S Truman's name stands for nothing. That's why it is often written without a period after it. His parents chose the S to avoid favoritism, because both his grandfathers had names beginning with S.

———

President William Howard Taft weighed 350 pounds. He got stuck in a bathtub in the White House and someone had to be called to pull him out. He then had a special tub made. It was so big that, when it was delivered, four White House workmen climbed into it and had their picture taken.

———

Franklin Pierce, the fourteenth President of the United States, was an alcoholic. His wife undertook to control his behavior, and her influence led him away from the drunken pranks and tavern brawls that marked his youth. After her death, he spent his last years succumbing to his drinking problem.

———

Not more than a half-dozen people in the country knew that President Theodore Roosevelt had lost the sight of his left eye. He was struck in the eye during a vigorous boxing exercise with a young army officer, in 1904, and his vision became dimmer and dimmer until there was no sight at all from 1908 on. T.R. was sensitive over the defect, and carefully avoided giving the impression that he was using only one eye.

———

The chief drafter of the U.S. Constitution and twice President of the U.S. was a lightweight on the scales. James Madison weighed in at only one hundred pounds. He was the shortest President, at five feet four inches.

———

During one five-week span in 1841, three different men served as President of the United States. Martin Van Buren finished his term on March 3. The following day, his successor, William Henry Harrison, was inaugurated. Harrison died after only thirty-two days in office, and John Tyler became President on April 6.

———

The first inaugural address of President Franklin Roosevelt was broadcast by radio and resulted in the unprecedented number of 500,000 pieces of mail to the White House.

———

Abraham Lincoln was convinced all his life that he, like his mother, Nancy Hanks, was illegitimate, and he observed that "bastards are generally smarter, shrewder, and more intelligent than others." Not until after his assassination was it proved that Lincoln had been legitimate.

———

Only one President subsequently served in the House of Representatives. John Quincy Adams, President from 1825 to 1829, was elected to the House in 1831, remarking that "No election or appointment conferred on me ever gave me so much pleasure." He served until his death in 1848, from a stroke suffered in the House chamber.

———

One President, Franklin Delano Roosevelt, was related to eleven Presidents, six by marriage, five by blood. Theodore Roosevelt was F.D.R.'s fifth cousin, and was President—and in attendance—when F.D.R. married cousin Eleanor, in 1905. The others to whom F.D.R. was related were Washington, the two Adamses, Madison, Van Buren, the two Harrisons, Taylor, Grant, and Taft.

———

President Lincoln's successor, Andrew Johnson, never went to school. He had not learned to write and could barely read when his wife undertook teaching him these skills.

———

Only one President subsequently became Chief Justice of the Supreme Court. William Howard Taft, President from 1909 to 1913, ran for reelection against his will, and finished last in a field of three, behind the victorious Democrat Woodrow Wilson and Theodore Roosevelt, who had come out of retirement to run on the Bull Moose ticket. Taft achieved his life's ambition when he was appointed Chief Justice by President Warren G. Harding in 1921. He served until ill health forced him to resign in 1930, a month before his death.

It took the Franklin Delano Roosevelt Memorial Commission twenty-three years (1955–78) of study and 500 designs and a $1.7 million expenditure to agree on a site and an architectural plan for commemorating the nation's only third- and fourth-term President. The memorial is slated to be a 1,000-foot-long granite wall, which will meander between the Tidal Basin and Potomac River in Washington, D.C.

About two-thirds of U.S. Presidents have served in various branches of the armed forces or state militia units. Only five have served in the Navy, and they are the five most recent Presidents—Kennedy, Johnson, Nixon, Ford, Carter.

On his inauguration day in 1829, Andrew Jackson had to climb over a wall and enter the Capitol from the basement in order to avoid boisterous mobs that thronged the Capitol in celebration.

President James Garfield seems to have had a premonition of his assassination. Two days before a disappointed office-seeker murdered him in 1881, Garfield asked Robert Todd Lincoln, a son of the late President, to relate his memories of Lincoln's assassination.

The U.S. technically had two Presidents when Rutherford B. Hayes was sworn before the designated date, the only time this has happened. To blunt the possibility that Samuel Tilden would forcibly assume the office after losing the Presidency to him by one controversial electoral vote, Hayes, while dining with President Grant at the White House on the eve of the scheduled inauguration, slipped with Grant and Chief Justice Morrison B. Waite into the Red Room and quietly took the oath of office. The next day, Hayes officially was administered the oath of the President on the east steps of the Capitol building.

Abraham Lincoln was distantly related by marriage to Paul Revere. Lincoln's father, Thomas, was the cousin of Amos and Jedediah Lincoln, both of whom were sons-in-law of Revere. Thomas was a carpenter, like his successful Boston cousins, but unlike them he was unsuccessful and shiftless.

President Lincoln's only son to live to manhood—Robert Todd Lincoln—was at hand at the assassinations of three Presidents: his father's, Garfield's, and McKinley's. He was called to the house where his father was dying; he arrived only moments after Garfield was shot in the capital and McKinley was shot in Buffalo.

For the first thirty-five years, the U.S. President was not elected by the people. Popular vote was first made a part of the Presidential contest in the election for the nation's sixth President, in 1824, but fewer than five percent of the electorate participated in the voting. Prior to 1824, the electoral college alone selected the President, the candidates having been chosen by party caucus. In the 1824 election, the state legislatures nominated the candidates.

Andrew Johnson, who served as Lincoln's second-term Vice-President, and later as President, was nearly lynched by a mob as he was returning home to Tennessee from Lincoln's first inauguration because he was the only Southern Senator who was loyal to the Union on the eve of the Civil War. A mob in Virginia dragged Johnson from a train and put a noose around his neck. They released him only when the suggestion was made that he be allowed to return to Tennessee, which—as his home state—should have the privilege of hanging him.

James K. Polk was the first "dark horse" to be elected a President of the United States. His name was not even mentioned during the first seven ballots at the Democratic National Convention of 1844. He did not receive a single vote until he was suggested as a compromise candidate when a stalemate developed between former President Martin Van Buren and Lewis Cass on the eighth ballot. On the ninth ballot, Polk was nominated.

After George Washington (1732–99) was elected President, he proposed he should receive no salary, but only be reimbursed for his expenses, as he had been during the Revolution. Congress, however, fixed a salary of $25,000 a year. Although Washington indeed drew only his expenses over the first four years of his Presidency, they amounted almost exactly to what the salary would have been.

In the territory and new state of Tennessee, he was solicitor at twenty-two years of age, U.S. attorney at twenty-three, a Congressman at twenty-nine, a U.S. Senator at thirty, and a justice of the state supreme court at thirty-one. He gained these positions without particularly strong political ambitions, and he readily resigned each after brief tenure. Andrew Jackson went on to become the seventh U.S. President and served two full terms.

John Tyler, tenth President of the United States, later served as a member of the Confederate House of Representatives for a brief period before he died in 1862. He's been the only President to renounce the Union.

Though it was not diagnosed until he had returned to Washington, Abraham Lincoln was suffering a mild case of smallpox when he delivered his historic address commemorating the new cemetery at Gettysburg, Pennsylvania, in November 1863.

Swift to set an example, President Theodore Roosevelt in his fifties (January 1909) didn't "spare the horse" when he rode a hundred miles over rough roads to Warrenton, Virginia, in order to shame the Army, which had complained of an order to keep physically fit.

After being shot in the chest by an insane saloonkeeper who opposed his third-term candidacy, Theodore Roosevelt ("bleeding like a wounded bull moose") went on to finish the speech he was delivering in Milwaukee, in 1912, before he accepted medical care.

The U.S. was without a working President for the last seventeen months of Woodrow Wilson's second term. After his disabling stroke, Wilson lay or dozed in the White House, unable to carry out his duties. No move was made to remove the President from office. His wife, Edith, was supposed to have unobtrusively performed many of the Presidential functions.

The Republican party wanted to know if its potential candidate for President in 1920, Warren Harding, of Ohio, had anything in his present life or in his past that might, on disclosure, result in a cause célèbre, embarrass the Presidency, or cost the candidate the victory. Harding said he was as clean as a hound's tooth. He won the nomination and the national election. It later was revealed that Harding, who was married, had at the time a mistress who was to bear him a child.

The media made a big deal out of two little words nestling in Governor Franklin D. Roosevelt's acceptance speech at the Democratic Presidential nominating convention in Chicago in 1932. The words were "new deal." F.D.R. had flown in a flimsy trimotor airplane from Albany, New York, to Chicago to accept the nomination rather than follow tradition and acknowledge it weeks later. The nation was gripped by the Depression, and Roosevelt was seen as the man on the white horse, the savior. He told the cheering convention: "I pledge you, I pledge myself, to a new deal for the American people." The phrase "new deal" had meant little to the nominee, and to his speechwriters, but columnists and cartoonists quickly ballooned it into a rallying cry. The day after the speech, there appeared a cartoon by Rollin Kirby showing a "man with a hoe" (the title of Edwin Markham's famous poem of protest against exploitation of labor) looking up puzzled but hopeful at an airplane labeled "New Deal." So effective was "New Deal" that politicians have tried to create a winning catch phrase in each election thereafter.

James Buchanan has been the only bachelor to serve as President of the United States.

President Andrew Johnson's "crime" that led to impeachment proceedings against him was that he carried out his duty to obey the Constitution as he understood it. He was acquitted by one vote in May 1868. On March 2, 1867, the U.S. Congress had passed the Tenure of Office Act over Johnson's veto. Still, he tried to force his Secretary of War, Edward M. Stanton, out of office because Stanton was suspected of undermining Johnson's programs. Despite the fact that Johnson did not fire Stanton, Congress acted against Johnson for trying.

William Henry Harrison rode into the White House in 1841 on the impetus of a brief but bloody battle against an Indian stronghold near Tippecanoe Creek, Indiana, on November 7, 1811. The battle was celebrated as a great victory and made Harrison a national hero. Actually, it was indecisive, and U.S. military losses were far heavier than those of the Indians.

When he became governor of New Jersey in 1911, Woodrow Wilson had never before held public office. One year and ten months later, he was elected President of the U.S.

The man who cast the single vote that elected Thomas Jefferson President over Aaron Burr—William C.C. Claiborne (1775-1817)— had been elected to Congress before he was of constitutional age.

———

Charles Willson Peale, painter of more than 50 American Revolutionary contemporaries, was a master tinker. For George Washington's inauguration in Philadelphia in 1793, he built a triumphal arch. As the general rode beneath, Peale's daughter Angelica pulled a concealed string and with accurate aim dropped a laurel wreath on the first President's head.

———

So short (five feet six inches) and chubby was John Adams that he was known as "His Rotundity." His Presidency was sandwiched between those of two six-footers: Washington (six-two) and Jefferson (six-two and a half).

———

Not until Herbert Hoover was President, in 1929, did the U.S. Chief Executive have a private telephone in his office. (The telephone had been invented fifty-three years earlier.) The booth in a White House hallway had served as the President's private phone before one was installed in the Oval Office.

———

Twenty percent of U.S. Presidents were born in the same state: Virginia. Nearly 40 percent were born in either Virginia or Ohio: eight in Virginia, seven in Ohio.

———

Only two Presidents of the United States, James K. Polk and Woodrow Wilson, have been elected without winning the vote of their home state.

———

To thwart a suspected assassination attempt by secessionists in volatile Baltimore, President-elect Lincoln changed his travel plans for reaching Washington for his inauguration. He left Harrisburg, Pennsylvania, after a speaking engagement, by night instead of by day as originally announced, and was escorted by a heavily armed friend. He arrived in Baltimore, switched trains in the wee hours of the morning, and embarked safely for the capital.

———

Until 1826, white people in the United States were sold as indentured servants who would be freed after a certain period of time. Andrew Johnson, who became President in 1865, was a runaway white slave;

advertisements appeared in newspapers in an attempt to get him back.

————

When he was nominated for President at the Republican convention in 1880, James A. Garfield did not get a single delegate vote on the first ballot. He got one vote, from a delegate from Pennsylvania, on the second, third, fourth, and fifth ballots. He did not get a single vote in the fourteenth, fifteenth, sixteenth, seventeenth, and eighteenth ballots. He won the nomination on the thirty-sixth ballot, with 399 of the 756 votes, the largest number of ballots cast at a Republican convention up to that time. Garfield won the Presidency, squeezing past with a plurality of 9,464 votes out of a total of almost 9 million cast. He was assassinated the following year.

————

Not until 1845, when the issue was payment for naval vessels ordered by President John Tyler, did Congress override a Presidential veto. Congress had passed a bill providing that no revenue cutter could be built unless an appropriation law was passed by Congress. Tyler vetoed it on grounds that a contract for two revenue cutters already had been let. On March 3, 1845, the Senate overrode the veto, 41 to 1, and the House of Representatives overrode it, 127 to 30.

————

John Quincy Adams, when his alma mater, Harvard, conferred a doctor of laws degree upon President Andrew Jackson, Adams's successor in the White House, said: "Myself an affectionate child of our alma mater, I would not be present to witness her disgrace in conferring her highest literary honors upon a barbarian who could not write a sentence of grammar and hardly could spell his own name."

————

In 1848, when Zachary Taylor was nominated for President by the Whig Party, prepayment of postage was optional. When Taylor's supporters did not receive a response to their letter offering the nomination to Taylor, they thought he was not interested. It was later determined that the notification had been sent "collect on delivery," and the popular hero of the Mexican War made it a practice to accept only prepaid mail. (Prepayment of postage became compulsory in 1855.)

————

The longest Presidential inaugural address—nearly two hours—8,445 words, almost twice as many as any other President's—was delivered during a snowfall by a hatless, coatless William Henry Harrison in 1841. He died of pneumonia exactly a month thereafter—his was the shortest administration. Forty-eight and fourteen Presidencies later, Harrison's grandson Benjamin Harrison successfully withstood torrential rains and strong winds during *his* inaugural.

———

Technically speaking, the twelfth President of the United States was David Rice Atchison—which would make Zachary Taylor the thirteenth (and Jimmy Carter the fortieth). Atchison was President for a day. James Polk's four-year term had ended constitutionally at noon, Sunday, March 4, 1849; his successor, Zachary Taylor, did not take the oath of office until Monday, March 5; from noon Sunday until the inauguration Monday, there was no President Polk and no President Taylor. Vice-President George Dallas had resigned as president of the Senate on the previous Friday and Missouri's Senator Atchison was elected by the Senate to fill his place *pro tempore*. The Constitution declares that, in the absence of a President and a Vice-President, the Congress can name a substitute. Atchison, as president of the Senate throughout that weekend, was therefore the legal President of the nation until Taylor was sworn. On his monument in Missouri is written: "David Rice Atchison, 1807–1886, President of the U.S. one day."

———

Two Presidents of the United States, George Washington and James Monroe, were unopposed in their quest for the Presidency. Monroe's second election would have been unanimous except for a single dissenting ballot in the Electoral College. It was cast to keep Washington the nation's only unanimously elected President. Until 1824, there was no popular vote.

———

Though Lyndon B. Johnson's Presidential message of January 8, 1964, was only 3,059 words long, twenty-four writers worked six weeks on the draft and made about sixteen major revisions.

———

President Millard Fillmore's mother feared her son might have been mentally retarded.

———

Probably the least politically active of all first families were the Eisenhowers. Until General Eisenhower became the Republican candidate for the Presidency in 1952, Mrs. Eisenhower had never voted, nor was there any record that General Eisenhower had ever voted. Both major political parties had had hopes that Ike would be their candidate.

———

Sarah T. Hughes was the first woman to swear in a U.S. President. A Federal District Court judge, she administered the oath to Lyndon B. Johnson in Texas soon after President John F. Kennedy's assassination there in 1963.

A committee of the first Senate of the United States voted to have the President referred to as "His Highness." The full title selected was "His Highness the President of the United States of America and the Protector of the Rights of the Same." The House of Representatives did not agree, and the title remained simply "Mr. President."

President James Garfield (March 4, 1881, to September 19,1881), ambidextrous and schooled in classical languages, could write Latin with one hand and Greek with the other—simultaneously.

Almost half a century passed before a man born in the United States rather than in the English colonies became President in 1837—Martin Van Buren, the eighth.

Although George and Martha Washington never lived in the official "White House" (it wasn't built until after he left office), the Virginia plantation that Martha Curtis Washington inherited from her first husband was called the White House. It was in this White House that George and Martha were married. John and Abigail Adams also lived in another "White House." Theirs was in Brattle Square, Boston, and they moved there in 1768. The Adams family was much happier there than in the White House in Washington, D.C., which was half finished when they moved in near the end of Adams's Presidential term. No rooms were completed. There was no bell system, so the Adamses had to shout for servants. With no place to hang out her laundry, Abigail Adams strung up clothes lines in the great unfinished audience room.

In 1947–48, three future Presidents of the United States, Lyndon B. Johnson, John F. Kennedy, and Richard M. Nixon, served in the House of Representatives. In 1833–34, three future Presidents— James K. Polk, Millard Fillmore, and Franklin Pierce—also served together, along with former President John Quincy Adams.

The sixteenth President of the United States, Abraham Lincoln, was the first to be assassinated, but the seventh President, Andrew Jackson, was almost the first. A house painter, Richard Lawrence, was able to get within six feet of Jackson at a funeral service in the Capitol rotunda. Lawrence aimed two pistols and pulled the triggers. Both guns misfired. Lawrence was seized and jailed and later committed to a mental hospital, where he was diagnosed as a monomaniac.

None of the twenty-five U.S. Presidents between the second, John Adams, and Woodrow Wilson, made an appearance before Congress. Wilson broke the century-old precedent on April 8, 1913, emphasizing before a joint session his determination to lead in legislation and to use all his powers as President and leader of the Democratic party.

A campaign issue in John Quincy Adams's unsuccessful reelection campaign of 1828 was the White House expense account: $50 for a billiard table, $6 for billiard balls, $23.50 for chessmen.

Theodore Roosevelt was the first U.S. President to ride in an automobile and the first to fly in an airplane, among many other firsts.

In the fourteen years before the election of 1788 that made George Washington the first President of the United States under the present Constitution, the nation had fourteen different Presidents. They were elected and they served an average of a year apiece, in the period from the First Continental Congress (1774) to the last session of the original Congress (1789). The first President was Peyton Randolph, a Virginia aristocrat, unanimously elected at the first session of Congress in September 1774. John Hancock served two widely spaced terms, including one in absentia.

The first U.S. President to be born in the twentieth century didn't take office until 1961—John F. Kennedy (1917–1963).

At the time of his inauguration as President of the United States, George Washington was the only head of state of a major country in the world who was not a crowned monarch. There are now far more presidents than monarchs.

John Quincy Adams, sixth President of the U.S. (1825–1829), served the United States in an official capacity for fifty-five years, beginning as private secretary and clerk to the American minister in Russia in 1781 at the age of fourteen.

After being inaugurated earlier in the day as President of the U.S., Thomas Jefferson returned to his boarding house and found at dinner, "every accustomed seat in the dining room taken. No man present rose to offer the President his seat, until the wife of John Brown, the senator from Kentucky, offered to yield hers at the more desirable end of the table." But as any Southern gentleman would have, Jefferson declined.

———

The only tie in the history of American Presidential elections occurred in 1800. Thomas Jefferson and Aaron Burr each received seventy-three electoral votes. This occurred because the members of the Electoral College could vote for two men. The top vote-getter became President; the second, Vice-President. The Republicans had planned to have several electors split their tickets so that Burr would be second to Jefferson in the voting, but each thought others would do so—and none did. The tie forced the election into the House of Representatives, which gave Jefferson the majority by one vote, but only after thirty-five ballots.

———

An American President cannot be arrested unless he willingly agrees. When Ulysses S. Grant was stopped while speeding in his carriage in the capital, Grant urged the policeman to take the appropriate action. The President was taken to the police station, but the speeding charge was dropped.

———

One of the best-kept secrets about U.S. Presidents was the operation for cancer of the mouth that Grover Cleveland underwent in 1893. The operation was performed aboard a yacht cruising New York's East River. Not even the Vice-President knew about it. Cleveland's quick recovery helped to conceal the surgery, which did not become publicly known until a doctor published an account after Cleveland's death.

———

He
—lost his job in 1832.
—was defeated for the legislature in 1832.
—failed in business in 1833.
—suffered a nervous breakdown in 1836.
—was defeated for speaker of the Illinois state legislature in 1838.
—was defeated for nomination for Congress in 1843.
—lost renomination to Congress in 1848.
—was rejected for land office in 1849.

—was defeated for the Senate in 1854.
—was defeated for nomination for Vice-President in 1856.
—was defeated for the Senate in 1858.
—became the sixteenth President of the U.S. in 1861.

If he had been defeated for reelection in 1916, President Wilson planned to try to turn the government over immediately to his successor, Charles Evans Hughes, rather than spend five months as the lame duck chief executive.

On May 27, 1943, Edwin Barclay, grandson of American slaves and president of the Liberian Republic, became the first black man to appear as a guest of honor before the United States Congress and be officially introduced from its rostrum. He was repaying the call President Franklin Roosevelt had made to Liberia after the Casablanca Conference.

The true name of President Ulysses Simpson Grant was Hiram Ulysses Grant. The Congressman who recommended Grant for West Point in 1839 thought his first name was Ulysses and guessed that his middle name must be his mother's maiden name, Simpson. Grant adopted the name and used it thereafter, going down in history as Ulysses Simpson Grant.

Abraham Lincoln had a dream on the eve of his first election as President. In a large mirror, he noticed two distinct images of himself, one imposed on the other. One image was much paler than the other. Lincoln told his wife about the dream, and she interpreted it to mean that he would be elected to a second term but would not live through it.

Andrew Jackson married the same woman twice. When he was a young lawyer in Nashville, he and Rachel Robards, a divorcee, became man and wife, although her divorce (unknown to them) was not final. Three years later, after the Jacksons learned the true state of affairs, they were remarried. When Jackson ran for President, he was hounded with scurrilous retellings of the story, and his wife died on the eve of his election. He became permanently embittered.

When he received the cable from Admiral George Dewey reporting the capture of Manila, President William McKinley had to look up the location of the Philippines on a globe. "I could not have told where those damned islands were within 2,000 miles," he confessed later.

————

Vice-President-elect Andrew Johnson didn't hold his liquor well, and seemed clearly drunk at his inauguration in 1865. Those who opposed Johnson, especially when he succeeded the assassinated Lincoln to the Presidency, never allowed the public to forget the gaucherie.

————

Abraham Lincoln claimed that a widely circulated photo of him made in early 1860 by Matthew Brady helped him to become President. The photograph, Lincoln said, "dispelled the opposition based on the rumors of my ungainly figure." Cartoons had led the citizenry to think of Lincoln as a gangly and crude backwoods boy, and the photograph showed him to be "a man of human aspect and dignified bearing."

————

When future U.S. President William Howard Taft was president of the Philippine Commission in 1900, Secretary of War Elihu Root cabled him to ask how he was—Root had heard that Taft was ill. Taft, who weighed over 350 pounds, reassured Root by cabling that he was much better and that he had, in fact, just returned from a twenty-five-mile ride on horseback. Elihu Root cabled back: "How is the horse?"

————

Former President Ulysses Simpson Grant's six-week visit to China in 1879 seemingly made little impression upon his hosts, though he was the most important American to have visited the country and he was borne in an imperial palanquin into the heart of Peking's Forbidden City. No mention of the visit appears in the daily records of the court. Grant—who had been chief commander of the Union Army in the U.S. Civil War—told the ruling regent of the Manchu Court that "any course short of national humiliation or national destruction is better than war. War, especially in the East, would be a misfortune—a great misfortune." Prince Kung responded: "A great misfortune to the outside powers as well."

————

The president of Korea apologized to Lyndon B. Johnson when "only" 2 million people were on hand to greet the visiting U.S. President. "I'm sorry, President Johnson," the Korean chief declared, "but this is all the people I have."

————

For all his charismatic authority, President Lincoln could not inspire the American people with his vision of amortizing the abolition of slavery over forty years. The President twice proposed a Constitutional amendment that would end the Civil War immediately and pay off slaveholders by 1900, at which time all slaves would be granted their freedom.

———

All U.S. Presidents have worn eyeglasses, although many of them—including Lincoln—didn't like to wear them in public.

———

In 1844, during his successful Presidential campaign, James K. Polk was smeared with the charge that he had branded his initials on the shoulders of forty-three slaves.

———

The only professional scientist who became the head of a nation was the chemist Chaim Weizmann, who became president of Israel when it was founded in 1948. He remained President until his death in 1952.

———

Bolivia was liberated from the rule of Spain in 1825. Between then and 1925, the nation had over forty presidents, six of whom were assassinated while still in office. Over the same one hundred years, Bolivia had 187 armed revolts. Between 1828 and 1871, there were nine different constitutions.

———

During his successful come-from-behind Presidential election campaign in 1948 against the Republican front-runner, Thomas E. Dewey, President Harry S Truman conducted a thirty-five-day, 31,000-mile "whistlestop" campaign, delivering 356 speeches.

———

No President of the United States was an only child.

———

When the federal excise tax on whiskey enraged western Pennsylvanians so much that they initiated the Whiskey Rebellion of 1794, President George Washington as commander-in-chief of the United States Army donned his Revolutionary War uniform, raised a force of 12,000 men, rode to Fort Cumberland, and stopped the rebellion cold.

———

PRESIDENTS' WIVES

American First Ladies not only far outlive their husbands but have a mortality rate 10 percent lower than the general population of women, according to a Metropolitan Life Insurance survey. Presidents since 1860, even excluding those assassinated, have had a mortality rate 40 percent higher than their wives.

___

Andrew Carnegie personally paid pensions to widows of former Presidents before Congress decided that the responsibility was the country's and not a steel magnate's.

___

President Ulysses S. Grant's wife was cross-eyed and wanted to correct the problem. Grant refused to let her have the operation because he liked her that way.

___

When the First Lady, Eleanor Roosevelt, received an alarming number of letters threatening her life, soon after her husband, Franklin D. Roosevelt, took office as President of the United States during the Depression, the Secret Service insisted that she carry a pistol in her purse.

___

Abraham Lincoln's wife—like Lincoln himself—was born in Kentucky. During the Civil War, she was accused of being a spy for the South, for her brothers were members of the Confederate Army.

___

President Andrew Johnson's daughter, who ran White House domestic affairs in place of her invalid mother, bought two Jersey cows, which she kept on the White House grounds, to assure her family of fresh milk and butter.

___

President Calvin Coolidge did not allow his wife to supervise any details of White House life. He did it all. Even the menus and other housekeeping plans were submitted to him and not to the First Lady. She did not even buy her clothes without Coolidge's approval.

Martha Washington was nearly sixty years of age when she became "Lady Washington," as she was called during her husband's Presidency. She did not enjoy the role. She had not read widely, had slight interest in politics, and rarely made a public political comment. And she was a poor conversationalist. Privately, she wrote that she was "more like a state prisoner than anything else."

Two First Ladies practiced interesting economies by using the lawn of the White House. Mrs. William Howard Taft, as part of her penny-pinching for the kitchen, bought a cow, which grazed on the White House lawn; twice a day, milk from the cow was delivered to the White House kitchen. Mrs. Woodrow Wilson practiced stringent economies during World War I. Among her programs, she bought a flock of sheep to crop the White House lawn, and auctioned their wool for the benefit of the Red Cross. She was a good businesswoman—the auction netted $100,000.

Mary Todd Lincoln was tried for insanity before a jury after her husband's assassination. Her son Robert attempted to have her declared legally incompetent when she began suffering hallucinations and phobias, but the law required a trial before a person could be institutionalized. Mrs. Lincoln attempted suicide after she was judged insane by the court, and was taken to a sanitarium, where she received treatment. She improved to the point that another court reversed the insanity verdict in 1876.

PROPHETS

Fourteen years before the *Titanic* sailed on an April day in 1912 on her maiden voyage from Southampton to New York, a novel was published called *Futility* about an unsinkable and glamorous Atlantic liner, the largest in the world. Like the *Titanic*, the fictional vessel was triple-screw and could make 24–25 knots; at 800 feet it was a little shorter than the *Titanic*, but at 70,000 tons its displacement was 4,000 tons greater. Like the *Titanic's*, its passenger list was the crème de la crème, and of course there weren't enough lifeboats. On a cold April night, the fictional "unsinkable" vessel strikes an iceberg and· glides to the bottom of the Atlantic. The name of this liner, in the story by Morgan Robertson—The *Titan*.

The American inventor Samuel Pierpont Langley (1834–1906) spent $50,000 of government money between 1897 and 1903 in an attempt to devise a workable airplane. His three attempts were all failures. After his third failure *The New York Times* published a severe editorial castigating what it considered Langley's foolish waste of public funds on an idle dream. There was nothing wrong, by the way, with Langley's last plane except an insufficiently powerful engine. In 1914, that plane was fitted with a better engine and successfully flown.

Back about 340 B.C., Aristotle observed that dolphins gave birth to live young that were attached to their mothers by umbilical cords. For this reason, he considered dolphins and related creatures to be mammals. Biologists agreed with him—twenty-four centuries later.

In his speech accepting a Nobel Prize in chemistry—for his mass spectrograph and the knowledge it had given rise to—the English chemist and physicist Francis Aston envisaged a future in which the energy of the atom would be tapped by man, and he forecast the dangers involved in such an eventuality. But the year was 1922, and

Aston's views were considered the province of science-fiction writers.

———

The English chemist William Prout published an article in 1815 suggesting that all the chemical elements were built up out of hydrogen, the simplest of the elements. He realized this was a very far-out suggestion. To avoid sullying his reputation, he published his hypothesis anonymously. His authorship was discovered, however, and the notion was called "Prout's hypothesis." For exactly a hundred years, chemists "proved" over and over again that Prout was wrong— until it was discovered that the elements were really mixtures of slightly different varieties of atoms. Each variety is built of particles like the one that makes up the nucleus of the hydrogen atom. In that sense, the truth proved to be very close to Prout's hypothesis.

———

More than three-quarters of a century before Freud published his first major works, Dr. Benjamin Rush, who established the first free dispensary in the United States, sowed the seeds of "modern" psychoanalysis in his book *Diseases of the Mind,* in 1812.

———

Twenty-three centuries passed between the Greek philosopher Xenophanes' surmise that mountains on which seashells were found must originally have been covered by the sea and the Scottish geologist James Hutton's scientific deduction that made sober sense of what had seemed lunacy.

———

A completely automated grist mill was invented by the American Oliver Evans in 1793. The mill performed all operations without human labor. The millers, of course, opposed it, and it would be many decades before Evans's idea was fully accepted. In 1805, Evans suggested using the evaporation of ether for refrigeration, and again was decades ahead of his time.

———

While it was the deepest secret in the world, the atomic bomb was publicly described with considerable accuracy by Cleve Cartmill— a year and a half before it was announced officially. The description was included in a science-fiction story called "Deadline," in the March 1944 issue of *Astounding Science Fiction,* so virtually no one paid any attention.

———

Astronomers today have the very modern notion that the stars are suns and that they generally have planetary systems and that on some of them there may be life. A German archbishop, Nicholas of Cusa, said the same thing in 1450 A.D.—but almost no one listened.

———

Social Gospel, a nineteenth-century Protestant movement to apply principles of Christianity to social and economic problems of an industrial society, became a factor in the New Deal. The Reverend Endicott Peabody, founder of the Groton School and an advocate of the social responsibilities of the wealthy and powerful, preached this message to his students—one of whom was Franklin D. Roosevelt.

———

As early as 1868, Mahlon Loomis—experimenting with electricity—was able to carry on two-way conversations without wires over a distance of eighteen miles, between two mountains in Virginia. But he was unable to find financial backing for exploitation of his device.

———

The true size of the Earth was known seventeen and a half centuries before it was first circumnavigated. In 230 B.C., the Greek philosopher Eratosthenes worked out its circumference of 25,000 miles by studying shadows cast by the sun at different places on the same day.

———

The suggestion that a star could be so massive and have so strong a gravity that it would be invisible—that it would be, in other words, a black hole, a notion that we accept today—was first made nearly two centuries ago, by the French astronomer and mathematician Pierre Simon, Marquis de La Place.

———

The first person we know who realized the Earth couldn't be flat was the Greek philosopher Anaximander. About 560 B.C., he suggested the Earth had a cylindrical shape. By 350 B.C., the concept of a spherical Earth was so satisfying and so free of paradox that it was generally accepted by scholars even in the absence of direct proof. Eighteen more centuries were to pass before direct proof occurred—the lone surviving ship in an expedition once commanded by Ferdinand Magellan sailed completely around the globe.

———

The Roman poet Lucretius, in 56 B.C., published a poem in which he expounded the views of those Greek philosophers who believed the universe to be composed of atoms. All the works of the earlier atomists had vanished because their views were unpopular, and Lucretius' poem almost vanished, too. In 1417, however, one copy was discovered, copied, and eventually printed. Its views helped to persuade the chemists of early modern times to consider the atomic theory of matter, and those views won out eventually.

Among the first to suggest that clocks be moved ahead to extend daylight hours during the spring and summer was Benjamin Franklin. However, it was not until March 31, 1918, more than a century after Franklin's death, that Congress adopted the practice—during World War I, in order to save electricity. During World War I, daylight saving was also adopted in England, Germany, France, and many other countries.

A chaplain of the U.S. Senate—Edward Everett Hale—was the first to propose the artificial satellite, in 1870, in *The Atlantic Monthly*, in a story called "The Brick Moon." Brick as material for the satellite was selected because it might be able to withstand the heat of atmospheric friction. (Hale also wrote the classic short story "The Man Without a Country.")

About 3650 B.C, an Emperor of China, Hwang Ti, noted that "all the blood in the body is under the control of the heart . . . the blood current flows continuously in a circle and never stops." More than 4,000 years were to pass before experimental data—William Harvey's, in 1616—supported the theory that the heart functions as a pump and that blood circulates through the body.

Newton estimated correctly that the Earth would have a mass of 6,600,000,000,000,000,000,000,000 tons and a density of about five and a half times that of water. The fact wasn't demonstrated until one century after his estimate.

The first "horseless carriage" to be run by an internal combustion engine was built by the Belgian-French inventor Etienne Lenoir, in 1860. It ran on illuminating gas. Lenoir also hitched a similar engine to a boat, and produced the first motorboat. The so-called Lenoir engine wasn't efficient enough, and the inventor died poor.

The first Greek to observe ocean tides, in the Atlantic in the early third century B.C., was the navigator and astronomer Pytheas, who also produced the correct explanation for them. He was 2,000 years ahead of his time, for it took that long for tides to be attributed (by Newton) properly to the influence of the moon. Until Newton's time, most scholars refused to believe that the moon could have any effect on the ocean, especially because one tide each day took place when the moon was not even visible in the sky.

———

H. G. Wells wrote of an atomic weapon in "The World Set Free" in 1914. His name for the device was "atomic bomb."

———

The U.S. and Great Britain were warned in February 1945 that if the German people surrendered to the rapidly approaching Russian army, the Russians would drop "an iron curtain" between their occupied lands and the West, remorselessly keeping away all non-Soviet, or outside, influences. The exhorter was Joseph Goebbels, whose chilling picture of Soviet domination was designed to bemuse the Western Allies in the final days of the war. Many political leaders before Goebbels had used the phrase "iron curtain" as well, but it took Winston Churchill to make it memorable. Ten months after the end of World War II, the former British Prime Minister addressed himself to the dangers he perceived, and one of the greatest, he said, was the "iron curtain" that indeed had descended across the Continent, "from Stettin in the Baltic to Trieste in the Adriatic," just as Goebbels had predicted. Churchill had originally used the phrase "iron curtain," in May 1945, in a telegram to President Truman, but the telegram was then top-secret.

———

RELIGION

By insisting that the Puritans enforce their law against Quakers rather than accepting their terms for freedom, Mary Dyer of Newport, Rhode Island, was hanged on Boston Common on June 1, 1660, and became the only woman resident of the colonies in America to die for the cause of religious freedom. Mary was three times banished from the Colony of the Massachusetts Bay for her beliefs, twice on pain of death should she return. On her third visit to Boston, she watched the hanging of two fellow Quakers, then was placed upon the gallows for her own execution. At the last moment, with the noose about her neck, she was reprieved, to be sent back to her home on the condition she not return. But she was back in Boston the following May. She again was offered reprieve if she would remain outside the colony, and again she refused. This time she was hanged for her challenge of the law of banishment of Quakers.

A room with bath is perpetually reserved in one of Java's best hotels for the goddess of the South Sea, Njai Loro Kidul.

December 25 was not celebrated as the birthdate of Christ until the year 440 A.D.

Francis Asbury, the first U.S. Methodist Episcopal bishop, covered 270,000 frontier miles between 1771 and 1816, preaching to pioneers in the American West. He preached anywhere he could attract a crowd—at camp meetings, on riverboats, in bordello parlors, and from church pulpits.

A nation other than modern Israel was the first to adopt Judaism as its state religion. The pagan Khazars, a Turkic people who had migrated from Asia to southern Russia, established a kingdom on the Volga River and in the eighth century A.D. adopted Judaism. (They may have done it to maintain a neutral posture in the wars between

Christians and Muslims.) The kingdom was destroyed two centuries later by invading troops from Kiev.

In 1831, a persuasive religious enthusiast from New England named William Miller began preaching that the world would come to an end on April 3, 1843. He said his reckoning was based on a thorough study of the Bible, and he convinced thousands of Americans. When Judgment Day rolled around, his followers gathered on hilltops and in cemeteries—and waited. Many had burned their possessions or given them away. When April 3 passed uneventfully, Miller named a new date, October 22, 1844. Many loyal followers met again at that time. The Millerite movement then declined. Cynics asserted that on each supposed last day of the world Miller's woodshed and pantry were full.

Sticking to their belief that the Lord alone giveth and the Lord alone taketh away, the Mormons refused help from the U.S. government during the Depression of the 1930s. They were the only American farm cooperative (so called because the land, though owned by the Church, was worked by Church members) to do so.

Many odd beliefs grew around the sacrament of the Mass in the medieval church. People believed that the Host (the consecrated wafer of the Eucharist—the bread used is pure, white and unleavened and baked in small disks) had magical power; they would carry it secretly away from the church and use it to cure swine fever, put out fires, fertilize fields, make love charms, protect a criminal from discovery, and so on. The practice was popular among average churchgoers in England, but more so—according to John Lake (1624–89), bishop of Chichester—among "witches . . . sorcerers, charmers, enchanters, dreamers, soothsayers, necromancers, conjurers, cross-diggers, devil-raisers, miracle-doers, dog-leeches and bawds."

In medieval times, church bells were often consecrated to ward off evil spirits. Because thunderstorms were attributed to the work of demons, the bells would be rung in an attempt to stop the storms. Lots of bellringers were killed by lightning.

Despite the fact that the church during the Renaissance frowned on the occult as bordering on heresy, Pope Julius II set the time of his coronation in 1503 according to astrological calculations.

Although Buddhism began and first flourished in India, it had by 1200 all but disappeared there, but had won huge numbers of followers in Ceylon, Burma, Thailand, Tibet, China, and Japan. (Less than 1 percent of the 1977 estimated Indian population of 622,200,000 were Buddhists.)

———

Suspension of the construction of the Washington Monument, at the 153-foot level, was forced by the anti-Catholic Know-Nothing movement, which was offended by Pope Pius IX's gift of a block of marble from Rome's Temple of Concord. The suspension lasted twenty-six years. Work resumed in 1880 and the monument was completed in 1888.

———

Discrimination against Roman Catholics in citizenship and public life was legal somewhere in the United States until 1835, when the last anti-Catholic law of colonial times was repealed.

———

Ten years before Henry VIII broke with the Roman Catholic Church and established the Church of England over the issue of his divorce, he wrote a book entitled *Assertion of the Seven Sacraments,* which attacked Martin Luther's theses and affirmed his loyalty to the pope. The pope granted Henry the title "Defender of the Faith" for having written this scholastic work. The king kept the title after breaking away from Catholicism—as have his successors to this very day.

———

Missionary diplomacy—the influence in foreign countries of U.S. missionaries and their supporters—had strong and sometimes violent effects. Protestant missionaries in Hawaii were strong influences for annexation of the island to the U.S. In China, Protestant and Catholic missionaries caused U.S. troops to be involved in suppressing the Chinese Boxer Rebellion, in 1900. Protestant efforts to overturn the rule of Catholic Spain in Cuba were a contributing factor to the Spanish-American War.

———

A visitor in 1946 to the Greek Orthodox monastery of St. Catherine's, founded in the sixth century at the foot of Mount Sinai (Jabal Musa in Arabic), learned that the monks there did not know of World War II and that some had not heard of World War I.

———

Jesus of Nazareth was born four to eight years before he was "born." (His birth was in the reign of Herod, who died in 4 B.C., four years "Before Christ.") In 534 A.D., the first man who calculated the year of Jesus' birth made a mistake—and we've been stuck with it ever since.

———

The Chinese Emperor Kublai Khan, a clever politician, observed not only the holy days of his nation, but those of the three major faiths of the West—Christmas and Easter for the Christians, Passover and the Day of Atonement for the Jews, and Ramadan for the Muslims.

———

In the sixteenth century, many Christians gave up the Catholic faith and became Protestants. The rejection of the lavish ritual of Catholicism often took on extreme forms. In England, elaborate ceremonies and processions were banned to keep religion pure. Later, in 1647, a law was passed by Parliament that abolished Christmas and stated that it was to be a day like any other day. Some people felt, however, that this law went too far. Sometimes, entire congregations were arrested for protesting the abolishment of Christmas.

———

Mithraism, one of the dominant religions of the Roman Empire, was practiced more than Christianity in the second century A.D. Named for the ancient god Mithras of Iran, who was originally a minor figure of Zoroastrianism, Mithraism became essentially a soldier's religion. Its ethics were rigorous, loyalty was inculcated, and fasting and continence were prescribed. It was a mystery faith. Converts entered by rites that involved bathing in the blood of a freshly killed bull. Mithraism became far more popular and important in Rome than it possibly could become in Persia under the hostile eyes of the orthodox Zoroastrian priesthood.

———

In early eighteenth-century Portugal, the Church owned two-thirds of all the land.

———

A woodsman's ax was the only implement used to shape the twenty-two silvery-scaled onion domes of the wooden Church of the Transfiguration at Kizhi, Russia. It is located on an island in Lake Onega near Leningrad.

———

Nearly four centuries before Columbus's first voyage across the Great Ocean Sea, the first bishop of America was appointed. Named by Pope Paschal II, Eric Gnupsson had in his province Greenland and Vinland (America.)

———

In biblical days, it was forbidden to sell a synagogue for subsequent use as a tannery, bathhouse, immersion pool, or urinal. The institution of the synagogue probably dates to the Babylonian exile of the sixth century B.C. The returnees to Jerusalem brought with them the basic structure that was to develop by the first century A.D. into the well-defined institution known from then to this day.

When a statue of native-born Copernicus was unveiled, finally, in 1839, in Warsaw, no Catholic priest would officiate at the occasion though the world-shaking astronomer had been a canon of a cathedral in East Prussia and had in 1543 dedicated to Pope Paul III his revolutionary treatise on the way the universe really works.

St. Mary-Magdalen dei Pazzi (1566–1607), the Florentine mystic and Carmelite nun, preached so volubly during her ecstasies that she had to be provided with six secretaries, who wrote under her dictation for hours and sometimes for whole days at a time.

Queen Mary, in 1555, banned any version of the Bible in English translation, commanding "that no manner of persons presume to bring into this realm any manuscripts, books, papers, etc., in the name of Martin Luther, John Calvin, Miles Coverdale, Erasmus, Tyndale, etc., or any like books containing false doctrines against the Catholic faith."

After St. Francis's death in 1226, his followers who attempted to continue to embrace a life of poverty were burned at the stake as heretics. The Church had no desire to encourage poverty because it had become committed to the financial power structure of Europe.

The Egyptians attacked the Jews on a holy day in 320 B.C. An army led by Ptolemy I of Egypt attacked Jerusalem on the Sabbath. But unlike the Israelis in 1973, the ultra-pious Jews in those days refused to fight on the Sabbath, even in self-defense, and so Jerusalem—which had withstood Sennacherib and Nebuchadnezzar with admirable tenacity—fell easily to Ptolemy.

By "deciphering" the Book of Revelations, a minister in Lochau—in what is now East Germany—proclaimed that the world would end on October 18, 1533. When it didn't happen, the minister—a Michael Stiftel—was given a thrashing by the townspeople.

No other country has as diverse religious groups as the U.S., which has at least 52 major denominations with membership exceeding 100,000. The *Yearbook of American and Canadian Churches* lists 223 sects, cults, and denominations, not counting groups such as the First Church of Christ, Scientist, which provide no membership statistics.

Piles of skulls of dead Greek Orthodox monks are stacked in St. Catherine's monastery near the foot of Jabal Musa, the traditional Mount Sinai (at the mouth of the Gulf of Aqaba), the holy site revered as the place where God spoke to Moses from the Burning Bush. Christian monks since about 250 A.D. have lived and prayed at St. Catherine's, and it is their wish even today to have their own heads added to the piles.

A Baptist church in Hammond, Indiana, reported a record attendance of 12,350 worshipers in December 1972. The church employed a fleet of sixty-eight buses, picking up people over a radius of fifty miles. Their advertised program for "Heaven Sunday" included Carl McIntire, and an organist without arms or legs, a karate expert, a former Hollywood stunt cowboy, an ex-football hero, a rodeo star, Santa Claus, and a ventriloquist.

The great British physicist Robert Boyle (1627—91), who was the first to study gases scientifically, was a fairly religious youth who became even more devout the rest of his life after being frightened by a thunderstorm in Geneva. In middle age, he learned Hebrew and Aramaic. He wrote essays on religion and financed missionary work in the Orient. In 1680, he was elected president of the Royal Society, but would not accept because he disapproved of the form of the oath. Through his will, he founded the Boyle Lecturers, not on science but on the defense of Christianity against unbelievers.

No clergyman attended the U.S. Constitutional Convention, and the Constitution itself contains no religious references, not even a mention of God. The Founding Fathers even added these strong words in the Bill of Rights two years later: "Congress shall make no law respecting an establishment of religion, or prohibiting the free exercise thereof."

In 963 A.D., Athanasius established the famous monastery on the sharp peak of Mount Athos in northeastern Greece. Though the monastery is dedicated to the Virgin Mary, no woman has ever been allowed on the mountain.

————

A chief tenet of John Humphrey Noyes's utopianism held that the pleasures of sex and the bearing of children were events that might be separated in the interests of his community, which was called Oneida and located in New York State. Withholding of male orgasm would satisfy the tenet. Older women of Oneida initiated boys into the art of *coitus reservatus* and older men instructed the young women. Carefully chosen couples were permitted to have children, who then were raised by the community instead of by the parents, in the manner proposed by Plato. This religious society of "perfectionists" was established in 1848. It prospered economically by making steel traps and silverware. It was reorganized in 1881 as a joint stock company and the social experiments were abandoned.

————

Thomas Aquinas was kidnapped by his own family. After an education at Monte Cassino and at the University of Naples, Thomas joined the new Dominican order in 1244. His family objected, kidnapped him, and held him in custody. He escaped, and made his way to Paris. His philosophical system remains the basis of Catholic teaching to this day. By upholding reason as a respected method for extending the boundaries of human knowledge, he helped to make science respectable again in Christian Europe after it had been considered pagan for a long period. He was canonized in 1323, a mere half-century after his death.

————

Various gatherings of bishops in southern France in 990 A.D. tried to set up a "Truce of God," a subjection of warfare to rules. The chief rule called for converting all ecclesiastical property and persons into a kind of neutral territory that was not to be touched. Eventually, this was extended to a total prohibition of warfare from Wednesday evening to Monday morning of each week, and on numerous fast and feast days as well. In the end, as much as three-fourths of the year was put off limits to fighting—in theory.

————

The Society of Jesus has never officially adopted the term "Jesuit," and the popes in their official documents about the society have never used the term. In an unofficial way, however, members of the Society refer to themselves as Jesuits.

————

The Jews and the early Christians started the day at sunset. "Christmas Eve" means, accordingly, the first part of Christmas Day, and it was only later that it came to be considered as the evening *before* Christmas. The same goes for New Year's Eve.

––––––––

Michael Faraday (1791–1867), the great English chemist and physicist, was a member of the Sandamanian Church, a tiny sect of fundamentalists. He was invited to dinner with Queen Victoria on a Sunday in 1844, which meant he would have to miss services. After an agonizing period of uncertainty, he decided it was necessary for him to obey the Queen. His fellow church members excommunicated Faraday as a result, and would not reinstate him until he had undergone considerable penance.

––––––––

The Shakers, a Utopian religious group that was at its height in the late eighteenth and early nineteenth centuries, were nearly self-sufficient and quite innovative. Living in rural communes concentrated mostly in the northeastern U.S., they made their own shoes, silk, and clothes. They invented the circular saw, the common clothespin, an apple parer, the first one-horse buggy, a four-wheeled dumpcart, a rotary harrow, the automatic spring, a washing machine that later was used by hotels, and the needle with an eye in the middle that later was adapted to the sewing machine.

––––––––

In a single century, from 1170 to 1270, the French working classes built some 80 cathedrals and 500 large cathedral-type churches. Notre Dame in Paris, the first great Gothic cathedral, was built by an effort of the entire community. Inspired by Christian faith, manual laborers, master artists, serfs, merchants, and princes worked from 1163 to 1300 to complete this cathedral.

––––––––

In a church in Czechoslovakia, there is a chandelier made of human bones. The ceiling is festooned with the remains of former worshipers.

––––––––

During the high Middle Ages, there was, on the average, a church for every 200 people. The area covered by religious buildings took up a large part of every city. In the English cities of Norwich, Lincoln, and York, which had populations of between 5,000 and 10,000, there were fifty, forty-nine, and forty-one churches, respectively.

––––––––

The story of Noah's Ark was written earlier than the biblical version—in the Sumerian *Epic of Gilgamesh*. The "Noah" of this epic is Utnapishtim, who is supernaturally warned to build a boat in which to survive the deluge. Similarity extends even to the sending out of birds to see if dry land has appeared.

————

Provided they agreed to look after their own poor, Jews were to be welcomed in New York by the stern and narrow-minded Dutch governor Peter Stuyvesant, on orders from the Dutch West India Company.

————

Pope John XXIII served as a sergeant in the Italian army during World War I.

————

Muslims are forbidden to drink liquor. Saudi Arabia's prohibition law requires that foreigners' liquor cabinets, when not in use, must be sealed. Violation by two Britishers in 1978 led to 200 strokes with a cane and a ten-month prison sentence.

————

While there is no law that forbids the mentioning in Swiss newspapers of suicide as a cause of death, suicides are not specifically mentioned in many cases. The reason for such omissions is related particularly to Catholic doctrine that regards suicide as sinful.

————

Lionel Nathan Rothschild (1808–79), of the prominent family of European bankers, became in 1847 the first Jewish member of the British House of Commons, but he did not assume his seat for eleven years, until Parliament finally let him take the oath in a manner acceptable to his Jewish faith.

————

SALTY FACTS

The first systematic chart ever made of an ocean current was published by Benjamin Franklin in 1769. Franklin was aware that American ships took two weeks less to cross the Atlantic Ocean than did British ships. He learned that when traveling to Europe Americans steered to take advantage of the eastward current, and that on the return journey they attempted to avoid the current. Using temperature measurements and observation of changes in water color, Franklin had a chart drawn that showed the course of the great current, which he named "Gulf Stream." British captains ignored the chart of this "river in the ocean" for many years, but Americans found it valuable.

You cannot easily drown in the Dead Sea or in the Great Salt Lake. Because of salinity, the water is so buoyant that it is difficult to even get under the surface.

Salt has never turned up in a primitive rock formation. All salt deposits are of aqueous origin. All of the 350,000 cubic miles of salt deposited in the earth is sea salt—that is, it all came from the sea in the past.

Each year, 9 million tons of salt, more than 10 percent of all the salt produced in the world, is applied to American highways for road de-icing. The cost of buying and applying the salt adds up to $200 million.

So visibly polluted with globules of unknown composition had the mid-Atlantic Ocean become that Thor Heyerdahl and his crew drifting across the ocean in 1971 were reluctant to dip their toothbrushes in the water.

Captain William Bligh (1754–1817), who became well known as the victim of his crew's mutiny on the ship *Bounty*, was the victim of another rebellion. In 1808, when governor of Australia, Bligh tried to eliminate rum smuggling. A "Rum Rebellion" occurred and officers of the New South Wales Corps arrested Bligh, took over the government, and held him prisoner until a new governor arrived the following year.

––––––––

Every cubic mile of seawater holds over 150 million tons of minerals. There are 350 million cubic miles of seawater on the planet.

––––––––

The oceans of the world are so vast and deep that if Earth had an absolutely level crust, the sea would form an envelope over 8,800 feet deep.

––––––––

Salt helped build the Erie Canal. A tax of 12½ percent on New York State salt, plus tolls charged for salt shipments, paid for nearly half of the $7 million construction cost.

––––––––

The English naval hero Viscount Horatio Nelson chose to be buried in St. Paul's Church in London rather than in the national shrine of Westminster Abbey because he had heard that Westminster was sinking into the Thames.

––––––––

There is a salt mine in the Polish town of Wieliczka, near Cracow, that has been in operation for nearly 1,000 years.

––––––––

In the mid-seventeenth century, Polynesians built double-hulled canoes, carried by sails made from woven coconut fibers, that could sail more than 1,000 miles in all kinds of weather. The wooden hulls, sometimes eighty feet long, were lashed together and a deck house built between them.

––––––––

Joshua Slocum was the first person to sail around the world alone. When he was fifty-one years old, he left Newport, Rhode Island, in 1895, in his thirty-six foot oyster boat *Spray*, returning three years and two months later after sailing 40,000 miles.

––––––––

Two men rowed across the Atlantic in 1896. George Harbo and Frank Samuelson set out from New York in an open boat, took turns at the oars, and reached Britain's Scilly Isles. They were fifty-five days at sea and covered 3,000 miles. (Provisions included canned meat, 250 eggs, a hundred pounds of sea biscuits, nine pounds of coffee, and two tanks of fresh water. The adventurers also had a small stove and five gallons of kerosene for its operation.)

––––––––

SHARPS
AND FLATS

In addition to the use of the British national anthem, "God Save the Queen," in Britain and other Commonwealth countries, the anonymously written tune itself has been used for a patriotic song or national anthem in other countries (including, in the past, Germany, Russia, and Sweden; and currently, the United States, Switzerland, and Liechtenstein). In total, it has been used by about 140 composers (including Haydn, Beethoven, Weber, and Brahms).

When Girolamo Frescobaldi (1583–1643), the great keyboard virtuoso, was appointed organist at St. Peter's in Rome, in 1608, 30,000 flocked to his first performance there.

New York's original Metropolitan Opera House was started because of a feud between the Astors and the Vanderbilts. In 1880, the Astor-dominated Academy of Music Opera House refused William Henry Vanderbilt's offer of $30,000 for a box for the season. He retaliated by forming a syndicate to build what was to become America's most important and influential opera theater.

Because the middle finger on each hand was considered too short, Ignace Jan Paderewski, the famous Polish pianist, composer, and statesman, was told by a teacher that he could never expect to be a competent pianist.

Before the mechanical clock was invented in the fourteenth century, the most complex machine was the pipe organ installed, about 950 A.D., by Bishop Aelfeg in his cathedral in Winchester, England. The organ had 400 pipes, and seventy men were needed to operate the twenty-six bellows.

If a deaf person understands the physics of sound, he or she can tune a lute, a viol, a spinet, or any stringed instrument. The sound made by a vibrating string depends on its length, its mass, and how much it is stretched.

———

Ironically, one of the Confederacy's rallying songs in the U.S. Civil War, "Dixie," was written by a Northerner, Dan Emmett, of Ohio.

———

The French horn is a descendant of the medieval hunting horn, which was shaped into a loop so that it could more easily be carried and played on horseback. The tube of the modern horn is from twelve to sixteen feet long. Before the introduction of its three valves, the horn could produce only a limited number of tones. In order to get different tones, players had to remove part of the tube and replace it with a larger or smaller one, these parts being called "crooks." Players were expected to carry nine of them, allowing them to play a complete range of keys.

———

At the age of two, William Schwenck Gilbert was kidnapped from his parents in Naples, Italy, and ransomed for £25. He wrote kidnapping episodes in two of his operettas with Arthur Sullivan—*The Gondoliers* and *The Pirates of Penzance*.

———

Irving Berlin, America's most prolific songwriter, has never learned to read music or to write it. He hums or sings his songs to a secretary, who takes them down in musical notation.

———

Many composers have written "musical puzzles," compositions that were amusing to them, if not to their listeners, who probably did not recognize them as such. Haydn's Piano Sonata in A, for example, contains a minuet *al rovescio* ("in reverse"), in which the second part is exactly the same as the first, but played in reverse. Similarly, in one section of Arnold Schoenberg's *Pierrot Lunaire*, the music goes forward to a midway point and then works its way exactly backward. Paul Hindemith has gone them one better. In *Ludus Tonalis*, the Postlude is, with the addition of a final chord, the same as the Prelude, but the score is played upside down and backward.

———

Gioacchino Rossini—perhaps ridiculing composers who would excuse their lack of creativity because of the lack of suitable subjects—declared: "Give me a laundry list and I'll set it to music."

———

There were at least fifty-two musicians in the family of Johann Sebastian Bach.

———

Beethoven was half-deaf most of his life. He was completely deaf when he composed his greatest work, the Ninth Symphony.

Much of operatic star Enrico Caruso's fame came from his recordings, a new industry when he first began. In 1902, he recorded ten songs for the Gramophone and Typewriter Company, for which he was paid £100, a fee considered exorbitant by the recording company. Later, they were very glad they had made the deal; their net profit amounted to about £15,000.

When Charles Ives's *Concord* Sonata and Fourth Symphony are performed, a specially sized block of wood is used by the pianist for striking complex chords correctly.

So shy was Franz Peter Schubert that his first meeting with Ludwig van Beethoven was his last. Schubert had written a set of variations on a French tune for four hands and dedicated it to Beethoven, to whom he wanted to present the score personally. A meeting was arranged. Because he was deaf, Beethoven handed a piece of paper and pencil to Schubert so that a particular bar of music could be explained. Schubert became so nervous at the request that he fled from Beethoven's home and the two composers never again met.

Mozart composed, wrote down, rehearsed, and performed within five days his *Linz* Symphony, the Symphony in C Major, K. 425.

The great tenor Enrico Caruso was performing in San Francisco on April 17, 1906, when the famous earthquake occurred. The terrified tenor took just one thing from his shattered room, a picture of President Theodore Roosevelt, personally autographed to Caruso. Later, when he tried to get on a train with the other members of the opera company, the guards didn't recognize him and wouldn't let him pass. But Caruso showed them his treasured picture, was issued a boarding pass, and made his way to safety.

The original hurdy-gurdy was one of the most popular musical instruments of the medieval period. Known as the organistrum, it was a stringed instrument with a resined wheel that, turned by means of a crank, rubbed across the strings. Haydn wrote five concertos and several nocturnes for latter-day hurdy-gurdies, which combined these features with those of a small organ. These works were written for the king of Naples, who fancied himself a virtuoso on the instrument.

Francis Scott Key wrote "The Star-Spangled Banner" to be sung to the tune of a popular English drinking song, the "Anacreontick Song" or "Anacreon in Heaven," which had been composed by John Stafford Smith for the Anacreontic Society of London. Anacreontics wrote poems in the style of the Greek lyric poet Anacreon (ca. 521 B.C.). Percy Scholes's *Oxford Companion to Music* notes that "the nation defied has furnished the music for the defiance—a proceeding happily unresented by either party."

Both Arturo Toscanini and Leonard Bernstein got their big opportunities as conductors when they were called upon to substitute. Toscanini, a cellist at the time, took the podium at the opera house in Rio de Janeiro and conducted Verdi's *Aida* from memory. Bernstein substituted for an ailing Bruno Walter in Carnegie Hall, and his performance as conductor made the front page of newspapers in New York the next morning. He had been, under Walter, an assistant conductor of the New York Philharmonic.

Serge Diaghilev and Igor Stravinsky both studied law in St. Petersburg. Diaghilev hoped to become a composer, but was advised against it by Nicholas Rimsky-Korsakov. He instead became the father of modern ballet. Rimsky-Korsakov encouraged Stravinsky's musical interests, and Stravinsky became the father of modern music.

For $500, Stephen Foster sold to the leader of the Christy Minstrels the right to claim authorship of the song "Old Folks at Home," one of the most popular songs ever written. Christy held the right for a quarter of a century.

Bach's Six Concertos for Orchestra—the *Brandenburg* Concertos—were written for the margrave of Brandenburg, a prince who loved music, concertos in particular. When the margrave died, the *Brandenburg* Concertos were said to be worth twenty-four groschen. Eight groschen were worth $1.50 in those days (1721), so the value for six of the most distinguished pieces in all of music was only $4.50.

Francis Scott Key wrote many other songs. Many were on religious themes, for he was a devout lay reader in the Episcopal Church. Still being sung is his hymn "Lord with Glowing Heart I'd Praise Thee."

At the pinnacle of his concert career, the renowned pianist and composer Ignace Jan Paderewski (1860–1941) headed the Polish government, in 1919. He also headed the Polish government in exile during the early years of World War II.

————

More of Mozart's compositions are still in active use today than the works of any other composer in history—with the possible exception of J.S. Bach. But some of Mozart's most important works—by today's standards—have suffered long periods of neglect. For example, for twenty-three years, beginning in 1917, the Metropolitan Opera did not give a single performance of *The Marriage of Figaro*.

————

Nicolò Paganini (1782–1840) had a twisted stance on the concert stage, a spectacular bowing technique, and an awesome mastery of the fingerboard that may all have been attributable, at least in part, to an affliction that he had inherited. It is believed that he exhibited the effects of Marfan's syndrome (named after the French pediatrician Bernard-Jean Antonin Marfan), which is characterized by a tall, thin body with underdeveloped muscles but with unusually long extremities and hypermobile joints. These enabled him to perform musical feats beyond the capacities of ordinary men.

————

Irving Berlin, one of America's great songwriters, taught himself to play the piano by practicing on a piano in a saloon where he worked as a singing waiter. He could play only in one key, the key of F-sharp.

————

Maurice Ravel (1875–1937), one of the greatest of modern French composers, referred to his most famous work, *Bolero*, as "seventeen minutes of orchestra without any music." He limited himself to an eight-measure theme that he repeated, with different orchestral colors, for the entire piece.

————

Only one person walked with Mozart's coffin from the church to the cemetery for its burial in an unmarked pauper's grave.

————

One of the earliest operas was composed by a woman, Francesca Caccini. Performed on February 2, 1625, in Florence, Italy, in honor of a visit by the Polish Prince Sigismund to the Medici court, it was a gala spectacle that wound up in a *ballo à cavallo*, a ballet performed on horses.

————

Though he could have used the money—2,000 livres was "a considerable sum, I admit"—Mozart declined the post of organist at Versailles, in 1778. One reason: He did not like French music.

A musician signed the Declaration of Independence. He was Francis Hopkinson, generally thought to be the first native-born American composer. His *Temple of Minerva* (1781), an "oratorical entertainment" resembling opera in style, won the approval of most of his contemporaries, including George Washington.

It has been estimated that the songs of composer Irving Berlin are worth more than $100 million. His song "White Christmas" had sold 113,067,354 records and 5,588,845 copies of sheet music in the United States and Canada alone, as of May 1978. He has composed some 3,000 songs, publishing nearly 1,000.

To make their parades more glamorous, the Sybarites taught their horses to dance rhythmically to music. But when the Sybarite cavalry charged Croton, a city seventy miles to the south of Sybaris in Italy on the Gulf of Taranto, in 510 B.C., the men of Croton struck up a lively dance on their pipes and the Sybarite horses promptly fell to dancing. The charge was broken up, and the demoralized Sybarite army was slaughtered.

Beethoven composed his Third or *Eroica* Symphony in honor of Napoleon, whom he admired. When Napoleon proclaimed himself emperor, an enraged Beethoven tore out the dedication to Napoleon and substituted "To the Memory of a Great Man."

The celebrated Budapest Quartet played an "unforgettable" work at a concert in New York honoring the memory of Bela Bartok (who had died on Central Park West). It was unforgettable, remembers the critic-composer Robert Evett, "because in the last movement of the Bartok *First Quartet*, which is a long one, someone got lost and stayed lost for at least ten full minutes, during which interval the music played was not the *First Quartet*, but some chaotic nightmare created for the occasion and surely impossible to duplicate. When the players got organized sufficiently to finish the piece more or less together, they were received not with boos and catcalls but with a prolonged standing ovation complete with cheers and bravos."

Only once, and in the right hand, is a white key played in Frederic Chopin's Étude for Piano in G-flat Major, Opus 10 No. 5, called appropriately—and what else!—the *Black Key Étude*.

During its first performance, on Christmas Eve 1818, in an Austrian village church at Oberndorf, "Silent Night" was performed by soloists who were accompanied by a guitar, the organ bellows of the church having been gnawed away by mice.

"The Star-Spangled Banner" bore another name when it was first published in September 1814 in the Baltimore *Patriot*; it was called "The Defence of Fort McHenry." The title was changed about a month later.

The Russian composer Sergei Prokofiev composed an opera, *The Giant*, when he was only seven years old—using only the white keys.

As a young man, Arturo Toscanini ran for political office in Italy—as a candidate of the Fascist Party.

Irving Berlin wrote his patriotic masterpiece, "God Bless America," for the Ziegfeld Follies. But after finishing it, he withdrew the song because he decided it didn't belong in a lavish girl show. It was not publicly performed until twenty years later, when Kate Smith introduced it, on radio, on Armistice Day 1938.

Mozart's librettist sailed to America and became a grocer in Philadelphia. Lorenzo Da Ponte, who had written for Mozart *The Marriage of Figaro, Così fan tutte,* and *Don Giovanni*, was up to his ears in debt when he left Europe in 1808. After then failing as a grocer, he went to New York and in 1830 became professor of Italian at Columbia University.

Though he dreaded seasickness, the Viennese waltz king Johann Strauss agreed—after receiving, in advance, a payment of $100,000 in gold—to sail to Boston and conduct there, in 1872, a supermusical called the World Peace Jubilee. The concert took place in a shed for 100,000 patrons. Strauss had to lead 20,000 musicians and choristers; to start everyone on time and to have them end all together, Strauss gave his beat to 100 subconductors.

Although "The Star-Spangled Banner" was written by Francis Scott Key during the War of 1812, it was not adopted as the national anthem of the United States for more than a century, until 1931.

For thirteen years, Peter Ilich Tchaikovsky was financed by a wealthy widow, who stipulated they never meet. And they didn't.

Beethoven as a child made such a poor impression on his music teachers that he was pronounced hopeless as a composer. Even Haydn, who taught him harmony for a time, did not recognize Beethoven's potential genius.

Although the song "Auld Lang Syne" is usually attributed to Robert Burns, it was known at least a century before he published it in 1796. One of his letters says, "It is the old song of the olden times, which has never been in print. . . . I took it down from an old man's singing."

During the Renaissance, music for the Mass was originally based on a Gregorian chant, around which complex melodies were woven. But later, composers introduced popular tunes of the day, including two titled "Good-bye, Lover" and "Kiss Me." They got away with it by changing the rhythms of the tunes, covering them with so many other melodies that the songs were not recognized.

Johann Sebastian Bach must have liked to walk. He walked the 230 miles from Arnstadt to Lübeck, Germany, in order to hear the organist Buxtehude. On another occasion, he walked 25 miles to Halle in the hope of meeting Handel, arriving just after Handel had left the town by coach.

Both Scarlatti and Chopin were inspired by cats. When Scarlatti's cat struck certain notes on the keys of his harpsichord, one by one, with its paws, Scarlatti proceeded to write "The Cat's Fugue," a fugue for harpsichord in D minor. While Chopin was composing Waltz No. 3 in F major, his cat ran across the keys of the piano, amusing Chopin so much that he tried for the same sounds in what is called "The Cat's Waltz."

The French composer Maurice Ravel suffered an injury to the brain in an automobile accident. He died in 1937 as a result of a neural operation, which he feared could not help him but hoped might aid science.

———

If we divide electromagnetic radiation into octaves—as we divide the sound waves produced by a piano—we are able to detect eighty-one octaves. Of these, the best-known electromagnetic radiation, visible light, makes up exactly one octave.

———

Mozart comes closest of all musicians to being the universal composer. During his short lifetime (he died at thirty-five), he wrote operas and symphonies, chamber music and church music, solo and concert works for virtually every instrument—plus mechanical clocks and musical glasses. (Ludwig von Köchel made a thematic catalog of Mozart's works and published it in 1862. Mozart's works are usually identified by their numbers in this listing—for example, the Piano Concerto in B-Flat, K595. The *Köchel Listing* catalogues 626 authentic works.)

———

The composer John Cage's *Imaginary Landcape No. 4* (1953), never sounds the same way twice. It is scored for twelve radios tuned at random.

———

SKY WATCHERS

The telescope was invented in 1608 when a young apprentice was playing games. While his master, the spectacles-maker Hans Lippershey, was away, the apprentice amused himself with lenses and suddenly found a combination that made things seem closer. He showed this to Lippershey, who enclosed the lenses at two ends of a tube.

———

The speed of rotation of the Earth's surface increases steadily from zero at the poles to a bit over 1,000 miles an hour at the equator. (New York City's latitude travels only about 790 miles per hour.)

———

Perhaps the astronomer with the sharpest eyes was the American E. E. Barnard. In the 1890s, he thought he detected craters on Mars; but he didn't announce this formally. He didn't think anyone else would see them and he feared he'd be laughed at. But he was one hundred percent right. It took seventy years and the development of rocket-powered Mars probes to demonstrate the fact.

———

Astronomers at first tried to compensate for poor lenses by making very long telescopes and sometimes by using lenses suspended in air without a tube. In 1722, James Bradley used a telescope 212 feet long. In the preceding century, the French astronomer Adrien Auzout had considered building one 1,000 feet long. He thought it might enable him to magnify things so greatly he would see animals on the moon.

———

On October 2, 1933, the light of the moon was received through Galileo's 3½-centuries-old original telescope and was used to switch on the lights of the Century of Progress Exposition in Chicago. Photoelectric devices transformed the moonlight into electricity and the resulting current closed the illumination circuit of the exhibition.

———

Radio telescopes are now more important than ordinary light tele-scopes. The first was built inadvertently by an engineer, K.G. Jansky, employed by Bell Telephone to locate the source of static on tele-phones. By accident, in 1931, he detected radio waves from space. The second radio telescope was built in 1938 by an amateur, Grote Reber, in his backyard in Wheaton, Illinois. It was not until after World War II that professional astronomers began to take radio tele-scopes seriously.

Astronomers classify stars by their spectra, to which they have given letter designations. It turned out that to put the stars in order of decreasing temperature, the spectra would have to be listed as O, B, A, F, G, K, M, R, N, and S. To make it easier to remember the order, a mnemonic device was created: "Oh, Be A Fine Girl; Kiss Me Right Now, Sweetheart."

An Irish amateur astronomer, the Earl of Rosse, built a telescope with a lens six feet across in 1845. It was called the Leviathan and was the largest telescope built to that time. But he built it in Ireland and the weather there was so bad he could hardly ever use it.

The German optician Joseph von Fraunhofer built magnificent re-fracting telescopes in the early 1800s. He discovered dark lines in the solar spectrum, founding the important science of spectroscopy. He made important studies on light refraction and was a major sci-entific figure. But he didn't have a university education, and thus was not allowed to address scientific meetings.

In the 1580s, the Danish astronomer Tycho Brahe built the best astronomical observatory and made the best astronomical instru-ments the world had seen. They included astrolabes and other de-vices for measuring the distance between two close stars. No one could possibly have done better. But just twenty years later, the telescope was invented and Brahe's beautiful instruments were never used again.

Through the largest telescope on Earth and in the most favorable circumstance, it would not be possible to see an object on the moon much smaller than half a mile across.

During World War II, it was possible to get the best look yet at the Andromeda galaxy. The reason: Los Angeles was blacked out at the time, making it possible for the hundred-inch Mt. Wilson telescope near L.A. to be employed to maximum advantage through the fully darkened skies.

The English astronomer James Bradley, whose measurement of the diameter of Jupiter led astronomers to realize just how much larger some of the planets were than Earth (for so long regarded as the massive center of the universe), is supposed to have turned down a salary increase after he had become an astronomer royal in 1742. He observed that, if the position of astronomer royal were made too lucrative, no astronomers would be appointed to it—only politicians or noblemen.

On every sunny day for seventeen years, the German astronomer Heinrich Samuel Schwabe sketched sunspots. His patience was rewarded in 1843 when he was able to announce that the sunspots waxed and waned in number according to a multiyear cycle. He was only a year off, the cycle being eleven years rather than the ten that Schwabe had stated.

In 1800, a group of German astronomers, suspecting the existence of a small planet in an orbit between Mars and Jupiter, carefully parceled out the sky and arranged which astronomer should look where. While they were organizing themselves carefully, an Italian astronomer, Giuseppe Piazzi, found the "planet," Ceres, quite by accident, on January 1, 1801—the first day of the nineteenth century. It was the earliest known asteroid. The German astronomers kept looking anyway, and by 1807 found three more asteroids: Pallas, Vesta, and Juno. (Since then, 1,700 more asteroids have been discovered.)

The English astronomer Jeremiah Horrocks was a curate. He calculated the date for the next transit of Venus across the sun, and it turned out to be November 24, 1639, which fell on a Sunday. He got through the services with extraordinary speed, then raced across the fields to his instruments. There was a happy ending! He got there in time to make the observation.

In the early 1400s, the greatest astronomer in the world was a Mongol prince, the grandson of the conqueror Tamerlane. The prince's name was Ulugh Beg. In 1428, he built an observatory in Samarkand, and later prepared a star map and planetary tables that were the best up to that time. No one heard of him in Europe, however. By the time his work was translated into Latin, in 1665, the telescope had been invented and Ulugh Beg's work no longer had value.

The French astronomer Charles Messier (1730-1817) was interested in finding comets. He occasionally mistook hazy objects that weren't comets for the comets he was looking for. In exasperation, he made a list of 102 objects for comet hunters to avoid. The objects he listed are what he is now famous for, for they are much more important than comets. Messier 13 is the great Hercules Cluster of a million stars; Messier 31 is the great Andromeda galaxy of half a trillion stars. Messier did, however, discover twenty-one comets, none of them of any importance.

Maria Mitchell (1818–89) discovered a new comet in 1847. This brought her world fame and election as the first woman member of the American Academy of Arts and Sciences in 1848. Taught astronomy by her father, she discovered the comet while she was a librarian in Nantucket. In 1865, she was made Vassar College's first professor of astronomy, a post she held until 1888.

Tycho Brahe felt it beneath the dignity of a nobleman, which he was, to write books, but he fortunately overcame this snobbish impulse and published the fifty-two-page work *De nova stella*, "Concerning the New Star." The greatest naked-eye astronomer, Brahe wrote in 1572 about the flaring-out of a star that had exploded and increased enormously in brightness in the constellation of Cassiopeia. "Tycho's star" remained visible for a year and a half, growing brighter than Venus, before fading out. Brahe's book struck a blow to the Aristotelian notion that the heavens were perfect and unchanging.

The bibliography of variable stars—it includes about 200,000 references—and the catalog of some 300,000 stellar spectra by the Harvard astronomer Annie Jump Cannon were described by Harlow Shapley, longtime director of the Harvard Observatory, as constituting "a structure that will probably never be duplicated in kind or extent by a single individual."

William Herschel (1738–1822), the German-English astronomer who discovered the planet Uranus and became the most famous astronomer of his time, was a music teacher to begin with and entered astronomy as a hobby. Because he couldn't afford to buy good telescopes, he made his own—the best instruments in the world. He would sit grinding the lenses for hours and hours while his sister Caroline read aloud to him to distract him and fed him a mouthful at a time. Caroline went on to do astronomical work of her own, discovering eight comets, and lived to the age of ninety-eight. She devoted herself entirely to William and to his son, John (another great astronomer), and never married.

Galileo became totally blind shortly before his death, probably because of damage done to his eyes during his many years of looking at the sun through a telescope.

A war was ended by a solar eclipse—and became the oldest event on Earth that can be dated to the exact day. The armies of Lydia and Media were preparing for battle in Asia Minor when the eclipse occurred. Sobered by the event, the two nations signed a peace treaty. Modern astronomers have fixed the date of that eclipse at May 28, 585 B.C.

The largest refracting telescope, the forty-inch Yerkes telescope, was built in 1897, and is still in use. All larger telescopes are of the "reflecting" variety, using mirrors rather than lenses.

The villagers of Gonesse, France, were sure their visitor from the sky was the work of Satan himself, and they attacked it with pitchforks, then tied the wheezing, deflated *carcasse* to the tail of a horse, whose dashes over the countryside tore it asunder. "It" had been a rubberized-silk hydrogen-filled balloon—one of the first, in the year 1783.

The telescope was first used in 1608 as a war weapon to spy on enemy ships at a distance. The Netherlands (where the telescope was invented) was at war with Spain, and the Dutch leader, Maurice of Nassau, wanted to keep the invention secret.

An English lawyer, Chester Moor Hall, worked out in 1733 the principle of an "achromatic" telescope by putting together a lens with two kinds of glass. To keep it secret, Hall had two lensmakers work on the two halves of the lens. Each lensmaker turned out to be busy, and subcontracted his job; each used the same subcontractor—and the secret was out.

It took many years for the German astronomer Johann Kepler to make his observations of the heavenly bodies and work out the computations that led to his discovery in 1609 that the planets moved in elliptical orbits. In 1973, a computer given Kepler's data performed the necessary computations in eight minutes.

―――――

The Hale telescope, the 200-inch, 20-ton mirror at Mount Palomar Observatory in California, had to be cooled for nearly a year after it was cast. It then was ground and polished on and off for eleven years. By the end of the process, over five tons of glass had been worn away and 62,000 pounds of abrasives had been used in creating the desired shape and surface.

―――――

Even two centuries ago, an "iron curtain" cloaked scientific achievement in Russia. The reason then was that so few Westerners understood Russian. In 1761, the Russian chemist Mikhail Lomonosov became the first to observe the atmosphere of Venus (during its transit across the sun), but the discovery remained unknown outside the country for 150 years. Lomonosov was the founder of Russian science, and would have been renowned if he had lived in western Europe. He published the first history of Russia, prepared the first accurate map of the country, wrote a Russian grammar that reformed the language, helped to found the University of Moscow, and wrote poems and dramas.

―――――

There are massless elementary particles called "neutrinos" which are emitted during the decay of certain other particles and pass effortlessly through the solid earth. The study of the sun by means of its emission of neutrinos is essential in gaining additional astronomical information.

―――――

There is only one constellation of the heavens that in olden times was reported to be named for a human object: Coma Berenices, "Berenice's Hair." While her husband, Ptolemy III, ruler of Egypt and Cyrene, was off at the wars, Berenice prayed for his safe return and, to ensure it, about 247 B.C., had her long hair cut off and dedicated to the gods in a temple of Aphrodite. The hair was stolen, but the astronomer Conan of Samos was tactful enough to explain it had been taken by the gods to heaven. He pointed out some faint stars that, he insisted, represented her hair.

―――――

The year is previewed in Bhutan by astrologers. If a particularly unlucky coincidence of signs for a combination of day and date is discerned, the calendar is fixed so that the day and date do not occur as they occur elsewhere. Bhutan, in the east Himalayas, has been known to skip a whole month, e.g., there might be no December, but then there are two Januarys.

Nicholas Copernicus (1473–1543), the Polish astronomer, maintained that the stars showed parallaxes (alterations in the relative apparent positions of objects produced by a shift in the position of the observer—used in astronomy to determine distance), but that they were too small to be measured. Observational evidence supporting this Copernican system of planetary motion was not collected until three centuries after his death.

Astrology was not the "father" of astronomy (astronomy is much older), but it was closely tied to the development of mathematics, medicine, chemistry, and biology. Mathematics supplied the tools for understanding and predicting the movements of heavenly bodies upon which astrological forecasts were based. Observations and experiments in medicine and the life sciences were spurred by astrological predictions concerning life, death, and health.

Sir William Herschel, who dethroned the sun as the motionless center of the universe (as Copernicus had dethroned the Earth as the motionless center more than two centuries earlier), doubled the extent of the known solar system and became the most important and successful astronomer of his time. Before his time, only 100 nebulas had been known. Sir William's catalog contained about 2,500. He also discovered the planet Uranus and the sixth and seventh satellites of Saturn. But he believed that the moon and the planets were inhabited, that the luminosity of the sun might be confined to its atmosphere, that under the sun's belt of fire was a cold, solid body that might even be inhabited, and that sunspots were holes in the atmosphere through which the cold surface could be seen.

The diameter of the first distant star to be measured, Betelgeuse, is approximately 240 million miles, making it 250 times bigger in diameter than our sun. Twenty-seven millions of our sun could fit into the body of Betelgeuse. The measurement was made by the American physicist Albert Abraham Michelson, who won the Nobel Prize in 1907, and is known especially for his determination of the velocity of light.

Girolamo Cardano (1501–76), the great mathematician, was a firm believer in astrology. He went a little too far, however, when he tried to cast the horoscope of Jesus; *that* had him imprisoned for blasphemy for a while. On the other hand, he cured a Scottish cardinal of asthma by forbidding him to use feathers in his bed—the first case of an understanding of what we now call "allergy." There is a story (probably false) that Cardano predicted astrologically the day of his own death. When the day, September 21, 1576, found him in good health, he committed suicide.

———

The German astronomer Johann Bayer (1572–1625) felt it was blasphemous to have the constellations named for characters in Greek mythology. He introduced a new system in which the northern constellations were named after people in the New Testament and the southern constellations after people in the Old Testament. It didn't catch on.

———

The island of St. Helena, in the South Atlantic, 1,200 miles west of Africa, has had at least two famous residents. Prior to Napoleon's exile in the early 1800s, Edmund Halley was there, in 1676, to map southern skies.

———

At an eclipse of the sun, the Ojibwa Indians of North America and the Sencis of Peru shot flaming arrows into the sky, hoping thus to rekindle the light. At the autumnal equinox, ancient Egyptians held a festival called "the nativity of the sun's walking stick" in the belief that the declining sun needed a staff to lean upon.

———

Tycho Brahe, the most prominent astronomer of the late sixteenth century, was extraordinarily quarrelsome and arrogant. Over a point in mathematics, he foolishly engaged in a midnight duel that cost him his nose. He was only nineteen years old at the time (1565). For the rest of his life (thirty-six years) he wore a false nose of metal.

———

The first man to determine the distance from Earth to a star was the Scottish astronomer Thomas Henderson. He did it at the Cape of Good Hope, in 1835. He decided to wait till he got back to Scotland before publishing his results—but by that time the German astronomer F. W. Bessel had also determined the distance of a star and had published it. Bessel therefore got the credit, which as a rule goes to the first who publishes, not the first who discovers.

———

In 1704, the English astronomer Edmund Halley (1656–1742) noticed similarities in the paths of the comets of 1531 and 1607 with the comet of 1681 which he himself had first observed. He declared they were the same comet and predicted it would return about 1758. It returned in 1759—seventeen years after Halley's death—and it has returned twice since then, in 1835 and in 1910.

————

In his search for a trans-Neptunian planet—that is, one with an orbit lying beyond that of Neptune—Clyde Tombaugh at the Lowell Observatory found himself at times struggling with a single photographic plate that contained as many as 400,000 stars. His mission, using many plates, was to see if any of the stars had moved.

————

SOLAR SYSTEM

As recently as half a century ago, there was no clear understanding as to why the sun shines. The discovery that it is due to nuclear-fusion reactions was not made until the 1930s, by Hans Bethe and Carl von Weizsacker.

At its center, the sun has a density of over a hundred times that of water, and a temperature of 10–20 million° C.

In 435 B.C., the Greek philosopher Anaxagoras suggested that the sun was not just a small glowing circle of light. He maintained that it was a glowing rock a hundred miles across. For that outrageous statement, he was exiled from Athens.

The rings of Saturn are not solid, flat discs as they appear to be in illustrations. They are made up of billions of tiny particles, probably ice-coated rocks. Each ring circles Saturn at a different speed. The rings are only about ten miles thick. In 1978, rings were unexpectedly discovered around Uranus and Jupiter.

The pressure at the center of the sun is about 700 million tons per square inch. It's enough to smash atoms, expose the inner nuclei, and allow them to smash into each other, interact, and produce the radiation that gives off light and warmth.

Want to reach the outermost planet of the solar system in twenty-five years instead of in the forty-seven years that a direct flight would take? If yes, be sure to be launched first toward Jupiter. Passing through that giant planet's gravitational field, your spaceship would receive an added boost on its way to that most distant planet, Pluto.

The sun is colossal. It contains 99.8 percent of the total mass of the solar system. More than one million Earths would be required to match its volume.

———

The most dramatic astronomical discovery in the last half of the nineteenth century was the "canals" of Mars, in 1877. People speculated about them and tried to use them as proof of intelligent life on Mars, and they inspired H. G. Wells to write the very first "star wars" book, *The War of the Worlds,* in 1898. The canals turned out to be only an optical illusion.

———

The pressure at the center of the Earth is 27,000 tons per square inch. At the center of the giant planet Jupiter, the pressure is three times as great.

———

There is a correspondence between the fluctuation of agricultural production and sunspot variations. Production of wheat, for example, reaches high figures during sunspot maximums and low figures during sunspot minimums.

———

The moon is always falling. It has a sideways motion of its own that balances its falling motion. It therefore stays in a closed orbit about the Earth, never falling altogether and never escaping altogether.

———

The least massive star known is Luyten 726-8B. It has only 0.04 percent the mass of the sun, and it barely shines. It is only forty times as massive as Jupiter. Somewhere in that forty-fold difference in mass is the borderline between planets and stars.

———

Some subatomic particles discovered by nuclear physicists have a lifetime of just a few trillionths of a trillionth of a second. In this moment, light—which travels from moon to Earth in 1¼ seconds—moves to no more than the width of a proton.

———

During an eclipse of the sun in 1868, spectral lines were located that were attributed to an unknown element that was called "helium," from the Greek word for "sun." Thirty years later, helium was discovered on the Earth.

———

The sun is about midway in the scale of star sizes, but most stars are smaller ones. Only 5 percent of the stars in our galaxy are larger than the sun. (That's five billion larger stars, however.)

———

At a height of a hundred miles, air is only a billionth as dense as it is on the Earth's surface. Even so, the total amount of air that is higher than the hundred-mile level comes to 6 million tons.

———

Jupiter is the largest planet, and it has the shortest day. Although Jupiter has a circumference of 280,000 miles, compared with Earth's 25,000, Jupiter manages to make one turn in nine hours and fifty-five minutes.

———

The heaviest known meteorite to fall to Earth—the Hoba West meteorite—lies where it fell in Africa. Weighing about sixty tons, it is not likely to be moved.

———

Polaris, in the tail of the Little Bear constellation, is the closest visible star to true north and thus is referred to as the North Star. By about 2100 A.D., the wobble of the Earth's axis will slowly begin pointing the North Pole away from Polaris. By the year 14,000 A.D., the new North Star will be Vega.

———

Millions of meteorites fall against the outer limits of the atmosphere every day and are burned to nothing by the friction.

———

The discovery of Neptune was announced in 1846. But when astronomers checked, they found the record of an observation of the planet as far back as 1795 by astronomers who, believing it to be a star, recorded the position routinely.

———

Every year, it takes the moon two-thousandths of a second more to circle the Earth than it took in the previous year, as it slowly recedes from the Earth. Long before the moon recedes to much more than its present distance, the sun will have come to the end of its existence as a normal star.

———

Total eclipses of the moon are considerably rarer than total eclipses of the sun. However, a total eclipse of the moon can be seen from anywhere on the side of the Earth facing the moon. A total eclipse of the sun can only be seen from a narrow band about a hundred miles wide at the most. The person who doesn't travel is sure to see a far greater number of lunar eclipses than solar eclipses.

———

The sun's total lifetime as a star capable of maintaining a life-bearing Earth is about 11 billion years. Nearly half the time has passed.

———

The moon fits snugly over the sun. It is a sheer astronomical accident, and it is what makes a total eclipse possible. The moon is just large enough to cover the sun completely, at times, as seen from the Earth. It is also small enough so that during the sun's obscuration the corona, especially the brighter parts near the body of the sun, is completely visible. There is no astronomical reason why moon and sun "fit" so well. The Earth, among all the planets, is the only one blessed in this fashion.

———

One of the planets lies on its "side"—Uranus—and there is no adequate explanation as to why. The extreme axial tip of Uranus is 98° as it revolves around the sun. The axis of Earth is tipped at 23.5°, Mars at 24°, and Jupiter at only 3°.

———

It was as late as 1835 that the mass of the planet closest to the sun, Mercury, was finally determined. The determination was made from the effect of Mercury's gravity upon the orbit of the close-passing Encke's comet, the first short-period comet to be discovered (and the comet with the shortest period, as it turns out). A number of comets have orbits of known periods of revolution. Some of these range from dozens to hundreds of years. About forty-five have short periods of less than ten years.

———

Saturn's rings are briefly invisible to astronomers every fourteen years. At that time, the plane of the rings (which are not solid but consist of discrete particles) is tipped to that of the Earth's orbit, and they are seen edge-on—that is, they are so thin that they then can't be seen at all from the Earth, which is hundreds of millions of miles distant.

———

The first Greek astronomer to suggest the sun was the center of the solar system was Aristarchus of Samos, about 290 B.C. No one took him seriously, and his writings no longer exist. The only reason we know of him is that Archimedes (whose writings do exist) referred to Aristarchus as holding this apparently nonsensical notion.

———

A giant solar flare temporarily knocked out Britain's entire radar system during World War II. The flare also gave the first indication of the existence of solar cosmic rays. The flare apparently had sent out a flood of microwaves toward the Earth that succeeded in handily drowning the man-made radiation that fed the radar system. Thus, it was discovered that the sun radiated in the radio-wave region of the spectrum. By the time World War II was over, astronomers were ready to turn to radio astronomy in earnest.

The Earth and the moon circle each other. The center of gravity about which both circle is located 1,000 miles beneath the surface of the Earth. The center of the Earth makes a small circle about that center of gravity every 27⅓ days. The center of gravity always remains on a straight line between the center of the moon and the center of the Earth. The Earth's turning about the center of gravity is a third motion, in addition to its turning about its axis (rotation) and its turning about the sun (revolution).

Mars' Olympus Mons (Nix Olympica), which is over 300 miles wide at the base, is twice as wide as the largest volcano on Earth—the one that makes up the island of Hawaii. The top of the crater of Olympus Mons is over 40 miles wide.

A system of Martian canyons dwarfs anything on Earth. It stretches across a distance equal to the full breadth of the U.S. The canyons are up to four times as deep as the Grand Canyon, and up to six times as wide.

Jupiter's Great Red Spot is 25,000 miles wide. The spot may be the vortex of a hurricane that has been whirling for at least seven centuries.

Uranus nearly came to be named Herschel—for its discoverer in 1781, the German-born English astronomer Friedrich Wilhelm Herschel. The proposal was defeated when it was decided that planets would not be named for persons. (Herschel dropped the Friedrich and changed the Wilhelm to William after becoming an Englishman.)

In the entire history of the solar system, 30 billion comets may have been lost or destroyed. That amounts to only 30 percent of the estimated number that remain.

Jupiter is two and a half times larger than all the other planets, satellites, asteroids, and comets of our solar system *combined*.

The tails of comets generally point away from the sun whether the comet is approaching the sun or receding. Tiny dust particles surround a comet. They are swept into a long tail by the solar wind, which consists of subatomic particles speeding outward from the sun at speeds of hundreds of miles per second.

———

Though Mars at its closest approach to Earth is only 34.6 million miles distant in a straight line, each of the Viking spaceships had to travel 440 million miles on an elliptical orbit for a guided landing on the red planet.

———

If we imagined the entire solar system shrunk in size to the point where it would fit in the island of Manhattan, the sun would be only a foot across. On the same scale, the nearest star, Alpha Centauri, would be 5,500 miles away from Manhattan—that is, in Jerusalem.

———

Every 584 days, Venus passes between Earth and the sun. In that interval, Venus rotates exactly five times on its axis. This means that every time Venus passes between Earth and the sun, it presents the same face to Earth. Astronomers can't figure out why this should be. Either Earth's gravity has an effect on distant Venus, which seems unlikely, or it is a pure coincidence, which also seems unlikely.

———

It has been estimated that at least a million meteors have hit the Earth's land surface, which is only 25 percent of the planet. Every last trace of more than 99 percent of the craters thus formed has vanished, erased by the effects of wind, water, and living things.

———

Pluto's lone moon, discovered in 1978 by astronomers at the U.S. Naval Observatory, is apparently only 12,000 miles above the surface of the planet and in synchronous orbit. An observer on Pluto would always see the moon in the same place in the sky, and the moon would not be seen at all by an observer on the opposite side of the planet. (Thirty-three moons in all have been detected around seven of the planets—Venus and Mercury are not known to have a satellite.) In discovering Pluto's moon, astronomers learned that Pluto itself is much smaller and lighter than had been believed—it is one-eighth the weight of Earth's only moon—and is, therefore, not heavy enough to exert the gravitational pull on "neighbors" Uranus and Neptune that would be sufficient to account for irregularities in their observed motions. It is believed that something else—one or more massive objects, possibly even a "new" planet—must be beyond Pluto's orbit and causing the perturbation of the orbits of the outer planets.

———

A man bicycling on the moon could, for a while, easily keep up with the sharp-edged frontier between night and day, whose maximum speed is about 10 miles per hour. On Earth, at the equator, the night-day frontier moves along at 1,000 miles per hour.

———

A neutron star consists of matter so compressed that subatomic particles, chiefly neutrons, are in actual contact. If the sun were squeezed into a neutron star, it would be something like 8 miles across instead of 865,400 miles. A 1-pound object placed on the surface of a neutron star would weigh 20 trillion pounds.

———

Not one single science-fiction story—not even by me—placed craters on Mars prior to their discovery. On the surface of Mars there are some four times as many craters as on our moon.

———

Myriads of small meteors fell on the French town of L'Aigle on April 26, 1803, finally convincing the doubting Thomases of the French Academie des Sciences and astronomers everywhere that stories of "stones from heaven" were more than mere medieval superstition and old wives' tales. In other words, they should be studied seriously.

———

Olaus Roemer struggled with a puzzle in 1675. The satellites of Jupiter seemed to move around their planet at irregular times. In trying to solve the problem, the Danish astronomer found he had to assume that light traveled at a finite speed, and in so doing he was the first to work out the speed of light. The speed of sound, which is only a millionth as great, wasn't worked out for another sixty-three years.

———

Copernicus knew of the astronomical views of the Greek Aristarchus, who believed that the motions of the heavenly bodies could easily be understood if it were assumed that all the planets, including Earth, revolved about the sun and that the stars must be infinitely far away because they seemed motionless. Copernicus mentioned Aristarchus' views in a passage in De revolutionibus orbium coelestium that he later eliminated, as though not wishing to compromise his own originality.

———

The comet of 1843 swung around the sun at a distance of only 80,000 miles above its surface. Nothing we know of has ever approached the sun more closely. The comet would have evaporated completely, of course, if it had stayed that close, but under the lash of the sun's gravity it swung around that mighty orb in about an hour and began to recede.

Only one satellite in the solar system holds a dense atmosphere—Titan, at 3,000 miles across the largest moon of Saturn. It is probably almost entirely ice. Prebiological organic chemistry may be in progress. Because of its moderately dense atmosphere and low gravity, Titan would be the easiest object to land on in the entire solar system.

The planet Neptune was discovered by mathematics. Because the planet Uranus did not move according to theory, there had to be a gravitational pull that was not being taken into account. Two men, John C. Adams in England and Urbain J. J. Leverrier in France, calculated where a planet *ought* to be to account for Uranus's movements. An astronomer, John G. Galle, in Berlin, on September 23, 1846, looked at the spot they had indicated, and discovered Neptune in less than an hour.

By projecting the image of the sun onto a white screen, Joseph Henry in 1848 was able with sensitive measurements of heat to show that sunspots were cooler than the rest of the sun—an ingenious scientific demonstration.

Afternoon temperatures on Mars go up to about 80° F. in some areas, and down to −190° F. at night.

Maps that show the solar system need to be updated if they were published before 1979. The reason: Pluto is no longer the most distant planet from the sun; Neptune now is. In its 248.8-year orbital revolution around the sun, Pluto crossed Neptune's orbit in December 1978. Neptune and Pluto resume their more familiar positions in March 1999 as Pluto journeys to its farthest point from the sun, over 4.5 billion miles away.

SPORTS

Though a U.S. Army officer, Abner Doubleday, is generally hailed as having invented baseball at Cooperstown, New York, in 1839. Games called "baseball"—embodying the idea of hitting a ball and running bases—were mentioned in English publications as early as 1744 and in America fourteen years before the Declaration of Independence. Jane Austen's heroine in the 1818 novel *Northanger Abbey*, for instance, "prefers cricket, baseball, to books."

A pole vaulter, when he lands, may absorb up to 20,000 pounds of pressure per square inch on the joints of his tubular thigh bones.

Between 1920 and 1932, the Finnish track star Paavo Nurmi (1897–1973) set twenty world running records and won nine Olympic gold medals.

Between 1882 and 1887, Hugh L. Daly played second base and shortstop and pitched for several major league baseball teams. As a pitcher, he won seventy-four games, including a no-hitter, and he registered a long-standing record of striking out nineteen batters in a game. Not bad for a man with only one arm.

So ferocious had the game become that during the football season of 1905 at least nineteen players died in college and high school contests.

Track star Jesse Owens beat a race horse over a 100-yard course in 1936. The following year, Olympic hurdler Forrest Towns beat a prize cavalry horse, trained as a running jumper, in the 120-yard hurdles, using only five hurdles to give the horse's longer stride a fair chance.

Until Michael Murphy proposed the idea, in 1908, sprinters on track teams had never taken a crouching start. A crouching start allows sprinters to push off into full stride and top speed almost immediately. Murphy coached Yale University, the University of Pennsylvania, and U.S. Olympic track teams.

No one has explained the Minoan art depicting the bull acrobats of ancient Crete. If we can believe this art, an acrobat would face a charging bull, grasp its horns, and do a somersault over its back to the ground. The problem is that the feat appears to be impossible. No daredevil has been reckless enough to attempt it, at least not in our time.

Basketball is the only major sport entirely of American origin. It was invented in December 1891 by James Naismith, a Canadian and an instructor at the YMCA Training School (later Springfield College) in Springfield, Massachusetts. His students complained about the boring daily gymnasium class in marching and calisthenics. After much thought and trial and error, Naismith devised a game with two peach baskets and a soccer ball. In a few years, basketball was being played throughout the country; and after World War I, it became a major international sport.

Prize fights prior to the turn of the century lasted up to more than a hundred rounds (rounds were often determined by knockdowns)—with the fighters using bare knuckles (no gloves).

The first formal rules for playing baseball required the winning team to score twenty-one runs.

Two brothers from Lancashire, England, brought the cotton industry to Moscow in 1903. One of the brothers founded the first Russian football (soccer) team, the Morozovtsi, which held the Russian national football championship until 1914.

The Italian Tazio Nuvolari, considered by many to be the boldest and greatest automobile racing driver of all time, won the 1930 *Mille Miglia* by a flick of the light switch. Driving an Alfa-Romeo, he trailed the faster Maserati driven by Achille Varzi. With the last part of the race finishing in the dark, Nuvolari turned off his lights, leading his opponent to believe he was so far ahead that he eased off to a slower speed. Nuvolari rapidly overtook the unsuspecting Varzi. With a few miles to go, Nuvolari switched on his lights, flashed past the Maserati, and won.

The Metropolitan Museum of Art, in New York, houses the largest collection of baseball cards: 200,000.

A Russian, Nikolai Sologubov, helped the U.S. team win the Olympic ice-hockey championship in 1960 at Squaw Valley, California. The U.S. had never won the hockey title. All the team needed to do after unexpected victories over Canada and the Soviet Union was to defeat Czechoslovakia in the final game. After two periods, the Americans, playing lethargically in the thin air high in the Sierra Nevadas, were trailing, 4-3. During the intermission between the second and third periods, Sologubov, who spoke no English, went to the U.S. dressing room and, through gestures, suggested the Americans inhale oxygen. They did, and when they returned to the ice, they were revived and eager enough to rout the Czechs, 9-4, and win the title.

In a dual track-and-field meet on May 25, 1912, Lafayette College had forty-eight men on its unbeaten squad and Carlisle Indian School (no longer in existence) had six. But one of the six was Jim Thorpe, probably the greatest all-around athlete the U.S. has had. He won the high jump, broad jump, shotput, discus, 120-yard high hurdles, and 220-yard low hurdles. He "slumped" to third in the 100-yard dash. His teammates contributed five other victories and Carlisle won, 71 points to 41.

The knuckleball baseball pitcher Hoyt Wilhelm hit a home run in his very first time at bat in the major leagues, and never hit another in more than 400 times at bat in his twenty-year career with many teams, from 1952 to 1972. In his second season, he hit a triple and never hit another, and two doubles and hit only one more. His career batting average was .088.

O.J. Simpson had a severe case of rickets and wore leg braces when he was a child. Glenn Cunningham was badly burned when he was eight years old and was told he would never walk again; in fact, it took him more than two years simply to straighten out his right leg. Simpson went on to set ground-gaining records in the National Football League, and Cunningham went on to become one of the greatest all-time mile runners, holder at one time of five world track records.

During the baseball rivalries between the two major leagues in the 1890s, the Pittsburgh Nationals, taking advantage of a technicality, signed a player from another club. The Nationals' president, J. Palmer

O'Neill, was called J. "Pirate" O'Neill, and his club became—the Pirates.

———

Billy Sunday, famous as an evangelist after 1903 and reported to have converted more than a million people during his career, was a professional baseball player from 1883 to 1891 with Chicago, Pittsburgh, and Philadelphia teams.

———

New York Yankee pitcher Ron Guidry became baseball's first player to make his batting debut in a World Series game, when he strode to the plate in the fourth game of the 1977 Series. Because of the American League's designated-hitter rule, which allows a team to substitute in the batting lineup a slugger for the (usually) weak-hitting pitcher, Guidry had never gone to bat in a regular-season game. The rule did not apply in that Series. (Guidry laid down a perfect sacrifice bunt.)

———

Ty Cobb of the Detroit Tigers played slightly more than a score of baseball seasons in the American League. He banged out 4,191 hits and posted a lifetime batting average of .367. As of the beginning of the 1979 season, Rod Carew was the leading active baseball batter with 2,082 hits and a lifetime average of .334. Few modern players average .300 or last as long as fifteen years, let alone Cobb's more than twenty.

———

Grand Duke Alexander, third son of the Russian Czar, went to Nebraska in 1872 to hunt buffalo. He brought along railroad cars, including two sleepers, a diner, and a refrigerator car stocked with grouse, quail, and caviar. His guide was U.S. Civil War General Philip Sheridan, and the rest of the staff included General George Custer, Buffalo Bill Cody, and 1,000 Sioux.

———

In 1959, for the first time in his remarkable career, Ted Williams of the Boston Red Sox batted under .300, hitting only .254 and ten home runs. The highest-paid player in sports that year (his salary of $125,000 would seem paltry by today's terms), he was offered the same contract by the Red Sox to play the next season, and he refused. He signed only after management agreed to cut his salary by 28 percent ($35,000), the maximum decrease allowed under baseball's rules. His view was that he had always been treated fairly and he didn't deserve as much as the Red Sox were offering. Ted Williams was one of the greatest natural hitters in the history of baseball. He had a lifetime batting average of .344 and hit a total of 521 home runs during his career. In 1941, Williams's batting percentage was .406 (no one since then has hit .400), which means that he hit safely at least four out of every ten times. Today, a player is considered a good hitter if he bats .275 to .300.

In Thailand, kite flying is a big-league sport with established teams, umpires, official rules, and a national championship. The competition involves fighting between kites controlled by teams of up to twenty men.

In 1954, Roger Bannister overcame physical and psychological barriers and became the first human to run a mile in less than four minutes. He did it in 3:59.4, in Oxford, England. Within two months, the four-minute mile was beaten again, as it has been over 50 times since Bannister's unprecedented feat.

Before they were allowed to compete in the state of Indiana, boxers and wrestlers in 1954 had to swear under oath they were not communists.

For sixty-two years, baseball's greatest slugger, Babe Ruth, alone held the record (nine) for pitching the most one-season shutouts in the American League. In 1978 he became the co-holder, with Ron Guidry, of the record.

To boost attendance, the St. Louis Browns of the American League signed up a midget in the 1951 season. Eddie Gaedel was three feet seven inches tall, and wore a uniform numbered ⅛. He went to bat only once, in a game against the Detroit Tigers, and walked on four pitches. Midgets are now banned by the major leagues. (The Browns that year also hired a team psychiatrist. The next year, they moved to Baltimore.)

There are more than 10,000 golf courses in the U.S.

Most professional sports have "iron men"—athletes who play most of the game. The basketballer Wilton Norman Chamberlain—at over seven feet, "Wilt the Stilt"—was probably king of the iron men. A regulation game in the National Basketball Association is forty-eight minutes, but in one season Chamberlain played an average of more than forty-eight minutes a game—because of overtime periods. In his 13 seasons in the NBA, he logged 47,859 minutes, or just under 798 hours. Chamberlain never fouled out of a game.

———

STOP THE PRESSES

Although freedom of the press is guaranteed by the Constitution, the Lincoln administration not only censored the news but closed down publication of the New York *News* for anti-administration editorials, in 1861 and again in 1863, for alleged spy activity. When the New York *World* satirized Lincoln in 1863, the paper was shut down and its editors arrested on Lincoln's personal orders.

Credit for inventing the quoted interview goes to Anne Royall, the first crusading American woman journalist. She interviewed every U.S. President from John Quincy Adams to Franklin Pierce, and exposed graft in federal departments and incompetence among employees high and low. She campaigned for Sunday mail service and against whipping in the Navy. She had a leg broken in Vermont by an irate Congregationalist, was horsewhipped by a young man in Pittsburgh, and fled Charlottesville, Virginia, with a mob of students at her heels.

The Detroit *Free Press* offered each of 120 households in Detroit and its suburbs $500 if the members of the household would not watch television for a month. Ninety-three of the families said no. Almost all members of the six families eventually chosen for the test were at times depressed, bored, and nervous.

Karl Marx and Friedrich Engels, the fathers of communism, wrote 500 articles for the New York *Tribune*, from 1851 to 1862.

The press response to President Lincoln's Gettysburg Address was primarily one of disdain; the Chicago *Times*, for instance, felt Americans should be embarrassed by the "dish-watery utterances."

In the 1530s, a printing press was set up in Mexico City, and the first Mexican newspaper was published there in 1541.

A French term for wartime propaganda, *bourrage de crane*, means "brain-stuffing."

―――――

The Ladies' Home Journal had to include a reference to whiskey and champagne—two beverages that were taboo in the magazine in the mid-1890s—in order to get the right to publish Rudyard Kipling's story "William the Conqueror."

―――――

The New York *Sun*'s circulation reached a record peak when it printed a week-long series of articles (by the British-American Richard Adams Locke) purporting to reveal that Sir John Herschel—through the world's largest telescope—had discovered life on the moon. Furry batlike creatures "were evidently engaged in conversation; their gesticulation . . . appeared impassioned and emphatic . . . they were capable of producing works of art and contrivance." The hoax was perpetrated during a heat wave and a circulation war in 1835.

―――――

The three newspapers with the largest daily circulation in the world are all Russian. They are *Pravda*, 10 million; *Komsomolskaya Pravda*, 10 million; and *Izvestia*, 9 million.

―――――

Three hundred and fourteen acres of trees are used to make the newsprint for the average Sunday edition of *The New York Times*. There are nearly 63,000 trees in the 314 acres.

―――――

Horace Greeley did not originate the quote by which he is best known. "Go west, young man" was originated by John Babsone Lane Soule in an article in the *Express* of Terre Haute, Indiana, in 1851. Acknowledging the source of the quote, Greeley reprinted and extended it in an editorial in his famous newspaper, the New York *Tribune*. "Go west, young man," Greeley wrote, "and grow up with the country."

―――――

The first newspaper to be published in colonial America was *Publick Ocurrences Both Foreign and Domestic*. It appeared on September 25, 1690, but was shut down immediately by the Massachusetts governor and council because the publisher, Benjamin Harris of Boston, had not obtained a license.

―――――

The journeyman printer of the sixteenth century in Europe worked twelve to sixteen hours a day, printing from 2,500 to 3,500 sheets, an average of one printed sheet every twenty seconds. This rate was not exceeded until the late eighteenth century, and then only modestly. It wasn't greatly exceeded until November 29, 1814, when the London *Times* produced the first newspaper printed on a mechanical press that could turn out 1,100 sheets an hour.

The first known political cartoon, printed in 1747 in a pamphlet called *Plain Truth*, published by Benjamin Franklin, is credited with raising 10,000 volunteers for the Pennsylvania Militia.

Benjamin Franklin founded the first foreign-language newspaper published in America, the German *Philadelphia Zeitung*, in 1732. It expired after only a few issues.

A substantial proportion of the printers and newspaper publishers in colonial America were women. Six women served as official printers to provincial governments. John Zenger's wife ran his newspaper while he was in jail in 1734 on a libel charge in the first freedom-of-the-press case in the colonies.

The first newspaper in Turkey was founded in 1831. By midcentury, there were more newspapers, but all were officially censored and all controversial and troublesome stories were changed or omitted. Regicide and similar crimes could never be reported. When U.S. President William McKinley was assassinated in 1901, it was reported he had died of anthrax. When the King and Queen of Serbia were murdered in 1903, Turkish readers were told they had died of indigestion.

Extraordinary precautions were taken to prevent photographers from showing the public what occurred on the floor of the New York Stock Exchange. The first published picture, which appeared in *Pear's* magazine in 1907, was made through the empty sleeve of a coat that concealed the camera from the sharp eyes of the exchange's guards.

A disastrous hurricane in 1772 swept over St. Croix and is described as having "blown Alexander Hamilton into history." The hurricane made such a vivid impression on young Hamilton that he wrote a long letter to his father, then living on St. Vincent Island. A minister named Hugh Knox saw the letter and had it published in the *Royal Danish-American Gazette*, where it received much acclaim. Through Knox's efforts and other helping hands, it was arranged for Hamilton to attend Columbia (then King's) College. He was on his way.

American cattle barons grabbed land every way they could. One favorite method was to advertise in the local paper. The *Glendive Times* (Montana), of April 12, 1884, carried this ad: "I, the undersigned, do hereby notify the public that I claim the valley branching off the Glendive Creek as a stock range. Chas. S. Johnson." Western papers in the 1870s and 1880s carried columns of such ads which read like legal notices. They had no legal value whatever, but they worked.

———

Apparently because it could not locate a copy in any of its libraries, the Soviet Union was obliged to ask the Hoover Institution on War, Revolution and Peace, at Stanford University, for a microfilm copy of its original edition of the first issue of *Pravda* (dated March 5, 1917).

———

Seven days before the Wright brothers first flew a powered heavier-than-air ship, in 1903, an editorial in *The New York Times* said that "time and money spent in airship experiments are wasted."

———

When a vigilante organization raided a communist bookshop in Oklahoma City in 1940, it seized a number of publications thought to be "advocating violence" and publicly burned them at the city stadium. Among the publications picked for destruction were the Declaration of Independence and the Constitution of the United States.

———

An American woman became the most famous reporter of her time. In 1889, Nellie Bly traveled around the world to "race" against the fictional male hero of *Around the World in Eighty Days;* she beat him by eight days. Accompanying her fame was a scandalous fact: Miss Bly traveled alone. When she died, in 1922, she was buried in an unmarked grave. (In 1978, the New York Press Club dedicated a stone to Nellie Bly at Woodlawn Cemetery in New York City.)

———

The woman who has appeared most on the covers of *Time* magazine is the Virgin Mary—ten times.

———

When her husband was elected President in 1932, Eleanor Roosevelt was editor of the magazine *Babies*.

———

Elizabeth Cochrane Seaman—better known as the adventurous and enterprising journalist Nellie Bly–had herself committed under a pseudonym for ten days to New York's Blackwells (now Welfare) Island. The narratives she wrote for the New York *World* in 1888 resulted in a grand-jury investigation of the asylum's neglect of its patients and in subsequent improvements in their care.

———

STRANGE HAPPENINGS

An American student, Charles Martin Hall, then twenty-two years old, heard his chemistry teacher say that anyone who could devise a practical way of isolating aluminum from its ores would grow rich. Hall went home to his own laboratory, experimented, devised such a method—and grew rich. That very same year, 1886, a French chemist, Paul Heroult, devised the very same method. He was twenty-two years old also. Both Hall and Heroult died twenty-eight years later; each one died one month past his fifty-first birthday.

An international "kingdom of occultism" took in parts of France, Switzerland, and Germany in the eighteenth century. Freemasons, Rosicrucians, and assorted mystics traveled through this underground "kingdom," exchanging ideas and describing their visions. A sorcerer like Alessandro Cagliostro (1743–95) could always rely on other occultists to give him secret lodgings in centers like Lyons, Strasbourg, and Zurich.

Helen Keller (1880–1968), blind and deaf from an early age, developed her sense of smell so finely that she could identify friends by their personal odors.

The slave Henry Brown escaped from Virginia in 1858 by hiding (with a box of biscuits and a bladder of water) in a box that was shipped from Richmond to Philadelphia. There, he popped out into "the free world." He was forever after known as "Box" Brown.

A black cook named Tillman commandeered the last prize ship taken by a Confederate privateer during the Civil War. One night, Tillman killed the captain and mates of the prize crew with an ax, and then forced the survivors to sail to Sandy Hook in New York Harbor, where he turned them in. The feat gained him and his ax a job with Barnum's circus.

Upton Sinclair's blistering novels of social protest ripped the fabric of American industry at the start of the century. Three decades later, Sinclair's cousin Wallis Warfield Simpson ripped the fabric of British royalty by becoming the great and good friend of King Edward VIII. (Fear of a threat to constitutional procedure forced Edward's abdication. in 1936, and a year later he married the divorcée.) Both Sinclair and Simpson were Baltimorians.

Nearly 87 percent of the 103 people asked in a poll in 1977 were unable to identify correctly an unlabeled copy of the Declaration of Independence. (The poll was conducted at a shopping area in Fort Lauderdale, Florida.)

The two greatest writers in their respective languages—William Shakespeare and Miguel de Cervantes—died on the very same day in the very same year, April 23, 1616. They probably did not know of each other. Two men who knew each other well—the second and the third Presidents of the U.S., John Adams and Thomas Jefferson— died on the very same day in the very same year, the Fourth of July in 1826. Adams's last words were: "Jefferson still lives." Jefferson had died, however, a few hours earlier. (The fifth President, James Monroe, also died on a Fourth of July—1831.)

The Soviets are buying skateboards from the United States—but not for recreational purposes. They see them as an answer to some of the country's transportation needs, because the boards are less expensive than bicycles and require little storage space. The first boards went to school instructors so they could train pupils how to ride them.

The German chemist Emil Fischer worked on important tissue compounds, the sugars and purines, and was awarded a Nobel Prize in 1902 for that work. Despondent over Germany's defeat in World War I (and over the loss of two of his three sons and his own ill health), he killed himself shortly after the war's conclusion. A young assistant of his was Hans Fischer—no relation—who also worked on important tissue compounds, the porphyrins, and was awarded a Nobel Prize in 1930 for that work. Despondent over Germany's defeat in World War II (and over the destruction of his laboratory by air raids), he killed himself shortly after the war's conclusion.

The Sûreté, the French precursor and modern counterpart of the FBI, was founded in 1812 by a man who had been Public Enemy Number

One of the Paris rogues' gallery. Eugene-François Vidocq, a thief and outlaw, evaded the police for years, turned police spy, joined the force as a detective, and used his knowledge of crime to establish a new crime-fighting organization, the Sûreté.

———

Without a parachute, a Russian survived a 21,980-foot fall from a damaged plane. Lieutenant I. M. Chisov fell on the steep side of a snow-covered mountain and slid to the bottom, breaking his pelvis and damaging his spine.

———

The Vikings established a colony on the southwestern coast of Greenland that lasted about four centuries, from 982 to nearly 1400. The colonists routinely got their wood from North America by sea (there was none on Greenland), even though that land had not yet been "discovered." In the late 1300s, the Black Death ravaged the northlands, the Eskimos attacked the colony, the climate grew colder, and the colonists finally died or left.

———

The carpenter who built the first stocks in Boston in 1634, a man named Palmer, was the first to occupy them. When he submitted a bill for 1 pound, 13 shillings, the town elders thought it to be excessive and had Palmer charged with profiteering. He was found guilty, fined 1 pound, and sentenced to spend a half-hour in the stocks that he had recently constructed.

———

To help determine on what floor it should have its offices in one of the two 110-story skyscrapers of the World Trade Center, in lower Manhattan, a Japanese company hired a soothsayer to throw dice.

———

At the "worker control room" at Matsushita Electric Company in Japan, workers beat, with bamboo sticks, dummies of their foremen, thereby letting off steam, grievances, and tensions before heading for home and kin, presumably for a more peaceful weekend. (Matsushita's business grew by 30 percent a year for twenty-five consecutive years.)

———

When Alexander Graham Bell was working on the telephone in 1876, he spilled battery acid on his pants and called out to his assistant, "Watson, please come here. I want you." Watson, who was on another floor, heard the call through the instrument he was hooking up, and ran to Bell's room. Bell's were the first words anyone spoke on the telephone. In 1915, when the first transcontinental telephone line was opened, the first person who spoke into it was Bell on the East Coast. His words were, "Watson, please come here. I want you." This time Watson couldn't come. He heard the plea, but he was in California, 3,000 miles away.

———

There was rioting in England when the Gregorian calendar was adopted and September 3, 1752, became, just like that, September 14. Many people insisted they had been deprived of eleven days.

———

A young man named Steve Brodie began telling friends around New York's Bowery in 1886 that he was going to jump off the Brooklyn Bridge as a stunt. For several months he talked about it, and on July 23, the day of the event, he spent a long time in a tavern getting ready. A friend drove him in a wagon to the center of the bridge and left him there. A policeman saw an object fall in the dark to the East River below and a rowboat picked Brodie out of the water. Brodie became famous and opened a saloon where people listened to him describe his deed. There is no proof that he did jump or that he did not. Another young fellow, named Larry Donovan, later made the leap before witnesses. He survived, and was fined $10 for obstructing traffic.

———

The world's largest building without internal supports is the Goodyear Airship hangar, in Akron, Ohio—it has 55 million cubic feet of air. Clouds form in the top of the structure during sudden temperature changes, and it rains.

———

During the Gold Rush days in California, Charlie Parkhurst was a stagecoach driver, taking passengers and gold shipments along dangerous roads. Charlie smoked cigars, chewed tobacco, played cards, and drank. He shot dead two highwaymen. Charlie retired and went into the cattle business in Santa Cruz, California. On December 31, 1879, some neighbors found old Charlie dead at home. When they got around to dressing the body for burial, they discovered that Charlie Parkhurst was a woman.

———

In 1929, the U.S.S.R. decreed a week of five days. In 1932, the U.S.S.R. decreed a week of six days. By 1940, the seven-day week had been restored.

———

Because many scientists believed they owed a debt of gratitude to John Scopes for his role in the internationally publicized Tennessee "monkey trial," they helped to establish a scholarship at the University of Chicago so that Scopes could study geology there. Scopes had been tried for teaching evolution in a Dayton, Tennessee, school in the face of a state statute that prohibited the teaching of theories contrary to the accepted biblical interpretation of man's creation. Controversial trial lawyer Clarence Darrow defended Scopes, and former Presidential candidate William Jennings Bryan worked with the prosecution. Scopes was convicted. When his case went before the Tennessee Supreme Court on appeal, Scopes was so engrossed in his studies that he had little interest in the proceedings, and did not bother to return to Tennessee. The high court reversed the lower court's decision that Scopes be fined $100.

The two most illustrious people in England at the close of the sixteenth century never set foot outside of "this royal throne of kings, this scepter'd isle, this earth of majesty, this seat of Mars, this other Eden, demi-Paradise; This fortress built by Nature . . . this little world; this precious stone set in the silver sea . . . this blessed plot, this earth, this realm, this England." The two were, of course, Queen Elizabeth and William Shakespeare; their achievements, however, have to this day influenced all of the world.

Once in the history of the U.S., a governor—instead of the President—issued a declaration of war against another nation. There was much argument over an uncertain Maine–Canada (New Brunswick) boundary that had persisted since the Treaty of Paris (1783). When Canadian lumberjacks began to build a road along the Aroostook River, American lumberjacks moved in to stop them. Tension rose. Governor John Fairfield of Maine declared hostilities and mobilized the state militia, and New Brunswick mobilized its militia. The bloodless "Aroostook war" ceased when President Martin Van Buren sent General Winfield Scott to arrange a truce in 1839. The present border was agreed upon in the Webster–Ashburton Treaty.

The world's first iron bridge, built at Coalbrookdale, Shropshire, England, in 1782, was the product of three generations of Darbys. Abraham Darby I developed the use of coke; his son manufactured cast iron; his grandson built the bridge.

A Harvard student on his way home to visit his parents fell between two railroad cars at the station in Jersey City, New Jersey, and was rescued by an actor on his way to visit a sister in Philadelphia. The student was Robert Lincoln, heading for 1600 Pennsylvania Avenue. The actor was Edwin Booth, the brother of the man who a few weeks later would murder the student's father.

One man has been punished for libel both in the U.S. and England. In his native England, the fiery anti-establishmentarian and master of vituperation William Cobbett was sued for attacking, without evidence, abuses in the military. He was imprisoned for two years. In the U.S., Cobbett joined the Federalists in attacking the Republicans, and was sued, in 1799, for $5,000 by Dr. Benjamin Rush.

During the reign of Alexander II in Russia (1881–94), many liberal reforms were instituted, including a judiciary system operating in open courts, oftentimes with juries. But in 1878 a young girl, Vera Zasulich, assassinated the governor-general of St. Petersburg in reprisal for punishment of a political prisoner. She was tried and acquitted by a jury. As a result the government abolished jury trials in political cases.

Eleven days before the statute of limitations was to expire on the Brink's robbery in Boston, Massachusetts, that netted nearly $3 million in January 1950, one of the robbers confessed and betrayed his fellow robbers.

When a suspension bridge was being built over the gorge near Niagara Falls, New York, there was no way a boat could carry the necessary suspension wires across the violent waters. The builders of the bridge were inspired to offer $5 to the first boy to fly a kite from the American to the Canadian side. It worked. Once the kite string made the crossing, a succession of heavier cords and ropes tied to the kite string was pulled over until the first length of cable finally spanned the river.

The snow-capped "land of the thunder dragon"—Bhutan, north of India—issued a postage stamp that is actually a tiny phonograph record. It plays, naturally, the Bhutanese national anthem.

In July 1585, 108 Englishmen landed at Roanoke Island off the coast of North Carolina. Sponsored by Sir Walter Raleigh, the settlers built a fort and houses, planted crops, and sought gold. Hurricanes and hostile Indians forced them to return to England within a year. In 1587, another 118 colonists arrived, among them the parents of

Virginia Dare, the first English baby to be born in the New World. The leader of the colony, John White, sailed back to England after a few weeks in order to get more provisions. When he returned to Roanoke in 1591, he found it deserted. The word "CROATOAN" was carved on a tree, and no one to this day knows what happened to the settlers.

———

Minoru Genda, a Japanese general who helped to plan the attack on Pearl Harbor, was awarded the United States Air Force Legion of Merit in 1959. This occurred when Genda was head of the new Japanese air force, and after he had test-flown Lockheed's F-104 Starfighter in California. His recommendation was a factor in Japan's purchase of the planes.

———

The classical period of Mayan culture lasted for six centuries and then collapsed for reasons that have never been explained. Theories range from an epidemic to bad farming methods that exhausted the land. The mystery is that the great Mayan cities flourished at the beginning of the ninth century and were ghost towns by its end.

———

Until the U.S. Post Office laws were strengthened in the 1870s, a big and profitable mail-order business was the selling of mechanical devices to help gamblers to cheat. Known as "advantage tools," these devices included marked cards, loaded dice, cutters and trimmers for shaving edges on cards, sleeves and vests for holding extra cards, and "shiners" or "spies" for reading the opponents' cards.

———

Oak Island off the coast of Nova Scotia has a mysterious deep shaft that has resisted exploration because the water cannot be pumped out. All that has been discerned is that the shaft was dug and lined with logs in the eighteenth century by an unknown band of men.

———

In 1695, two scientists obtained a diamond from a rich patron and heated it by using a lens to focus light on it. The diamond disappeared. Diamond is made of carbon, and it burns just as coal will when it is heated strongly enough.

———

Columbus was returned to Spain in chains after his third trip to the New World. He was charged with tyrannical mismanagement of the Haitian colony. On his fourth voyage, he tricked the Indians by predicting an eclipse he knew would occur.

———

The celebrated seventeenth-century pirate William Kidd was a wealthy landowner in New York.

All the time that the public prosecutor's office in Germany was searching for the family of Adolf Eichmann, it was duly registered in Buenos Aires with the German embassy, whose staff maintained rare discretion.

U.S. Congressmen expressed surprise on learning in 1977 that it takes fifteen months of instruction at the Pentagon's School of Music to turn out a bandleader but merely thirteen months to train a jet pilot.

After being evacuated to England in 1961, the "primitive" people of the island of Tristan da Cunha voted two years later to return to their homes, though they would have only a remote chance of rescue if the 6,760-foot-high volcano on their island in the South Atlantic, about midway between South Africa and South America, erupted again.

On the night that John Wilkes Booth killed President Lincoln in Ford's Theater in Washington, D. C., he also intended to assassinate General Grant. The Grants had been invited to accompany the Presidential party to the theater, but declined in order to visit their children at school in New Jersey.

Winston Churchill was born in a ladies' cloakroom in the ancestral castle of Blenheim. His mother was attending a dance there when she prematurely delivered.

Returning to his Minneapolis home from a political meeting in 1947, Mayor Hubert Humphrey was shot at three times. The would-be assassin has never been traced.

Four months after falling off the *Orient Express* while wearing only pajamas, sixty-four-year-old Paul Eugene Louis Deschanel resigned as president of the French Republic. He miraculously had survived the mishap, which occurred on the way to Lyon, in 1920, but he was unable to survive the merciless satires in night clubs and newspapers.

George Washington's mother caused him embarrassment during the Revolutionary War by complaining in public that she was starving. Actually, he was satisfactorily providing for her, but she was a cold woman, probably with Tory leanings, who deprecated her son's achievements and refused to appear at either of his inaugurations.

Mark Twain was born in 1835 when Halley's comet appeared. He predicted that he would die when Halley's comet next returned to scare everyone—and he did, in 1910. Superstitious people bought anticomet pills at $1 a box. The comet returned in 1986.

Two psychologists at Edgewater College, Cincinnati, Ohio, studied 34,318 criminal offenses committed over a one-year period in Hamilton County (Cincinnati), and reported in 1976 that eight categories occurred more frequently during or near the full-moon phase. The categories were rape, robbery and assault, burglary, larceny and theft, auto theft, offenses against family and children, drunkenness, and disorderly conduct.

There has been a blue moon. When a large amount of fine dust was sent into the upper atmosphere by huge Canadian forest fires in 1950, the dust caused a blue coloring in various parts of the world. Cars turned on their headlights in the daytime, and at least one daytime baseball game was played under lights. In some places, people even reported a blue sun. The phenomenon lasted at least two days.

STRANGE RULES, LAWS, AND CUSTOMS

The town of High Wycombe in Buckinghamshire, England, carries on the multi-century custom called the "Weighing-in Ceremony." In early May, the town's mayor, mayoress, deputy town mayor, deputy mayoress, town clerk, and district councilors representing wards in the town's boundaries are weighed in order to learn if they have grown fat at the public trough. (The ceremony was banned when Cromwell and the Puritans came to power, in the seventeenth century, and revived in the nineteenth century.) The present weighing machine was a gift of a greengrocer. It consists of a red plush seat suspended from an overhead dial with a spring resistance. The whole is suspended from a large brass tripod, and it is known as jockey scales.

Over the centuries, playing cards have been put to strange uses. They became the first paper currency of Canada when the French governor, in 1685, used them to pay off some war debts. In 1765, the year of the Stamp Act—when every pack of playing cards was being taxed one shilling—they were used for class admission at the University of Pennsylvania. Napoleon used them as ration cards during the French Revolution.

It was proposed in the Rhode Island legislature in the 1970s that there be enacted a $2 tax on every act of sexual intercourse.

In 1853 Illinois passed a law that required any black entering the state and staying more than ten days to pay a fine of $50. If he could not pay, the black could be sold into slavery for a period commensurate with the fine.

When the X-ray was discovered by Wilhelm Roentgen in 1895, some journalists were convinced that the primary user of the revealing shortwave radiation would be the "peeping Tom." The titillating publicity led to legal and mercantile steps. Two examples: A law introduced in New Jersey forbade the use of "X-ray opera glasses," and merchants in London sold X-ray-proof underwear.

A law was passed in England requiring all corpses to be buried in a wool shroud, thereby extorting support for Britain's flagging wool trade. The act was repealed 148 years later, in 1814.

The U.S. Internal Revenue Service allows deductions of thousands of dollars for installation of an elevator in the home, but not a single penny for the heating and lighting of an exercise space in the basement (let alone for the construction of such an area). Prescriptions for possibly addictive medications are deductible, but vitamins that could well be supplementing a deficient diet are not. Vanity surgery—facelifts, breast enlargements, eye tucks, nose jobs, and the like—is allowable, but fees for a health club or for weight-reducing programs are not. The tobacco industry can write off its advertising expenditures, but an individual may not deduct the expense of enrolling in a course to break the smoking habit.

In 1795, the National Convention in revolutionary France decreed a new calendar to educate the public to new ideas such as eliminating wasteful holy days, including Sundays and saints' days. It was identical to that used in ancient Egypt: Each year was divided into twelve months of thirty days each, with five extra days at the end of the year; each month had three ten-day "weeks." This calendar was repealed in 1805, mainly because of the confusion caused by its abolition of the seven-day week. It had wreaked havoc with the traditional system of religious observances, festivals, and market days.

Even the shadow of a lower-caste person in India may be considered a defilement if it falls on a Brahman, a member of the highest or priestly caste. Although current Indian law forbids the caste system, in practice many people who held these notions still hold them today.

Only 15,000 out of the 35,000 population of the tiny mountain principality of Andorra, wedged between France and Spain, could call themselves full citizens until recently. To become a true Andorran, tradition required the passing of three generations or the marriage of a daughter recognized as the "heiress" of a family.

The Tinguian people of the Philippines have their own way of kissing. They put their lips close to each other's face and quickly inhale.

———

As artists and traders in medieval cities began to form organizations, they instituted tough initiation ceremonies. Journeymen in Bergen, Norway, were shoved down a chimney, thrown three times into the sea, and soundly whipped. Such rites made belonging to the guild or corporation more precious to those who were accepted, and survived.

———

The average age of Elizabethan and Jacobean brides was about twenty-four and their bridegrooms around twenty-seven. The primary reason for delayed marriages was to limit births among poorer people. The higher the social status, however, the younger the age at marriage.

———

A 180-square-mile land of deep valleys and high Pyrenees Mountains—the principality of Andorra—is ruled by two foreign sovereigns: the bishop of the Spanish town of Seo de Urgel, south of the Andorran border, and the President of France. Seven centuries ago, a Spanish bishop and the French Count of Foix settled a long-term land dispute by agreeing to become co-princes of the Andorran valley. The Spanish title was handed down the centuries to the present bishop. On the French side, the title was passed to the kings of Navarre, then to the kings of France, and now to the presidents of France.

———

Wanton cruelty in the treatment of slaves was forbidden by the Code of Hammurabi, one of the most famous of ancient documents. It was promulgated in the King's name in Babylonia sometime between 2100 and 1800 B.C. The code, however, stipulated that slaves were to be branded on the forehead and forbidden to hide or mask the mark.

———

Common in Europe and the British Isles during the Middle Ages and later even in the New World was the practice of trying and condemning animals for injuring or killing a human being. For instance, the French parliament, the highest court in the land, ordered the execution of a cow. It was hanged, then burned at the stake.

———

As in Abraham's time, it was the custom among men in Rome, when swearing to tell the truth, to place one's right hand on one's testicles. The English word "testimony" is related to this custom.

When a Chinese bystander ashore was killed accidentally by a cannon salvo of greeting from an English ship, during the early days (1830s) of the China-Western trade, the English were forced to turn over to China the hapless gunner, who was promptly strangled. (Strangling was thought by the Chinese to be a less severe punishment than, for instance, beheading, because the body would not be permanently disfigured.)

In the Andes, time is often measured by how long it takes to chew a quid of coca leaf. Sometimes, and not just in the Andes, a destination is said to be so many cigarettes away.

The minister of education in the bureaucracy of post-Napoleonic France could boast that he knew, given any hour, what every teacher in every school in the nation was teaching. A similar scholastic regimentation existed in each province of Germany into the twentieth century.

Charles Bradlaugh (1833–91), an English atheist, fought against the requirement to take oaths on the Bible. He was elected to the House of Commons in 1881 and refused to take the oath necessary for being seated. He was expelled, and was reelected and expelled again, in 1881, 1882, 1884, and 1885. He finally won his point and was allowed to affirm instead of swear. In 1888 a law made affirmation sufficient in the English courts.

The *Titanic* had a sister ship—the slightly lighter *Olympic*, which was built first. Upon being launched, the *Olympic* collided with the British cruiser *Hawke* and had to steer to Belfast for repairs. The Right Honorable Alexander Carlisle, the designer, was to remember a conference where lifeboat capacity was discussed for "five or ten minutes," whereas the time allotted for the discussion of decorations for the liners ran up to five hours.

Captain William Kidd sailed in 1695 as a pirate-hunter commissioned to help clear the Indian Ocean of buccaneers. But he captured and plundered legitimate merchantmen, made the mistake of returning home to England, and was hanged for a pirate himself.

THAT'S ENTERTAINMENT

Charlie Chaplin broke into show business at age five because his mother, a music-hall performer, lost her voice during the performance and had to leave the stage, and Charlie went on and sang a well-known song. Halfway through the song a shower of money poured onto the stage. Charlie stopped singing and told the audience he would pick up the money first and then finish the song. The audience laughed. This was the first of millions of laughs in Charlie Chaplin's fabulous career.

Ethel Barrymore of Broadway's "royal family" of actors often played royalty in her plays and movies. In·one of her silent films, she had the role of a Russian princess. Among the extras was a Russian emigre tailor. He was Leon Trotsky, who moved up to become a leader of the Bolshevik Revolution—which put an end to royalty in Russia.

The American chemist Robert Hare discovered that a blowpipe flame acting upon a block of calcium oxide—which is lime—produces a brilliant white light that could be used to illuminate theater stages. We speak of someone who faces the glare of publicity as being in the limelight.

Perhaps the most economical form of makeup ever used by actors was known in England as "Sadler's Wells makeup." All the actor needed for this makeup was a couple of empty tobacco tins into which he or she scraped some paint from the walls to use in coloring the face. For shadowing, the actor merely ran his finger along the shelf under the dressing table and applied dust directly to the face.

In the mid-1960s, the motion picture director-producer Stanley Kubrick wanted from Lloyd's of London an insurance policy protecting against losses should extraterrestrial intelligence be discovered before completion and release of his far out motion picture *2001: A Space Odyssey*. Lloyd's didn't take the chance.

———

England's fun-loving Prince of Wales, who later became King Edward VII, was fond of practical jokes. Once he went on stage to play the role of a corpse in a scene in Sardou's *Fedora* when Sarah Bernhardt was weeping over the body of her murdered lover. (Mme. Bernhardt and the Prince were long-time friends. On the occasion of his coronation, she was invited to be one of a group of beautiful lady friends of the new king who were seated in what was called "the King's Loose Box.")

———

Not until 1959 was a play by a black woman produced on Broadway. Twenty-nine-year-old Lorraine Hansberry's *A Raisin in the Sun*, about the problems (comic and serious) of a black family in modern America, was successful and has been made into a motion picture.

———

By 1929, two years after introduction of the "talkies," motion pictures in the United States were attracting 100 million patrons every week.

———

A fifteen-minute radio serial, *Amos 'n' Andy*, which went on the air every week-night at 7:00, was so popular in the 1930s that most movie theaters throughout the United States changed curtain time to 7:15, because hardly anyone would go to the movies until they had heard the latest *Amos 'n' Andy* episode. (In those days, the feature film was always preceded by a newsreel, at least one comedy, a cartoon, a travelogue, coming attractions, and perhaps a specialty two-reeler. One had plenty of time to arrive before the main show began.)

———

The large number of drunken workers and children sparked a temperance movement in England after the 1850s. Temperance cafés, restaurants, and refreshment houses featured food or nonalcoholic beverages at modest prices. The first temperance music hall was founded in 1880 in a popular quarter of London. It became the Old Vic Theatre.

———

Northwestern University conferred an honorary degree on a dummy of the wooden variety—on ventriloquist Edgar Bergen's dummy, Charlie McCarthy.

———

The Nobel Prize-winning (1962) American biochemist James Watson, whose work with Britain's Francis Crick led to discovery of the molecular structure of deoxyribonucleic acid (DNA), the stuff of which genes are made, was a Quiz Kid on the popular radio show.

The great French actress Sarah Bernhardt was obsessed with death. As a teenager, she made frequent visits to the Paris morgue to look at corpses of derelicts dragged up from the Seine, and she begged her mother to buy her a pretty rosewood coffin with white satin lining. The coffin became part of the Bernhardt legend. Occasionally, she slept in it, and eventually she was buried in it when she died at seventy-nine.

The most extravagant and glamorous shows ever seen on Broadway were the Ziegfeld Follies. The reason was the beautiful Ziegfeld girls. Almost half of the costs for these expensive productions went for their costumes. These Broadway beauties slouched around the stage and hardly ever smiled. In fact, Dolores, the most famous of Ziegfeld girls, never once smiled on-stage in her ten years with the Follies.

Most plant pollen is highly inflammable. It will ignite and explode when placed on an extremely hot surface. In the early days of modern theater, artificial lightning was produced by throwing pollen grains of the club moss onto a hot shovel.

Charles Didelot, a Frenchman, staged ballets in St. Petersburg and had a profound influence upon Russian ballet. In 1796, he devised a system whereby dancers could be lifted into the air on wires, giving the illusion of flight. By means of wires, Didelot could lower a ballerina to the floor so that she seemed poised on the tips of her toes. Ballerinas soon after learned to dance on their toes without wires.

The English indirectly owe the preservation of Shakespeare's birthplace to P.T. Barnum. In the 1850s, the Stratford-on-Avon cottage was neglected, and its living room was a butcher shop. When Barnum began to negotiate to acquire the house and ship it in pieces for display in his museum, the English were horrified and banded together to buy it; they made it a national monument.

When Maxwell Anderson wrote the play *Elizabeth the Queen* for Alfred Lunt and Lynn Fontanne in 1930, many revisions were necessary, but none were forthcoming. The Philadelphia run was a disaster. The next stop was Baltimore, where the play opened during a torrential rain. The next morning, Anderson finally showed up with the precious rewrites. He confessed that he could write only when it rained. In his Rockland County, New York home he had a sprinkler system over his studio roof so he could have the sound of rain falling whenever he wanted it.

In the 1920s and 1930s, Charlie Chaplin was probably the most celebrated man in the world. On a visit to his native London, the motion-picture comedian received 73,000 letters in just two days.

In 1967, both Laurence Olivier and Peter Ustinov were nominated by the Television Academy for the same Emmy award. Olivier was not able to be present, so he requested that Ustinov should accept for him if he won. Ustinov was superstitious about preparing an acceptance speech in advance for himself, but he was prepared to accept for Olivier. It was Ustinov who won the award and, stammering and changing a word or sentence here and there, he used the Olivier speech for his own acceptance.

During the Elizabethan age, plays were usually printed without credit to the author. All of Christopher Marlowe's plays that were printed in his lifetime, for example, appeared anonymously. Only because of a casual reference by a fellow playwright two decades later is it known today that Thomas Kyd wrote The Spanish Tragedy.

Shakespeare never gave up acting while he was writing thirty-seven plays. It was his livelihood. He was one of the "principal comedians" who acted in Every Man in His Humour by Ben Jonson in London in 1598. Two years after the first performance of Hamlet, his name appears on the list of "principal tragedians" who acted in Jonson's Sejanus. Eight years before his death in 1616, Shakespeare was among the "men players" who arranged to use the Blackfriars Theatre.

A U.S. television network's dramatic representation of the trial of Nazi judges was sponsored by the natural-gas industry. The word "gas" was excised from the script, but a few "gases" slipped by; those had to be blipped by technicians before the program was broadcast.

The master of theater realism was the producer David Belasco. For The Easiest Way, in 1908, he bought the entire interior of a dilapidated boardinghouse—furniture, carpets, gas fixtures, and the faded wallpaper—and transferred it to the stage. In 1912, for a play entitled *The Governor's Lady,* Belasco bought the furnishings and equipment of a Childs restaurant for his set. He even had coffee brewed in the coffee urn so that the aroma would fill the theater.

In the early 1900s, Rector's was the most popular and fashionable after-theater dining place in New York. But in 1908, the heroine in the play *The Easiest Way* gave up trying to be virtuous and decided to return to a life of sin. The last line of the play was, "I'm going back to Rector's to make a hit and to hell with the rest." These words so shocked the public that Rector's business fell off, and five years later it was bankrupt.

Anyone who thinks that theater tickets are expensive today might consider what happened in 1854. That was the year the famous Academy of Music opened on New York's 14th Street. The prices ranged from $3 to $40 per seat.

The nineteenth-century New York theaters, with their gas lights and inflammable scenery, were prone to fires. One of every four theaters of this period burned within four years of being built. The Bowery Theatre, which opened in 1826, was destroyed four times and rebuilt. Showman P.T. Barnum was burned out of his theaters twice in three years; both times his valuable animals were incinerated or let loose on the streets. The greatest toll of human lives in a nineteenth-century theater fire in New York resulted from the burning of the Brooklyn Theatre in December 1876 during a performance of *The Two Orphans.* Firemen searching the ashes found 289 bodies—people from the gallery who had suffocated before they could escape. Many theaters, fortunately, burned down when they were empty.

Clare Boothe Luce was not allowed by her husband, Henry Luce, founder of Time, Inc., to participate in the development and running of *Life* magazine, though she had created the concept. She turned instead to writing the Broadway play *The Women.* It ran for 657 performances on Broadway, was translated into twenty-six languages, and was twice made into a movie.

The fabled entertainer George M. Cohan not only produced, directed, and starred in productions, but he wrote them as well. He did his writing at night, completing as many as 140 pages at a single sitting. He wrote songs for his musicals after he had written the books for his musicals. Someone else made the musical notations for him while he whistled such now famous melodies as "Over There" and "You're a Grand Old Flag." If he couldn't get enough peace and quiet at home, he would go to the railroad station and hire a Pullman-car drawing room on a train going far enough away for him to complete his work.

———————

Alfred Lunt became very nervous if he played to a theater with any empty seats. He was really only happy with an audience that included standees. One night, during the run of *Idiot's Delight,* there were a few empty seats. So the playwright Russell Crouse got out a dummy that had been a prop in another play, dressed him, stood him up in the back of the house, and told Lunt there were standees. Lunt was delighted, and told Crouse after the performance that "one standee was so interested in the play that he hardly moved at all."

———————

Everyone has heard of Hollywood's voice-dubbing. In the movie musical *Singin' in the Rain,* the lesser art of foot-dubbing was applied: After Gene Kelly completed his famous tap dance in the rain, the director still needed the sound of sloshy tapping feet. Instead of having Mr. Kelly dance again for the sound track, two young ladies put on their tap shoes and, tapping in bucketsful of water, produced the required sounds to match the tapping seen on the screen. One of these tappers was the late Carol Haney, assistant to Mr. Kelly, and the other was Gwen Verdon, choreographer Jack Cole's assistant. Both of these foot-dubbers later became Broadway dancing stars.

———————

Silent-movie superstar Mary Pickford was known as "America's Sweetheart," but she was adored all over the world. On her frequent trips abroad, she would be mobbed by hordes of overenthusiastic fans. In Paris, when she visited Les Halles, the open-air market, her fans became so threatening that two butchers had to lock her in a meat cage until the police could rescue her. Later, in Alexandria, Egypt, her car was nearly wrecked by stevedores who wanted her to autograph their ears so they could have the signature permanently tattooed.

———————

Throughout her long and enormously successful career, Sarah Bernhardt never trusted any of her money to a bank. She insisted upon being paid in gold coins, which she carried with her in a battered chamois bag. From this bag she paid her company, servants, and creditors. When there were too many gold coins for the bag, she put the overflow in a chest under her bed.

––––––––

The partisan supporters of the American actor Edwin Forrest and the British actor William Charles Macready clashed violently outside the Astor Place Opera House in New York in 1849—Macready was playing *Macbeth* there—and twenty-two people were killed in the confrontation.

––––––––

After months of discussion and planning, it took Richard Rodgers only five hours to compose the overture, the ballet music, and the songs for his first big Broadway musical hit with Oscar Hammerstein, *Oklahoma!* (The show tried out on the road under the title *Away We Go.*)

––––––––

In shooting the acclaimed film *The Lost Weekend,* about an alcoholic, the outdoor filming was done in New York City and the interiors were done in Hollywood. The latter included an exact duplicate of a Third Avenue bar, P. J. Clarke's. On Stage Five at Paramount Pictures Clarke's was reborn, complete to the dusty stuffed cat on the top of the telephone booth. Ray Milland, who starred in the film, tells that for one week every afternoon at five o'clock the door of the set would open, a man would walk up to the bar (whether filming was going on or not), order a straight bourbon, chat about the weather, plunk down fifty cents, and stroll out. It was the writer Robert Benchley, who was homesick for New York.

––––––––

Florenz Ziegfeld got his first job in show business with Buffalo Bill. One of the features of the famous Wild West show was a shooting contest with the sharpshooter Annie Oakley. The sixteen-year-old Ziegfeld was in the audience and volunteered to compete. When he beat Annie Oakley, Buffalo Bill offered him a job, and Ziegfeld accepted without telling his parents. The job didn't last very long because the irate elder Ziegfelds brought their runaway boy back almost immediately.

––––––––

During the pre-Broadway tour of the 1936 musical *Red, Hot and Blue!,* Cole Porter had to do a lot of rewriting. Rather than hire a professional stenographer to take his dictation and transcribe the changes, he used the services of one of the stars of the show—Ethel Merman. Before she went into show business, Miss Merman had been a secretary. Porter described her as "among the best steno-graphers I ever had."

When the Broadway musical *Annie Get Your Gun* was being pro-duced, the production staff, including director Joshua Logan, decided that the leading man and leading lady needed one more duet. At a meeting they asked composer Irving Berlin to write it. When the meeting broke up, Mr. Logan went right home, and when he walked in the front door of his apartment the phone was ringing. It was, of course, Irving Berlin, who proceeded to sing the just-written "Any-thing You Can Do, I Can Do Better." Berlin had created the whole song, words and music, in the ten to fifteen minutes it took him to ride home in a cab.

The first motion picture copyrighted in the United States showed a man in the act of sneezing. (The year was 1894.)

Showman Florenz Ziegfeld believed in getting just what he wanted. When his show *Whoopee* was about to open in Pittsburgh, the star, Eddie Cantor, came down with laryngitis and was unable to speak. Ziegfeld found out that the best throat doctor in Pittsburgh was re-covering from a near-fatal car accident. He stormed into the man's sickroom, gave him a check for $1,000, and had him put on a stretcher and into a waiting ambulance. Eddie Cantor sat on the floor of his hotel room while the doctor painted his throat and gave him other medication from the stretcher. The show opened as planned.

In 1957, Frank Sinatra was quoted as describing rock-and-roll as "phony and false" and "written and played for the most part by cretinous goons." But when Elvis Presley finished his army stint three or so years later, Sinatra paid him $125,000 to appear for six minutes on a television special.

Acting was once considered so frivolous an occupation that author-ities in Virginia, in 1610, forbade the immigration of actors from England. Because of the evils that were thought to be associated with the craft, the cast of the first English play in colonial America in 1665 was arrested in Virginia, but acquitted. The play was *Ye Bare and Ye Cubb,* written and produced by three amateurs.

The usual technique of making a motion picture is to do it in short "takes" lasting from five to fifteen seconds each. The film then is put together by splicing the takes. In filming *The Rope,* Alfred Hitchcock made a unique experiment. He did the entire movie in a "single shot." It was not really a *single* shot, because each reel of film runs ten minutes and there was a pause at the end of each ten minutes to reload the camera. The pause was "covered" by a closeup of someone's back or a table. The new take began at the point the previous one ended. When something went wrong during a ten-minute segment, the scene had to be done over. When *The Rope* was completed, there was no cutting required. The various reels had only to be spliced.

———

Julian Mitchell was the director most frequently used by Florenz Ziegfeld to stage his musical extravaganzas. He did his job brilliantly in spite of the fact that he was deaf. In order to judge the dancers' steps or calculate the rhythm of a scene, he would put his forehead or his ear to the piano to feel the tempo. One of the stars who worked for him, Hazel Dawn, remembered one time when a great thunderstorm had broken out while he was working with a chorus and he complained, "Why are you girls shuffling your feet?"

———

After becoming Emperor of Rome, Nero's dearest ambition was to sing in public, according to the Roman chronicler Suetonius. After taking lessons, he made his debut in Naples. An earth tremor shook the theater, causing some of the audience to depart while Nero continued singing. At a later performance elsewhere, he had the gates locked so no one could leave while he was on stage. Some women gave birth in the stands. Some men, tired out with listening and applauding, furtively leaped over the walls. Three clever citizens tricked the guards into letting them through an exit: one pretended to be dead and the other two carried him out.

———

All of Mary Pickford's success came from playing the roles of young girls (and occasionally young boys). Even though she was only five feet tall, the sets for her pictures were especially built to enhance her slightness. All furniture and props were scaled one-third larger than life-size, doors and windows were bigger than normal, and doorknobs were placed higher.

———

During his career as an actor and light-opera singer, DeWolf Hopper recited "Casey at the Bat" at least 10,000 times.

———

The stellar cataclysm in the motion picture *2001: A Space Odyssey* was filmed by Stanley Kubrick in an abandoned corset factory in

New York City. The "cataclysm" was a close-up of paint dripping in a bucket.

———

A tambourinelike instrument used in minstrel shows was made from the jawbone of a horse or ass—from which the instrument got its name, "bones." When the bone was thoroughly dried, the teeth were so loose they rattled and produced a sound as loud as a castanet. Every minstrel troupe had a "Mr. Bones."

———

In the early days of silent films, there was blatant thievery. Unscrupulous film companies would steal a film print, reshoot a scene or two, and release it as a new production. But the Biograph company, to identify and protect its productions from piracy, put the initials AB (the company's trademark) somewhere in every scene—on a door, a wall, or window.

———

Sideshow performers in ancient Greece used to amaze their audiences by pressing a spot on a goat's neck—pinching off the artery leading to the brain—and causing it to go to sleep. Releasing the pressure would allow the goat to wake again. (The trick still works today.)

———

George S. Kaufman began his career as a newspaperman, going to work on The New York Times in September 1917. For most of his years on the Times, Kaufman was the drama critic, a job he continued to hold even when he became a successful playwright. The newspaper business seemed steadier to him than the fly-by-night life of the theater. He didn't resign from the Times until August 1930. In fact, he wrote twelve of his greatest hits while continuing his $80-a-week job on the Times.

———

There are songs in all of Shakespeare's plays except The Comedy of Errors. That play was the basis for a Broadway musical in 1938 that won the Pulitzer Prize: The Boys from Syracuse, by Richard Rodgers and Larry Hart.

———

Rin Tin Tin, for years the most famous dog in the world, was born to a war-dog mother in a German trench in France during World War I. Deserted when the Germans retreated, the German shepherd puppy was found by an American officer who happened to be a police-dog trainer from California. He trained Rin Tin Tin when they returned home. The dog was so intelligent he came to the notice of

Warner Brothers, which signed him up for what turned out to be a long career as one of the biggest box-office draws of the silent screen.

Cole Younger, a notorious Western outlaw, spent twenty-five years in a Minnesota jail, and emerged to say he was a changed man. He made a good income on the lecture circuit, attracting large audiences who came to hear him on "What Life Has Taught Me." He said it had taught him to be good.

Cat's cradle is one of the most universal games in the world. It is played in almost every culture. What is somewhat a puzzle to ethnologists is that widely scattered peoples—Maoris of New Zealand, North American Indians, Arctic Eskimos, and Africans, for instance—make figures of string between their hands that are exactly the same.

Twenty years before the Mayflower dropped anchor off Cape Cod in 1620, Spanish explorers near present-day El Paso, Texas, put on a performance of a *comedia* dealing with an expedition of soldiers.

Elsa Maxwell was a unique phenomenon in the twentieth-century social world. Starting without beauty, money, or social connections, she made herself into the social arbiter-supreme. Her contacts with the wealthy and titled of the international set were so extensive that when the Waldorf opened in New York in 1931, she was given a suite rent-free in hopes of attracting a rich clientele. Both the Ritz Hotel and Maxim's restaurant in Paris never presented Miss Maxwell with a bill when she honored their premises.

UNIVERSE

The universe is so vast in relation to the matter it contains that it can be compared with a building twenty miles long, twenty miles wide, and twenty miles high that contains only a single grain of sand.

The nearest star we know of that exploded as a supernova is the one that gave rise to the Gum Nebula (named for Colin Gum, an Australian astronomer who discovered it in 1950). At its peak, the star may have blazed as brightly as the full moon. That was 11,000 years ago, however, and there were only Stone Age men to observe and admire it—or to be frightened.

The night sky may appear to be full of stars, but actually only about 3,000 stars are visible to the naked eye. They can be seen without a telescope because they are either extremely luminous or relatively close to Earth. The closest star to Earth, not counting the sun, is Alpha Centauri, which is at a distance of 4.3 light years, or 25 trillion miles.

All the stars comprising our galaxy, the Milky Way, revolve around the center of the galaxy once every 200 million years or so. At the distance at which our sun is located from the center, Earth and the rest of our solar system are moving at a speed of about 170 miles per second around the center.

The brightest star in historic times was the supernova of 1054, the Crab Nebula. It was far brighter than Venus. It was bright enough to be visible in daylight and to cast a shadow at night. We know of it through the astronomic records of China and Japan. No European seemed to have taken note of it at the time.

Cepheid stars vary in brightness in such a way that they can be used to measure the distance of very far-off objects. The first Cepheid was discovered by a nineteen-year-old named John Goodricke, in 1784. He died two years later. The youngest observer in astronomical history, Goodricke was a deaf-mute.

———

Photographs of galaxy M-82 showed it to be undergoing an enormous explosion in its core. Jets of hydrogen up to 1,000 light-years long were streaming outward in all directions. The explosion probably had to be going on for 1.5 million years.

———

If all the atomic nuclei in the entire known universe were squashed together, it would make a ball small enough to fit inside our solar system. In fact, it would stretch out to the asteroid belt and still have all the mass of the entire universe.

———

The closest star to the sun, Alpha Centauri in the southern celestial hemisphere, is never visible in the sky north of about 30° Northern Latitude. Though it is the third-brightest star in the sky, it was not seen by the ancient Greeks nor by the chief observatories of the medieval Arabs at Cordova, Baghdad, and Damascus, all located north of the 30° line.

———

In the constellation Cygnus, there is a double star, one of whose components has such a high surface gravity that light cannot escape from it. It is Cygnus X-1, which many astronomers believe to be the first "black hole" to be detected.

———

The second-brightest star in the constellation Perseus dims and brightens quite perceptibly. Every two days and twenty-one hours, the star, Beta Persei, rapidly loses a full magnitude of brightness for a brief period, and then as rapidly regains the loss. This cycle is the most notable variable among the naked-eye stars. It sometimes has been called the "Demon Star," a sign that something might have been considered to be wrong with it. The Arabic name for the star is Algol, "the Ghoul," again indicating something chilling.

———

Carbon, hydrogen, nitrogen, and oxygen—the four basic elements that make up all but 1 percent of terrestrial matter—are also the basic elements of the stars of the Milky Way. Which is why George Wald, the Nobel Prize-winning professor at Harvard University, tells his students that if they learn their biochemistry here on Earth, they would be able to pass examinations on Arcturus as well. Life, consisting of common elements, after all, is likely to be fundamentally the same chemistry everywhere.

———

A massive star has a shorter lifetime than a less massive star. The more massive a star, the more tightly its gravity pulls it together, the hotter it must be to keep it from collapsing, and the more rapidly it uses up its hydrogen fuel. The reason there are so few really massive stars is that they do not live very long, as little as a million years. For comparison, our sun has an expected lifetime of about 11 billion years.

———

A neutron star is so small and has such a powerful gravitational pull that it can turn on its axis in a second, or even in a thirtieth of a second without tearing itself apart.

———

Though the effort proved negative, Project Ozma for three months in 1960 marked the first attempt by man to detect intelligent life in another world. The radio telescope at Green Bank in England tracked Epsilon Eridani and Tau Ceti for signals of intelligent origin.

———

The Greek philosopher Thales (624–546 B.C.) is the first man in history to ask the question "Of what is the Universe made?" and to answer without introducing gods or demons. In later centuries, when the Greeks made up lists of the "seven wise men," Thales invariably was placed first.

———

The first pulsar (a celestial object that emits brief, sharp pulses of radio waves instead of the steady radiation associated with other natural sources), discovered in 1967, never varies in its timing by even as much as a hundred-millionth of a second. Its pulse is registered every 1.33730109 seconds.

———

Science is accustomed to puzzles. In 1669, a Dutch physician, Erasmus Bartholinus, discovered that a transparent crystal of Iceland spar split light into two parts; every line looked like a double line. It didn't fit the then-current theory of light as a stream of particles, and the effect remained a total puzzle for 139 years. A French physicist, Etienne L. Malus, finally solved the puzzle in terms of the new wave theory of light.

———

The diameter of the sphere of the observable universe—25 billion light years—is nearly four times that thought correct as recently as three decades ago.

———

As late as 1820, the universe was thought by European scientists to be 6,000 years old. It is now thought to be between 15 billion and 20 billion years old.

———

A "shell" of TV and radio signals carrying old *Gangbusters* and *Lone Ranger* and *Howdy Doody* radio and television programs is expanding through the cosmos at the speed of light, sweeping past the stars.

———

UNITED STATES

The District of Columbia, which has a single, non-voting seat in the House of Representatives, has a population (700,000) that is greater than that of any one of seven states: Alaska, Wyoming, North Dakota, South Dakota, Nevada, Delaware, and Vermont. The district also pays more in taxes than any one of eleven states.

In 1638, Sweden founded a colony in the New World—New Sweden, in the Delaware River Valley.

During the colonial period in North America, a package was not always shipped by the most direct route. A package from Virginia that was destined for Massachusetts might be shipped to London, where it would be transferred to an English vessel for delivery to Boston.

The "American" log cabin got its start in Sweden, where such a building had been popularly used for centuries, and was taken to America by the Swedish colonizers of New Sweden, which is now Delaware.

Robert R. Livingston and James Monroe sailed for Paris for the sole purposes of buying a small piece of French-held land in the West— New Orleans—and for expanding waterway traffic. They ended up buying half a billion acres of wilderness: the Louisiana Purchase.

Because he had a free pass to ride the railroads, a former conductor, Edwin Drake, became the first man to sink a well in the United States that struck oil (August 27, 1859). Because Drake's trip wouldn't cost them anything, a group of businessmen in New Haven, Connecticut, sent him to western Pennsylvania, where "rock oil"—petroleum— had been found floating on ponds. Drake convinced an old salt driller, "Uncle Billy" Smith, that because oil also was obtained when people bored for salt water, one should simply bore for the oil.

————

The population of New Hampshire increased only 8.3 percent between the start of the War of Independence and the 1970 census. In the same 194 years, the total population of the original thirteen states, which included New Hampshire, increased from 2,616,000 (estimated) to just under 75 million—a gain of 2,767 percent.

————

In the United States only eighty miles separate the highest point of land in the lower forty-eight states and the lowest point. Mount Whitney on the eastern border of Sequoia National Park in California is 14,496 feet high, and a pool called Badwater in Death Valley is 280 feet below sea level.

————

Until the late nineteenth century, there was no uniform system of timekeeping in the U.S. Time was determined locally except for railroad time, and each railroad had its own standard usually based on the local time of its headquarters city. There were at least seventy-five different railroad times. The resulting confusion and the growth of complex rail networks led Congress to call an international conference in Washington, D.C., in 1884, to establish a common prime meridian for regulating time worldwide. Greenwich in England was chosen as the prime meridian, and the world was divided into twenty-four time zones.

————

The name "United States of America" was coined by a man who lived the last years of his life in disrepute and whose bodily remains eventually were lost—Thomas Paine. Paine had lived his first thirty-seven years in London, mostly in poverty, and only a happenstance meeting in London with Benjamin Franklin encouraged his move to America. Later, in 1776, he wrote his popular revolutionary tract, *Common Sense.*

————

Many American cities were equipped with electric lighting before Thomas Edison invented the incandescent lamp. A device known as the arc lamp, brighter and more glaring than Edison's bulb, had been invented in the early nineteenth century by Sir Humphry Davy. By the 1870s, it was in use in lighthouses, public buildings, and factories. The Edison bulb's softer glow made electricity more desirable. By 1885, most U.S. electric companies were switching to incandescent lighting.

————

The first nation to receive foreign aid from the United States was Venezuela. In 1812, Venezuela, fighting for its independence from Spain, suffered a severe and damaging earthquake. Congress appropriated $50,000 to help the victims.

Congress, in 1870, granted naturalization rights to whites and to people of African descent, but not to Orientals. This law was confirmed by a Bureau of Immigration and Naturalization decree in 1911 and again by the Immigration Act of 1924, which stopped all immigration from Japan. It was only after Congress passed Public Law 414, in 1952—granting Japanese aliens the right to become U.S. citizens—that the last regulations discriminating by race were abolished.

The first automobile to cross the U.S. took fifty-two days in 1903, to go from San Francisco to New York.

The U.S. in many ways does not measure up to its image of advanced medical care. There are sixteen other countries, including all the Scandinavian countries, France, and Spain, in which a newborn baby has a better chance to survive the first year.

Morocco was the first country to recognize the United States (1789).

By law, the U.S. Census Bureau may not share information about an individual with any other federal agency, let alone with an outsider. As a result, the bureau refused to turn over to government authorities a list of all the names it had of individuals of Japanese origin when the U.S. was rounding up persons of Japanese descent in California and herding them into internment camps after Pearl Harbor.

When Alaska and Hawaii became the forty-ninth and fiftieth states of the U.S., their principal cities became the two most expensive cities in the nation in which a family can live "comfortably." According to the U.S. Department of Labor in 1978, it cost the average family $24,019 a year to live comfortably in Anchorage and $20,883 in Honolulu. One of America's oldest cities, Boston, ranked as the third most expensive: $20,609. New York and northeast New Jersey were fourth: $19,972. Texas may be the millionaires' state, but two of its cities ranked among the least expensive cities for a family to live comfortably: Austin, $14,776; Dallas, $15,313.

It was an English chemist—James Smithson, bastard son of a lord—whose bequest led to the founding of the Smithsonian Institution in Washington, D.C., "for the increase and diffusion of knowledge among men." No one knows why he selected the U.S. as the seat of his largesse. He had no acquaintances in America and seemed to have only a couple of books relating to America. When President Andrew Jackson informed Congress that he had no authority to take steps toward accepting Smithson's gift of $500,000, a tedious ten-year proceeding and debate ensued. Senator John C. Calhoun expressed the opinion that "it was beneath . . . dignity to receive presents from anyone." It took until August 1846 to establish the institution. Smithson's body, interred in Italy, was fetched and now rests in Washington.

———

The budget of the U.S. Department of Health, Education, and Welfare—$200-billion—is larger than the combined operating expenses of all the governments of the fifty U.S. states combined.

———

The U.S. has profited greatly twice at the hands of a nation that viewed Great Britain as the enemy. In 1803, France, aware it could not hang onto the vast Louisiana Territory, sold it to the U.S. (at about 2½ cents an acre) rather than have it fall to Great Britain. In 1867, Russia sold the 586,400 square miles of Alaska to the U.S. (at less than 2 cents an acre). The logical purchaser would have been Great Britain, whose dominions in Canada bordered the land on the east, but Russia considered Great Britain to be an enemy. (Britain had won the Crimean War against the Russians and sided with the Confederacy in the U.S. Civil War.)

———

Most freed slaves remained in the South immediately after Reconstruction, but some venturesome ones moved westward. About 40,000 black homesteaders began new lives on the plains of Kansas, Iowa, Nebraska, and Oklahoma in 1879.

———

After an act of Congress, in 1808, prohibited African slave trading, at least a quarter of a million more slaves were illicitly imported into the U.S.

———

Texas has 254 counties. Alaska, which is more than twice as large, hasn't any.

———

Jews first came to America in 1624, when two Jewish men and one Jewish woman arrived in Virginia. On the eve of the Revolution about 1,500 Jews lived in the colonies but in none were they allowed to vote or to hold public office.

————

Mail-order frame houses were popular in the U.S. in the mid-1850s. The exact-size boards, nails, etc., bought by catalog, were shipped mainly to the Far West. One hundred portable wooden houses were sent by pack mules across the Isthmus of Panama, then by ship to California. One hundred and seventy-five were sent around Cape Horn to the West Coast. In San Francisco, a three-and-a-half story hotel—a hundred rooms, ten shops—was similarly ordered and put up in a hurry.

————

Pennsylvania was named not after the Quaker William Penn, but after his father, Admiral William Penn. Charles II owed a large debt to Admiral Penn, whose son agreed to cancel the debt for a grant of land in America on the Delaware River. The new proprietor was alluding to his father when he called the grant "Pennsylvania"— "Penn's Woodland."

————

Among the memorable quotations of the 1920s are "Public service is my motto" and "I want peace, and I'm willing to live and let live." They were spoken by Al Capone when he was the most notorious public enemy in America and the most murderous of Chicago gangsters. He also said, "The American system of ours . . . gives each and every one of us a great opportunity if we only seize it with both hands and make the most of it." Arguing sharply against communism, Capone said, "We must keep America whole and safe and unspoiled."

————

In the U.S., about 48 billion metal cans, 26 billion bottles, 65 billion metal bottle caps, and seven million automobiles are junked each year.

————

Pornography is a $4 billion business in the U.S. annually.

————

Woodrow Wilson's Vice-President, Thomas Riley Marshall—who is credited with saying during a Senate debate on national needs that "what the country really needs is a good five-cent cigar"—was the first man in nearly a century to serve a second term as Vice-President. In 1828, two-term John C. Calhoun became the only Vice-President to serve under two Presidents (John Quincy Adams and Andrew Jackson); Calhoun later became the first Vice-President to resign.

————

The first operable gasoline-powered automobile in the United States—assembled by J. Frank and Charles E. Duryea—was still considered as such an oddity two years after its introduction in 1894 that it became a principal attraction at the Barnum & Bailey circus, where it was displayed like some freak.

———

Beginning in 1882, immigrants had to pay to enter the United States. A tax of 50 cents per person was imposed that year; it was increased to $2 in 1903 and to $4 in 1907.

———

May 10, 1869, marked the completion of the first single-track transcontinental railway in the U.S. as well as the giveaway by Congress of 155 million acres to railway promoters and buccaneers. In addition to land, promoters received millions of dollars in U.S. subsidies and bonds. Some of these found their way into the pockets of the congressmen who had given them away.

———

Eskimos use refrigerators to keep food from freezing.

———

The United States has about 3,600,000 square miles of land, and on it more than 3,600,000 miles of highway have been constructed—a mile of road to each square mile of land. The paved area is as large as the state of West Virginia.

———

The U.S. state of Maine has 3,500 miles of coastline.

———

In 1813, Major George Armistead, commandant of Fort McHenry, placed an order for a flag "so large that the British will have no difficulty in seeing it from a distance." In fulfilling the commission for that flag, subsequently celebrated as "Old Glory" and "The Star-Spangled Banner," Mary Pickersgill and members of her family sewed over 400 yards of bunting into a banner 30 by 42 feet, costing $405.90. This was the flag that Francis Scott Key saw "was still there." It hangs today in the Smithsonian Institution.

———

There are half a million more automobiles in Los Angeles than there are people.

———

In the Old West, in the second half of the 1800s, nearly one cowboy in three was either Mexican or black. (About one cowboy in six or seven was Mexican; a similar proportion was black.) Most of the blacks had been slaves on Texas ranches, where they had been taught the skills of roping and riding.

———

The U.S. Automobile Association was formed in 1905 for the express purpose of providing "scouts" who could warn motorists of hidden "police traps."

———

A community for the purpose of "educating blacks for freedom" and to help make possible their resettlement outside the U.S. was established by Frances Wright and others on the Wolf River near Memphis, Tennessee, in 1825. Called Nashoba, it was unsuccessful due to poor management and hostility of outsiders. It was abandoned within five years.

———

A century and a half ago in the United States, all postal rates were determined not by weight but by the distance the mail had to travel. During the period 1825–38 the rates were 6 cents for a trip up to 30 miles, 10 cents for 30 to 80 miles, 12½ cents for 80 to 100 miles, 18¾ cents for 150 to 400 miles, and 25 cents over 400 miles. Today, most U.S. mail rates are related only to weight. A few categories such as second class (magazines) and fourth class (packages) have rates based on weight and zones (distance shipped).

———

Every year, dirt costs the United States $4.9 billion. That is the estimate by the U.S. Council for Environmental Quality of the damage to vegetation and the works of man caused by airborne dirt.

———

Nearly 43 percent of convicted criminals serving prison sentences in the U.S. are rearrested within a year of being released from prison.

———

A replica of the head and the torch of the Statue of Liberty sat on the grounds of the Philadelphia Exposition celebrating the U.S. centennial in 1876, and later in Madison Square on lower Fifth Avenue in New York. (The statue itself, a gift from France, was delayed by the Franco-Prussian War.) A decade passed before funds were raised for the erection of the statue on Bedloe's Island, now called Liberty Island, in New York Harbor.

———

The American Colonization Society was formed, in 1816, by the Reverend Robert Finley of New Jersey, for the purpose of establishing in Africa a colony to which the 200,000 U.S. blacks freed by slave-holders or born to free parents could be sent. Prominent slaveholders like Calhoun, Clay, Randolph, and Jackson supported the Society because they feared the threat to slavery posed by free blacks. Congress was persuaded to lend aid for land purchases. In all, about 15,000 blacks left America for the colony, which came to be called Liberia. The capital is named Monrovia, for President James Monroe.

_____

Four states have active volcanoes: Washington, California, Alaska and Hawaii, whose Mauna Loa is the world's largest active volcano. Hawaii itself was formed by the activity of undersea volcanoes.

_____

The U.S. has had three different names. It was known as "The Congress" until the Articles of Confederation was ratified in 1781. Under the Articles, the U.S. was then called "The United States in Congress Assembled." Under the present Constitution, the country is known as "The United States of America."

_____

Two Americans, John Reed and William Haywood, are buried in the Kremlin. John Reed wrote the book *Ten Days That Shook the World* (1919), considered the best eyewitness account of the Russian Revolution. Big Bill Haywood, an American labor leader, was one of the organizers of the radical Wobblies, the Industrial Workers of the World. When the U.S. entered World War I, Haywood was arrested for sedition and tried, convicted, and sentenced. He jumped bail in 1921 and fled to Russia, where he died.

_____

Half of the people of the U.S. live in just eight of the fifty states: in Pennsylvania, Massachusetts, Michigan, California, Illinois, Ohio, New Jersey, and New York.

_____

No one seemed to know for certain at the time what the U.S. had bought in the Louisiana Purchase. The details of the boundaries were not clear, and much of the territory was unknown and unexplored. The purchase turned out to total 883,072 square miles, or 565,166,080 acres, which is seven times larger than England, Scotland, and Ireland combined. It was also larger than the combined areas of France, Germany, Italy, Spain, and Portugal.

_____

The Pony Express, which has lived in legend for more than a century, lived in fact for less than two years. Indian raids curtailed service on the 1,966-mile route between St. Joseph, Missouri, and Sacramento, California, and the transcontinental telegraph finally obviated it in late 1861.

———

To avoid speculation in rarities, the U.S. Post Office intentionally printed 10 million defective stamps honoring the late U.N. Secretary-General Dag Hammarskjold after a printing error was discovered in the original fifty-stamp pane.

———

In the United States there are over 100,000 labor-union officers, elected democratically every year, in the 115 national unions that comprise the AFL-CIO. About 450,000 general membership meetings of unions are held annually.

———

In 1978, more than a thousand deer were accidentally killed in Connecticut by automobile drivers. Only 948 were killed by hunters.

———

The official manual of the Internal Revenue Service of the U.S. is an agglomeration of 38,000 pages. It has appropriately been described as "the world's most confusing publication."

———

Although the first permanent English settlements in the United States were established on the east coast, the Spaniards' Palace of the Governors in Santa Fe, N.M., built in 1610, is the oldest public building still standing in the United States.

———

There were several threats of secession by states of the U.S. before the Civil War: in 1798, when Federalist efforts to control criticism of the government caused Jefferson and Madison to formulate the Kentucky and Virginia Resolutions that developed the states' rights position (later used as justification for nullification and secession); in 1812, when the Federalists opposed the war and New England threatened secession; in 1832, when South Carolina promulgated an Ordinance of Nullification in a contest over a protective tariff.

———

A copy of the U.S. Constitution was burned in 1854, on the Fourth of July, by the main speaker at a public demonstration in Boston. In tolerating slavery, he said, the Constitution was "blood-stained . . . a covenant with death and an agreement with hell . . . a compromise with tyranny." The speaker was William Lloyd Garrison the abolitionist. Eventually, the Constitution was amended.

———

The Bill of Rights barely received the necessary votes in 1791 to be ratified as part of the U.S. Constitution; approval of three-quarters of the fourteen states was needed, and only the eleven required votes were obtained. The last three of the fourteen states that belonged to the United States at that time—Georgia, Massachusetts, and Connecticut—did not ratify the Bill of Rights until its 150th anniversary in 1941.

The first department store that opened in the United States is still in operation. It is the Zion's Co-operative Mercantile Institution, founded by Brigham Young in Salt Lake City in 1868.

So outraged were Bostonians that the U.S. military (army and navy) in 1854 had forced the return of the slave Anthony Burns to his Southern master, that a fund was raised for the purchase of Burns—and he was then set free. The U.S. had spent at least $100,000 in extraditing Burns.

Though the U.S. has less than 6 percent of the world's population, its share in the consumption of the world's resources amounts to nearly 60 percent.

Congressman Thaddeus Stevens was so dedicated to helping the newly emancipated blacks achieve rights and economic aid after the Civil War that when he was dying he ordered that he be buried in a cemetery among blacks so that even in death he might demonstrate his devotion to equality.

When Vice-President Spiro Agnew resigned his office in 1973, he was not the first Vice-President to do so, although he was the first to be compelled to do so. John C. Calhoun, Andrew Jackson's Vice-President, resigned in 1832 so he could be named senator for South Carolina. This move made it possible for Calhoun to lead the fight of the Southern states for states' rights and the doctrine of nullification.

There have been communist settlements in the U.S. The followers of Etienne Cabet founded several. Cabet (1788–1856) was a French utopian socialist who, when exiled from France in 1834, went to England where he developed his form of communism in his famous book *Voyage en Icarie* (1840). He came to the U.S. and his disciples founded several colonies. Icaria, founded in Corning, Iowa, in the year of Cabet's demise, survived until 1898. Other settlements were shorter-lived.

———

The state of South Carolina voted to secede from the United States more than a quarter of a century before it actually did so, in 1861. After the reelection of Andrew Jackson as President in 1832, the state legislature voted to leave the Union if the U.S. continued to collect tariffs. But when Jackson prepared for a civil war, South Carolina backed down and rescinded its vote.

———

The first draft-card burners were members of the International Workers of the World, during World War I. The I.W.W. was the first great working-class American protest movement, flourishing from 1905 to 1920. Nicknamed the Wobblies, they fought for the poor, the hungry, the downtrodden, and the dispossessed. They set the pattern for sit-ins and other types of demonstrations that were utilized by civil-rights groups and war protesters half a century later. Leaders of the Wobblies were intellectuals and Marxists, poets and singers. They gave America such songs as "Casey Jones," "Dump the Bosses off Your Back," and "Solidarity Forever." They failed in their aims—overthrow of the capitalistic system—but they created a new awareness of the right to protest.

———

The first "dude-ranch" trip took place in May 1843 when the West was still "wild." A column of riders, pack mules, and covered wagons filled with tents, India-rubber boats, costly wines, potted meats, jams, and other expensive food and gear headed west across the Missouri plains. About forty young American sportsmen, including doctors, lawyers, businessmen, and scientists, signed up for a summer of fun and hunting in the greatest wilds of all, the Rocky Mountains. Sir William Drummond Stuart, a Scottish nobleman, was the organizer and leader of the "sporting expedition to the West." Besides hunting and fishing, the "sportsmen" went exploring and held horse races with the Indians, while the guides did all the necessary chores.

———

The coastline of Alaska is longer than the entire coastline of the lower forty-eight states of the United States.

———

When the U.S. was sixty years old in 1836, Narcissa Prentiss Whitman and Eliza Hart Spalding were perhaps the first women to cross the continent. They reached Oregon that year in a party organized by the American Board of Commissioners for Foreign Missionaries. The success of the expedition stimulated emigration to the territories in the Northwest.

———

U.S. CIVIL WAR

During the Civil War, the Confederate army had all the cotton it needed for uniforms, but no opium to kill the pain of the wounded. The Union Army had plenty of opium, but no cotton. Throughout the war, North and South exchanged opium and cotton. President Lincoln had been authorized to trade with the South when it would be of benefit to the Union.

———

Robert E. Lee, general-in-chief of the Confederate armies that fought to maintain the institution of slavery in the U.S., freed his own slaves, having found that "slavery is a moral and political evil in any society, a greater evil to the white man than the black."

———

The Emancipation Proclamation, President Abraham Lincoln's executive order dated January 1, 1863, abolishing slavery in the Confederate States of America was probably not legal according to U.S. civil law. To remedy any deficiencies in the proclamation's legal status, the Thirteenth Amendment to the Constitution was introduced in Congress in 1864 and ratified in 1865. It abolished slavery or involuntary servitude in the United States or anywhere under U.S. jurisdiction. The Proclamation had had little impact, for Lincoln had no authority in the Confederacy.

———

Richmond-born Elizabeth Van Lew was sent to private school in Philadelphia, where she became an abolitionist and persuaded her father to free the family's fifteen slaves. One of the slaves was sent to Philadelphia to be educated. When the Civil War broke out, the former slave returned to work as a servant in the home of Confederate President Jefferson Davis, gathering valuable information for the Union Army.

———

Furious at Great Britain's support of the Confederacy during the U.S. Civil War, many Americans wanted Canada as reparation. But Canada was a self-governing British dominion, and it became difficult to argue its annexation to pay a British debt. The U.S. demanded $2 billion, and eventually settled for $15.5 million, which the British paid in full within a year. The situation was known as the *Alabama* reparations claim. The ship *Alabama* and other Confederate privateers had been outfitted and supported by Great Britain.

At the mere nod of his head, Jefferson Davis could have had a senatorial seat after President Andrew Johnson's Christmas 1868 amnesty had put an end to Davis's treason trial. But the erstwhile president of the Confederacy refused to accept citizenship or to enter the government again (he had been Secretary of War and a Senator from Mississippi). He was given a hero's funeral when he died in New Orleans in 1889.

The vindictive U.S. Secretary of War Simon Cameron made sure that no one would again want to live in Robert E. Lee's house south of Washington, D.C. Soldiers' graves were dug close to the house, and the area later was confiscated. Today, the site is the national military cemetery at Arlington, Virginia.

Barbara Fritchie, whose reported heroism in facing down General "Stonewall" Jackson and his Confederate army marching through Frederick, Maryland, in 1862, was celebrated in John Greenleaf Whittier's widely popular ballad, probably never met or even saw the Confederate general. She was ninety-five years old and bedridden when she supposedly protested the dragging of the Union flag in the dust: " 'Shoot if you must this old gray head, but spare your country's flag,' she said." The ballad was popular with Southerners as well, for the chivalry of the Confederate general was noted by Whittier: " 'Who touches a hair of yon gray head, dies like a dog! March on,' he said." Jackson was killed in the war, and Fritchie died before the ballad achieved national circulation and they could attest to its authenticity.

Confusion reigned during one of the first major battles of the U.S. Civil War because the Union and Confederate flags were similar in appearance. At the Battle of Bull Run, in the spring of '61, the Union flew the Stars and Stripes and the Confederacy flew a flag with seven stars and three stripes. The Confederacy quickly adopted a new pennant.

More than 3,000 Union soldiers were quartered in the U.S. Capitol when they were stationed in Washington to defend the city during the Civil War.

Henry Morton Stanley—who later became famous for saying, "Dr. Livingstone, I presume?"—fought in the U.S. Civil War, on both sides. In 1856, he had moved from Great Britain to New Orleans, the home of his adoptive father. He enlisted, at the age of twenty-one, in the Confederate Army, was captured after a year's service, and imprisoned. In exchange for his release, Stanley agreed to join the federal artillery. After being discharged because of poor health, he served impressively as a ship's writer in the federal navy.

Major General Leonidas Polk, who led Confederate troops in the Mississippi Valley during the Civil War, was the Episcopal bishop of Louisiana when Jefferson Davis appointed him to the command. An 1827 graduate of West Point, Polk had resigned from the army to study for the ministry.

Long-term idealism won over short-term advantage in Britain's response to the U.S. Civil War. The British did not side openly with the Confederacy, though the ruling classes would have liked to, if only to weaken the U.S. and throw the Americas all the more open to British exploitation. Oddly, the textile workers in England, who were thrown out of work when the factories shut down for lack of cotton, rallied in great demonstrations against the very Confederacy that could have put them back to work. The reason for the workers' protest: they disapproved of slavery.

Civil War general William Tecumseh Sherman, renowned for the most controversial campaign of that war, the devastating Union army sweep through Georgia in 1864, the "march to the sea," had been superintendent of a new military academy in Louisiana (now Louisiana State University) from 1859 to 1861. When Louisiana seceded in January 1861, Sherman resigned, despite his love for the South and its people, and was commissioned a Union infantry colonel.

A woman, Elizabeth Van Lew, was rated by General Grant as his most efficient secret agent during the Civil War. Known as "Crazy Bet," this supposedly demented daughter of a well-to-do Richmond merchant passed information to Union commanders and arranged daring prison escapes for Union soldiers, hiding the fugitives in a secret room in her mansion overlooking the James River.

Only once during the Civil War, at the Battle of Nashville, December 15–16, 1864, did a Union commander win a total victory over a major Confederate army, ending its usefulness for the rest of the war. That officer was General George Henry Thomas, who also was one of only fifteen Union officers voted the thanks of Congress for war service.

In April, 1865, with the Civil War over, thousands of Union soldiers were gathered at Vicksburg on the flooded Mississippi waiting to be sent home. Among them were soldiers freed from Southern prison camps. The men were so eager to get home that when the steamboat *Sultana* landed at Vicksburg, the soldiers jammed aboard the ship; 2,300 men squeezed into a space meant to carry 376. The boat puffed upstream against a strong current, and was further slowed by defective boilers. About three days later, at two in the morning, the boilers exploded and the ship caught fire and sank. Seventeen hundred men died in one of the worst steamship accidents.

In England, there are about 500 Civil War buffs who congregate in the countryside on weekends, divide up into regiments—Union and Confederate—and reenact the battles of Shiloh, Chickamauga, Gettysburg, etc.

The U.S. Civil War broke out on April 9, 1861, but the first soldier did not die in battle until six weeks later. The combatants made up for the slow start. In four years, up to 700,000 men were killed.

President Jefferson Davis, in a message to the Confederacy in November 1864, urged that 40,000 slaves be purchased outright and enlisted into the army; after the war, they would be given their freedom.

Senator Andrew Johnson of Tennessee, who had also served as governor, maintained an unswerving pro-Union stand in Congress during the Civil War crisis. He was the only senator from a seceding state to remain in the Senate over the protests and vilification of his constituents. (Lincoln made him governor of the reconquered Tennessee in 1862 and his vice-presidential partner in the election of '64.)

To stave off the Civil War, Senator John J. Crittenden of Kentucky proposed, unsuccessfully, that the country be divided along the old Missouri Compromise line (the southern boundary of Missouri), with slavery forever barred in any territory north of it and forever guaranteed against federal action in any territory south of it. When war erupted, one of the Senator's sons became a general for the Union and another became a general for the Confederacy.

"There is Jackson, standing like a stone wall!" said Bernard Elliott Bee about Confederate general Thomas Jonathan Jackson at the First Battle of Bull Run, in 1861. Bee was later killed in the battle, and "Stonewall" Jackson, as he was everafter known, was killed accidentally by fire from his own troops after routing the federal right wing at Chancellorsville, in 1863.

Troops returning from Gettysburg restored order in the New York City draft riots of 1863, but by then 1,200 people had been killed.

The Confederate soldier who pulled the lanyard that fired the first shot of the war at Fort Sumter—Edmund Ruffin—committed suicide after the Confederacy had surrendered at Appomattox.

Raphael Semmes, who had resigned his commander's commission in the U.S. Navy to serve in the Confederate Navy as captain of the *Alabama*, sank or captured more than eighty Union vessels from 1861 to 1864.

In the 1850s, Ulysses S. Grant, under pressure of allegations of intemperate drinking, resigned his U.S. Army commission. He farmed and worked as a clerk in his father's leather store in Illinois. He later led the Union Army to victory in the Civil War.

Before he accepted command of the Confederate Army in the U.S. Civil War, General Robert E. Lee had turned down a similar offer to command the Union Army.

Less than 25 percent of the white U.S. population were members of the slaveholding planter class in the old South. The 1860 census records show that under 400,000 heads of households were listed as owning slaves. Assuming five persons in each of their families, the class as a whole was much smaller than usually believed—only 2 million people. Nonslaveholders were generally small farmers, artisans, tradesmen, and poor whites. Usually, they were more anti-black than the slaveholders. (If they didn't keep the blacks at the bottom of the heap, they themselves would have been there. In turn, the house blacks—the slave aristocracy—despised the "poor white trash.")

———

The first time that an enormous amount of clothing was needed all at once was during the Civil War, when the Union needed hundreds of thousands of uniforms for its troops. Out of this need came the ready-made-clothing industry.

———

The first battle of the Civil War was also the quickest and most bloodless battle of the war. Major Robert Anderson surrendered Fort Sumter in the harbor of Charleston to Confederate General P.G.T. Beauregard, who had fought for the U.S. alongside Anderson in the Mexican War. In the day-and-a-half siege, no one was even wounded.

———

Robert E. Lee was a superintendent of West Point but had never commanded in battle when he became commander of the Confederacy's Army of Northern Virginia during the Civil War.

———

Confederate officers were allowed, after Appomattox, to keep their swords—the symbols of their honor—and officers and troops were allowed to keep their horses so they could use them back home to help in planting crops. "This will have a very happy effect upon my army," General Robert E. Lee said on learning of the Union's decision.

———

The first fatalities in the Civil War did not occur on the battlefield. Four members of the Massachusetts militia were stoned to death by a Baltimore mob of Confederate sympathizers, on April 19, 1861.

———

The reputed creator of baseball, Abner Doubleday, is celebrated for another reason: he aimed the first Union defense shot from Fort Sumter, in the harbor of Charleston, South Carolina, in the exchange that ignited the Civil War. A West Point graduate, Doubleday served as a Union general through the war.

———

During the Civil War, George Washington's home at Mount Vernon, Virginia, was treated as neutral territory by arrangement between the Union and the Confederacy. No armed soldiers invaded the house.

———

When Union general William Rosecrans and Confederate general Braxton Bragg met at Murfreesboro during the Civil War, each adopted the same tactics, holding his right in place and wheeling in a flanking maneuver to the left. They thus exchanged places on the battlefield and confronted each other again, but in opposite directions. The Battle of Murfreesboro was as indecisive as this maneuver.

———

Abraham Lincoln and Jefferson Davis were inconspicuous officers in the Black Hawk Indian War of 1832. Thirty years later, they were commanders-in-chief—Lincoln of the Union Army against Davis of the Confederacy during the U.S. Civil War.

———

Giuseppe Garibaldi, hero of Italian national unification, was asked twice by President Lincoln to head a Union army in the U.S. Civil War. Garibaldi had two conditions: that he be made commander-in-chief and that the abolition of slavery be made an official goal of the war. Lincoln was not ready in 1861 to agree with the goal, and, according to the Constitution, only the President can be commander-in-chief.

———

Just before the Civil War, the Republican Party led Congress in passing a proposed amendment to the Constitution that would have denied the federal government the power to abolish or interfere with slavery in those states in which it already existed. The measure was sent to the states for ratification, in March 1861, with the approval of newly inaugurated President Lincoln. Three states had ratified it when the outbreak of the war made the amendment meaningless.

———

WEATHER

New Hampshire's Mount Washington, which is only 6,288 feet in altitude, is often considered to have the worst weather in the world. Its severe combination of wind, storm, cold, and icing is the result of its location where two storm tracks meet, one from the Arctic and the other from the tropics. The highest wind velocity ever recorded on Earth—231 miles per hour—swept across the summit of Mount Washington in April 1934. More than thirty people have died there as a result of sudden changes in the weather.

It is said that no two snowflakes are identical, but all snow crystals can be classified into seven basic shape categories. Most recognizable as a typical snowflake is the six-pointed star; other common shapes are the column, the needle, and the hexagon. Each crystal's individual shape is determined by the temperature and humidity of the air in which it is formed.

In living memory it was not until February 18, 1979, that snow fell on the Sahara. A half-hour storm in southern Algeria stopped traffic. But within a few hours all the snow had melted.

Lightning strikes the Earth a hundred times every second, from the 1,800 thunderstorms in progress at any given moment.

Continental snow cover would advance to the equator, and the oceans would eventually freeze, if there were a permanent drop of just 1.6 to 2 percent in energy reaching the Earth.

In 1816, there was no summer in many areas of the world. In parts of New England, snow stayed on the ground all year. Crops there and in Europe were ruined. Volcanic dust from the eruption of Tomboro in Indonesia that blocked the rays of the sun has been blamed for the unusual weather as well as for the red and brown snow that fell in the United States, Hungary, and Italy.

Most grandfather clocks with metal pendulums lose time in warm weather. This phenomenon occurs because most solids expand when heated. In the case of the clock, the higher temperature makes the metal pendulum longer, and thus slower.

An average of 140 tornadoes occurs every year in the United States. But there were a record 90 in one day alone, in a region extending from Ohio to Georgia, in the spring of 1974.

Lightning is more likely than not to strike twice in the same place. Like all electric currents or discharges, lightning follows the path of least resistance.

Because air is denser in cold weather, a wind of the same speed exerts 25 percent more force during the winter than it does during the summer.

Due to friction with the surface of the planet, the wind retards or accelerates the spin of the Earth very slightly. A peak in the seasonal slowing of the planet is most evident during the northern winter.

Seventeen and one-half inches in circumference and 1.67 pounds in weight: that's the size of the largest hailstone known to have fallen in the U.S. It struck during a severe storm at Coffeyville, Kansas, in September 1970.

The fastest temperature change on record is a rise of 49° F. in two minutes, from −4° to 45° F. in Spearfish, South Dakota, January 22, 1943, between 7:30 and 7:32 A.M.

Lightning kills more people in the United States than any other natural disaster: an average of 400 dead and 1,000 injured yearly.

Weather hazards (rainstorms and snowstorms, floods, tornadoes, hurricanes, etc.) cost the U.S. $11.6 billion in property damage and over 1,000 lives annually.

The chinook, a wind phenomenon that occurs over Montana in the U.S. and Alberta in Canada, is capable of raising the temperature more than 30° F. in three minutes. Damp sea air from the Pacific Ocean drops rain and snow as it passes over the Rockies. The dry air then tumbles down the eastern slopes, becoming compressed as it does so, and, as a consequence, incredibly hot. One February, the temperature in Calgary rose from −14° to 76° F.

The Sahara is not the perpetual oven of baking sand, as many believe. It has the typical continental climate of alternating hot and cold seasons. Its high temperatures range up to the 136.4° F. (58° C.) recorded at Al Aziziyah, Libya, and as low as 5° F. (−15° C.) in the Tibesti mountains in midwinter.

Gigantic snowfalls may be crippling to big cities, but at least in New York City they have a tendency to fall mainly on the days most convenient for the urban population. A study of the biggest snows in the last sixty-eight years shows that 54 percent of them fall on Friday or Sunday, when the cleanup can be accomplished with minimum inconvenience to those millions who must go to work and school. According to the law of averages, only 28.6 percent should have fallen on these two days.

A person working in downtown Manhattan will have 16 percent more rain than his family at home on Long Island. He will also be drenched by more thunderstorms. Rainfall is greater in this inner city than in the surrounding suburban area because of pollution factors in the city. Another example of how man's treatment of the environment affects the weather is found in La Porte, Indiana, a town downwind from the industrial Gary-Chicago area. It gets 246 percent more rain than the surrounding area because of the pollution blowing its way.

In 1755, Benjamin Franklin pursued a small tornado for three-fourths of a mile on horseback, repeatedly lashing out with his whip in an effort to dissipate the storm.

The date of June 2, 1953, was selected for the coronation of Queen Elizabeth II because meteorologists said it was the most consistently sunny day in the calendar. However, the weather is no respecter of royalty and, of course, it rained.

Though 25,000 surface weather observations are made every day around the world, though there are 10,000 land stations and 6,700 ships with weather-measuring equipment, and though more than 1,000 daily measurements of winds and temperatures in the air are made from balloons, no more than 20 percent of the globe is considered adequately covered.

———

Rain contains vitamin B_{12}.

———

The behavior of certain animals can be successfully used in weather prediction. Fiddler crabs have been seen burrowing inland two days before a hurricane. In the northwestern United States, foresters have sometimes predicted snow by observing elks, which gather beneath sheltering trees two or three days before a blizzard.

———

Observations of increased rain after U.S. Civil War battles led to abortive experiments with weather control. Cannon volleys were fired into clouds in order to induce rain.

———

When the hot wind called *sharav* arrives twice a year in Israel, there are marked increases in restlessness and irritability among people and animals. The ionic balance of the atmosphere apparently changes with the arrival of the "ill wind," and excess positive ions are trapped at ground level. The effect on humans of excess positive ions is an increase in serotonin, one of the body's neurotransmitter substances. Excessive serotonin is known to make a person nervous, irritable, and depressed.

———

On June 10, 1958, a tornado was crashing through El Dorado, Kansas. The storm pulled a woman out of her house and carried her sixty feet away. She landed, relatively unharmed, next to a phonograph record titled "Stormy Weather."

———

Nearly 100 pollution-filled, weather-beaten years in New York have done more damage to Cleopatra's Needle—a granite obelisk covered with hieroglyphics—than did 3,500 arid years in Egypt.

———

Residents in a small village in Scotland schedule their television viewing according to the tides. At low tide, the nearby mud flats absorb the broadcast "waves."

———

With the information received from 3,000 U.S. weather stations, a computer performs 10 billion arithmetical operations in printing out the twenty-four-hour national weather forecast. It is estimated that a hundred-day forecast would require a trillion arithmetical operations.

———

WHAT A WAY TO GO

Archduke Francis Ferdinand of Austria was an extremely vain man. When he went to a great occasion, he had himself sewn into his uniform so there would not be a single crease to mar his appearance. Unfortunately, the Archduke was wearing one of his sewn-on uniforms when he was shot in Sarajevo, on June 28, 1914. It was impossible to unbutton his uniform. By the time scissors were found, the Archduke had bled to death.

———

In 1911, a suburban tailor named Teichelt, who had invented a bat-wing cape that he believed would enable him to fly, applied for permission to fly from the Eiffel Tower. The proprietors of the tower reluctantly gave permission, provided that Teichelt obtain police authorization and that he sign a waiver absolving the tower proprietors. Incredibly, the police gave permission. At eight o'clock, on a cold December morning, Teichelt—accompanied by a handful of well-wishers and press photographers—climbed to the level of the first platform, stepped over the edge, and plunged to his death.

———

When the "mad monk" Rasputin was assassinated in Petrograd (Leningrad), in 1916, his assassins first fed him cakes and wine laced with enough cyanide to kill several men. Rasputin ate and drank, and showed no ill effects. Then Prince Felix Yussupov shot him through the chest and clubbed him on the head with a lead-filled walking stick, and the conspirators threw him into the Neva River. When the body was recovered, the autopsy revealed that Rasputin had drowned.

———

As a young man, Maximilien Robespierre opposed the death penalty, giving up the opportunity for a brilliant legal career because he had scruples about serving in a court that sentenced condemned persons to the scaffold. But on gaining control of the French Revolution, in

1793, Robespierre launched the Reign of Terror that sent hundreds to the guillotine—before he himself died beneath its blade.

The Donatists of fourth-century North Africa were so committed to the idea of martyrdom that they would stop strangers and demand to be killed by them. Since the strangers were threatened with death if they refused, the Donatists found martyrdom easy enough to come by.

The city morgue in the Bronx, New York, has been so busy at times that next of kin take numbers—as in a corner bakery shop—and wait in line for their body-identification call.

At the Pan-American Exposition in Buffalo, in 1901, President William McKinley received a line of citizens, shaking hands with each. In the line was a man with a handkerchief covering one hand. Neither of the two Secret Service men guarding the President was curious enough to take a look at what might be under the handkerchief in the hand of the man—Leon Czolgosz, an anarchist. What he had was a loaded revolver, and when the President thrust his right hand out for the shake, Czolgosz fired twice. McKinley died a week later.

About 13,700,000 people died in battle during World War I. The year-long influenza epidemic that followed killed even more. At least a billion people were ill and at least 20 million died.

Through the door and the windows, would-be assassins poured seventy-three bullets into Leon Trotsky's bedroom in his fortresslike house in Mexico City. Thanks to a moment's warning, Trotsky and his wife escaped unscathed by hiding under their bed. Later in the same year, which was 1940, Trotsky was slain by one man, using an ice pick, who had wormed himself into the confidence of the old Russian revolutionist. The assassin went by the alias Jacques van den Dreschd, but his true identity remains unknown.

How many of us, at the moment of death, will have the composure to say something memorable and impeccably phrased? And what will motivate us? French revolutionist Georges Jacques Danton may have been conceited or just bitter when he said, under the guillotine: "Be sure you show my head to the mob. It will be a long time before they see its like." Nero's case was clearly conceit: "*Qualis artifex pereo*"—roughly, "What an artist the world is losing!" Sir Walter

Raleigh, feeling the edge of the ax, mused matter-of-factly, " 'Tis a sharp remedy, but a sure one for all ills," as did Anne Boleyn when she said, "The executioner is, I believe, very expert, and my neck is very slender." Louis XVI may have been forgiving rather than sarcastic when he said, on the scaffold: "May my blood cement your happiness." The deaf Beethoven must have welcomed a better world with the words "I shall hear in heaven." Denis Diderot was philosopher to the end: "The first step toward philosophy is incredulity."

The story of the Temple Mound Indians of the Mississippi Valley, known for their extensive archaeological remains, is a mystery. At the height of their cultural achievement, around the sixteenth century, they developed an apocalyptic death cult, and before the invading Spanish could conquer them, their entire society had died out. No satisfactory explanation for their disappearance has been found.

The chief theme of Joseph Conrad's novels is the demoralizing effect of isolation. Conrad's personal experiences were the basis for this. While the Polish-born Joseph (1857–1924) was still young, for instance, his mother voluntarily became a political prisoner so the family could accompany Joseph's father in exile. It took three months to make the coach trip from Poland to Siberia.

The greatest funeral for a gangster ever held in Chicago was for a flower shop entrepreneur named O'Banion. The shop, at the corner of State and Superior Streets, was a front for O'Banion's bootlegging and hijacking operations. Ten thousand mourners were in attendance, and the most expensive wreath—it cost $1,000—came from Al Capone, who had ordered that O'Banion be rubbed out.

The sheriff of Bannack, in the Idaho Territory (now Montana), and the most-wanted outlaw in the area were one and the same man. Henry Plummer kept the peace by day and led a gang of bandits and murderers by night. In January 1864, vigilantes captured the gang, and Plummer was hanged.

Someone maliciously shouted "Fire" at a copper miners' Christmas party in Calumet, Michigan, in 1913. Panic ensued and seventy-two lives—mostly children's—were lost.

In London in 1812, a gambler, having lost his money and his clothes, staked his life on the next roll of the dice. He lost again, and agreed

to let the winner hang him. When rescued from the rope by a passerby, the gambler was incensed because he held to the code that a gambling debt should be paid.

———

The British abolition of the death penalty was triggered by a case in which the star witness was a mass murderer. John Christie in 1950 testified that John Evans had killed his own wife and son, and Evans, despite his insistence that he was innocent, went to the gallows. In 1953, it was discovered that it was Christie who had killed a number of people, including probably the Evanses. (Christie was tried and executed.) The revelation that an innocent man, Evans, might have been hanged caused such revulsion against executions that Parliament voted to end them.

———

The most ancient report of a solar eclipse is in Chinese records. The eclipse came without warning, according to legend, because the royal astronomers, Hsi and Ho, were too drunk to make the necessary computations. They were executed—the only astronomers known to have been killed for dereliction of duty.

———

One of the most atrocious murders of the nineteenth century was committed by a Harvard professor. When Dr. John Webster of the medical school owed Dr. George Parkman a large sum of money, he killed Parkman and dismembered him, hiding the parts in a well. A suspicious janitor opened the well and found them. Webster was tried and executed.

———

On August 12, 1895, Minnie Dean became the first woman to be hanged in New Zealand. Her crime was "baby farming." She would adopt unwanted babies for a certain fee and then dispose of them, a "service" she began in 1889. The police caught on to Minnie after six years and found her to be most certainly guilty when they dug up three bodies of infants in her flower garden.

———

"Thugs" were originally religious mystics of India. Banded together in a secret society, and devoted to the sinister goddess Kali, they performed countless ritual murders by twisting a rope around the victim's neck. The society was broken up in the nineteenth century.

———

In winter, gravediggers in Siberia pour kerosene over the frozen ground and set it afire. When the kerosene burns off, they dig away the layer of thawed soil. They then pour more kerosene, burn it, and dig some more. They keep this up until the ground has been pried open enough to accept a coffin.

––––––

From the 1850s to the 1880s, the most common reason for death among cowboys in the American West was being dragged by a horse while caught in the stirrups.

––––––

Pierre Belon (1517–64), a French naturalist, wandered all over the hostile shores of the eastern Mediterranean, where Christians were not exactly welcome in those days, studying plant and animal life. He came through it all without a scratch. Back in Paris, he went to the Bois de Boulogne to gather herbs and was waylaid by robbers and killed.

––––––

A common taboo is that royal blood should not be spilled on the ground. When Kublai Khan defeated his uncle Nyan, he ordered him placed in a carpet and tossed to and fro until he died. In 1688, the king of Siam executed a kinsman by having him placed in a large mortar and pounded to death with a pestle so that no blood would touch the ground.

––––––

Having survived a barrel ride over Niagara Falls that broke "nearly every bone" in his body, in 1911, Bobby Leech embarked on a lecture tour around the world. In New Zealand, he slipped on a banana peel and died of complications from the fall.

––––––

Medical treatment, during the seventeenth and eighteenth centuries, was aimed at ridding the sick of "vile humours" by vomiting, purging, and bleeding. The treatment was often the immediate cause of death. Some prescriptions called for "letting" more blood than is now known to exist in the whole body.

––––––

The Sui, who ruled China briefly, around 600 A.D., devoted much of their reign to constructing the Grand Canal, a waterway 100 feet wide, lined with roads and trees, and stretching for 1,000 miles. The canal was completed in less than twenty-five years, at a terrible cost in human life. Almost 5.5 million people were involved in the construction, and it has been estimated that 2.5 million died due to the harshness of the working conditions. The canal, extending from Peking to Hangchow, is as navigable today as when it was built almost 1,400 years ago.

––––––

The English sociologist Herbert Spencer was a Darwinian who proceeded to discredit the Darwinian view among people who felt kindness, pity, and mercy to be virtues. Arguing the theory of "survival of the fittest," Spencer declared that people who were unemployable or burdens on society should be allowed to die rather than be made objects of help and charity.

In early America, death was often the most public and most dignified event in an individual's life. It was considered important to "die well," surrounded by friends, neighbors, and relatives—witnesses to last words and wishes, which would be treasured as sacred.

Every four or five years the Malagasy of the Indian Ocean island of Madagascar, off southeast Africa, retrieve their dead from tombs that are half above ground and half below, expose them to the sunlight, toss them and catch them, and then wrap them in a new silk for reinterment. It is called *famadihana,* and it is a time of much celebration, with singing and dancing.

Parsis, the religious community of India that stresses education and practices Zoroastrianism, believes that the sooner the dead body is picked clean of flesh, the sooner the spirit will be released. Parsee dead are placed on platforms—towers of silence—where they are ravaged quickly by vultures.

In seventeenth-century Russia, the Great Schism (the Raskol) left the dissenting religious group (the Raskolniki) in such despair that many of its members sought death rather than wait for the end of the world they had predicted would occur before the end of the century. Between 1672 and 1691, there were thirty-seven mass immolations in which more than 20,000 Raskolniki voluntarily burned to death. They had thought it senseless to remain on Earth and risk being contaminated by heresy.

After Spartacus's gladiatorial revolt had been suppressed in 71 B.C., no less than 6,000 recaptured slaves were crucified on miles of crosses all along Rome's main highway, the Appian Way.

The Greek city-state Thebes had suffered for four years under the Spartan yoke when a small party of Theban men dressed as women and joined a drinking party the Spartan commanders were giving. The "women" drew their knives and slaughtered their hosts, and the

Spartans gave up the territory about 379 B.C.—the "Trojan horse" by another name.

In early England, suicides were interred in unconsecrated ground on the north side of the churchyards or at the crossroads with a stake driven through their bodies to keep them from rising and haunting the neighborhood. The latter practice did not end until 1823, when a murderer and suicide was staked and buried in St. John's Wood. Thereafter, such interments were forbidden by law.

Hatto II, archbishop of Mainz, Germany, was said to have found a unique solution to the great famine of 914 A.D. According to the chroniclers, he gathered in a barn at Caub a large number of the exceedingly poor and oppressed, under the pretext of feeding them there; once the crowd was inside, he set fire to the structure. His rationale: If the poor were sent to their heavenly reward, the famine would cease sooner. Years later, Hatto may have gotten his just reward—he was said to have been eaten alive by hordes of mice.

There was an apocalyptic manner about the most intellectual of the fathers of the American Revolution, James Otis (1725–83), who inspired the Committees of Correspondence. (These committees were set up to collect and dispense information to kindred souls throughout the colonies. Otis's views were the basis for continuing attacks upon acts of Parliament that regulated colonial commerce and taxation.) He wished, in his later years, that he would die in a truly unexpected, heaven-sent way, and he did.—He was killed by a bolt of lightning.

The greatest disaster in circus history occurred in Hartford, Connecticut, on July 6, 1944, when fire swept through the Big Top. A total of 168 men, women, and children died in the fire, and nearly 600 were injured. At the moment when the fire broke out, the audience was watching the performance of the Flying Wallendas. Disaster seemed to stalk this high-wire-performing family. In January 1962, while performing in Detroit, Michigan, a fall from the high wire resulted in two dead and one critically injured. The tragic Wallenda story ended in March 1978 when the patriarch and founder of the act fell to his death while walking a high wire in a high wind in San Juan, Puerto Rico.

In a number of cultures—among Indians of Central America, the Thracians of antiquity, and others—when a child was born, its family sat around wailing over the woes the child must endure, ticking off every calamity that could befall humankind. But when death occurred, the survivors laughed and joked on behalf of the deceased, whom they saw as departing for eternal bliss. Sometimes a favorite wife or consort was slain so she could share her loved one's paradise.

Every day in the U.S. about a hundred people over the age of fourteen commit suicide, a 50 percent "jump" in the last decade.

Burns are second only to traffic accidents as the cause of accidental loss of life in the U.S.: about 6,000 fatal burns a year.

Twenty-one people were killed by a wave of molasses in Boston, Massachusetts, in 1919. Over 2 million gallons of melted sugar, weighing 13,500 tons, had been stored in a tank in the harbor. The tank ruptured, for reasons never fully determined, and the wave, cresting at fifty feet, swallowed eight buildings.

Louis XVI and Marie Antoinette might have escaped from France in 1791 except for a delay to change coach horses at Sainte-Menehould. The King and Queen got out of the coach to wait, and were recognized. Two horsemen who rode ahead to Varennes gave the alarm that caused the fugitives to be stopped and returned to Paris—and eventually to the guillotine.

The French chemist Eugene Chevreul was born in 1786 and died in 1889 at the age of nearly 103. No other important scientist has lived to such an age. He remained active into his nineties, when he studied what we now call gerontology (the science of old age), using himself as a subject.

Stephen Decatur, U.S. naval hero of the Tripoli campaign and of the War of 1812, was challenged in 1820 to a duel by a fellow officer, Commodore James Barron, who was nearsighted. To accommodate his opponent, Decatur agreed to exchange shots at only eight paces. Barron killed him.

It's dangerous being a critic. The great French chemist Antoine-Laurent Lavoisier turned down a chemical treatise as worthless. The writer was a lawyer named Jean-Paul Marat. Marat later was one of the influential radicals of the French revolutionaries, and he saw to it that Lavoisier was made increasingly unpopular. In 1794, Lavoisier was guillotined. When pleas were made that such a distinguished scientist should be saved, the presiding judge declared, "The Republic has no need for men of science."

Some scientists really are absent-minded. The great French physicist André Marie Ampère (an important contributor to electrical theory; "amperes" are still the unit of current flow) was invited to have dinner with the Emperor Napoleon; Ampère forgot and never showed up. Maybe Ampère's absent-mindedness had something to do with the sadness of his private life; his father was guillotined in the French Revolution; his wife, with whom he was deeply in love, died after they had been married only a few years. When Ampère was dying, in 1836, he chose the inscription to be placed on his tombstone. It was *Tandem felix*—"Happy at last."

Nearly half of us die within three months after our last birthday, according to a study conducted by a Brigham Young University sociologist, Philip R. Kunz. Following up on a random sampling of 747 obituaries published in Salt Lake City during 1975, Kunz found that 46 percent of the deaths came within three months after a birthday and 77 percent during the first six months. Only 8 percent came during the three months *preceding* a birthday. People seem to look forward to birthdays as a goal to be achieved. The period following a birthday is anticlimactic and can lead to depression and loss of the will to live.

Francis Bacon (1561–1626), the Elizabethan champion of the scientific method, died in pursuit of a better way of preserving food. He had caught a severe cold while attempting to preserve a chicken by filling it with snow.

A great philologist was executed for murder in 1759. Eugene Aram had proved that Latin was not descended from Greek, and that Celtic belonged to the Indo-European language system. Unable to make a living from his scholarship, he murdered Daniel Clark—possibly with money as a motive, possibly because Clark had seduced his wife— and paid for the crime on the scaffold.

Henry Cavendish, one of the great scientists of the 1700s, was painfully shy and could barely speak to one person—never to two. He was so afraid (or shy, or something) in the presence of women that he communicated with his female servants by notes only. If one crossed his path in his house, she was fired on the spot. He built a separate entrance to his house so he could come and go without meeting anyone. In the end he insisted on dying alone.

In 1705, John Smith, a condemned robber, fell through the drop at London's Tyburn gallows, and dangled at the end of the rope for about fifteen minutes. Suddenly a courier came galloping up with a reprieve. The hanged man was cut down, found to be still breathing, and resuscitated. He lived for some years after that, and was called "Half-hanged Smith."

Robert Goddard was the father of the space age, having launched the first liquid-fuel rocket in 1926, from an aunt's farm in Worcester, Massachusetts, and developed a general theory of rocket action. When captured German rocketeers were brought to the U.S. after World War II and were questioned about rocketry and its development, they asked with incredulity why the U.S. didn't already have the answers from Goddard. The U.S. had to admit that it had neglected Goddard. He died in 1945 before the neglect could be corrected and ergo, before the U.S. could benefit.

The terrible toll (more than 50,000 deaths) attributable to automobile accidents in the U.S. each year is accepted or ignored, but one airplane crash with 100 deaths makes headlines.

During their first winter in the New World—and a rugged winter it was—the Pilgrims secretly buried their dead in Cole's Hill in Plymouth. The reason for the secrecy: The Pilgrims did not want the Indians to know how much the settlement had shrunk in population.

George Eastman (1854–1932) was born poor and had little chance for schooling. Thanks to the profit of the company he founded, Eastman Kodak, he was able to contribute over $100 million to various educational institutions. Eastman committed suicide rather than spend his last years in loneliness and without the prospect of further accomplishment.

Though the charges of atheism and treason and corruption of young people were justified (in a sense), Socrates would have been acquitted at his trial, in 399 B.C., if he had made the least attempt to defend himself rationally. He deliberately goaded the jury of 500 men until they voted the death sentence in spite of themselves, and even then the majority was small, 280 to 220. "The gadfly of Athens" spent a month between sentence and execution, refusing to escape, although escape could easily have been arranged. He had always been far more interested in the right code of behavior, in understanding the workings of virtue rather than of the heavenly bodies. When he drank the poison hemlock, Socrates believed that in his seventy years he had lived a good life. Most people have agreed with him.

William Walker, a proslavery American adventurer, "colonized" Nicaragua in 1855, was "elected" president there a year later, and was recognized by U.S. President Franklin Pierce, who had vacillated between recognition and the probability of antagonizing Great Britain. Walker was shot by a firing squad in Honduras in 1860 before he could carry out his plan to conquer Central America.

Robert Cavelier La Salle (1643–87) really put in the mileage for France. Exploring North America, he traveled the whole of the Mississippi to the Gulf of Mexico (claiming the entire valley for France); traveled the whole of the Mississippi all the way back to Quebec; sailed back home for refinancing; sailed to the New World again, landing by mistake on the Texas coast instead of in the Mississippi delta; walked thousands of miles looking for the Mississippi; then sailed for Canada, got lost, storm-buffeted, and found himself back in the Gulf of Mexico. Such was the long-drawn-out weariness of the mission that on the third unsuccessful attempt La Salle's men mutinied against more hardship and murdered him.

The first martyr to science of whom we know was the Roman scholar Pliny the Elder. He was in charge of the Roman home fleet, stationed near the Bay of Naples in 79 A.D., when Vesuvius erupted and buried the towns of Pompeii and Herculaneum. In his eagerness to observe the eruption, Pliny went ashore. By delaying his leaving, he was trapped and was killed.

In 1885, Louis Pasteur saved the life of a nine-year-old boy, Joseph Meister, who had been bitten by a mad dog. It was one of the most famous medical triumphs. Fifty-five years later, in 1940, Meister was gatekeeper of the Pasteur Institute. When the Nazis captured Paris, a Nazi officer ordered Meister to open Pasteur's crypt. Rather than do so, Meister killed himself.

Charles Byrne was born in 1761 in Littlebridge, a town in Ireland. He grew to over seven feet in height as a result of a tumor on his pituitary gland. A surgeon, John Hunter, wanted Byrne's body for his museum and at one point offered him a large sum of money. Byrne was frightened at the idea of dissection after death and refused. Hunter hired a fellow by the name of Hewison to follow Byrne everywhere. When Byrne died of tuberculosis, in 1783, Hewison was right there to bribe a guard at the undertaker's. The final price settled on was £500, supposedly the most ever paid for a body.

———

Mithradates (c. 131–63 B.C.), the great king of Pontus and enemy of Rome, is said to have swallowed toxic substances systematically, increasing the doses until he made himself immune from assassination by poison. Ironically, when he was defeated and cornered by the Romans, he tried to commit suicide by poison, only to find that it had no effect. He had to get a soldier to kill him with a sword.

———

Joe Hill (1879–1915), Swedish-American union organizer, radical, folksong writer, and now legendary hero, was executed by firing squad after being tried and found guilty (some say framed) of murdering a Salt Lake City, Utah, man. Thirty thousand people attended his funeral in Chicago. On the following May Day, his ashes were scattered in every state (except Utah) and many countries.

———

True heroes are indeed rare. Unique is Edith Stein, who went to her death in Auschwitz wearing the Star of David on her nun's habit, after offering herself as a sacrifice in an effort to save others. She was born into a German Jewish family in 1891; became assistant to the philosopher Edmund Husserl in 1916; converted to Catholicism in 1922 and took her vows as a Carmelite nun twelve years later; and wrote philosophical works and taught at German universities. When the Nazis rounded up Jews for extermination, Edith Stein proudly identified herself as Christian and Jewish, and in 1942 was gassed. Twenty years after her death, the Vatican began the formal canonization procedure for Sr. Teresia Benedicta a Cruce (the name she took)—which would make her the first "Jewish Catholic" saint of our time.

———

Kepler calculated that the first voyages to the moon would take four hours, and thought that the passengers, in order to endure the trip, would take narcotics.

———

Alexander Graham Bell devised a metal-locating tool to help find the assassin's bullet in President James Garfield in 1881. The device was workable, but didn't work on this occasion because no one had thought of removing the steel-springed mattress on which the President was lying. The metal, it turned out, interfered with the search. The unsanitary methods used in attempting to locate the bullet caused infection to spread through Garfield's body and resulted in his death.

———

Prince Borghese drove an Itala from Peking to Paris in 1907. During the trip, a defunct tire had to be replaced, and it was—by a wooden wheel fashioned by a *muzhik,* a Russian peasant.

———

Suttee—the immolation of a widow on her husband's funeral pyre—existed in India as a pious custom for centuries. Thousands of women "volunteered" to be burned every year. In the nineteenth century, the British imposed stiff penalities for those who participated in the rite, and eventually suppressed it.

———

WHAT'S IN A NAME

The Marquis de Lafayette, who fought with the forces of George Washington during the Revolutionary War, and his wife had the same first name: Marie.

Count Rumford (1753–1814), who was the first to develop the modern theory of heat, was born in the American colonies (Wolburn, Massachusetts) but was a Tory during the Revolutionary War and spied for the British, reaching the rank of lieutenant colonel in the British army. He left with the British forces and spent the rest of his life in Europe. In 1791, he was made a count of the Holy Roman Empire. He chose his title from the name of the town, Rumford (later Concord), New Hampshire, where his wife was born. He did not entirely forget his native land. When he died in 1814 (while Great Britain was fighting a second war with the now-independent United States), he left most of his estate to the U.S. and endowed a professorship in applied science at Harvard.

The U.S. nickname "Uncle Sam" was derived from "Uncle Sam" Wilson, a meat inspector in Troy, New York. During the War of 1812, Wilson's "U.S." stamped on meat barrels prepared for the U.S. Army was interpreted by some workmen to stand for their boss, "Uncle Sam," and the legend grew. (In newspaper cartoons during the Civil War, the figure of Uncle Sam took on the appearance of President Lincoln.)

Michael Faraday (1791–1867), whose discovery of electromagnetic induction led to the development of electrical machinery for industry, refused a knighthood. He declared, "I must remain plain Michael Faraday to the last."

During his career, Vladimir Ilyich Ulyanov employed at least 151 pseudonyms. The best-known was Lenin (1870–1924).

The palace where the king of Egypt lived was the *per-o*, "the big house." When the Egyptians began referring to the king by his place of residence, "pharaoh" (for *per-o*) came into the language. It is as though Jimmy Carter were called "whitey" for White House.

The most common name in the world is neither Ching nor John. It's Muhammad.

A common American coin, the nickel, is named for the Devil. It is so called because it contains the metal nickel, which was called that by German miners of the 1700s because it interferred with the smelting of copper. They called it *Kupfernickel*—"copper Devil," or "Devil's copper." (We still speak of the Devil as "Old Nick.") A related metal, cobalt, presented similar trouble, and the German miners got the name from the earth spirit *Kobold* because it was thought cobalt was copper that had been bewitched.

The original name for the United Nations was "Associated Powers." Prime Minister Winston Churchill effected the change to "United Nations" by quoting Lord Byron to President Roosevelt:
"Millions of tongues record thee, and anew
Their children's lips shall echo them, and say—
'Here, where the sword united nations drew,
Our countrymen were warring on that day!'
And this is much, and all which will not pass away."

A book of maps is called an atlas because the innovative sixteenth-century Flemish geographer Gerardus Mercator's book of maps detailing various portions of Europe sported on its cover a picture of the Greek titan Atlas holding the world on his shoulders—and this book became known as the atlas.

By the time he was eight, Carolus Linnaeus (1707–78) had gained the affectionate nickname of "the little botanist." He went on to classify living things in a particularly methodical way. For example, he gave the human species the name of *Homo sapiens*, "thinking man," though he confined this classification to man's body alone. (He considered man's soul to be outside the animal kingdom.) Linnaeus's interest in sex led to a curious byproduct: He was the first to use the Mars and Venus symbols for "male" and "female."

Assassins originally were members of a secret order, a Muslim sect, in Persia and Syria. Their leader, called the Old Man of the Mountain, would serve them opium, later confused with "hashish" (which became "assassin"), and then dispatch the men to kill his enemies. They were given the "hashish" and treated to great sensual pleasures. It was supposed to be a sampling of the pleasures of Paradise, where they would go if they died while performing their duties. The assassinations stopped after the Mongols stormed the sect's Alamut base in Persia, in 1256, and killed most of the Persian branch of the sect. But the sect, however, continued. Its leader today is the Aga Khan.

The male Maya Indian would change his name twice as he was growing up. His original name was linked with the date he was born. He would get a new name, describing a personal feature, when he was initiated into manhood. On marrying, he would take on his formal name.

The name "Inca" originally did not refer to a race or to a nation of people. When Francisco Pizarro landed in South America in 1532, "the Inca" meant king or ruler, and by extension one of his ancestors or relatives.

The Colosseum received its name not for its size, but for a colossal statue of Nero that stood close by, placed there after the destruction of his palace.

Natives of Papua, New Guinea, who deposit their money in the bank at Port Moresby don't get numbered accounts. Instead, they are identified by the names of fish and birds or other natural objects. One bank customer is called "sawfish" for instance; another, "hornbill." Each depositor keeps his symbol secret.

Some of the names by which Bangkok is known are Great City of Angels, the Supreme Warehouse of Divine Jewels, the Great Land Unconquerable, the Grand and Prominent World, the Royal and Delightful Capital City Full of Ninefold Gems, the Highest Royal Dwelling and Grand Palace, the Divine Shelter and Living Place of the Reincarnated One . . . .

The original name of Los Angeles was El Pueblo de Nuestra Senora la Reina de los Angeles de Porciuncula—"The Village of Our Lady the Queen of the Angels of 'Little Portion.' "

Before Charles de Gaulle's death in 1970, French families were not free to choose any name they wished for their children. The ministry of the interior, in charge of licenses and records, kept a list of names of both sexes, and given names had to be chosen from that list.

A bicycle racer earned his nickname of Charles "Mile-a-Minute" Murphy after proving he could pedal a mile a minute if wind resistance was eliminated. A smooth board track was laid between rails of the Long Island Rail Road, a hood was attached to the end of a passenger car, and on June 30, 1899, Murphy pedaled a measured mile behind the moving car in 57¾ seconds—faster than any automobile at the time.

In the eighteenth century, wealthy visitors so thoroughly enjoyed the mineral springs and baths in the fashionable watering town of Spa in the Ardennes in southeast Belgium, near the German border, that the name of the town soon became a lowercase English noun.

The *Mayflower*'s Pilgrim Fathers didn't realize they were Pilgrim Fathers for another five decades, or until William Bradford wrote of the Plymouth plantation: "They knew they were pilgrims." Because of this phrase, first printed in 1669, the hearty band that landed on wintery Cape Cod in 1620 are now called Pilgrim Fathers.

Four of the chemical elements are named after a hamlet of Ytterby near Stockholm. The elements are erbium, terbium, yttrium, and ytterbium—the minerals containing them were located in Ytterby. In contrast, France, Germany, Russia, and the United States have one element apiece named in their honor. They are francium, germanium, ruthenium, and americum. Great Britain has none.

About 1,500 years after they occupied parts of Spain, the Vandals, a German tribe, are still present in name: the region in the south known as Andalusia is merely "Vandalusia" with the initial letter missing.

The Ghana of today is not the same Ghana of yesteryear. Today's Ghana was once the Gold Coast, on the Gulf of Guinea in West Africa. Ancient Ghana was situated between and to the north of the Senegal and Niger rivers and to the west of Timbuktu. The word "ghana" was a title meaning "war chief," and the area got its name from Africans from the north who would trade with "ghana." Ancient

Ghana lasted around 1,000 years, until about 1240 A.D., when it crumbled and disappeared.

––––––––

When Adolf Hitler was in power in Germany, policemen and farmers were not allowed to call their horses by the name "Adolf."

––––––––

"To Oslerize" became a byword in newspaper columns, letters, and cartoons when the Canadian physician Sir William Osler (1849–1919) delivered his valedictory address at Johns Hopkins University in Baltimore. He said, "My . . . fixed idea is the uselessness of men above sixty years of age, and the incalculable benefit it would be in commercial, political, and in professional life, if as a matter of course, men stopped work at this age." One periodical headlined its story, "Osler Recommends Chloroform at Sixty."

––––––––

Although some 200,000 surnames are used in Sweden, fully 40 percent of the population share just twenty of them, all ending in "son." Johansson is the most common name. The Swedish government urges people with the most common names to change them. It has worked out a computerized list of Swedish-sounding words and urges name changers to adopt new names drawn from combinations of those for natural objects. Among the popular names in use are Bergkvist ("rock-twig") and Malmstrom ("ore-river"). Names adopted from towns or railroad stations are forbidden.

––––––––

There are at least 2.4 million people in the U.S. named Smith, and over 1.8 million named Johnson, and over 1.6 million named Williams or Williamson, and over 1.4 million named Brown, and over 1.3 million named Jones. Keeping up with the Joneses would appear to be easier than keeping up with the Smiths.

––––––––

In 1935, "Iran" became the new name for what had been Persia, which was the new name for what had earlier been Iran.

––––––––

In ancient Rome, there were fewer than twenty first names for males, among them Caius, Marcus, Quintas, Lucius, and Decimus. For that reason, people were further identified by two additional names denoting their gens (or clan) and family. For example, Caesar's full name was Caius Julius (of the Julian clan) Caesar (of the Caesar family).

––––––––

WOMEN'S RIGHTS

Although colleges for women had been established in the United States as early as 1819, the first women's colleges to give an education comparable with that in the best men's schools were Vassar Female College (now Vassar College), chartered in Poughkeepsie, New York, in 1861; Wellesley, near Boston, Massachusetts, in 1870; Smith College, Northampton, Massachusetts, in 1871; and Bryn Mawr, Philadelphia, Pennsylvania, in 1880. The first coeducational college to offer the same education to women as to men was Oberlin College, Ohio, which granted the bachelor's degree to three women in 1841.

———

When Jane Addams (1860–1935), the American social worker and reformer, wrote her entry for *Who's Who*, she proudly listed "Garbage Collector" among her chief achievements. A corrupt Chicago bureaucracy was endangering the health of the slum people by failing to pick up the garbage, so the "Lady of Hull House" assumed the responsibility herself.

———

To prove that girls could master such subjects as mathematics and philosophy without detracting from their health or charm, Emma Hart Willard founded the Troy (New York) Female Seminary, in 1821.

———

For founding a birth-control clinic, in 1917, Margaret Sanger was jailed for a month in a workhouse.

———

Not until 1932 was a woman elected to the Senate. She was Hattie Caraway, Arkansas Democrat. The first appointed woman Senator was Rebecca Felton, a Georgia Democrat, in 1922.

———

Dorothea Dix, the nineteenth-century educator and first superintendent of U.S. Army nurses, recommended as nurses only women who were strong and not too good-looking.

———

No woman held a Presidential cabinet position until 1933, when Frances Perkins became secretary of labor. She served a dozen years. Before her appointment in Washington, Miss Perkins was industrial commissioner for New York State.

———

Epicurus (341–241 B.C.), to whom good and pleasure were synonymous, was the first important philosopher to accept women as students.

———

Mercy Otis Warren (1728–1814), at a time when women rarely played any part in public life, became a propagandist for the U.S. revolutionary cause, a confidante of John Adams, and an admired ally of most of the Massachusetts rebel leaders. She was a pioneer feminist who argued that women's alleged weaknesses were due simply to inferior education.

———

For several years, in the small town of Tweed, Ontario, there was a council consisting solely of women. This was the only known such case of female leadership in North America. In 1967, several men ran for office in Tweed solely on the basis of their gender, and one was elected.

———

In rain forests near the border of Brazil and Venezuela, the Yanomamo tribe had a unique practice: Until a woman gave birth to a son, she killed her female infants, and she could do away with *all* unwanted children, regardless of sex, once the first son was born.

———

To the Athenians of the Golden Age, women were inferior creatures, only dubiously superior to domesticated animals, and with nothing in the way of human rights. To these cultivated Athenians, it seemed virtually self-evident that male homosexuality was the highest form of life, because that was the only way in which a male could love an equal.

———

At a time when the education of girls in most prominent families was concentrated on needlework, music, dancing, and languages, Aaron Burr insisted that his daughter, Theodosia, learn serious subjects rather than ornamental ones "to convince the world what neither sex appears to believe—that women have souls!"

———

In seventeenth- and eighteenth-century America, women were employed in all of the same occupations that men were, and men and women earned equal pay. A female blacksmith charged the same as a man to shoe a horse. Women sextons and printers were paid the same rate as men. Women were silversmiths, gunsmiths, shipwrights, and undertakers.

Along the east coast of America, Indian women's councils could veto a declaration of war by refusing to supply moccasins and field rations. The decision whether to kill a captive or adopt him into the tribe was always made by women.

While women have often fought alongside their men, the only authenticated Amazon army was the fighting women of the West African kingdom of Dahomey. Formed into an army by King Agadja in the early eighteenth century and trained into a serious fighting force by King Gezo a century later, they were eventually crushed by the French, in 1892. But for nearly two centuries, the fighting women of Dahomey had been feared by the neighboring kingdoms. The army numbered about 2,500—all were officially wives of the king—and carried bows and arrows, blunderbusses, and other firearms. Their huge knives were well known. Their main strategy was surprise. Effective as they were in warfare, they killed only in self-defense.

Margaret Brent (ca. 1600–ca. 1671) was an early American feminist. She went to Maryland from England, in 1638, and was the first woman in Maryland to hold land in her own right. She served as agent for Lord Baltimore, and, under the will of Governor Leonard Calvert, was made executor of his estates.

The first woman governor in U.S. history was Mrs. Nellie Taylor Ross. She was elected governor of Wyoming in 1925.

The only male speaker at the first women's rights convention, in Seneca Falls, New York, in the summer of 1848, was Frederick Douglass, former slave, abolitionist, editor, and spokesman for American blacks. Men who supported the feminist movement were called "Aunt Nancy Men" (meaning milksops), and worse.

The first woman governor in the New World was Isabel De Soto, who acted as governor of Cuba from 1539 to 1542 in the absence of her husband, the Spanish explorer Hernando De Soto.

The constitution of the state of New Jersey, adopted in 1776, gave property-owning women (only widows and spinsters could own property) the right to vote in state elections. However, voting by ineligible females—that is, young girls and married women—and, in the election scandal of 1806, by men in drag led to "election reform." In 1807, all women were disenfranchised.

A woman agreed in 1952 to play in organized baseball, with the Harrisburg, Pennsylvania, Senators of the Interstate League. However, minor league commissioner George Trautman, with the support of major league baseball commissioner Ford Frick, unilaterally voided Mrs. Eleanor Engle's contract.

The Territory of Wyoming allowed women to vote in territorial elections in 1869. When the territory became a state, in 1890, women's suffrage was written into the constitution so that women could vote in local and state elections. (They still could not vote in a national election.) Colorado allowed women's suffrage as early as 1893; Utah and Idaho, in 1896.

At the turn of the century, one-third of all the U.S. states—there were then only forty-five—did not allow wives to claim their own earnings, and one-quarter of the states denied wives the right to own property.

In 1781, a black woman, Elizabeth Freeman, who had been a slave in Massachusetts for thirty or forty years, was struck on the arm with a hot poker as she was defending her sister from their mistress's wrath. She ran away. In Great Barrington, her master sued for her return and lost the case, which was decided on the basis of the Bill of Rights to the Massachusetts constitution holding that all men were born equal.

Ten thousand dollars was offered by Marion Hovey, of Boston, to the Harvard Medical School, to be used to educate women on equal terms with men. A committee approved the proposal, but the Hovey offer was rejected by the board of overseers. The year was 1878.

Though she was a Nobel Prize winner (and soon would become the first person to win two), Marie Curie (1867–1934) was denied membership in the august French Academy simply because she was a woman.

Belva Ann Lockwood (1830–1917) ran for President as the candidate of the Equal Rights Party in 1884 and again in 1888—at a time when women could not vote in a national election. As the first woman to practice law before the Supreme Court, she won a $5-million settlement for the Cherokee Indians, and she introduced the first Southern black to practice before the Court.

Victoria Woodhull, the radical feminist who ran for the Presidency in 1872, feared that she would die if she went to bed in her old age. She spent the last four years of her life sitting in a chair. (She died at the age of eighty-nine in 1927.)

Abigail Adams wrote her husband, John, in 1776: "If particular care and attention is not paid to the ladies, we are determined to foment a rebellion, and will not hold ourselves bound by any laws in which we have no voice or representation."

During the American Revolution, many brides did not wear white wedding gowns; instead, they wore red as a symbol of rebellion.

Two female pirates, the English Mary Read and the Irish Anne Bonny, joined forces in 1719 when they found themselves quite by chance disguised as men on the same sloop. (Each had been notorious before their encounter.) Together with a privateer, a Captain Rackham, they took command of the ship. When their vessel was captured, after many acts of piracy, the two women were among the only three pirates who fought it out on deck rather than surrender. When Rackham was hanged, Anne told him, "If you had fought like a man, you need not have been hanged like a dog." The women were committed to prison after pleading pregnancy. Mary Read died there of a fever; she would have been hanged after giving birth. Anne Bonny's fate is not certain.

As early as the thirteenth century in Lübeck, the free Hansa city in Germany, women were given the same legal status in business as men. They were also allowed to belong to workers' guilds.

There are fifteen nations that had given women the right to vote before the U.S. did in 1920. The earliest were New Zealand, in 1893, Australia, in 1902, and Finland, in 1906.

China was, at times, relatively progressive in its attitude toward the education of women. They were allowed to study at medical schools during the reign of the Yuan emperors, which was from 1260 to 1368. Harvard Medical School did not enroll women until 1945.

Jeanette Rankin of Montana was elected in 1916 as the first woman member of the U.S. House of Representatives. She was elected again in 1940. During each of her two separate terms, Congress declared war (in 1917 and 1941), and she was the only Representative to vote against both declarations.

Margaret Higgins Sanger, the birth-control pioneer, was one of eleven children.

A woman collected a federal pension for a war disability incurred in 1776, and is the only Revolutionary War veteran to be buried at the U.S. Military Academy, West Point. Margaret Corbin followed her husband to war and served in the field. He was killed, and she was crippled for life, during action at Fort Washington, New York.

The generally accepted start-up date for the Industrial Revolution is roughly 1750, but it took a century for development of the first product that specifically lightened women's household tasks. It was Elias Howe's sewing machine.

The first female telephone operator was Emma M. Nutt, who started working for Telephone Dispatch Company in Boston, on September 1, 1878. Prior to that, all operators were men.

The women's suffrage amendment to the U.S. Constitution reached ratification by exactly one vote in the state of Tennessee, which became the thirty-sixth state to ratify it and therefore meet the Constitutional requirement that three-fourths of the states had to ratify it before it would become law. Harry Burn, a twenty-four-year-old Tennessee representative, cast the decisive "yes" vote after receiving an exhorting note from his mother. On August 26, 1920, the Nineteenth Amendment became effective.

She was eighty-seven years old when she became the first woman U.S. Senator, and she served for only a day, November 21, 1922. Rebecca Latimer Felton, a Democrat and the widow of a Georgia representative who had opposed reactionary machine politics, had long worked for women's suffrage, which became national law in 1920. She was appointed for a day to the Senate in a token gesture by the governor of Georgia, who had opposed the suffrage movement. "The word 'sex' has been obliterated from the Constitution," Mrs. Felton said on accepting her appointment. "There are now no limitations upon the ambitions of women."

———

WORDS

Writing under the pseudonym Lewis Carroll, English mathematician Charles L. Dodgson coined dozens of new nonsensical words in *Alice in Wonderland, Through the Looking Glass,* and his nonsense poems. Many of them are now part of the English language, like "chortle" and "galumph." He called them "portmanteau" words, forming most of them by telescoping two others and suggesting something from each. In *The Hunting of the Snark,* for example, the snark was reminiscent of both a snake and a shark. Wordmongers today have borrowed Carroll's technique and come up with portmanteau words like "brunch," "smog," and "guesstimation."

Literacy in Iceland is 100 percent. Every Icelander must graduate from school in order to get a job, and he has to be able to speak three languages. (The "native" language, namely Icelandic—which is the ancient language of the sagas—is spoken in no other country.)

The man who devised an alphabet of raised letters for use by the blind was himself blind from the age of three—Louis Braille (ca. 1809–52). (The Braille system, which evolved from Charles Barbier's method of writing with points, has sixty-three combinations of six raised points.)

One of the greatest orators of all time—Demosthenes (384?–322 B.C.)—was once a stutterer who stubbornly trained himself out of it, reportedly by putting pebbles in his mouth and practicing speaking aloud.

The Polish actress Helena Modjeska (1844–1909) was popular with audiences for her realistic and emotional style of acting. She once gave a dramatic reading in her native tongue at a dinner party of people who didn't know Polish, and her listeners were in tears when she finished. It turned out she had merely recited the Polish alphabet.

Various ancient peoples speaking a group of related languages were described in the Bible as having descended from Shem, one of the sons of Noah. The German historian August Ludwig von Schlozer suggested in 1781 that these languages be called "Semitic."

The literal meaning of "lady"—in its Old English form "hlāēfdīge" (through the Middle English "lafdi, ladi")—is "loaf-kneader."

Hardly anybody speaks Russian in the province of Georgia, where Joseph Stalin was born. Russians from elsewhere find they have to learn Georgian, the official language, which is known as Gruz, in order to communicate there. When the Moscow government tried to make Russian mandatory, in 1977, there were riots—and the Soviets backed down.

The word "million" didn't come into being until around 1300. Until then, the largest number word was "myriad," which was Greek for 10,000. Archimedes, in calculating the number of poppy seeds in the entire universe as he knew it, used expressions meaning "myriads of myriads of myriads . . . "

Spartan youngsters were taught to be terse in speech. They were supposed to act rather than to talk; if they really had to talk, the less said, the better. The district surrounding the city of Sparta (and the first area Sparta came to dominate) was named Laconia. To be terse in speech, therefore, is to be laconic.

The French philosopher René Descartes (1596–1650) speculated that monkeys and apes have the ability to speak but maintain their peace to avoid being put to work.

Winston Churchill's prodigious memory made it possible for him to repeat verbatim a lecture or a whole Shakespearean play.

The inhabitants of a slum called Trastevere, near Rome, speak a dialect all their own. They claim to have more than two thousand vulgar words to describe the human genitalia.

In eighteenth-century London, architecture went through a phase of being imitation Greek. The increasingly prosperous middle classes built town houses with Greek-temple touches—Attic, or Athenian, architecture. Peaked roofs were placed over the main structures (as in Greek temples), and they were supported with pillars in front. That was the particularly Attic part of the house, and, in consequence, a room immediately under a peaked roof became an "attic."

Throughout the ancient civilized world, men and women alike wore flowing clothing. When this drapery got in the way of work, it could be raised and bound in a belt or sash, hence the biblical phrase "to gird one's loins," meaning to get ready for work.

During Chinese Deputy Prime Minister Teng Hsiao-ping's meetings with President Jimmy Carter in Washington in early 1979, the U.S. did not have anyone fully qualified to provide a simultaneous interpretation from English to Chinese. Mr. Teng's interpreter, Chi Chao-chu, could do it, however, and thus served both parties. Mr. Chi is an official of the Chinese Foreign Ministry, and a Harvard graduate. President Richard Nixon, during his visits to China, also did not have the services of an American interpreter, and had to rely on his hosts for interpretation.

The much-quoted exhortation "The only thing we have to fear is fear itself" was not original with the just-inaugurated Franklin Roosevelt in 1933. It originated with Francis Bacon three centuries earlier, and was echoed by Montaigne and Thoreau.

The phrase "What a guy!" is a cry of derision in Great Britain and a cry of admiration in the U.S.

All the world's main alphabets have developed from an alphabet invented 3,600 years ago in the Middle East and known as the North Semitic Alphabet.

In a twelve-year effort—in a singular feat of original scholarship—the Cherokee silversmith Sequoyah (ca. 1770–1843) created an "alphabet" (a syllabary of eighty-six characters) for the Cherokee language. His nation adopted it, and in just seven years was transformed into a literate society with a weekly newspaper. The sequoia tree is his living memorial.

A London teacher made the proposal that English, in addition to Latin, be taught in the classrooms of Renaissance England. No one paid much attention. The feeling was that English was just a patois that everyone knew and wasn't used for scholarly books.

There are over 170 different nationalities and more than 200 languages and dialects spoken in the Soviet Union.

The practice of linking characters of the alphabet to produce the small letters used today in writing originated in the monasteries of the Middle Ages. Scribes found it easier to write whole words without lifting their pens from the paper. They connected the individual characters instead of writing a character, lifting their pen, and writing another character, and on and on.

Ameslan could be said to be the fourth most widely used "language" in the United States. Ameslan is an acronym for the American sign language used by the deaf. The first three most widely used languages in the U.S. are English, Spanish, and Italian.

Although the official language of India is Hindi, there are fourteen regional languages that are officially recognized for conducting national affairs. In addition, there are approximately 170 other languages and over 500 dialects. Of the Indian population of over 548 million, only about 134 million understand Hindi.

Most of the Carib Indians who once inhabited the lesser Antilles, West Indies, had three different languages. One language was used by the men, but women could use it when speaking to a man. The second language was that of women; men would only use it when mocking the women or quoting them. The third language, never learned by women, was used by men in councils of war.

A greater variety of languages existed in North America at the time of the Spanish invasion than in all the countries of the Old World put together. There was an even greater variety in South America than in North America. The most conservative guesses put the number of mutually unintelligible languages in North America at from 500 to 1,000, and in South America at at least twice that.

Just because a word is in common use today doesn't mean it has been around for a long time. There was no word "scientist" until it was coined by the English scholar William Whewell, in 1840. Sometimes it is the meaning that is new. The word "energy," for example, had been around for a long time, but it was not applied in the modern sense—as a term in physics—until 1807.

―――――

"Philologically, the word 'Kodak' is as meaningless as a child's first 'goo.' Terse, abrupt to the point of rudeness, literally bitten off by firm and unyielding consonants at both ends, it snaps like a camera shutter in your face. What more would one ask?" —Inventor George Eastman, discussing the origin of the name of his camera, Kodak.

―――――

In the fourteenth and fifteenth centuries in England, the costliness and scarcity of plain pins caused Parliament to limit their sale to the first two days of January. Women saved money throughout the year for this purpose—hence the term "pin money."

―――――

The inhabitants of the city of Soloi in ancient Cilicia (now Turkey) became so famous for their peculiarities in speaking the language of the conquering Greeks that a piece of bad grammar is today called a "solecism."

―――――

The word "hussy" in the sixteenth century was perfectly respectable; it meant simply a housewife, derived from the short form of the Old English *huswif*. Only one century later, the word had come to mean a bold and shameless woman.

―――――

Georges Schmidt, of the translation service of the United Nations, can translate sixty-six languages and speaks thirty fluently.

―――――

The average daily issue of the *Congressional Record* carries more than 4 million words—the approximate equivalent of twenty long novels. It is printed and published *overnight*.

―――――

In the original *Oxford English Dictionary* there is a twenty-three-page essay on one word—"set"—written by Henry Bradley.

―――――

Today, hospitals are thought of as places involved with medical and surgical care and cure. In the Middle Ages, "hospital" meant a place of shelter and rest for travelers, and, later, a charitable institution providing for orphans, the aged, and the infirm—a "hospitable" place. This early meaning survives in our words "hostel" and "hotel."

―――――

Edward Everett, the ardent Unionist, a former American minister to the Court of St. James's and a former president of Harvard College, was well known for his oratorical skills. On November 19, 1863, he delivered his best-known wartime oration. The occasion was the dedication of the national cemetery at Gettysburg. After Everett had spoken for two hours, President Lincoln got up and spoke for two minutes, delivering the famous Gettysburg Address.

———

Among the thousands of languages spoken around the world, about 175 languages are spoken natively by at least a million people. The ten largest languages each have over 100 million native speakers. They are, in descending order, Chinese, English, Russian, Spanish, Hindi, Bengali, Arabic, Portuguese, German, and Japanese.

———

The word "noon" comes from the Latin *nonus*, which means "nine." Originally, it referred to the ninth hour of the day counting from sunrise, which, on the year-average, is at 6:00 A.M. This put *nonus* at 3:00 P.M., or halfway between midday and sunset. What was originally the middle of the afternoon has come to mean the middle of the day itself.

———

It took twenty years for the Accademia della Crusca to put together the first dictionary of the Italian language, which was published in 1612. The French Academy spent four years simply deliberating how to proceed with a dictionary of the French language: most of the forty members of the Academy then spent more than half a century— fifty-five years, to be precise—writing it; publication was in 1694. Samuel Johnson wrote his *Dictionary of the English Language* mainly by himself, in a few years—one of the monuments of English scholarship. He wrote the definition of more than 40,000 words and handled more than 200,000 illustrative quotations, of which 114,000 were included in the dictionary, published in 1755. The first edition of the *Oxford English Dictionary* took forty-eight years to compile; the editor, James A. H. Murray, had worked on the dictionary for thirty-five years by the time he died in 1915; not until 1928, almost seventy years from the time the Philological Society had resolved to prepare a new English dictionary, did the last part appear. Currently there are thirteen volumes, 15,487 pages, 414,825 defined words, and 1,827,306 illustrative quotations.

———

Winston Churchill's "blood, sweat, and tears" of World War II had a long tradition. John Donne, in 1611, wrote, "Mollify it with thy tears, or sweat, or blood." Lord Byron, in 1823: "Year after year they voted cent per cent, Blood, sweat, and tear-wrung millions—why? for rent!" Lord Alfred Douglas, in 1919: "It [poetry] is forged slowly and patiently, link by link, with sweat and blood and tears." Churchill himself first used the phrase in 1931 in writing about the armies of the czar, before the Russian Revolution: "Their sweat, their tears, their blood bedewed the endless plain."

"Journal" does not contain a single letter of the Latin word from which it is derived: *dies*, "day." Among the intermediate steps in its development were the Latin *diurnus*, the Italian *giorno*, and the French *jour*.

Language reflects the things that occupy us most. In the Solomon Islands, in the Pacific Ocean, there are nine different words for the various stages of the maturation of a coconut, but there is no one word that corresponds to our "coconut." In contrast, one word is applied there to the four meals of the day.

In the first half of the seventeenth century there was a small but busy fur-trading district on Manhattan Island that was visited by many different people. By 1644, eighteen different languages were spoken at the bustling lower tip of Manhattan.

A major contributor to the first *Oxford English Dictionary* was a longtime inmate of Broadmoor Criminal Lunatic Asylum. Dr. W. C. Minor, incarcerated for a street murder brought on by a persecution mania, submitted 12,000 sources in one year alone. (He had been a surgeon-captain in the Army of the North in the U.S. Civil War and suffered his first mental breakdown when ordered to brand a soldier who had deserted.)

In New Guinea, home of the last direct survivors of the Stone Age, there are 700 cultures, and 700 languages and dialects are spoken. Villages within five miles of each other speak different tongues. A day's canoe trip of fifty miles could expose the traveler to ten or more languages.

Some odd words enter into the scientific vocabulary. When the rotation period of a neutron star changes suddenly, it is called a "glitch." Why? A Jewish astronomical observer noticed a change in the regularity of the pulse of a star, as though there had been a sudden slip. In referring to this colloquially he used the Yiddish word for "slip," which is *glitch,* and the designation stuck.

To the early Greeks, foreign languages seemed to be a meaningless succession of syllables, like "bar-bar-bar." They called all foreigners *barbaroi* ("stammerers"), and in English this became "barbarians." At first, there was no particularly derogatory meaning to the word. It simply stood for "foreigner." After all, the Greeks were encountering foreigners like the Syrians, Egyptians, and Babylonians, all highly cultured people.

A forty-five letter word connoting a lung disease, pneumonoultramicroscopicsilicovolcanoconiosis, is the longest word in *Webster's Third New International Dictionary.* The longest word in the *Oxford English Dictionary* means the act of estimating as worthless—floccipaucinihilipilification, which has twenty-nine letters.

The Scottish writer Robert Bontine Conninghame Graham, who had won a seat as a Liberal member of Parliament in 1886, was suspended from the House of Commons for having had the audacity to use the word "damn" in a public speech.

Thales, the Greek philosopher, noticed that amber decorations on spinning wheels attracted threads, feathers, and light objects through what is now known to be static electricity. The Greek word for amber is *elektron,* from which William Gilbert, physician to Queen Elizabeth I, coined the word "electricity."

The fame of the Czech physiologist Jan Evangelista Purkinje rests not on his work in medicine or in microscopy but on a single word: "protoplasm." He coined the word partly because of his theological training. The word's root means "first formed," which is how Adam is described in the Bible. In 1839, Purkinje referred to the gelatinous embryonic material in the egg as the protoplasm, which has come to mean quite generally the living material within the cell: that is, the "first-formed" material.

"Crystal" is from a Greek word meaning "ice." When the first quartz crystals were found, so amazing was their quality of transparence that they were assumed to be ice that for some reason could not melt. The word "crystal" was used to mean "transparency" rather than a natural geometric solid. That is why we speak of a fortune-teller's "crystal," though it is just a sphere of glass that has no crystalline shape at all. However, all quartz is not transparent. It may be translucent or opaque; it may be colored or colorless.

A germ is not necessarily a bacterium; it is *any* small scrap of life. That's why egg cells and sperm cells are called "germ cells." And why the little bit of living protoplasm in the wheat kernel is called "wheat germ."

The word "curfew" is derived from an old French word that means "cover fire." In Europe during the Middle Ages, a curfew was a metal cone or shield that was used to put out the hearth fire in the evening. The word "curfew" came to mean the end of the day's activities.

Oliver Wendell Holmes (1809–94), American poet, philosopher, and physician, invented the word "anesthesia" for the process by which ether and other substances were found to remove sensations of pain.

At least fifty years before the beef-cattle industry boomed in Texas, vaqueros whose range was Spanish California set the style, evolved the equipment and techniques, and developed much of the vocabulary that later was used by the American cowboy.

The word "ozone" got its name from the Greek *ozo*, which means "I smell." (Ozone is the most reactive form of oxygen. It is an unstable, pale bluish gas with a penetrating odor.) Christian Friedrich Schönbein, a German chemist, thought the smell of electricity, produced in the laboratory by passing dry air between two plate electrodes connected to an alternating current of several thousand volts, was somewhat like chlorine. Thinking he had a chlorine-like substance, perhaps even chlorine in combination with other elements, Schönbein coined the word ozone, in 1840.

It would be improper for a scientist to name a discovery after himself. Thus, when the French chemist Paul Émile Lecoq de Boisbaudran discovered a new element in 1874, he named it "gallium" after Gallia, the Latin name for what is now France. However, *le coq* is "the rooster" in French, and *gallus* is "rooster" in Latin. There is at least a suspicion that Lecoq de Boisbaudran was doing a little crowing on his own.

Though it is believed that Columbus was from Genoa, he never wrote in any form of Italian, not even to Genoese. He wrote only in Spanish.

The bloody battle of Magenta in northern Italy between a combined Franco-Sardinian army and an Austrian army in 1859 gave its name to the beautiful red-purple dye and color synthesized by French chemists shortly after the battle—magenta, the color of blood.

German was the official language of Prague until 1860. The city had been settled by Germans in the thirteenth century. When the newly created Czechoslovakia became a republic in 1918, Prague became its capital.

At a gathering of Russian Communist leaders in Brussels in August 1903, Lenin managed through his eloquence to get a majority to vote on his side. With a sure propaganda touch, he immediately labeled his group the Bolsheviks, "the majority." Subsequently, the group won few votes, and was actually a minority, but the name "Bolsheviks" stuck, adding to the prestige of Lenin's followers.

Mudslinging dates back to the time of the Romans. White togas were worn by all candidates for office in the Roman senate. Citizens threw mud at an unpopular candidate until his toga became *toga maculosa* (a toga defiled with mud). Cicero referred to the victims as "polluted senators." They were no longer to be "candidates"—which means, literally, "white ones."

One legal term for having sexual intercourse with someone else's spouse—i.e., adultery—is "criminal conversation."